The
World Council of Churches
and
The Catholic Church

JOHN J. MC DONNELL, C. M.

Toronto Studies in Theology
Volume 21

The Edwin Mellen Press
New York and Toronto

John J. Mc Donnell, **The World Council of Churches and the Catholic Church**

ISBN 0-88946-765-X

Toronto Studies in Theology
Volume 21

The Edwin Mellen Press
P.O. Box 450
Lewiston, New York 14092

Printed in the United States of America

οἰκοδομήσω
μου τὴν ἐκκλησίαν

-Matthew 16

CONTENTS

FOREWORD

Within this century Protestantism has generated a phenomenal, driving movement toward Christian unity. The movement influenced every part of the Christian world. At mid-century this drive produced a new, globally-oriented, mainly Protestant institution named the *World Council of Churches*. At first, a few Orthodox Christians labored within the movement; most stood unmoved by it. Pope Pius XI assessed the originating currents as a move of conflicting voices; he warned Catholics against it. Some thirty years later, Pope John XXIII sent observers to the Third World Assembly (1961) of the new Council of Churches.

Pope John himself had already convoked the twenty-first Ecumenical Council (Vatican II, 1962-1965) of the Roman Catholic Church to which he also invited observers from the Orthodox and Protestant Communions. Vatican II had in view *all of Christianity* and more. On the other hand, the World Council's center in Geneva constructs its agenda holding in its view *all of Christianity* and more. Are these two Christian ecumenical bodies—the ancient one and the new one—converging, competing, colliding or just briefly running parallel courses with some sharing of interest on the Christian and global pilgrimage? These questions prompted this inquiry.

The Protestant pioneers of the movement: Methodist layman John Mott, Episcopalian Bishop Charles Brent, and Swedish Lutheran Bishop Nathan Soederblom proposed hereic but divergent Christian visions and courageously sought to realize them. Although the visions differed, they contained a precious element in common: belief in Christ. What is common holds the World Council of Churches together, but the difference in the pioneers' visions, and priorities among them, diffuse the member-Churches' efforts to achieve the goals originally envisioned, namely: Mott's *mission* for world Christianity, Soederblom's one Christian voice for *peace*, and deeper still, Brent's vision that both the mission and the voice for peace belong to the *one Church of Jesus Christ*.

The inquiry sought to describe the origins of, and the rationale for, the modern movement; it sought to determine its present and, possibly, its future stance. The study explored the motions toward unity in the midst of the dividing pressures still fragmenting the Christian people. If the modern movement's prime goal is the reintegration of Christian unity,

then its antithesis is Christian division. Can joint work-
projects of divided Christians yield the unity Christ wants;
or is the principle that can produce unity mainly operative
at the theologically deeper level of faith and order? Light
was sought mainly in the documents and in the published positions of the leaders of the two World bodies. The movement,
of course, is still going on! As a movement it must reach
its goal, terminate in some new relatively stable structures
or dissipate. Do the decisions and actions of the two major
bodies forecast how the movement must end as it contemplates
the twenty-first century?

My interest in this great movement which involves all Christians began fifteen years ago. The teaching of courses in
ecclesiology and ecumenical work on the Brooklyn diocesan
Christian Relations Committee deepened the interest. Over
the decade and a half span my gratitude extends to more per-
sons than I can name. Yet gratitude must be expressed to Rev.
Dr. Lee A. Belford of New York University for his consistent
encouragement and support. My Vincentian *confrères*, The
Reverend Doctors and/or authors, Thomas Mallaghan, John B.
Murray, Philip Dion, John McKenna, John Freund and Francis
Sacks gave assistance and support in many different and generous ways. Without the encouragement and support of Fr.
Mallaghan I would neither have started nor completed this work.
Dr. Herbert Richardson of the Edwin Mellen Press patiently
supported the realization of the project. Una Crist contributed the labor of typing in a joyful spirit and Mary Quinliven
graciously spent painstaking hours in proof-reading. The emphases, the phrasings, and any errors in either judgment or
fact are mine.

Finally, it is my hope that this work may in some small way
assist in the enormous task of the reintegration of the Christian unity intended by Christ.

John J. Mc Donnell, C.M.

January 1985

The
World Council of Churches
and
The Catholic Church

CHAPTER ONE

RELIGIOUS BACKGROUND OF THE UNITY MOVEMENT

The atmosphere of Protestant-Catholic relations has changed dramatically in a very short time. So short, in fact, that many Christians embraced by this religious atmospheric change from chill to fair are still groping for conversational words and understanding compatible with their new relationships.

During the four and a half centuries since the Protestant Reformation, the rapport between the Protestant and Roman Catholic world communities was more readily characterized as hostile, polemical, contentious, or at best indifferent, rather than by such Christian terms as brotherly, charitable, or friendly. But within a time period of about a decade, in America as well as in divided Europe, both groups, Protestant and Roman Catholic, have looked at the other in a new light and have begun to dialogue about Christian faith and activities in a climate of greater calmness and even cooperative interest.

This is not to say that the wounds and scars of the contentious centuries have disappeared, or that the descendants of men who in the early sixteenth century were brothers in the faith have renewed or fully rediscovered their neglected brotherhood. It is only to say that the religious climate has warmed considerably. The directional arrow now points toward the unity of Christian brotherhood whereas it had become fixed for centuries in the position of polemical divergence.

Because this change of climate was so long overdue, because it was so welcome, many assumed that the steps needed for the reunion would be quickened as those of a child returning home after an unwanted absence. Thoughts of reunion led to a swell of popular enthusiasm. Speeches and articles oversimplified the reality. The Christians coming together knew each other, but largely in caricature. Each focused on the other's faults. And this mutual negative side had been contemplated for a very long time. Anglican theologian John MacQuarrie cautions, "Christians have been a long time growing into division, and we must expect that it will take them time to grow into unity."[1]

The heading or rubric under which this historic and dramatic

1

change of climate continues to take place, is the "modern ecumenical movement." Very much has been written about this movement in recent decades. The problem in researching this subject is not lack of material, but rather an overwhelming quantity of publications. All too frequently, however, these
writings use the concept of *ecumenism* so broadly (that is,
with so much social, cultural, and sociological content) that
its primarily doctrinal and religious significance is almost
smothered. Yet, for the Roman Catholic Church and many member
churches of the World Council, absence of Christ's doctrine
means that there is no such thing as ecumenism. For them, absence of doctrine means no ecumenism!

In the origins of the modern movement, and especially of the
Roman Catholic Church's sense of the movement, ecumenism's
goal appears to be the reintegration of Christian unity in the
one Church of Jesus Christ. If this be so, then Christ's will
for his Church is intrinsic to the ecumenical problem. Questions of belief, worship, and authority have blocked any reintegration more radically than cultural and sociological questions. The search for clarity in the doctrinal concept of
ecumenism is of prime importance. The principal world leaders
(such as the heads of the World Council and the popes) and
their institutional documents provide primary source material;
leading Protestant, Orthodox, and Catholic theologians uncover
the background, significance and implications of official documents.

Consideration of *the terms* used in the expression, "Modern
Ecumenical Movement" is needed to focus the phenomenon in
question. The words "movement" and "modern" require only
brief mention; but the term "ecumenical," because of its specifying character and long history, requires a more complete
examination.

Terms

A generic word such as *movement* describes the dramatic religious turnabout which involves ongoing changes of attitude,
differences of activity, and continuing process of study and
dialogue between official church bodies. This phenomenon
started with isolated meetings among differing Protestant
groups; these meetings induced a widening sequence of writings
and activities, such that the pressure for change in some way
touched the majority of the world's Christian groupings. Words
of lesser breadth than movement appear to be inadequate.

The term *modern* in "modern ecumenical movement" distinguishes
the movement under consideration from other activities throughout Church history which have consistently been qualified with

the adjective, "ecumenical." Probably the millenial use of
this adjective to describe councils of the Apostolic Christian Church since the Council of Nicea in 325 A.D. is the
most widely known use of the word ecumenical. The adjective
modern distinguishes the present movement from activities
connected with the twenty-one ecumenical councils ranging
from Nicea to the first Vatican Council in 1870. The *modern*
movement which arose in the Protestant community is, however,
wider than any given ecclesial institution; it seriously engaged the attention of the second Vatican Council (1962-1965)
of the Roman Catholic Church.

This term *modern* is generally held to signify the date-span
from 1910 to the present. Both Protestant and Roman Catholic
commentators generally agree that 1910 can be viewed as the
starting point of the present-day ecumenical movement. The
widely quoted Protestant work, *A History of the Ecumenical
Movement, 1517-1948,* edited by Ruth Rouse and Stephen C.
Neill, also estimates that the modern movement started in
1910.[2]

In agreement with Rouse and Neill, George H. Tavard a leading
Roman Catholic observer of the movement, thinks that "The
World Missionary Conference of Edinburgh inaugurated twentieth
century ecumenism in 1910."[3] The Edinburgh conference took a
global point of view, and it was suffused with a cooperative
spirit, noted by Tavard.

Samuel McCrea Cavert, a Protestant scholar closely associated
with American and World ecumenism, would perhaps prefer a
slightly earlier date for the start of the movement in America, since the formal inauguration of the Federal Council of
Churches (FCC) occurred in Philadelphia two years earlier
than the Edinburgh Missionary Conference. However, it is
just about this same 1910 date that the dividing trend in
Protestantism, which Cavert terms "separatist denominationalism," is slowed and even partially reversed by the growing
forces of mutual understanding, cooperation, and federation.[4]
Cavert wrote that:

> The Twentieth Century has witnessed such an ac-
> celeration of the movement toward Christian unity
> in America,...that there...is good historical
> reason for calling the twentieth century the
> ecumenical era in America.

This may be identifying the era's beginning from hindsight if
Hugh T. Kerr is correct when he observes in his *Encyclopedia
Americana* article that it was not until 1925 that the word
ecumenical came into *modern* usage.[5] Kerr undoubtedly refers
to modern public usage and its identification with the move-

ment being considered, since the word was familiar in academic circles. In any event, neither Kerr's estimation nor
Cavert's "American viewpoint" observation conflicts with the
generally agreed-upon date of 1910 as the starting point of
the modern ecumenical movement.

The most significant term in the heading, "modern ecumenical
movement," is the word "ecumenical." Its special importance
for the overall inquiry requires a fuller consideration. This
word, which has a long history, started centuries before Christianity with the Greek word for house or habitation, namely
oikos. [6] The cognate verb, to inhabit, *oikeo*, has a partici-
pial form *oikoumene* which was used with the word for world,
ge, to mean "the civilized world" or the whole habitable or
inhabited globe. [7] The word, *oikoumene*, alone was also usable
as a substantive to convey the foregoing geographical senses.
After the time of Alexander the Great, *oikoumene* was used to
connote interchangeably the whole civilized world or the
whole Greek empire which embraced equivalently the same concept.

The original Greek-influenced Roman word changed the diph-
thong oi to oe and the k to c; it thus transliterated the
Greek word into *oecumenicus* and shifted its political reference to the "whole Roman world" after Rome had mastered the
civilized world. [8]

Outside of Palestine, the content of the New Testament was
spoken and written to the widely-dispersed Greek-speaking
Jews and to the interested Greek-speaking Gentiles. Thus,
the term *oikoumene* in the New Testament has mostly the same
sense as it did for the dominant Romans. Since the originators of the Modern Ecumenical Movement acknowledge special
dependence on the New Testament, it is worthwhile to note
the New Testament's uses of the term ecumenical.

The word appears in the New Testament at least fifteen times.
In most of its uses the sense is secular; in some of its
uses it involves Christian belief. Matthew (Matt. 24:14)
adds a theological dimension to the word, ecumenical, when
he notes that Christ's mandate extends to the *oikoumene*.
Luke (Acts 17:31) adds the transcendent dimension in pointing
out that God will judge the *oikoumene*. Paul (Romans 10:18)
and John (Rev. 3:10) similarly see the *oikoumene* in this added religious light.

Thus, the New Testament's use of the word *oikoumene* appears
to be largely similar to the popular sense in common Roman
use, with a theological dimension contextually added to it in
some New Testament citations.

The Roman use of the word "*oikoumene*" equivalently meant "the whole world" or "the whole Roman world." An easy transition for ancient Roman Christians after Christianity had been carried to all parts of the Roman world was to connote with the word *oikoumene,* "the whole Roman (and Christian) world," and later "the whole Christian world."

In some philological and psychological way, it appears that *oikoumene* (ecumenical) came to be attached to general Christian councils such as Nicea (325) and Constantinople (381)[9] which, in Patristic times, came to be referred to as general councils, ecumenical councils, or councils of the whole Christian world.

The sense of the word ecumenical in these contexts seems to be geographical, representational, and jurisdictional. The generality of geographical places was present, the teaching of Christ and the faith of the Church was thought to be represented, and the decrees of the Councils were thereafter generally held as binding in faith and discipline. The connection of things ecumenical with things theological is again made.

Following the end of the Roman Empire, the connection continued to be made to modify and identify the meetings at which the Church considered its doctrine and discipline. As the Modern Ecumenical Movement got underway, its relationship with Christian faith and Christian churches was still very much in evidence.

In the ensuing years, however, especially in the hands of the secular media, the word ecumenical was used to mean any kind of a coming together, even for entirely secular purposes. As Protestant scholar, William J. Schmidt, observed "...the term 'ecumenical' [is employed] in a variety of senses, a practice [one] cannot take lightly in view of the prostitution of the word by the so-called secular world."[10]

The senses of the word as used in the documents of the World Council of Churches and the Roman Catholic Church are commonly and substantially Church- and theology-related. Yet even in these senses, differences exist. Hence, it appears necessary to examine a series of commonly acceptable meanings for the term, ecumenical, in order to achieve and preserve clarity in the dialogues that refer to unity-oriented documents of the Roman Catholic Church and the World Council of Churches.

Willem Adolf Visser't Hooft, former General Secretary of the World Council of Churches, distinguished seven meanings in the course of its history for the word "ecumenical."[11] The first four are:

    (a)   Pertaining to or representing the whole
          [inhabited] earth.
    (b)   Pertaining to or representing the whole
          of the [Roman] Empire.
    (c)   Pertaining to or representing the whole
          of the Church.
    (d)   That which has universal ecclesiastical
          validity.

The meanings correspond substantially with the sense already
noted as the word passed from Greek to Roman use and thereafter into the vocabulary of the Church of Christ.

At first glance, the meanings appear to be parallel, with
only a different corporate reality as the focal point: first
the Greek world, then the Roman Empire, and finally the
Church. The content of the term, ecumenical, however, took
on new overtones in its use in the Church. The councils
characterized as ecumenical were deciding matters of belief
and actions. It was believed and taught that, despite the
all-too-human interplay of weakness which was present at each
such council's proceedings, God's special guidance and sanc-
tions, in some way, attended its conclusions and decrees.

It is this new dimension which supports an ecclesiastical
sense of *oikoumene,* "that which has universal ecclesiastical
validity," noted by Visser't Hooft. This added divinely-
authoritative dimension, with a waxing or waning of its bril-
liance for both individuals and eras, appears to have continued with some Christians down to the present times. When the
Roman and Byzantine Empires disintegrated, the term, ecumenical, freed of its political content, continued to have ecclesiastical and religious significance. Relieved of its
former ambivalence, the term's religious force emerged more
sharply.

It seems that three new connotations were added only within
this century. The remaining three of Visser't Hooft's seven
observed meanings have gained currency in the last four or
five decades. They are:

    (e)   Pertaining to the world-wide missionary
          outreach of the Church.
    (f)   Pertaining to the relations between and
          unity of two or more churches (or of
          Christians of various confessions).
    (g)   That quality of attitude which expresses
          the consciousness of and desire for
          Christian unity.[12]

Meaning (e) combines the missionary context of Matthew 24:14
and Romans 10:18 in the one word, *ecumenical*. This use arose
in Protestant circles, but seems largely to have remained
there. Among Roman Catholics the sense of universal missionary outreach is firmly attached to the word *Catholic* from
Christ's mandate to preach the Gospel to all nations.

Meaning (f) "pertaining to the relations between and unity of
two or more churches (or of Christians of various confessions)" reflects the original idea of "wholeness." Somewhat as the whole world was a unity, so the whole empire or
the whole church was one thing, or as the Latins would say a
quid unum. Thus, if any of these unities were divided the
healing of the divisions would again produce the whole or the
oikoumene. Again, the ecumenical councils were of, and for,
the whole church. Thus, when divisions were healed and unity
regained between Rome and the Orthodox, even for such brief
times as following the ecumenical Councils of Lyons (1274)
and of Ferrara-Florence (ended in 1445),[13] then the whole or
the *oikoumene* was again achieved. Thus "Church unity-seeking"
became derivatively the sense of ecumenical.

This sense of "Church unity-seeking" for the word ecumenical
generally seems not to have superseded, or become equivalent
to, the conciliar sense in Roman Catholic circles until very
recent times. It is rather among Protestants that the concept of "Church unity-seeking" has been so emphasized that it
appears to be emerging as ecumenism's foremost meaning in the
twentieth century.

As increasing numbers of Protestant Christians reacted
against the "separatist denominationalism" noted by Cavert,[14]
the vision of church reunion, especially within denominational lines, grew more attractive. This return to a unity, even
though only a denominational unity, was in the direction of
Christian wholeness and thus was directionally ecumenical.
The part was given the name of the whole.

In any event, some uses of the word ecumenical are intentionally limited to goals which contain some idea of being world-
wide, but are denominationally restricted. In Visser't
Hooft's article, he cites such a use by the Methodists: "...
who in 1881 held the first *Ecumenical* Methodist Conference
to represent the interests and discuss the affairs of world-
wide Methodism."[15]

This sense of pan-Methodism for the word ecumenical sharply
restricts the "universal-Christian-Church-concept" contained
in the centuries-old word. Pan-denominationalism and pan-
Christianity are two different things. Thus, uses of the
word ecumenical must be scrutinized for both direction and

goal. If the direction and goal of the context open-endedly
envision world unity of Christians, then the use of 'ecumenical' will appear as wholly consistent with history and tradition.

If, however, the use of the term, ecumenical, is at variance
with the traditional senses, that is, if it tends to block or
preclude the unity of *all* Christians, then one term is being
used in relation to different and possibly opposite goals.
Clarity in the use of 'ecumenical' helps to prevent confusion
and reduce dialogue tensions. If pan-Methodism, pan-Lutheran-
ism, etc. is the limited sense given to the word, ecumenical,
it is different from the totality signified by the term for
many centuries. If pan-Protestantism is the meaning contained, this again is a different sense and goal. If a pan-
Orthodox union is all that is meant, the word ecumenical is
limited. If a loose federation of churches teaching contrary
or even contradictory Christian doctrines is the sense and
goal of the term, it is again different. If the unity of all
Christians in one church is the sense and goal of the term,
it is clearly different from these other senses. Further,
the focus of dialogue shifts from sectarian interests to the
nature of the church that came from Christ. The term ecumenism primarily conveys the sense of *whole,* not merely *part.* It
has conveyed this sense for Christians since Nicea (325) defined the belief of the whole Church.

In all the possibilities mentioned, the concept of church is
implicitly contained or explicitly mentioned. In the formation process of the World Council of Churches, ecumenism, as
a term, was given world-wide currency. The Roman Catholic
Chruch examined its perennial use of the term and the new ecclesial implications of it at Vatican II. The arena of the
word ecumenism is *church.* If ecumenism's goal is a whole-
world church, or one church for the Christian world, or any
variation of church, then the concept *church* of the World
Council of Churches and of the Catholic Church is of primary
importance. Both bodies are in the first place concerned
with Christ's *Church.* The focus is thus theological. This
focus in no way intends to deny that the church is also a
sociological entity. However, unless the more fundamental
theological or doctrinal clarity of ecumenism's goal is
achieved, then ecumenical dialogue must remain burdened with
ambiguity and misunderstanding.

The final sense (g) observed by Visser't Hooft, namely "that
quality or attitude which expresses the consciousness of and
desire for Christian unity" points out the transfer of the
characteristic from the *object sought* of sense (f) to the
agents seeking Christian unity. Visser't Hooft also sees
this attitude as a composite of a desire for something which

does not exist (namely Christian Unity) and/or an awareness
of a certain Christian unity already existing and a desire
for it to increase. Finally, this personal and interior
state termed ecumenical is seen as popularly transferable to
the instruments ecumenically-minded people use in their communications, such as Ecumenical Press Service, Ecumenical Institute, Ecumenical Church Loan Fund, etc.[16]

This last observed sense (g) also reveals the current loose
and confusing dilution of the term to apply to any kind of
unity. Thus, "secular ecumenism," which when translated appears as "worldly one-worldism," may lay claim in some sense
to a redundant use of the original sense of *oikoumene*. Yet
in the context of traditional and modern Christian unity
goals, it must be confusing to anyone except those schooled
in ecumenical jargon.

Methodist Professor of Church History, William J. Schmidt,
summarizing and agreeing with Visser't Hooft's development of
definitions, observes that the word ecumenical has become an
"umbrella term" because so much "has been subsumed in that
one term."[17] Schmidt fears that such a catch-all sense of
the term ecumenical will rob it of its special Christian
unity connotation and will dull the sense of the uniqueness
of the Christian reality.

A partially similar and partially different development is
noted by Bernard Lambert, a Catholic theologian of Ecumenism.
Lambert sees the same original geographical (whole world) and
political (whole empire) senses, but discerns the word Catholic, descriptive of the Church for St. Ignatius of Antioch,[18]
as the early Christian word signifying the universality, or
all-Christians-in-the-world idea of Christianity. Searching
for the sense origins of the word *oikoumene* Lambert says:

> It appears that it was St. Ignatius of Antioch
> who, about A.D. 100, first used the word *KATHOLIKOS,*
> later adopted in the Nicene Creed, though it occurs
> nowhere in scripture, as the equivalant of the
> pagan *oikoumene*. It was only after the conversion
> of the Roman Empire that the word ecumenical came
> to be accepted by the Church in the same sense as
> Catholic,--as a designation of one of the charac-
> teristics of the universal church, namely orthodoxy,
> in opposition to whatever is partial, heretical,
> schismatic or sectarian.[19]

By the time of the Council of Nicea (325), the word *catholic* was
one of the attributes by which the Church identifies itself.
In requiring the use of the Nicene Creed, the Council fathers
of Nicea identified the church as "the Catholic and Apostolic

Church."[20]   In Nicea's canon number eight, the Church is repeatedly identified by the designation Catholic, thus: "to
enter the Catholic and Apostolic Church," "the teachings of
the Catholic and Apostolic Church," "the teachings of the Catholic Church," "the bishop of the Catholic Church."[21]   The
similar use of the term Catholic (universal) in the Nicene-
Constantinopolitan Creed, and the non-use of the word ecumenical, indicates that the universality of the church was conveyed by the term, Catholic.   The preference evidenced in
these data implied that *Catholic* was the common term until
the church was generally present throughout the Roman *oikoumene,* at which time the equivalence of the terms Catholic and
ecumenical would allow for their easy exchange.

In agreement with the modern note of Visser't Hooft's last
three senses of the word. ecumenical, namely (e) missionary
outreach, (f) any Christian Church unity, and (g) attitude of
unity, Lambert also perceives a shift in meaning:

> For a century now this word has enjoyed a singu-
> larly successful career among Protestants, but
> its meaning has changed. It no longer designates
> what is valid for the visible church as a whole
> ....Instead, it designates Christian universality--
> what concerns all Christians, what they have in
> common, what is believed by them, what includes
> all Christians.[22]

This change of meaning from the universal validity sense
(Visser't Hooft's "d") so traditional with Roman Catholics,
to a universal-interest-but-no-validity meaning of modern
Protestant Christian use is a troublesome pitfall in the present era of dialogue.   Thus, care is needed to observe which
sense of the word ecumenical is used.

Visser't Hooft's listing of the senses of the term ecumenical
may be summarized as:

        (a)   Geographical (whole world).
        (b)   Political (whole empire).

Senses (a and b) are *secular* in origin.

        (c)   Church representational (whole church represented).
        (d)   Universal church validity sense (whole church
              obligated).

Senses (c and d) are *ecclesiastical* in origin; they appear
also to be two different relationships of the same kind of
reality, such as an ecumenical council. Lambert's data indicate that the term Catholic (universal) was used to identify

the church prior to use of the word ecumenical (whole 'church'
world) and that it covered much of the same ground. The two
senses may be combined as the traditional ecclesiastical
sense which perdures to the present day.

     (e)   Missionary out-reach sense.
     (f)   Unity sense, partial or total; each needs
           identification.
     (g)   Unity attitude sense.

These last three senses (i.e., missionary outreach, partial
unions, and unitive attitude) are relatively recent uses
which have emerged in the Protestant sphere; they are spreading to some extent among Roman Catholics.

In some Protestant writings 'ecumenical' conveys Visser't
Hooft's last three senses. Nevertheless, perhaps in most
cases today, the meaning of 'ecumenical' is focused on partial
or total Christian Church unity.

An example of a use of the term ecumenical, which heavily emphasizes the "missionary out-reach" sense and tends to equal-
ize it with the "unity" sense (that all Christians be somehow
one), is the statement issued by the Central Committee of the
World Council of Churches at Rolle in 1951 concerning what
the committee saw as

> ...confusion in the use of the word 'ecumenical.'
> It is important to insist that this word, which
> comes from the Greek word for the whole inhabited
> earth, is properly used to describe everything
> that relates to the whole task of the whole church
> to bring the Gospel to the whole world. It there-
> fore covers equally the missionary movement and
> the movement toward unity, and must not be used to
> describe the later in contradistinction to the
> former.[23]

The easily remembered expression, "the whole task of the whole
Church to bring the Gospel to the whole world," is very useful
as long as it expresses the missionary function of the Church
as one entity. But writings on church unity tend to greater
clarity and force when the foregoing ambiguity of the term
ecumenical is avoided and the missionary function placed in
its proper order. A unified church will help to unify the
mission voice that speaks of *one* Christ to non-Christians. A
divided church must carry divisive and dividing voices.

In the introduction to Lukas Vischer's documentary history,
the Church-unity component is the principal, if not the exclusive, meaning of the word, ecumenical. The missionary

element was simply not germane to the unity-focus of Vischer's thought.[24]

Since the Church unity sense is largely common in World Council writings as well as Roman Catholic documents, the word ecumenical will refer specifically to Church-unity in this writing. Other implications of the word are in no way denied but are rather affirmed. The other connotations will be noted when the word ecumenical is used in a composite sense. Not infrequently the context itself will manifest and sometimes emphasize the precise sense used.

Past attempts to realize the given unity of the *Una Sancta* (Ecclesia)[25] indicated to Visser't Hooft the "church-unity" meaning of the term, ecumenical.[26] Similarly, the Church-unity concept is central in Lambert's discussion of the nature of the modern ecumenical movement. Considering an area of common agreement between Protestants and Roman Catholics, Lambert writes: "All are agreed that it [the modern ecumenical movement] can be defined as a movement dedicated to a quest for integrity and *unity*..."[27]

Another Catholic theologian who recognizes the prevalence of the Church-unity meaning which has spread beyond the Protestant milieu in which it emerged is George Tavard, who writes:

> The traditional meaning of ecumenical is equivalent to *universal*. More recently it refers to the movement of thought and action which is concerned with the reunion of Christians.[28]

Characteristics of the World Council/
Roman Catholic Dialogue

Three characteristics implicit in the "World Council/Roman Catholic" ecumenical dialogues need to be recognized. The characteristics are: (a) the movement is primarily a *Christian* movement; (b) the major focus of its inquiry is *theological*; and (c) theology among Catholics has an *ecclesial* relationship frequently harder to find in Protestant theological writings.

A. The Modern Ecumenical Movement is Primarily Christian

The principle reference point and common element among the major bodies engaged in the modern ecumenical movement is Christ. The word's modern inflation blurs its original thrust[29] but neither the World Council of Churches nor the Roman Catholic Church has withdrawn from the Christ-given motive and basis of its ecumenical activity.

This fact of Christ as the basis of dialogue naturally raises
the question of Judaism, Mohammedanism and other world religions. Both the World Council and the Roman Catholic Church
are explicitly interested in these other religious bodies.
But since the other religions do not see in Christ any basis
of unity, different bases are being explored and mapped out
for communication with non-Christians. Newspapers tend to
call all inter-religious activities (Christian or not) ecumenical, but its primary and strict sense is still needed to
identify unity among Christians, because Christ intends it.

This inquiry is chiefly concerned with the Protestant-Roman
Catholic relationship while yet aware that the Orthodox
Churches are definitely part of the modern ecumenical movement. In fact, Protestant-Orthodox relationships and Catho-
lic-Orthodox relationships themselves constitute an extensive
ground for further inquiry. The long history of Orthodox-
Roman Catholic relationships will not be the primary matter
considered. However, the Orthodox churches, in their relatively recent official relationships with Protestants in the
World Council, have expressed certain positions in World Council proceedings which shed light on similar Protestant-Roman
Catholic relationships. As the Orthodox were skeptical that
unity could come from Protestant divisions, so too was Rome.

The Modern Ecumenical Movement began among Protestants and
the World Council of Churches is wholly Protestant in origin.
The Roman Catholic Church feared that the new organization
would merely confirm division and canonize theological contra-
dictions. Catholic theologians became interested in the World
Council's theological positions and conversed with Protestant
theologians on those positions. Thus, the ensuing dialogues
are chiefly Protestant-Catholic in character.

As John Macquarrie observed regarding discussions about the
Church and questions connected to the nature of the Church:
"the fundamental dialectic in ecclesiology and in related
questions is the Catholic-Protestant one."[30]

The second element in the World Council/Roman Catholic dialogue is that its character is theological. Christ is basic
to the communication between the World Council and the Roman
Catholic Church; this means that both bodies are engaged with
each other on the basis of a mutual belief position concerning
Jesus Christ.

This Christian belief is a radical presupposition in ecumenical dialogue. Further, this common cornerstone-belief upholds
other beliefs concerning which both bodies have large areas of
agreement and also significant areas of disagreement. It is
on the basis of commonly-held beliefs that the World Council

of Churches is interested in the Roman Catholic Church and
vice versa. Elaboration and probing of belief positions is
what theology is about, hence the focus of ecumenical dialogue is theological. Therefore, a consideration of the nature of theology is necessary.

B. The Modern Ecumenical Dialogue is Essentially Theological

Theology has been traditionally enunciated as "*fides quaerens
intellectum*" (faith seeking understanding), since the time of
Anselm (1033-1109).[31] This formulation by Anselm has, in addition to its value of being brief, the other values of indicating that faith and theology are not identical things but
yet that true theology cannot exist without faith.

A modern Catholic elaboration of Anselm's definition identifies theology as "a wisdom acquired by human effort that considers, in the light of divine revelation, all the truth that
God has revealed."[32]

Distinguished Protestant scholar John Macquarrie, who is the
Lady Margaret Professor of Divinity at Oxford, in a somewhat
less formal idiom even more explicitly points up the faith-
basis of theology. Macquarrie defines theology as "the study
which, through participation in and reflection upon a religious faith, seeks to express the content of this faith in
the clearest and most coherent language available."[33] Condensing Macquarrie's statement to "lived faith seeking clear
expression" shows its close relation to Anselm's classical
definition. Anselm also was speaking of lived faith and the
relationship of the things believed with each other.

Macquarrie's fuller definition implies that two persons, say
a mother and her theologian-son, may have substantially the
same faith. The mother may not be able to express her belief
explicitly in its proper sources, implications and interrela-
tionships. Whereas the son, for whose theological education
she may be the sole support, should be able to unfold explicitly the understandable content of their common faith. Both
have the same essential faith, but the son, a trained theologian, can elucidate its content. The distinction between
faith and theology becomes clear to a student who fails a
test in theology and yet explains to anxious parents that he
has not lost his Christian faith.

Another well-known theologian, Karl Rahner, defines theology
in more modern-sounding terms, yet Anselm's expression is
contained in the underlined words. Rahner says that theology
is "the methodical *attempt* to secure an explicit *understanding* of what has been heard and *accepted as the word of God.*"[34]
Method has been added to Anselm's *seeking,* *understanding* has

been modified as explicit, and *faith* in the person has been
related to its source as the word of God.

In a more formal statement, Rahner, in conjunction with another dogmatic theologian, Herbert Vorgrimler, defines theology as "the conscious effort of the *Christian* to hearken to
the actual verbal *revelation* which God has promulgated in
history, *to acquire* a *knowledge* of it by methods of scholarship and to reflect on its implications." The words italicized highlight the Anselmian core definition and reveal the
elaborations of modern theologians. In the same place, Rahner
and Vorgrimler say that theology presupposes faith. They further stress that a gulf exists between a statement about divine things and the reality that is thus stated and that it
is "the duty of theology to allow this gulf to be sensed ever
more keenly as an assist to our poverty in understanding the
revealed reality itself."[35]

Although some differences of emphasis are involved in these
definitions, the common elements contained in their expression and their agreement with Anselm's requirement of *faith*
enable Catholic theologians, most of whom amplify the first
definition, to engage in ecumenical dialogue with the Protestant scholars who accept Macquarrie's definition, or some
equivalent of it.

Van A. Harvey, a Protestant theologian, in his *A Handbook of
Theological Terms* reflects the core theological notion of
Anselm when he says that theology "...involves a systematic
and rational clarification of Faith..."[36] Harvey's description indicates that theologians also do other kinds of work,
such as in linguistics, philosophy, etc., but presumably this
work is for their theology, which in turn seeks to understand
faith.

The theologians quoted are speaking of the Christian faith
and resting on the New Testament as one source. They identify Christian faith (theology's starting point) as a gift of
God, quoting various sources such as the Epistles of Paul,
Luke's Gospel or the Johannine writings.

A convenient affirmation of the Divine gratuity of faith occurs in Paul's letter to the Ephesians when, in speaking
about salvation through faith, Paul writes, "this is not your
own doing, it is God's gift." (Eph. 2:8).[37] Thus, faith is
God's gift and theology is man's responsive work with God's
gift. Briefly, man seeks to understand it, to plumb its
depths, to examine the interrelationship of the faith positions believed. Doing this work is doing theology. The theologians mentioned see God's self-revelation (variously explained) as the "sine qua non" of valid theology. If God's

part be denied, then theology is radically undercut and The
World Council of Churches-Roman Catholic Church dialogue is
falsely based.

A naggingly serious problem arises in theological dialogues
when a party to the conversations has given up or denies the
faith-base of theology. It is distress about this very faith-
absence which has a leading Catholic Scripture scholar, Xavier
Leon-Dufour, requesting that "Everyone who writes or speaks
about Jesus should openly admit whether he is a believing
Christian or not, because no one can speak about him without
being influenced either by faith or unbelief."[38]

Without Christian faith, there can be no Christian theology.
Without a Christian theological base, ecumenical conversations
about the re-union of churches must issue in mere business-
species merger talks for nonbelievers and a sense of frustration and betrayal for believers.

Such a concern as Leon-Dufour's rests on justifiable ground
when scholarly Scripture exegete Helmut Koester, at the very
end of *Trajectories Through Early Christianity* (co-authored
by chapters with James M. Robinson), enunciates that Christ
is nothing other than human. Koester says:

> The man Jesus of Nazareth was a human being who
> was fully subject to the contingencies and con-
> ditions of history. There is no way to escape
> this fact, in order to boast in the possession
> of any original formulation of revealed truth
> which is somehow less ambiguous and less subject
> to historical conditioning than the historical
> life,words and works of a *purely human man,
> Jesus*.[39]

One must acknowledge the clarity and forthrightness of this
statement while recognizing that such a position utterly
undercuts the belief basis fundamental to both the World Council and the Roman Catholic Church. These Leon-Dufour and
Koester statements serve mainly to point up the theological
character (with its implicit *faith* basis) as a radical presupposition to all ecumenical dialogue. The Roman Catholic
Church reaffirms its Christian belief position *explicitly* in
many of its official documents. The World Council of Churches, constituted of Church bodies holding some common Christian beliefs and some varying and even incompatible beliefs
about realities identified as Christian, manifests its belief
position more *implicitly* in its documents, and more explicitly in its prayer forms. In any event, both the World Council
and the Roman Catholic Church rest on Christian belief positions both for their existence and their mutual dialogue.

C. The Ecclesial Character of Theology Among Roman Catholics

A characteristic of theology coming from a Roman Catholic
source is that it is *ecclesial*; Catholic theology is intimately related to the life of the Catholic Church. A Catholic
theologian writes in the context of the Church's faith-life
that has been passed down from the time of Christ and His
Apostles to the present. He may push for one emphasis or another and may also intend to uncover a new insight contained
in the Scriptures or the Conciliar documents. He may even
criticize the Church in the light of Scripture. But he may
not deny doctrine held to be essential such as the trinity,
the divinity of Christ, the presence of Christ in the eucharist, nature of the Sacraments, etc.

This requirement of conformity to the doctrinal teaching of
the Church has been labeled inhibiting, yet also broadening,
because it is simultaneously a caution and also a demand that
the theologian see the continuity and unity of the faith from
Christ to the whole Church in which his theological writing
is presented.

The faith of the whole ecclesial body is related to the theologians' writings. Substantial contradiction of previously
defined faith expressions of the Church brings a theologian
into confrontation with other theologians and with the episcopal authority responsible for safeguarding the faith-life of
the local church. Thus, Edward Schillebeeckx writes "...far
greater importance is attached to the *fides ecclesiae,* than
to the finest syntheses of theologians, even though these
have a critical function with regard to the empirical form
in which the faith of the community appears."[40]

Further on, Schillebeeckx notes that "The Catholic theologian
is always only one small voice within a great movement which
began with Christ and the Apostolic Church with its Scripture
and has continued throughout the ages."[41] This consciousness
of being only one voice speaking within the stream of the
faith of the whole church is characterized by Schillebeeckx
as the "...ecclesial character of theology...."[42] Further,
Schillebeeckx was summoned to Rome by the Sacred Congregation
for the Doctrine of the Faith to defend the views on Christology in his book *Jesus, an Experiment in Christology.*[43]

This ecclesial character of Catholic theology is noted in
contradistinction to the independent (i.e., personal and non-
ecclesial) authority formerly and even now evoked by names
such as Karl Barth, Rudolph Bultmann, Dietrich Bonhoeffer and
so on. Many Catholics and perhaps even some Protestants do
not know from which reformed tradition they speak.

A further difficulty arises if the prevailing authority-

figures of the Protestant world present teachings which are
actually irreconcilable among themselves.   Is the Barth-Bult-
mann sharp divergence a development of the same difference
which divided Calvin from Luther and their followers down to
the present day? Robert Johnson of Yale, in writing about
Karl Barth's successor at Basel, speaks of Presbyterian
"Barth's kind of theocentrism."[44] He further notes that one
who wishes to preserve the valuable elements of Lutheran Bultmann's work must "...transcend the pervasive threat of theological agnosticism to which Bultmann's students seem in danger of succumbing."[45]

While observing the difference between the ecclesial nature
of Roman Catholic theology as contrasted with the personal
authority characterizing the Protestant theologian's position,
it must be acknowledged that all these men are most sincerely
seeking the truth of the Christian faith. Granting that
Christian faith rests on God's self revelation, differences
of perception, insight, understanding and explanation must
occur when human limitedness[46] probes the divine realities.
Finite minds use limited words to express previous insights
into these realities, but no words can exhaust the transcendent nature of the divine realities. Differences of insight
and expression seem proper here, but division leading to hostility appears both to contradict the gift of the One God,
and to render ecumenism futile.

In summary, the World Council/Roman Catholic dialogue within
the modern ecumenical movement is, from the previous discussion, characterized as (a) Christian (mainly Protestant and
Catholic); (b) essentially theological; and (c) the ecclesiological character of theology will appear more on the Roman
Catholic side.

Recognizing that the modern ecumenical movement is taking
place among believing Christians and is properly theological
in no way implies a denial that non-theological data, such as
cultural, political, psychological and economic factors, have
contributed both positively and negatively to the movement's
development.

Frequently, the factors are not entirely separable in a given
ecumenical event or decision, even though they may be distinguishable in concept. The intermingling of the foregoing
factors occasionally even functions as a contributing motive in
the ecumenical enterprise. Nevertheless, the removal of the
Christian theological basis from this modern movement will
utterly destroy it. Thus, it is necessary to pursue the Protestant and Roman Catholic concepts of modern ecumenism in the
light of its Christian and theological dimension.

The importance of theology to the modern movement calls for a
review of the historic divisions, mainly theological, which
disrupted overall Christian Unity and made the ecumenical
movement imperative.

A long-range overview sees first Arianism (IV Century), then
the division in the East between Rome and Constantinople in
1054, and finally, the centuries-later division in the West
between Rome and the Protestant Reformers (XVI Century) as
the three greatest ruptures among the followers of Christ.
Other divisions also appear but their influence was not so
great.

Divisions Among Christians

The Church was tested by divisive teachers from apostolic
times, as witnessed by the New Testament itself. [47]

A. New Testament Period

The scriptural writings warn against divisive teachings. Correction of abuses *within* the one Church was the only position
taken, however, rather than anything that was viewed as an
overall federation of separated churches holding contrary
Christian teachings. [48]

B. Patristic Period

The writings of the early fathers of the Church against divisive Gnostic teaching give witness of the efforts to preserve unity in the early Post-Apostolic period. [49]

Immediately after the last Roman persecution, the early Church
was critically tested concerning its fundamental belief about
the nature of Christ. This severe crisis, known as Arianism
from the doctrine of a man named Arius, testifies to the continuing tension between division and unity. But Arianism
was thought to be a rupture or an untenable party-position
within the Church. [50] From the ecumenical Council of Nicea
(325) there emerged mainly one Church. The small group supporting Arius grew, became significant, diminished, and 200
years later largely disappeared. The succeeding ecumenical
councils of Constantinople (381), Ephesus (431), and Chalcedon
(451) further testify to the continuing struggle to confront
and resolve divisive theological positions within the one
Church. [51]

Out of Ephesus, however, there emerged a group which followed
Bishop Nestorius to such an extent that it ultimately became
a new church. Thus, Nestorian Christians separated themselves

as a group from the main body of the Church on the basis of
dual-personality teachings about Christ. These Nestorian
Christians, numbering about a million souls, came down to the
present day in diminished form.[52]

These few items evidence the damaging presence of divisive
elements within the Church from its earliest years. The dividing doctrines were resisted; the dividing teachers were
reproved. If unyielding in holding a repudiated, heterodox
doctrine, some were even excommunicated. Meanwhile, the still
spreading Christian body continued to think of itself as the
one Orthodox Church.

Strangely, in this early period, Arianism caused the most
widespread division, but it almost totally disappeared as a
separate ecclesial reality. On the other hand, the much less
widespread Nestorianism came down to modern times as a small
group of separated Churches.

After Arianism the greatest rupture in Christian unity came
between the Christians who looked to Constantinople for leadership and those who looked toward Rome. In view of the doctrinal basis of division in Arianism and Nestorianism the
rupture between Rome and Constantinople appears to be far more
a drifting apart of cultural and political worlds than a division of faith. For centuries, the Church of Constantinople
maintained in depth and extent the same faith and sacraments
as Latin Rome. The Church of Constantinople continued to use
the name "Orthodox" signifying "true doctrine" as a sort of
public declaration that it maintained the true faith. "The
formal rupture came in 1054 and, in spite of several attempts
at union, has lasted till the present day."[53] The excommunication of 1054 was formally lifted by Pope Paul VI and Athenagoras, Patriarch of Istanbul, on December 7, 1965, the day before the close of the Second Vatican Council.

Writing of the common past and division of the Christian East
and West, Orthodox historian Georges Florovsky estimates:

> Yet there is justification for speaking of the
> undivided Church of the first millenium. Through-
> out that period, there was a wide consensus of
> belief, a common mind such as has not existed at
> any later date. Men were convinced that the con-
> flicting groups still belonged to the same Church
> and that conflict was no more than estrangement,
> caused by some grievous misunderstanding.[54]

In seeking a path toward reunion, such a consensus of belief
and such an awareness of original common mind must be advantageous.

The Ecumenical Councils which preceded Rome's first major-but-
temporary break with Constantinople are generally held to be
the common property of all later Christian groups, since the
present great divisions had not yet occurred. Thus Orthodox,
most Protestant churches, and Roman Catholics regard the formulation of the faith from Nicea, First Constantinople, Ephesus,
Chalcedon, Second, and Third Constantinople, and Second Nicea
as substantially corresponding with the Apostolic faith found
in the New Testament.

Thus,in many ecumenical writings, the first seven Councils
are referred to in a laudatory and unitive sense. The Patriarchal structure and Sacramental devotion of the Orthodox
Christian body finds a congenial and approving response from
Roman Catholic ecumenists.

Augustin Cardinal Bea, the first President of the Vatican
Secretariat for the Promotion of Christian Unity, observed
that the Orthodox have certain very deep advantages which aid
efforts at unity. He wrote:

> The Orthodox Churches have preserved unbroken the
> succession of their bishops from the Apostles and,
> along with that, valid sacraments, above all, the
> Eucharist. In doctrine they retain the ancient
> Apostolic and patristic tradition, and differ from
> the faith of the Latin Church only in a few points,
> particularly in their denial of the dogmas defined
> by Councils since their separation, such as the
> primacy and infallibility of the Roman Pontiff.[55]

Added to the doctrinal matter, however, is the division among
the Orthodox churches themselves which, after the collapse of
the Byzantine Empire, occurred on generally Nationalist
grounds. Thus "The 165 million Orthodox are today, for practical purposes, divided into sixteen national patriarchates
independent of each other, and frequently involved in mutual
disagreements, sometimes acrimonious."[56]

C. Sixteenth Century Divisions Among Christians

The eleventh-century East-West schism produced some major
problems obstructing the path of union; more obstacles and
more varied ones were produced by the disruption, commonly
referred to as the Reformation, which split the Latin West in
the sixteenth century.

It is acknowledged almost universally that the leaders of
the Reformation wanted reform, not division. As Stephen Neill
mentions in reflecting on the rupture of Western Christianity: "No
one at the time set out with the idea of producing divisions;

all the Reformers proclaimed their desire only for a sincere
and thoroughgoing inward reformation of the Church."[57]

Perhaps the "all" and the "only" in this passage are a bit
sweeping in their desire to affirm sincerity unambiguously,
but practically no scholars today seem to deny that renewal
and reform were the primary motives of the original reformation outbursts against abuses.

Neill gives his estimate of the relative extent and seriousness of the disruption when in the same context he says:

> The Reformation of the 16th century did, however,
> shatter such unity as Western Christendom had
> enjoyed, and did introduce divisions graver and
> more intractable than any which had entered in
> since the early days of the Church.[58]

If the divisions were "graver and more intractable," it may
well be that the abuses were "graver," more intolerable and
more widespread than Christ's Church had suffered in centuries.[59] Luther in November of 1518 made a formal appeal for
an ecumenical Council, but such a Council would have done
little good, estimates Catholic historian H. J. Schroeder.
The Fifth Lateran Council (1512-1517) had just ended without
producing efficacious reforms against current abuses; further,
the mood for self-discipline was hardly flourishing in the
hierarchy. Schroeder writes:

> There were not wanting bishops who expressed re-
> gret at the early dissolution of the council; yet
> it is difficult to see what would have been the
> advantage of its continuance. Only a few months
> later (October 31, 1517) Luther affixed to the
> castle church door his ninety-five theses. No
> council, certainly no council with Leo X at its
> head and surrounded by an array of corrupt cardi-
> nals and self-interested bishops, could have
> stemmed the storm of revolt. The evil was too
> widespread and its roots lay too deep to be de-
> stroyed overnight. Many salutary reform decrees
> had been enacted by this council of the Lateran,
> but unfortunately they were not enforced....It might
> be added that one of the most flagrant and crying
> abuses of the time, the traffic in indulgences,
> did not receive a word of condemnation from the
> council.[60]

Such conditions indicate a basis for the deep rupture in the
unity of Christians. The judgements in scholarly writings on
the abuses and divisions are tending to converge. Practically

all Roman Catholics and many Protestant scholars, however,
see the violation of Church unity as an unacceptable product
of the religious upheaval. This is not at all to deny the
political, economic and cultural factors which contributed to
the sixteenth century division which still plagues Christianity, but only to focus on the doctrinal elements without which
it scarcely would have been such an enduring catastrophe. Also, in the minds of the principal reformers and the counter-
reformation leaders at the Council of Trent (1545-1563), the
ultimate basis of the division was assessed as theological.

October 31, 1517 is generally acknowledged as the date symbolizing the origin of Protestantism, although the name
emerged twelve years later at the Diet of Speyer.[61] Soon added to this new ecclesial body, called Lutheran, were the Reformed in Switzerland, Anglican in England, Presbyterian in
Scotland, and Anabaptist in Holland.

A few decades in Western Europe saw an unprecedented dividing
of Catholic unity into many church-bodies differing in structure, some elements of belief, some elements of discipline and
authority and elements of worship. In a word, structure,
creed, code and cult were involved. All had been at least
nominally Catholic and united at the beginning of the sixteenth century. The dividing shock was convulsive. For many,
this experience must have been traumatic. Both sides anxiously emphasized the *differences* by which the opponents' formulations and practices of creed, code and cult varied from the
origins in scriptural and traditional Catholicism. Each side
continued to stress those same *differences,* even when, over a
century later, weariness of conflict settled over Europe. On
those same differences, moreover, the emphasis remained
through the post-Reformation era up until contemporary times;
historians divide the era into five periods.

First Period: A brief overview of this time between the Reformation and the beginnings of the modern ecumenical movement
identifies the *first period* of division as that between the in-
cident at Wittenburg in 1517 and the death of John Calvin in
1564. Calvin outlived Luther by almost a generation, and in
those years his influence was felt throughout the post-Reformation world. As Protestant historian John McNeill noted "The
death of Luther [18 February 1546] left Calvin the most effective leader of the Reformation."[62]

Second Period: A *second period,* which has an overall character consequent on the doctrinal emphases of the original Reformers, overlaps the first period a bit by extending from
the Peace of Augsburg 1555 to 1648, that is from the formulation of the religious-territorial defining principle *cuius
regio, eius religio* (whose region, his religion)[63] to the end
of the Thirty Years War.

This interval has the overall character of a territory-divid-
ing and confessional-defining period of the new religious
bodies. The Peace of Augsburg (1555) initiated a general set-
tling of the Churches' territories on the basis of political
boundaries. A National church concept is implicit in the
Augsburg principle. As John McNeill points out: "...the unity
of the Church tended to be conceived in national terms. Confessions of faith affirmed the Church's universality--but they
were national confessions."[64]

Stephen C. Neill, who estimates that the Reformation's divisions were about the deepest in the Church's history, calls
attention to the "agreement to remain divided" as a more basically burdensome condition. Neill's evaluation is:

> The most serious factor of all was the acquiescence
> in division, which became the basis of all post-
> Reformation settlements of religion. By 1555 it
> had become clear that the reformation was not going
> to capture the whole Church. By the Peace of West-
> phalia in 1648 the boundaries between Roman and non-
> Roman Churches were drawn almost exactly as they have
> remained to the present day.[65]

This second period (1555-1648) was characterized by scholastic
definitions of Reformation positions as well as by the *regio-
religio* boundaries. During this interval, "the movement was
signposted by a series of important confessions of faith...."[66]
Roman Catholic theologian Tavard notes a special importance
for one confession when he estimates that, "the Westminster
Confession, adopted in London by the Westminster Assembly
(1643-1647) became the *vade mecum* of American Puritans; and
thus Calvinist theology dominated the New World."[67]

By the end of the Thirty Years War (1618-1648), it had become
quite clear that distinctly different main types of Christian
communities were proceeding to the forms present today.

> On the left were the diverse groups of the ana-
> baptists, with a 'free church' tradition. Scanda-
> navia was Lutheran and Germany mainly so. France,
> Switzerland, Holland, Scotland and some other
> countries had churches of the Reformed type. All
> these stood in sharp contrast to the Roman Catholic
> Church and in less degree to the Anglican Reforma-
> tion.[68]

Other authors fill out the positioning of "middle" and "right"
suggested by historian Schmidt's use of the term "left" for
Anabaptist or "free church" position. But common agreement
does not prevail as to which churches belong in each category.

For example, historian Roland Bainton thinks "A convenient,
though arbitrary, classification places the Catholics on the
right, with their sacramental hierarchical system and their
union of Church and State."[69] He agrees with Schmidt's
placing of the "free Church" tradition on the left.

However, Bainton places all the remainder in the middle including Zwingli's group, which Luther assigned to the left,
and the Anglican Church which Crane Brinton assigns with the
Lutherans to the right.[70]

Brinton notes that model classifications such as these are
difficult because the possible bases of such divisions are
manifold and so composite that they are not easy to disentan-
gle. Furthermore, no single norm or test can, by itself and
without further specifications, produce an orderly spectrum
of positions for dynamic religious groups of people.[71]

In any event, both Bainton and Brinton conjoin their classifications to church-state relationships; both also indicate that
their categories are more free than iron-clad, and more for
practical use than for a theological distinction between
churches.

This very fact, however, that the churches are distinguishable on many bases, especially sacramental and ecclesiological bases, invites the analysis that the one Latin Church
came out of the Reformation as many churches, not merely as
groups of dissidents *within the one* universal church, nor as
one community of protest.

When writing of the nature of Protestantism, Bainton observes:
"There are, in fact, many Protestantisms. The ways of the
High-Church Episcopalian have little in common with those of
the convinced Unitarian or those of a primitive fundamentalist."[72]

In the same vein, after pointing out some of the characteristics of early Protestantism, Bainton goes on to say:

> ...the most obvious generalization you can make
> about Protestantism is that it is not a whole.
> Protestant unity, if it exists, must be sought
> among the abstractions and generalities of the
> spirit. In mundane matters of organization, ad-
> ministration, finance, in the outward signs of
> group experience, there is only the bewildering
> variety of sects.[73]

Without question there were ecumenical or unitive efforts on
both the Catholic side and the Protestant side, and also on

the part of diverging Protestant communions to unite with
each other. In the first century and a half, following the
Reformation, Christendom had been divided into two major and
many minor armed camps. As to the major combatants, historian Christopher Dawson notes:

> There could be no question of spiritual reconcil-
> iation so long as Catholics and Protestants were
> cutting one another's throats and calling in for-
> eign mercenaries to help in the work of mutual
> destruction....[74]

Precisions of doctrinal belief and reunion are hardly advanced by the heat of armed conflict.

Yet there were early ecumenical efforts; they tended to be
doctrinal formulations which softened the initial language of
theological division, or they sought ground shared prior to
the Reformation. One model of such yearning for "the good
old days" was the formulation by George Calixtus (1586-1656)
of a concept termed *consensus quinque saecularis* (consensus
of the original five centuries)that is, the consent which the
Church lived with in its first five centuries. This may be
termed "old ecumenism" because it is retrospective, a sort of
leap-froging back to idealized, distant times which implied
that the formulae of Christianity are unalterable and fixed,
and that the intervening insights and developments should be
discarded.

Calixtus' *consensus quinque saecularis* position rested on the
traditions of the "early Church" as its guiding principle.
Shying from doctrinal emphasis and stressing the elements of
Christian living and the teaching of the first four councils,
Calixtus, although schooled in Melanchton's thought, sought
to bypass the divisive theological disputations so corrosive
of sixteenth century unity.[75] This, of course, also meant
bypassing any valid and universally accepted advances
achieved. One critic judged that Calixtus' real aim was "the
unhistorical re-creation of an ideal dogmatically defined."[76]

Even so, Calixtus was a break-out figure from the prevailing
attitude of rigid orthodoxy. He placed special stress on
such elements as "belief in the value of Christian Synods,
and emphasis on Christian moral standards."[77] Calixtus' diminished attention to doctrine points up the trend to minimize
the truth-element of religion and to emphasize the pious-
living aspects. Calixtus liked the universal or Catholic element of the first five centuries and also the evangelical
theme of the early Church's consensus; thus his *consensus
quinque saecularis* may well be the forerunner of modern ecumenism's "Evangelical Catholicity."

Third Period: Following the period (1555-1648) which yielded
scholastic and territorial definitions of the different Reformation communities, and which saw a shift in emphasis from
doctrine toward moral perfection, a *third period* began which
was characterized by a movement known as *Pietism*. Dry academic definition and the hostilities of the Thirty Years War
left the weary Christian communities hungry for peace and the
refreshment of non-academic piety. Pietism responded to the
hunger. It emerged in the second half of the seventeenth
century (1648-1700); it influenced much of Europe and
America.[78]

German-born Pietism was a spiritual movement which first
spread throughout the Lutheran and the Moravian communities.
Instead of emphasizing doctrinal foundations, it concerned
itself with personal devotion and an experienced-attachment
to Christ.

Philip Spener (1635-1705) provided a theology of Divinely-
given rebirth, spiritual liberty, and light of the Spirit
which yielded religious ferment that penetrated beyond the
defined territorial and denominational boundaries.[79]

This permeating religious fervor was a source of ecumenical
or unitive feeling and action, for

> rebirth creates a new fellowship. It brings into
> being an invisible 'spiritual' Church which, as
> the true Church, reaches far beyond all the limits
> of all the historical and concrete churches.[80]

Pietism fostered the desire to spread the Good News, to engage in missionary work.

Fourth Period: The next *interval* (between the Reformation
and the Modern Ecumenical Movement's origin) is a period of
missionary movement. It had the overall character of Pietism
over a new *trans-confessional* thrust for ecumenism.

Pietism constructed a broad base for future unitive desires
by promulgating the doctrine that (a) every one united to
Christ participates in a new birth; (b) each individual is to
perfect himself in this new life, and the Church as a whole
will perfect itself and eschatologically be God's one kingdom,
one Church; (c) God is now bringing Christians and His Church
toward perfection; (d) *each individual* Christian's birth and
growth is primary, thus *biography* has new edifying importance;
(e) the free fellowship of true Christians should transcend
denominational territorial (state) boundaries.[81]

Unity of individual Christians with each other and, in an

analogous way, of Christian communities with each other flows
as a natural consequence from these essential points of Pietism. This unitive tendency springing from a heart-felt
piety can more easily demolish barriers of geography and age
than it can the more ageless and transcendent theological
walls. However, since piety itself is nurtured by doctrinal
belief, then in some way, pietism, even when most fraternal
and unitive, still nourishes within itself the divided denominational beliefs which gave it birth.

This developing movement, from Pietism into missionary outreach, seems to come to full flower under the generous, di-
recting hand of Count Nicolaus von Zinzendorf (1700-1760) who
thought that the *fellowship of those reborn* (i.e., Christians)
would give visibility to the Church which is otherwise invisible.[82]

Zinzendorf's emphasis may be termed a new ecumenical thrust
because it turned away more totally from intellectual precisioning of doctrine, and from analysis of the historic
divisions. Further, Zinzendorf's posture was more forward-
looking and conscious of practical unity in service than was
the position of the academic Calixtus whose gaze looked long-
ingly back to the first five centuries.

Schooled under the influence of Lutheran Pietism, Zinzendorf's
stress on generosity between churches made him an ecumenical
pioneer. He also inspired his Moravian Brethren to extraordinary missionary activity. In later efforts he aimed at a
Christianity without denominational names, while yet being
patient that denominations continue as long as they would
share with each other. He used the term *tropen* (from the
Greek word trope = a turning, containing the sense for
Zinzendorf, of a turning to each other) to express

> the belief that each particular Church has its
> own distinctive contribution to make the Church
> universal and that it is the duty of each Church
> to share its own special gift with all the other
> Churches.[83]

The most discernible product of Zinzendorf's Pietism was the
decisive inspiration found in it by Anglican John Wesley
(1703-1791) whose influence in this same period initiated the
Methodist Church.[84] It is an anomaly of history that Zinzendorf, who has been considered a significant pioneer of unity,
transmitted an influence which begot a new denomination, a
new division in Christianity.

As Calixtus marks the end of the period of definitions (1555-
1648), and Spener's doctrine captures the ideals of the period

of Pietism (1650-1700), so Zinzendorf exemplifies the fourth
period with its missionary activity nurtured by Pietism (1700-
1790s). The vast work of John Wesley, and the revivalist
movements, are significant religious events, but all that is
sought here is a brief characterization of the periods prior
to Modern Ecumenism, with an eye to influential models which
may throw some light on certain trends within the modern
movement.

Fifth Period: The terminal data of the 1790s is chosen because the pervasive movements of rationalism and secularism
caused modifications of attitudes in all the churches of Western Christianity and gave a new overall character to the *fifth
and final period,* the nineteenth century, before the emergence
of the Modern Ecumenical Movement.

Badly divided and socially enfeebled Christianity yielded the
field, by default, to secularism and the secular state.
Christopher Dawson estimates that:

> This is the age when the secularization of Western
> Culture was triumphant and when religion was con-
> sequently pushed out of social life and increas-
> ingly treated as a private affair that only con-
> cerned the individual conscience.[85]

The social impact of the Christian Churches was blunted. The
social implications of Christ's teaching were eclipsed. The
state's rules and laws began to have more influence on the
daily life than the Ten Commandments and the Sermon on the
Mount.

In tracing the divisive and unitive trends in Christianity,
the determination of such things as starting point, degree of
influence, high point and end, ranges from not easy to extra-
ordinarily difficult. Yet such trends are significant.

One such difficult composite of trends occurred in Western
Christianity leading up to and after the French Revolution.
Whether from the viewpoint of religion, economics, politics,
or culture, the period involves the searcher in the notice of
movements with names such as rationalism, humanism, liberalism, secularism, and "the enlightenment."

Most authors seem to use the terms somewhat freely without
trying to define sharply the concepts involved. One analyst
observes when considering *liberalism:*

> The word liberalism defies precise definition
> since its usage includes a variety of meanings
> in a number of different contexts. It may have,

> for example, at least personal, political, eco-
> nomic, religious, or theological connotations.
> The difficulty of defining liberalism precisely
> is further compounded by the fact that it has
> had somewhat different meanings in different
> historical periods. Nor is there agreement
> among scholars as to its historical origins.... [86]

This assessment seems to be relatively true of the other named
concepts also. Nevertheless, in the context of trends in
Christianity about the time of the French Revolution, the terms
mentioned are almost always used as having a common core. The
common core seems to be the "this human world" in contradistinction to the "that traditional Christian world."

To condense the expressions for sharper contrast, the basic
distinction seems to be between the "exclusively human" as
against "the Christian," with its supernatural or transcendent connotations. The emphatically human sought to exclude
what was Christian. The rational power excluded Christian
revelation from the field. Yet the exclusion was never complete; each world used insights of the other.

Thus it was that *rationalism*, as a movement, inveighed against
Christianity, yet many Christians cultivated some of the
values of rationalism; Christianity assimilated something of
liberalism; "the enlightenment" in a man such as Voltaire
wrote devastatingly against Christianity. Yet Christian in-
tellectuals, such as the men of the Oxford Movement, assimilated many of the insights of "the enlightenment."

In the context of Christian ecumenism it appears that: -*rationalism* viewed as a rejector of the Divine was corrosive of
all Christianity, -*humanism,* a rejector of the supernatural,
tended to undercut all Christianity, -*liberalism,* a rejector
of any restraint (and every commandment in some sense re-
strains), injured Christianity, -*secularism's* opposition to
the transcendent world scoffed at any claim of Christ's continuing presence.

While eighteenth century Christianity, especially the Protestant sector, was characterized by a flourishing Pietism and
missionary expansion of types such as that of Zinzendorf
(1700-1760) and Wesley (1703-1791), "The Enlightenment" with
its attendant secularism grew apace and prepared the ground
for the violent divisive eruption of the French Revolution.

"The Enlightenment," fostered by Francis Bacon's affirmation
of the inductive method, owes its growth and advance to such
factors as the break-through in natural science by Newton,
the extension of horizons through world travel and trade, the

ferment of Rene Descartes in philosophy and the absence of
Christian theologians from the arena of the ferment. It is
surprising to find that men, such as Robert Boyle (of Boyle's
law fame) and Isaac Newton, made serious theological assessments of their new discoveries.

Unfortunately, the mathematizing Cartesian and Newtonian viewpoints of theology yielded machine-like models of both man
and the universe. The Mechanistic philosophy praised God as
the Great Machine Maker, but simultaneously made Him more remote since He had created so wonderful a world-machine that
it ran by itself like a great clock and man could learn its
rules as Newton had. Making God thus remote is the stance of
Deism. Crane Brinton lucidly captures this counterpoint to
the heart-warming God of Pietism.

> Actually your deist is very firm about the exist-
> ence of God, remote and chilly though this God be.
> The deist's belief is the neatest possible reflec-
> tion of Newton's orderly universe spinning around
> according to law. The deist's God is the person
> responsible for planning, building, and setting
> in motion this world-machine....But once this
> necessary God had got the world-machine to running,
> he ceased to do anything about it. This clock-
> maker God has made his clock-universe, wound it
> up for eternity, and would let it run for eternity,
> according to the laws Newton had just made clear.
> Men in this universe are on their own. God has
> designed them as part of his machine, and has ar-
> ranged for them to run on, but with the special
> gift of getting to know by the use of their rea-
> son just how they run. Clearly there is no use
> praying to this clock-maker God, who could not if
> he would interfere with his own handiwork. Clearly
> this God never showed himself to Moses on Sinai,
> never sent his only begotten Son to earth to redeem
> sinful man - couldn't possibly have such a son.[87]

It only took a few generations to proceed from this rationalist concept of God thus remote to a total removal of God. The
stages of this progression may be named as Christian theism,
deism, agnosticism, atheism. This last stage was reached at
the moment in the French Revolution, so chilling for Christians, when a prostitute symbolizing reason was enthroned in
the Cathedral of Notre Dame in Paris.

A spectrum of Liberalism containing all the shades suggested
by terms deist, agnostic, and atheist thus threw its shadow
over the nineteenth century faith. The blood-shedding of the
French Revolution would pass, but the Rationalism, and

Secularism elaborated in this period would diffuse through
western Christianity, making it more and more conscious that
its sectarian divisions were rendering it helpless in its own
milieu. Deism rejected traditional Christianity.[88] Atheism
tried to replace Christianity with a secular humanism. Uned-
ucated folk were confused. Christopher Dawson discerns that
in this period of religious revolt, "more people were detached from the old religion than were converted to the
new."[89] This appears to be true to a massive extent when it
is realized that many millions of Americans, whose origins
are rooted in European Christianity, have no further connec-
tions with any Christian church.

One analyst is convinced that religious liberalism flows from
pietism. However, not all pietism turned into this liberalism: much of it vivified nineteenth century Protestantism in
revival meetings. It is rather that pietism easily crossed
denominational boundaries, thus it diminished the significance of doctrinal differences and, indeed, of doctrine itself. Doctrine was de-emphasized; personal feelings and
charitable acts were magnified.

In a sense the heart, the personal motivating reasons, became
the driver, while the head, the doctrinal discerner, was de-
moted. Thus, there was greater liberty to cross denominational boundaries or go outside of them altogether. Divine requirements were neglected, humanitarian goals were dispropor-
tionately praised. From the Christian tradition of true belief plus corresponding action, the emphasis shifted to "good"
human action alone, -to a humanitarianism that is good in some
secular sense. The purely human, secular norm superseded and
even muted the Divine norm.

It appears useful, even if oversimplified, to suggest that the
psychological sequence of emphases on the path to today's
secular humanism proceeded something like this: (1) doctrinal
conviction of the reformers to (2) devotional emphasis of
pietism to (3) the moral experiencing of Schleiermacher to
(4) social Christianity of the nineteenth century to (5) the
secular humanism of the twentieth century. By no means should
this suggested sequence of emphases intimate that all Christianity has cascaded down such steps from the common doctrinal
convictions of the Reformers. But stages, in some measure
like this, appear to have led many families, Christian in
their ancestors, into the position of post-Christian secularity.

As Pietism's emphasis on the heart must have refreshed the
generations weary of doctrinal conflict, so Friedrich
Schleiermacher's (1768-1834) emphasis on subjective *experience*
must have relieved those unable to confront the scathing

criticisms of the disbelieving Enlightenment. One suspects
that the recent Death-of-God end-point is finding in its own
time an equivalent reaction in the anxious search for transcendence among the nonchristian oriental religions.

Schleiermacher, a man learned in the ways of his time, sought
Christianity's value on a level that rationalist criticism
could not gainsay.

> ...an area must be found that is beyond the reach
> of analytic reasoning. Schleiermacher found it
> in experience. Thus religion consists in being
> 'one with the Eternal in the unity of intuition
> and feeling which is immediate.' Dogmas are sub-
> limated. Their formulas remain the same, but
> their substance changes.[90]

In analyzing the nature of "grace," a supernatural reality
for both the original Reformers and Roman Catholics,
Schleiermacher sees it *only* as a natural two-way interchange
between man and his world through intuition and feeling.
Thus "grace" and other such dogmatic-content terms will have
a different meaning in Luther's Pauline commentaries than in
the stream of Schleiermachian liberalism which flowed through
the nineteenth century.[91]

However, this very same liberalism became a sort of leveling
and smoothing factor and thus provided a humanist basis for
ecumenical exchange. The Pietism and Protestant missionary
expansion of the eighteenth century continued to flourish in
the nineteenth.

These common influences became the motivating bases out of
which both confessional and interconfessional *unitive* activities began to emerge by the mid-nineteenth century.

Some denominations with the same confessional base and origin
moved toward alliances in the closing decades of the century,
as the *Reformed* Churches' Alliance in 1875, the global Methodist Conference in 1861, and International Congregationalist
Council in 1891, and the Baptist groups in 1905.[92]

Prior to these denominational motions toward union were certain interconfessional activities and organizations which issued from revival pietism about the middle of the century.
First among these were small local groups of Protestants belonging to different denominations who met for common reflection, prayer and activity in London in 1844. In that same
year, the Young Men's Christian Association (YMCA) started.
Three years later, pietism produced the interdenominational
Universal Evangelical Alliance (1847). Incidentally, in the

previous year began the reign of the Roman Catholic Pontiff,
Pius IX (1846-1878), whose unitive reflections were directed
primarily to the Orthodox.

In 1895 John R. Mott (1865-1955) whose ecumenical activities
cover six noteworthy decades, founded for students an interconfessional (thus unitive) organization known as the World
Federation of Christian Students.[93]   The emphasis was on the
strength which comes from federating or uniting their individual Christian commitments; the outlook was a vision of the
world.

Mott, while a student at Cornell University in New York, was
inspired through evangelical work done there to make a decision for the Christian life.   He carried his idea of Christian world-unity to Protestant mission-agencies in Europe and
incorporated his vision into a mission organization so effectively that Ruth Rouse, co-author of the leading *History of
the Modern Ecumenical Movement,* says that John Mott is: "...
the man who, if any deserves the title, may be called the
pioneer of the Modern Ecumenical Movement."[94]

CHAPTER TWO

PROXIMATE BACKGROUND OF THE
MODERN ECUMENICAL MOVEMENT

Before continuing with pioneer John Mott, whose work in forming the World Missionary Conference in Edinburgh is the first
organizational step which in fact led toward the World Council
of Churches, it seems necessary to obtain a perspective of (a)
nineteenth century divisions and unity beginnings; (b) a possible scale or series of steps thought to lead toward total
unity; and (c) an overall preliminary picture of the ebb and
tide of ecumenism in the twentieth century.

Divisions Yield to Converging Activities

Without question the stirrings of desire for unity were present in the Protestant world of the nineteenth century but divisions still occurred. The motions toward unity were spas-
modic, small, and did not have much widespread influence
across the spectrum of Protestant denominational thinking. In
fact, some efforts to realize unity, as the Disciples of
Christ started out to do, ended instead in a further division,
the formation of a new denomination.[1]

Continuing separatist denominationalism more fully characterizes the nineteenth century than does the search for unity.
Further, the unity-model pictured rarely embraced the world
of Orthodox Christians or Roman Catholics, whose combined
membership accounted for three-quarters of the world's Christians who were convinced that they lived in the one true
Church of Jesus Christ.

The unity-agencies developed were, for the most part, task-
oriented, such as unions to aid Protestant Sunday Schools, or
to spread the Bible. Some initiatives for unity focused on
young adults. The effort to achieve a Christian commonality
brought together young *persons* on a basis which sought to
transcend denominational barriers, to cut across denominational boundaries, such as the Young Men's Christian Association
(YMCA). Similar inspiration founded the YWCA.[2]

The Student Christian Movement (SCM) and similar movements
arose about the turn of the century, generally from older

associations. Membership in an Evangelical Church, as the
basis for membership in the YMCA and YWCA, characterized these
non-ecclesial unitive movements as Protestant. These associations and movements supplied leaders and evangelical incen-
tives which influenced the beginning of the Modern Ecumenical
Movement, but the visible fruit of this continuous seeding
emerged not in the nineteenth century, but early in the twentieth.

However, these unitive movements were not enough to have an
overall impact or to characterize religious life in the nineteenth century. Continuing divisions overshadow the motions
of unity. For the most part, the freedom and benefits of
separate denominations were stressed, as smaller groups broke
away from anxious parent denominations. But each group's
leadership emphasized the good being sought as superior to the
suffering endured. Within a generation the debate cooled but
the denominational separations lasted.

This splitting process, based on linguistic, political, and
cultural as well as theological reasons, occurred overwhelmingly more in the New World than in the Old. This splintering
process brought Protestantism to this decade with very many
separate denominations.[3] The *Yearbook of American Churches*
lists more than 250 Protestant denominations.

Samuel McCrea Cavert, a Protestant scholar, whose years of experience in the Modern Ecumenical Movement lend weight to his
writings, observes:

> The diversity which has marked American religion
> is an amazing phenomenon. There are more than
> 250 separate denominations—some large, some
> very small—each having its independent organiza-
> tion. The ecclesiastical miscellany resembled a
> 'crazy quilt'....[4]

Cavert continues with the time and place setting of the division into denominations. "Most of this fantastic fragmenta-
tion took place in the nineteenth century, although it had
its beginnings in the colonial period."[5]

Further on, Cavert introduces another term to describe the divided state of Protestantism on the American scene. "Throughout the Nineteenth Century American religion was increasingly
pluralistic. It was, however, a pluralism within an almost
Protestant Circle."[6]

Some of the new denominations, such as the "Disciples of
Christ," were American-born. The Campbell brothers founded
the "Disciples" on a *scriptura sola* basis, and William Miller

founded the Seventh Day Adventists, with great emphasis on
Miller's own prophecy of Christ's imminent second coming.[7]

Cavert points out that other denominations were the result of
splits within the larger Protestant denominations. In 1810
Presbyterians separated over a revivalism issue. Congrega-
tionalism divided on a doctrinal Mystery of the Trinity in
1825. A Methodist division occurred over the problem of episcopal authority in 1830. Lutherans formed different denominations on the basis of strict versus liberal creedal interpretations in 1867.[8] Faith, Christian Scripture and theology
clearly were present in some of these separations.

Social issues contributed heavily to bitter divisions before
the Civil War, as Cavert notes.

> More dramatic and more fateful were the divisions
> occasioned by the National struggle over Slavery.
> The three largest denominations whose members were
> distributed between North and South all broke
> apart—the Methodists in 1844, the Baptists in
> 1845, the Presbyterians in 1857....[9]

Two years after his first volume, Cavert authored a second
historical review of the Modern Ecumenical Movement entitled,
"*Church Cooperation and Unity in America*." In his first
book, Cavert examined the cooperation which grew from seeds
planted earlier despite the nineteenth century's character of
spreading denominationalism. In his second volume, Cavert
looks at the growing cooperation in particular areas such as
mission, education, social tasks, mass communication, etc.

Cavert, interested in ecumenism, gives a brief assessment of
what he terms values and "the shortcomings of an anarchic denominationalism."[10]

> The denominational system, as it took shape in
> America, was not without important values. It
> made room for a rich diversity both of historic
> traditions and of ethnic characteristics. It
> fostered a spirit of freedom and creativity
> which encouraged each group to develop its own
> distinctive insights. It was effective in
> planning churches and schools across a vast
> unoccupied continent.
>
> But the intense individualism of the system
> tempted each denominational group to think more
> of its own advancement than of responsibility
> as a whole. This resulted in over-churching in
> many areas and underchurching in others. Worse

> than the wasteful inefficiency was the divisive
> influence on the life of the community. Instead
> of being a force for reconciliation the churches
> often added one more element of disunity. Most
> serious of all was an unconscious distortion of
> the Christian faith and life that arose from em-
> phasis on minor points of denominational differ-
> ence instead of concentration on the central
> meaning of the Gospel.[11]

What Cavert here irenically refers to as "an unconscious distortion of the Christian faith and life," is so serious to
those who hold precious the integrity of Christian faith that
the latter have been discouraged from entering into ecumenical dialogue with those espousing such distortions. Cavert
indicates that the divisions "arose from minor points of denominational difference...", whereas some of the splits already cited arose from profound theological differences, such
as those concerning the Trinity and authoritative interpretation of doctrine in the Church.

In any event, the divisions caused by denominationalism are
deep. They are probably as deep as the theological point of
difference is significant. At times, they appear so deep
that it is hard to see how large numbers of people accustomed
to such denominational mind-set from birth can humanly unite
with those from whom they have divided. Paul's opening salvo
to the Corinthians on the problem of factions, quarreling,
and division cautions Christians:

> I beg you, brothers, in the name of Our Lord
> Jesus Christ, to agree in what you say. Let
> there be no factions; rather be united in mind
> and judgment. I have been informed, my brothers,
> by certain members of Chloe's household that you
> are quarreling among yourselves. This is what I
> mean. One of you will say, 'I belong to Paul,'
> another, 'Cephas has my allegiance,' and the
> fourth, 'I belong to Christ.' Has Christ, then,
> been divided into parts? Was it Paul who was
> crucified for you? Was it in Paul's name that
> you were baptized?[12]

Perhaps motivated by such Pauline warning, not infrequently
for practical reasons as well, some unions and reunions have
in fact taken place, in Canada, India, the United States and
elsewhere. Cavert gives a brief summary of twenty-six such
unions and re-unions in the United States.[13] This involves
a relatively small number of the 250 dominations, but it is
significant that they have taken place at all. Further, the
fact that the number of such unions is ten percent appears to

indicate that the unitive trend may overtake the dividing
trend; the process has given a different character to American Christian life in this century.

The optimism of this joining trend, however, must be moderated by the fact that some of the unions occasioned further
divisions. A more careful examination reveals also that most
of the reunited church bodies were already in prior agreement
on questions regarding faith. Cavert observes that:

> Most of the unions have been within the bounds
> of a denominational family and have not had
> grave issues of faith and order to resolve.[14]

Cavert further indicates that only one union succeeded in
joining two church bodies with different structures (one
presbyterian and the other congregational). The United
States has not enjoyed the picture of any episcopally-structured church joining one whose clergy has not been episcopally ordained.

Realism applauds the unions achieved, yet sobers excessive
optimism; many extensive efforts to produce unity have ended
in frustration and failure. If it be difficult to unite
groups contained *within* congregational and presbyterian
boundaries, and if no church bodies in the United States have
as yet become one *across* episcopal boundaries, then one wonders how unity can be achieved across Patriarchal and Papal
boundaries.

Yet Christians, who believe that Christ transcends the merely
human realities, are convinced that their divided state is
unacceptable and even tragic. The enormous unity-effort
(manifested first by the formation and continuation of the
World Council of Churches in terms of personnel, time and
money, and later by the Roman Catholic Church) testifies to
the seriousness of the conviction that the divided state of
Christianity is unacceptable. The polemical atmosphere of
the past four centuries appears to be finished. But the end-
ing of the polemical era only ushered in a period of light
and growing cooperation; it did not automatically reveal the
sure path to Christian unity or even the minimum elements
that are essential for the achievement of that hoped-for
unity.

In his book, entitled *Protestantism,* Martin E. Marty suggests
that the Protestant divisions obstructing ecumenical hopes
are of the very nature of Protestantism.

Marty describes his work as "an historically informed theologically interested phenomenological study of Protestantism

as a religion."[15] He eschews a denomination-by-denomination
comparative study from Reformation origins in order to capture the sense of Protestantism as a whole. Marty does not
play down the heterogeneity of the picture as he searches for
elements which identify all Protestant groups. Oscar Cullmann's "rejection of the papacy" mark is acknowledged, but
Marty feels that Tillich's "prophetic protest" is a better
conceptual key in unlocking that which is common to all
Protestant denominations.[16]

In his admittedly difficult effort to capture Protestantism
as a whole, Marty sees dividedness as an ingredient of its
history. However, he does not correlate the observed pheno-
mena of dividedness with his accepted Protestant principle,
"prophetic protest."

Marty points out that Protestantism inherited the schism from
the Orthodox-Catholic split of the eleventh century. Protestantism itself "...by its very existence as a separate protest movement against Roman Catholicism...was an inevitable
contributor to Christian division."[17]

Marty estimates that a Protestant-Catholic unity would have
meant the loss of "prophetic protest" to the Protestants or
the diminution of identity and purpose to Catholics. He
feels that Modern Ecumenism was impossible in an earlier century.

Divisions within Protestantism have deeply troubled Protestant scholars.

> It has been split into Churches, sects, denomi-
> nations, parties, factions, emphasis groups and
> national entities—and at times such a premium
> was placed on 'the right of private judgment'
> that the meaning of Protestantism was reduced
> to autonomous and private forms of individual-
> ism....It is impossible to read extensively in
> Protestant history or to experience Protestant
> Church life almost anywhere in the world with-
> out coming soon to the sense that divisiveness
> belongs to the nature of Protestantism.[18]

It is this "sense that divisiveness belongs to the nature of
Protestantism" that strikes a sobering note when overly optimistic plans or schedules are proposed even for a reunion of
Protestant Churches which share the same statements of faith
and polity. If the path be difficult for those so close in
creed and structure, how much more difficult is the road ob-
structed with obstacles of creed, cult and code (with implications of structure contained under the titles of both

creed and code).

Marty indicates that he is not being merely rhetorical in his
view that "divisiveness" cannot be excluded from Protestantism's ecumenical considerations; the very concept of "reunion
among all Protestants" implies a return to, or regaining of,
a Protestant union previously enjoyed. Marty reminds his
readers:

> Such language has a kind of nostalgic ring,
> implying a fall from good old golden days when
> Protestantism was one thing and before evan-
> gelicals went their separate ways.
>
> Actually, there never was such a movement.
> Protestantism...is the name given by historians
> and others to a complex of events, personalities,
> and emphases bearing a few common features in-
> cluding most notably the rejection of Roman
> Catholicism.[19]

If Protestantism had had only one starting point and all later divisions were from within that one body, then there would
be a unity that Protestant ecumenism could perhaps recapture.
But the Protestant starting points were all from within Roman
Catholicism. Each of the Protestant originators, relatively
close in time, separated from the Roman Catholicism of their
prior lives in different countries and for different reasons.
Luther was a Catholic Priest in Germany, Zwingli a Catholic
Priest in Switzerland, Henry VIII the Catholic King of England, and Calvin a Catholic French layman who moved to Geneva,
to mention only a few leaders. Without question, abuses within the Church, even in high places, cried out for reform; but
the very Scriptures, appealed to for justifying reform, ruled
out division.

Marty perceives elements of unity-seeking and unity impulses
in some writings, formulations, and intentions of the original Reformers. He estimates that modern unity-seekers can
build on such elements and thus work out from unitive elements
intended in the primary reformation intent. They can further
build on the writings of the irenic spirits found among Protestants in each era since the reformation.[20]

More deeply still, the original Reformers did not discard all
the elements of their former Catholicism. On the contrary,
they sought to take the essential elements of the church body
they separated from and to discard what they saw as abusive
accretions.

As Marty observes:

> Far from being born as an individualistic pro-
> test, most of Protestantism inherited ancient
> doctrines of the Church. Reforms did not begin
> as carefree and casual destroyers of Catholic
> ecclesiastical symbolism...when they came to
> leave, or when they were excommunicated, they
> immediately set out to reconstruct the reality
> of the Church in their new situations.[21]

The original reformers varied considerably from each other in
knowledge of theology and perception of what was essential
for the continuation of the "one, holy, catholic and apostolic church" of Jesus Christ as affirmed in the ancient creeds.
All of the reformers discarded the papal authority and moved
their sights to other bases of authority, dominated by the
individual reformer's own interpretation. The reformers,
however, for the most part, preserved: the doctrine of the
trinity, the Bible as the word of God, the critical importance of Christ, baptism and the Lord's Supper. Despite the
fact that different interpretations for the latter items were
given by the different reformers, nevertheless, all these
elements give a commonality to most Protestant bodies, to all
the Orthodox groups and to Roman Catholics; these elements
distinguish Christians from all other religions in the world.

All these elements are faith-elements. They are dependent on
God's own revelation through Christ. Most Protestants believe these things; Orthodox Churches and the Roman Catholic
Church believe that transcendent realities are in these elements. Some of these beliefs and others related to them provided the theological foundation for: the start of the modern
ecumenical movement, the establishment of the World Council
of Churches, and the present relationship with the Roman
Catholic Church.

If ever there is to be a union in creed, worship and leadership, the foregoing elements must be taken into serious consideration; in these elements a more profound commonality
must be found than these separated bodies presently enjoy.
Outside forces such as secularism or communism can provide
motives for believing Christian bodies to unite, but these
forces cannot provide for Christians a basis of lasting union,
nor a vision to be achieved.

These elements mentioned as a basis of possible unity have
been, indeed, at the very starting point of actual past divisions. Mutually exclusive interpretations of the same element have led men to separate. The Luther-Calvin disagreement on the real presence of Christ in the eucharist is commonplace as a contributor to the division between Luther and
Calvin, and consequently in the division between the Lutheran

and Reformed churches.

An either/or polemical mentality characterized the early Reformation period, whereas a both/and perception of Christian realities could have in many instances (even if not all) avoided divisions. In any event, if a faith-union is ever to be attained, some minimum of common belief regarding essentials such as the eucharist must, after patient and calm examination, be achieved.

Marty, in his examination of Protestantism, examines phenomenologically such key elements as the Bible, the Church, orders, baptism and the eucharist from the point of view of sameness and difference among Protestants.[22] A broader view keeping the Orthodox and Roman Catholics in mind is taken by Oxford's John Macquarrie:

> ...if we consider the core, so to speak, comprising the vast majority of Christians, we find there an already existing unity which is quite substantial. Jesus Christ himself is the foundation of that Unity....He made such an impression that there grew up a community confessing that 'Jesus Christ is Lord' (Phil. 2:11) and, however differently this primitive confession may be understood by different people today, it is still the essential bond that holds the church together.[23]

Macquarrie goes on to cite the commonality of the New Testament baptism and the eucharist among the sacraments; creeds and ministry he mentions last, as containing perhaps greater ground of divergent interpretation.

The acknowledgement of the Lordship of Christ, proclaimed in scripture and homily from the time of the primitive community to the present, offered the early twentieth-century unity-seekers the renewed vision that the bond which held together each domination could once again hold the great majority of believing Christians together in a visible unity.

The vision, like the guiding star to the navigator, directs the course, even though it may be beyond reach. Perhaps this comparison is not so far-fetched in view of the mind-enlarging feat of landing spacecraft on Mars.

Yet, as this latter achievement in the physical order took enormous patience and innumerable, detailed steps, so the vision in the theological order can be seen as requiring patient and persevering work, a deepening Christian commitment, and a mutual Christian acceptance of others in the presence

of some unresolved differences. Many steps lie between the
present reality of division and the achievement of Christian
unity.

Cavert's Stages of Modern Ecumenical Activity

In his study of the modern ecumenical movement, Cavert perceived a series of relationships which have developed among
Protestants; this series rests on different types of cooperative and unitive activity. Viewed in an overall long-range
perspective, this series seems like a staircase, or a stage-
sequence leading toward closer union. These stages in fact
did occur, but Cavert does not canonize them as prerequisites
of final Christian unity.

Cavert highlights five stages of relationships through which
Protestants, first acting as individual persons and later as
official representatives of their respective denominations,
have come closer together. Practically all the stages except
the last are project-oriented. Differences of creed, worship,
or polity are so-to-speak off in the wings, while a particular project such as Bible distribution,or some secular project such as civil rights, occupies center stage. Through
the fourth stage, the separated denominations have kept their
full autonomy except for a particular project or area assigned
mutually to common agencies. In Cavert's final step, called
organic union, the united denominations lose their prior identity. Hindsight on this century's activities of the American
Protestant Churches reveals the following stages through which
some churches have passed. Cavert's analysis follows:

>   1. Undenominational and nondenominational de-
>   scribe activities at which Christians work to-
>   gether as *individuals* without affecting the
>   churches of their official agencies.
>
>   2. *Interboard* cooperation refers to the action
>   of denominational boards and societies in working
>   together in their specific fields, but without
>   involving decision by the denomination as a whole.
>
>   3a. Interdenominational (or interchurch) co-
>   operation goes beyond interboard action in indi-
>   cating measures taken by denominations as *corporate
>   bodies.*
>
>   3b. Federation goes beyond interdenominational
>   cooperation in implying a permanent and official
>   relationship of denominations as corporate bodies
>   under a constitutional *charter.*

4. *Federal union* goes beyond federation in
delegating to a central body a measure of
responsibility and authority in certain limited
fields, while the denominations retain full
autonomy in all functions not thus delegated.

5. *Organic union* is a form of corporate structure in which the denominations give up their
separate identities and become one united church.[24]

In his commentary on these stages of Christian cooperation
leading to an eventual union, Cavert joins 3a and 3b under
one heading: (1) the merely individual; (2) interboard or
interagency; (3) a limited association of the denominations
as churches identified as "federated association"; (4) a much
fuller association of the churches as well as some of their
agencies, without loss of each denomination's autonomy, this
is called *federal union*; and lastly (5) *organic union*, i.e.
church-mergers involving the loss of former denominational
identity.[25] Cavert's sequence remains confined to national
limits, that is, to the organizational formation of an organic, *national* church.

An example of each would be: (1) cooperation of individual
Christians regardless of denomination in YMCA work; (2) cooperation of Sunday School boards, regardless of denomination; (3) the formulation of the Federal Council of Churches
(FCC) in 1908; (4) the formation of the National Council of
Churches (NCC) in 1951; and (5) the merger of the Evangelical
and Reformed Church with the Congregational Christian Church
to become the United Church of Christ Church.[26]

In stages *one* and *two*, both of which flourished in the nineteenth century, the initiative was largely taken by Protestant *laymen* for both evangelical and practical reasons. Laymen were seeking mutual support in living their Christian
lives in a secularizing world; and denominational boards such
as Sunday School boards earlier, and home and foreign mission
boards later, solving their problems independently, and sometimes even competitively, decided that mutual cooperation
would mutually advance their Christianizing work.[27] These
works rather easily produced cooperation across denominational boundaries. Neither example involved the churches as
churches.

Stages *three* and *four*, i.e. the federated association (FCC)
and the federal union (NCC), each involved the action of
churches as corporate bodies. The different invited denominations sent appointed delegates to act under the name of the
sending denomination. However, the representative, generally
a layman delegated for the work, could in no way compromise

the absolute autonomy of his denominational church. The delegates came together to form a new *task-oriented* cooperative
organization which the joining denominational churches sub-
sidized with personnel and funds and whose services the churches could use or not as they chose.[28]

The first step to form a Federal Council of Churches (FCC)
was taken in 1900; the new, unprecedented Conciliar body of
thirty-three Protestant Churches held its first official
meeting in 1908.[29] This new multi-denominational structure
was intended to express a "catholic unity of the Christian
Church," to produce a "united service for Christ and the
world," to foster "fellowship" among the churches, "to secure
a larger combined influence for the churches of Christ" and
to help form autonomous, cooperative "local branches."[30]

The word "Catholic" expressed more of a hope than a fact
since most Protestant denominations were not represented and
the new agency was exclusively Protestant in foundation. The
delegates could have named the new structure the Protestant
Council of Churches or used this defining term in their
charter; however, they did not and thus from the FCC's point
of view left the way open for later cooperation and possible
membership of Orthodox or Catholic groupings.

The FCC's very openness toward membership of any Christian
grouping underscores the fact that the autonomy of the joining bodies was not threatened. Christian emphasis characterized the constituting speeches and documents but the creed,
worship and polity of the joining denominations were not part
of the new agency's agenda. During the days of its inaugural
meeting

> ...the Council surveyed the need for cooperation
> in all important areas except worship and doc-
> trine...evangelism, home missions, foreign mis-
> sions, Sunday School work, higher education,
> temperance, family life, Sunday observance[31]

were discussed.

This new Federal Council helped in one way to lessen denominational dividedness, but in another way it fostered its
growth. The council most easily handled social problems
(labor problems) which had nothing to do with denominational
differences, thus the sense of social division was diminished.
On the other hand, the churches, relieved of concern for problems they could not easily cope with, gained freedom to focus
efforts on their own identity and relationship with churches
of similar creed, cult and code. Strong denominational emphasis and loyalty thus becomes a barrier to the ecumenical

movement.[32]

The FCC helped to form autonomous local councils for local
problems, and autonomous state councils to consider problems
on that level. Thus, a loose conciliar structure outside the
structure of each denominational church was built. The churches could use the conciliar agencies but the agencies, kept
in existence by the member churches, could not speak for the
churches except in the event of consensus. The New Council
did not, and could not, reach the denominations in the elements of creed, cult and code which constituted them as churches. Thus, although the FCC is identified as a stage of the
ecumenical movement, and although it contributed toward the
diminution of Protestant denominational exclusiveness, it is
not of its nature a mechanism apt for producing organic
church unity.

The FCC drew Protestant Churches together as whole churches,
but not in each church's whole life, and especially not in
creedal, or worship life. It drew them together not as one
church, not as the "Catholic unity of the Christian Church,"
but as equal partners in facing and trying to solve common
public social problems.

This is very worthwhile indeed, but is this the goal of the
Modern Ecumenical Movement? Is not the desired union of the
churches primarily concerned with the unity of Christian
faith and the oneness of Christ's Church? Does the process
of forming new structures, local, state and federal (designed
from a single nation's political model) lead to the reintegration of the one church of Christ? Does not the character
of the structure as national hinder the emergence of Christ's
Church as transcendent to national boundaries?

The Federal Council was not itself a church or super-church.
It did not worship. By design it avoided questions of faith.
As it developed, its local, state and federal offices were
staffed by salaried and volunteer lay persons of different
denominations. This unprecedented structure, standing outside
of, and roughly parallel to, the local, regional and national
polity structures of the Protestant denominations, became, in
fact, a striking model of practical unity constructed out of
dividedness. As Christians submerged some differences, the
new pattern of hard-won unity suggested the unity of Christ's
one church. This sense of the unity of Christ's Church and
awareness of a structure that bypassed differences suggested
the vision that designed the World Council of Churches.

> The example of the American churches in forming
> the Federal Council was widely followed in other
> lands. Essentially the same type of federated

structure was adopted by other national councils, and also by the World Council of Churches
when its constitution was drafted thirty years
later.[33]

The new Federal Council sparked interest in cooperative effort across a broad front. Many previously isolated denominational boards joined other boards to form interdenominational agencies. This occurred with home mission boards,
foreign mission boards, local and higher educational boards.
These expanding interdenominational agencies, pursuing a
specifically limited interest for some churches, evolved
apart from, and independent of, the FCC and its internal
structures. As common problems were faced new agencies,
sometimes *ad hoc* and sometimes continuing, were formed to
connect the various interboard bureaus.

This picture of agencies connecting agencies outside of the
FCC structure contributed to the formation of the *fourth
stage* of Cavert's five stage analysis of the twentieth century ecumenical movement, namely the National Council of
Churches of Christ in the USA (NCC). Approximately the decade of the forties was needed to analyze the interrelations,
design a federation-type model including all the interdenominational agencies, sell the idea to the agencies, the denominational boards, and the denominations, and to vote the NCC
into being. Twenty-nine Protestant denominations voted positively to compose the still functioning National Council of
Churches in 1951.[34]

In effect, the NCC was constituted of the FCC and many of the
interboard agencies. Denominational barriers were clearly
becoming less significant. Inside the agencies, workers from
different denominations muted their differences. But agencies were composed of very few people; outside the agency was
the vast multitude of Protestant people primarily related to
the denominational church where they worshipped and were influenced in their family and religious lives. The denomination was concerned about its identity; the interdenominational agency was concerned about its task, and thus, muted denominational identities. The local church cultivated denominational identity or began to lose its meaning and its support; the agency cultivated non-denominational Protestantism.

The agency tended to minimalize the differences and emphasize
the common Christian elements. The common denominator of belief was the motivating fuel keeping the interchurch agency
going as a religious agency. The greater the denominational
differences, the less is the common denominator. The agency,
kept in existence by the funds of the denominations, could
in time undercut the very significance of the denomination's

meaning as a specific denomination. Presbyterian John Fry in
his book, *The Trivialization of the United Presbyterian
Church,* sees a loss of a religious sense of denomination in
recent years. The United Presbyterian Church has lost members, contributions, and a sense of purpose and direction in
the last decade.[35]

Without question these twentieth century stages of the ecumenical movement have contributed to further cooperation, a
diminution of divisiveness, and an increased amity in the
Christian religious atmosphere. Yet the troublesome theological question still intrudes itself: Is this leading to
the one Church of Christ? The separated denominations, while
members of the one NCC, will stand apart as churches. In
trouble, the divided churches look to their own existence;
the common effort diminishes.

In the recent recession, the general secretary of the NCC reported to the board of the 33 denomination-member Council
that the staff had to be cut by about one-third. In a four-
year period the Council's annual budget decreased by six
million dollars, from twenty million down to fourteen million.
A cut in staff of 190 persons left a working staff of 460
persons.[36]

Cavert's *fifth* observed *stage* of the modern ecumenical movement is that of organic union. In this step two denominations merge to form one united denomination. The process is
a church merger in which two become one. Some have succeeded;
some have failed. Some generally successful mergers have, in
the difficult joining process, produced a new splinter group
which started its own history as a separate denomination. The
overall projection is that the "church-merger process" will
continue until the last two denominations finally merge to
become the *una sancta* (the one holy) Church of Christ.

Are the Protestant denominations to become one church? As
Marty pointed out, there never was a Protestant Church. And
Cavert noted that the church mergers which have taken place
have mostly been of the same kind, i.e. the merging denominations have substantially shared the same creed, the same worship and the same polity. Episcopal churches stress their
historic continuity of bishops back to Apostolic times; Congregational Churches emphasize their democratic, non-episcopal character. A merger here seems to require that one
merging church (Congregationalist) give up a cherished position or the other (Episcopalian) an essential belief. If
theology is neglected, the joining is a mere political assimilation.

Ian Henderson views the process of the Church of Scotland

(Presbyterian) merging with the Church of England (Episcopal)
as an assimilation by a power-seeking bureaucracy. This long-
time professor of systematic theology at the University of
Glasgow sees the World Council of Churches as "an ecclesiastical power concentration."

Henderson views the emphasis on the unity of Christ's church
as "a ruthless and inveterate attack on denominations."
"Denominationalism," he maintains, is "the courageous abandonment of the nightmare dogma of the One Church."[37] Without
giving the reader his exegesis of the New Testament "Church,"
and while granting the value of the new amicable ecumenical
climate, Henderson nevertheless insists on the preservation
of denominational separatism.

Positions like Professor Henderson's notwithstanding, some
Protestant denominations in the United States, in Canada, and
in India have moved to the "organic union" stage of Cavert's
listing.

In Cavert's view the first four stages are ecumenical in
character because they lead to the summit of the faith stage;
thus they are ecumenical in a limited sense. Concerning the
fifth stage (and he has in mind all Christian churches) he
writes: "This is the pregnant stage in which the Churches are
finding themselves today, the *only* stage to which the term
'ecumenical' can be *fully* applied."[38] This is the critical
sense sought as World Council and Vatican II documents por-
tray it.

Ecumenism's Uneven Development

The overall *dividing* character of Protestant Church life in
the nineteenth century is seen by Cavert and others as yield-
ing to a *uniting* character in the twentieth century.

An overview of the periods of this century can be approximately related to the uneven development of the modern ecumenical movement. Cavert's wide sense of the term, ecumenical, is applied without distinction to varying degrees and
kinds of cooperation among persons and churches. Highlights
of some ecumenical events shed light on the formation of the
World Council of Churches. Cavert's work supports this condensed sketch.

If this century's two world wars and their post-war recovery
time be taken as single periods, then the time of this century in relation to modern ecumenism may be reduced to seven
periods. The thrust and the model for the modern ecumenical
movement come from Protestantism in the United States. However, by mid-century the focus and center of the modern

movement had shifted from the national arena (U.S.) to the
international scene.

The first period extends from the turn of the century to
World War I. The second period includes World War I and the
post war time, from about 1914 to 1925. The third is a short
period of the next four or five years. The fourth is the depression period almost covering the 1930s. The fifth period
embraces World War II and its recovery time; these events
placed their stamp on the forties. The sixth period, covering the fifties, is a time of ecumenical activity on both
national and international fronts. Finally, the seventh period finds the momentum of the ecumenical movement has focused
fully at the international level.

Until mid-century the initiative, the frame of reference, and
the American leadership was almost exclusively Protestant. In
preparation for construction of a large ecumenical center in
New York City, a charter for a nonprofit corporation was requested. The request indicates the overview then prevailing;
within a short time the view was widened to welcome non-
Protestant churches.

> The original charter of March 29, 1948 had been
> granted to 'the Protestant center.' A certifi-
> cate of Amendment was filed with the Secretary
> of State on July 9, 1956, changing the name to
> 'the Interchurch Center.'[39]

In the second half of the century, some Eastern Orthodox
churches entered the movement at different times and on varying levels. Thus the movement, in fact, became wider than
Protestantism.

Some Protestant Churches and the Roman Catholic Church officially entered the overall ecumenical movement but not its
organizations during the Second Vatican Council (1962-1965).
Certain Protestant churches still stand apart from the drawing together of the Christian communities which has characterized the Christian Church life of this century. The Protestant churches remaining aloof range in stance from open
hostility to doubt concerning the movement's final goal. One
outspoken theologian of this last position, Ian Henderson,
dedicated his book *Power Without Glory,* which alleges that
ecumenism serves the power-politics of the Anglican Church,
"...to the good Christians in every denomination who do not
care greatly whether there is One Church or not."[40]

To be more specific about the periods, the *first* one is characterized by an emphasis on the unitive spirit. The number
of interboard agencies increased and the high-water

ecumenical mark of the period was a determined eight-year
process of federating which produced the Federal Council of
Churches of Christ in America (FCC). This body constituted
the greatest single national cross-denominational event in
Protestantism in four centuries. The euphoria of this unitive venture in 1908 spurred cooperative efforts among Protestants, both in America and Europe, until World War I
abruptly ended this era.[41]

In the *second* period, national and international ecumenical
efforts were sharply overshadowed, curtailed and tested by
the War of 1914 to 1918.

> The outbreak of the world war was a disaster to
> the cause of Christian cooperation in interna-
> tional affairs. The war made communication be-
> tween the various Christian countries difficult,
> if not impossible; far worse, it destroyed to a
> large extent their inner Christian fellowship.
> On both sides churches and their leaders threw
> themselves into the conflict....In both warring
> camps men were firmly convinced that they were
> fighting in a just cause. The growing unity of
> Christendom was rent asunder.[42]

The post-war period extending from 1918 to about 1925 was
crowded with Church emergency efforts such as helping refugees, and clouded by the awareness that Church-union activity
had not impeded the traumatic hostility of war. The struggle
between fundamentalist and liberal interpretations of the
Bible also set back the ecumenical advance of this time.

Despite these extraordinary obstacles, some determined, far-
sighted Protestants managed to cling to and communicate plans
for international Christian cooperation and unity. Limited
progress was made in the countries preserved from the war and
in America, whose entry into it was delayed until April 1917.
However, international meetings to consider theological questions of Christian cooperation or church order became practically impossible. Such

> ...work in Europe and other parts of the world
> came almost completely to an end. Travel became
> impossible; contacts were broken; international
> life was for the time being at an end. It was
> only in North America that further progress was
> possible.[43]

War and its aftermath precluded large meetings, but not the
cultivation of ecumenical ideas.

Modern Ecumenism Takes Hold

In the *third* brief period between 1925 and 1929, the determination to seek unity, nurtured during the war and post-war
period, emerged on a conspicuous international level with a
will to continue in existence. Two groups commanded attention.

One group focused on the social life and work of the churches
and became known by the shorthand name of *Life and Work*. This
group felt that doctrinal questions would hinder unity and
that unity would be better served by Christian cooperation
in solving social problems, especially on the international
level.

The other group felt that any unity, achieved without confronting the differences of *faith* which divided Christians,
and the divisions built into Church structures resting respectively on Episcopal, priestly or congregational *order*,
would be inadequately based, and consequently futile for
ecumenism. This international group is referred to by the
shorthand name of *Faith and Order*. This period of expanding
international horizons was abruptly halted by the 1929 depression which ushered in a decade of world distress.

In the *fourth* period the debilitating depression confined
ecumenical efforts mostly to the local scene.[44] It allowed
only a few men the privilege of international travel to keep
ecumenical fires burning.

When the depression had sufficiently lessened, both the *Life
and Work* and *Faith and Order* movements held separate international meetings in the British Isles. In 1938, delegates
from the constitutionally-established international movements
embodied in Mission work, Faith and Order and Life and Work came
together to consider the establishment of a world body which
would coordinate their specific interests and consolidate
their frequently parallel or converging efforts. Thus was
born the committee which began the blue-print for the World
Council of Churches. World War II abruptly interrupted, but
did not abort, this world-envisioning initiative.

In the *fifth* period World War II and its aftermath overshadowed 1939 and the decade of the forties. Again, world travel
and communications were curtailed. But this time, various
ecumenically minded men and committees, established at pre-
war meetings, continued working to elaborate the structure of
a World Council of Churches; they made detailed plans for
bringing the World Council successfully into existence.

Ecumenism Prospers

The war, which prevented hasty action, yielded the time needed
for the slow maturation of the greatest Protestant world-wide
unitive event in over four centuries. In 1948, three years
after the end of the war, a constitutional Assembly of invited denominational churches was held in *Amsterdam*, Holland,
to vote into existence the World Council of Churches.[45]

The *sixth* period, the decade of the fifties, spurred by the
vision of a world-wide, inter-church Christian agency, gave
rise to voluminous ecumenical writings and initiatives. In
1954 the World Council held its second Assembly at *Evanston,
Illinois*. A wave of interest slowly engaged sizeable sections
of the Protestant world. The ecumenical movement broadly excited Protestant feelings as it peaked in the sixties; it
involved the Orthodox and Roman Catholics as well.

The *seventh* period, starting in the decade of the sixties,
emerged as a peak period of visible ecumenical activity. The
primary emphasis has shifted to the international scene.
Dampened by a counter-wave of anti-institutionalism fed by
the very unpopular Vietnam war, this period nevertheless
witnessed the widening of the Modern Ecumenical Movement to
embrace, in unequal ways, official Eastern Orthodox and official Roman Catholic interests and initiatives. Some of
the Orthodox Churches, in 1961, joined the somewhat modified
World Council at its third world-wide Assembly in *New Delhi;*
the Roman Catholic Church sent official observers to it.

Between the years of 1962 and 1965, the Roman Catholic Church
held the twenty-first ecumenical council, commonly referred
to as Vatican II. To this assembly, official Eastern Orthodox observer-delegates and official Protestant observer-delegates were invited; most of them went. The period continued
with the Fourth Assembly of the World Countil at *Uppsala,*
Sweden in 1968. The official delegations of the Orthodox
Churches and the observers of the Roman Catholic Church were
increased. The same relationships prevailed also at the
World Council's fifth international Assembly at *Nairobi,*
Africa in 1975; Orthodox were members, Roman Catholics were
observers.

The sixth World Assembly of the WCC at *Vancouver*, Canada, in
the summer of 1983, whole maintaining former relationships
with non-member churches, engaged its member churches and
interested observers in new considerations on Christian
Liturgy.

CHAPTER THREE

ECUMENISM RISES TO THE INTERNATIONAL LEVEL

Denominationalism has been briefly reviewed; Cavert's five
stages toward unity have been examined; and the ebb and tide
of ecumenism in the twentieth century has been sketched.
Next follows the rise of this unprecedented Christian movement to the world level. This rise took place through the
vision, conviction and sustained drive of a few pioneers.
The first originating person, as already indicated, was John
R. Mott.[1]

Back in 1806 William Carey, Protestant Missioner in Calcutta,
described a dream or a wish for a general association of all
denominations designed to meet about every ten years. He
predicted it would produce very important effects. This vi-
sionary wish, referred to as William Carey's "Pleasing
Dream," produced no known meetings. However, in the last
half of the nineteenth century, New York and London saw a
loosely related series of mission gatherings which cut across
denominational lines. One in New York in 1900 had the whole
world in view and was named the "Ecumenical Missionary Conference."[2]

Missions: John R. Mott

The expanding foreign missionary work and the wish of Protestant missionary agencies for a continuing center for consultation and cooperation made the next international, missionary gathering, set for 1910 in Edinburgh, most significant.
John R. Mott emerged as the giant of that meeting entitled
the World Missionary Conference.

Mott, a non-theologically-trained Methodist layman, was a
tireless reader, worker and organizer. He headed the first
commission to prepare for the conference. The 1910 Conference was better prepared than any which had preceded it.
Simultaneous preliminary studies by experts produced eight
written reports for the conferees. About six hundred people
received personal letters from Mott regarding the content
and conduct of the conference. The meeting was limited to
official delegates of Protestant Missionary agencies serving
non-Christian missions. The conference was consultative and

by definition avoided denominational differences of faith,
worship and church order. The envisioned target area of missionary work was proclamation of the Gospel to the whole
world (oikoumene). The mood was primarily practical. Reports touching this world vision, the church in all mission
places and the promotion of unity, struck a forceful ecumenical note among the conferees. In a rare move they voted to
stay in existence through the service of a *continuation committee* which should work toward the formation of a permanent
international council. Mott was chosen as its chairman.[3]

> The World Missionary Conference, Edinburgh
> 1910, was the birthplace of the modern ecu-
> menical movement. This was seen especially
> in relation to worldwide evangelism——the
> proclamation of the Gospel——and the planting
> of the Church throughout the world. While
> through the prosecution of Missions Protes-
> tants had been coming together as never be-
> fore, the Edinburgh gathering accelerated the
> pace. It cannot be said too often or too .
> emphatically that the ecumenical movement
> arose from the missionary movement and con-
> tinues to have at its heart world wide
> evangelism.[4]

The uninvited Orthodox and Roman Catholic worlds, representative of three-quarters of the world's Christians, were hardly
sanguine about this international Protestant group planning
"the planting of the Church throughout the world." In fact,
at this time, Protestants and other Christians were worlds
apart.

The Orthodox in the Moslem world were severely circumscribed;
the Russian Orthodox world of 1910 would soon be swamped by
the tidal-wave of communism. The Roman Catholic Church continued its own massive mission enterprises aware of the increasing divisions which were complicating the work of the
priests, brothers, and nuns in the mission fields.

Inquiries revealed that Protestant-Roman Catholic contacts in
the Kiangsi province of China during the pre-Communist period
were, for all practical purposes, zero. Probably the Protestant-Roman Catholic missionary communications ranged from
cooly-cordial to modestly-friendly and warm depending on the
personalities of the respective missionaries involved.

Edinburgh 1910, the Protestant starting point of the modern
ecumenical movement, was probably not even noticed by the
vast majority of the world's Orthodox or Roman Catholics.
Nevertheless, its work and that of its continuation committee

almost immediately began an ever-spreading influence. The
stone had been thrown into a corner of the pond and the ripples started spreading.

Within one six-month period, John Mott, the head of the continuing committee, "held a series of eighteen regional and
three national conferences in Asia—in Ceylon, India, Burma,
Malaya, China, Korea, and Japan."[5] Delayed but not stopped
by World War I, Mott unfolded his plan for a permanent international missionary organization. "The meeting at which the
International Missionary Council (IMC) was finally constituted was held in October 1921, at Lake Mohawk in New York
State."[6]

This early post-war constitutional meeting of the IMC enjoyed
the presence of over sixty representatives from more than a
dozen countries, mostly western; German missionary societies,
among others, did not attend. Thus, speaking graphically,
the representation was not as worldwide as the Council's intention. As time softened the war-embittered feelings, the
Council's membership increased. National missionary organizations, not churches, constituted the Council's membership.
The Germans sent delegates to the second IMC meeting at Oxford in 1923.*

John Mott headed the approximately decennial meetings
through Tambaram, retiring as the IMC head in 1941.[7] This
leader of an era, massive in frame, no stranger to superla-
tives, authoritarian at times, very direct and somewhat un-
imaginative, left an indelible global stamp on Protestant
mission work.[8]

A cardinal principle of Edinburgh 1910, was the exclusion of
"creed, cult and code" questions on which the conferees differed. The neglect of this principle probably would have
frustrated the meeting at that time. Yet some representatives there were convinced that sooner or later these difficult questions of faith, worship and church structure would
have to be faced. One delegate, Charles H. Brent, a missionary bishop of the Protestant Episcopal Church in the United
States, acceded to the temporary value of the excluding principle but stated in a significant speech:

>...that by its self-denying ordinance, which
>forbade discussion of differences of opinion

---

*Meetings and their documents are referred to commonly
by place and date, thus Jerusalem 1928 was the third meeting,
Tambaram 1938 was the fourth, Whitby (Canada) 1947 was the
fifth.

in doctrine and ecclesiastical structure and
practice, the gathering was failing to face
some of the basic issues confronting Christians.
Speaking from the floor he declared that he entirely accepted the wisdom of the decision that
questions of faith and order should not be included in the programme of the conference, since
that body was primarily concerned with practical
cooperation. Yet, he went on to say, Christians
could not rest content with cooperation between
separated bodies, and the causes of division must
be examined with a view of their removal. Characteristically, he expressed his intention to do
something about it; what he did is recorded in
the genesis of the Faith and Order Movement.[9]

Joint mission agencies had avoided questions of differing
creeds; education boards dodged them, the FCC had shunned
them, the World Missionary Conference ruled them out. They
had a threatening ring. Creed, code, cult differences con-
jured images of inflammatory arguments. Yet Charles Brent
felt they could be avoided no longer. Christians must meet
in Christian charity. In June 1910 Brent had resolved; in
October 1910 he brought his resolution to the General Convention of the American Episcopal Church.[10]

The convention unanimously resolved to set up a committee
that would arrange a meeting of all Christian communions
which profess Jesus Christ as God and Savior; the meeting
should then confer on matters of faith and order.[11]

Estimations of such a meeting ranged from "impossible" to
"productive of new divisions." Brent needed unfailing faith
and help. He had the faith. An Episcopalian layman, Robert
H. Gardiner, supplied untiring help as secretary of the newly-formed commission charged with production of the meeting.[12]
The Faith and Order Movement was started! The search for
the "lost gift of Church unity" (Brent felt it had been lost)
was begun. The way ahead loomed long and difficult, yet full
of interesting possibilities.

Life and Work: Nathan Soederblom

In the meanwhile the King of Sweden, who by law still had
final say as to the highest pastor of the National Church,
named 49 year-old Nathan Soederblom in May 1914 as the Archbishop of Uppsala and ecclesiastical leader of the Lutheran
Church there.[13]

Soederblom, a professor of the history of religions, assumed
his new post on the eve of World War I. As the storm clouds

burst Soederblom,from neutral Sweden, sought to get the
Church leaders of the belligerent nations to join in an appeal for Christian peace and unity.

> The attempt to secure a united Christian appeal
> for peace and a declaration of unity had failed.
> The refusals received from the belligerent coun-
> tries showed how deep the cleavage went even
> within the Christian Church. The peace appeal
> of November 1914...marks the starting point of
> what later developed into the Life and Work
> Movement.[14]

Toward the end of the war, and again after the war, the relatively unknown Soederblom launched a Christian Church peace
initiative. Soederblom's projection was interdenominational
and international. With Roman Catholics on both sides of the
war lines and Orthodox mainly on the eastern side, Lutheran
Soederblom's initiatives were those of a newcomer. His efforts failed, but Soederblom, himself, became fairly well
known.

Some saw Sweden's Archbishop as too closely allied to the
German side; this was especially true of the French Reformed
churches. Other churchmen, especially Roman Catholics, were
aware that he spoke as if he were spokesman for the whole
Christian world. As admirer Nils Karlstrom expresses Soederblom's position: "Unity in faith can exist even where confessions of faith are different."[15]

In a 1918 effort to convoke a representative Christian Assembly, the Swedish Archbishop expanded his invitation list,
without the customary courtesy of prior inquiry, to include
the Vatican as well as some Orthodox churches. However, so
many of the invitations were declined that Soederblom post-
poned the plan of convening an international Christian conference. At that time, he did come to know some of the Orthodox patriarchs, who indicated that their interest in a
meeting of churches was conditioned on affirmation of Christ's
divinity. They could share no ecumenical fellowship with
churches which denied Christ's divinity.[16]

A year later, in 1919, Soederblom addressed a committee meeting of an organization known as the "World Alliance for Promoting International Peace through the Churches." He proposed to this body the formation of an

> Ecumenical Council of the Churches which should
> be able to speak on behalf of Christendom on the
> religious, moral, and social concerns of men...
> [He felt] that it was impossible to wait until

> unity should be achieved in matters of faith
> and order before moving towards closer co-
> operation between the Churches...such an
> Ecumenical Council would not encroach on the
> independence of the individual Churches.[17]

The fact that the churches had been unable to stop the war,
or even to persuade the warring nations to seek a peace of
conciliation instead of a peace of conquest, gave force to
Soederblom's position. He wanted an international Christian
Church body to be a spokesman on international religious,
moral, and social questions. His position, that the faith
underlying the churches' differences was somehow the same,
led him to seek a quick path that avoided faith and order
questions. Yet religious, moral and social questions were
being faced and answered from faith. The nature of the churches he was calling to fellowship involved faith and order
questions.

The World Alliance Committee he addressed liked his idea but
felt that it was not the competent body to organize an *Ecumenical Council of Churches*. The Federal Council of Churches'
delegates supported Soederblom's idea. Such a council was
the natural top-story to its own conciliar edifice. The
Swiss representatives thought that it should be limited to
Protestant Churches; common international tasks were needed
to bring Protestants together.

At the World Alliance Meeting, Soederblom, a Swiss delegate
and a third delegate formed a committee to pursue the proposed concept. Some months later, seven others from the
United States, Switzerland, and Sweden were invited to join
them in the preparatory work for a conference in Stockholm
in 1925.[18]

Soederblom later approached the Lambeth Headquarters of the
Church of England to invite the Anglicans to the preparatory
committee as a founding body of the proposed Ecumenical Council. Lambeth would not consent unless the new council would
be truly ecumenical; it would not come unless the Roman Catholic Church and the Orthodox Churches were invited. Soederblom and his organizing committee entrusted the American
Protestant FCC members with the task of organizing a preparatory conference in 1920. The FCC committee sent invitations
only to Protestant Churches. Thus, the Church of England
took no part in the 1920 Geneva preparatory conference for
the proposed Ecumenical Council of the Churches.[19]

The word "ecumenical" in such a conference could express
neither a fact nor an intention. Even future invitations
would appear to be invitations to move under a Protestant

umbrella organization. The papers for the upcoming Stockholm
meeting would be formulated by Protestant theologians and
churchmen. Influential persons, who wanted neither Orthodox
nor Roman Catholic Churches there nor cared that much about
the Anglican position, had controlled the invitations. Also,
many Protestant churches were absent, yet the Geneva conference would speak about the obligations of "the Church" as if
it were representative of "the whole Church."

Some theologians at Geneva would argue that "the Church," the
Una Sancta, existed in each of the separated churches. They
believed that the *Una Sancta* was the one underlying common
bond, even though invisible, uniting all of them. It was out
of this context that the preparatory committee members felt
they could speak as "the Church." Soederblom himself held
that it was out of this great common existent unity that the
churches could speak as one to the transdenominational, international problems of the day.

Yet Soederblom, whose concept of the Church was wider than
that which restricted the invitations, argued that the scope
of the forthcoming Christian conference at Stockholm should
be universal. All Christian bodies should be invited. At
Geneva, in 1920, Soederblom

> ...strongly insisted that invitations should be
> sent to all Christian Churches. He pointed out
> that to convene an *ecumenical* conference of
> *Protestant* Churches involved a contradiction in
> terms. The Swiss contended that the point of
> view of the Roman Catholic Church was such as
> to make cooperation with it impossible. (Soeder-
> blom acknowledged that Rome would probably re-
> fuse the invitation, and continued.) If any
> communion were to be excluded *a priori* from the
> coming conference, those responsible for it
> would from the start have taken up a sectarian
> attitude.[20]

Soederblom's position won the day. He himself was entrusted
this time with the Committee on Arrangements. This committee
was later augmented by stages to become the International
Committee of Official Representatives. This latter committee
chose as the title for the upcoming Stockholm conference, not
Ecumenical Council of Churches, but Universal Christian Conference on Life and Work.

A letter of invitation was sent to the Pope who expressed
gratitude but declined the invitation. A delegation of notable men was sent to some Orthodox churches. Some of them
accepted; some declined.

The *Faith and Order* Movement, still in the process of formation, suggested to the *Life and Work* International Committee
that the two groups hold their constitutional meetings in
the same year, in the same city (Washington, D.C.) in succeeding weeks. The Provisional Committee declined this suggestion, replying that *Faith and Order's* goal was rather far
away, while *Life and Work* should be able to bring union for
international action quickly and without much trouble. In
declining the Faith and Order invitation the committee chose
to use the put-down expression "Doctrine divides, but service
unites."[21] The Faith and Order main interest is doctrine.

Despite conflicts, criticisms, and postponements, the Universal Christian Conference on Life and Work, now commonly referred to as *Life and Work* (L&W), met in Stockholm in 1925
with over 600 delegates of both churches and religious organizations attending from thirty-seven countries. Nathan
Soederblom, Lutheran Archbishop of Uppsala, had achieved it!
The Conference had accomplished the simultaneous crossing of
denominational and national boundaries for international
Christian consultation on political, social, economic, and
industrial problems at the international level. One writer
estimates that Soederblom himself was Stockholm 1925. No
Soederblom, no Stockholm! And further, no Stockholm, no
World Council of Churches as it is now constituted.[22]

Life and Work at Stockholm produced only one official statement. This one brief document noted both the past failure
of the churches and their future duty to apply the Gospel
message to every area and level of human life. The churches
must state the principles: individual Christians must carry
them out. Truth-seekers, youth, workingmen are allies in
this holy work. All will come together as they approach
nearer to the Crucified and Risen Lord.[23]

Life and Work had brought together official delegates of actual churches as well as delegates of church agencies such as
the FCC. These delegates were not the heads of the various
churches and organizations. They could neither speak nor act
for their respective bodies; they could only consult and
bring the sense of the assembly back to their sending organizations. The assembly had no authority to speak for the
churches; it could not mandate; it could only enunciate a position which the churches could accept, neglect or reject.

Life and Work at Stockholm voted unanimously to continue its
members' international relationships through a continuation
committee. This was a critically important structuring act.
In 1930, this committee was modified and constituted as a
permanent Council with the title "Universal Christian Council
for Life and Work." Its headquarters were in Geneva,

Switzerland.[24]

Stockholm was both praised and criticized. The praise came
from the social-minded who shared Soederblom's vision of
bringing the force of the churches and related organizations
to bear at the level of war and peace, international economics, etc. It was negatively judged by those who felt that
the churches were meddling in things that belong to politics.

Further, the Anglicans felt that their own one-shot Christian
Conference on Politics, Economics and Citizenship" (COPEC),
which had Anglicans, Catholics, Methodists on every commission and had produced influential documents in each field,
had done better. Finally, the Eastern Orthodox delegates
present

> ...could not fail to report the overwhelmingly
> Protestant character of the gathering, manifest
> in its membership, its worship and its discus-
> sions. It is therefore no wonder that in Ortho-
> dox countries interest in ecumenical developments,
> then as later, hardly went beyond a small circle
> of broad-minded leaders.[25]

The measure of support was greater than the negative criticism; thus, the initial achievement continued.

Under Soederblom as its first president, the continuation
body of Life and Work established an International Christian
Social Institute which published a quarterly, ran annual
seminars, and initiated studies probing into the nature of
Christ's one Church. The Continuation Committee, later named
the Council, did its work through commissions on: Church and
Labor, Cooperation among Theologians, International Christian
Press, Inter-Church Aid, International Work for Refugees, and
an International Protestant Loan Association.

Stockholm had aimed at crossing denominational barriers for
union in practical Christianity. It moved for the most part
to form particular subordinate service commissions as its
leaders became aware of pressing needs. The central body itself inclined toward becoming an overall Protestant service
agency.

Within the organization, opposing tendencies sought domination:
one, labeled "humanist ecumenism" pulled toward a neutral
organization for men of any, or even no, Christian convictions for international fellowship service; another wanted
the body as Christian to focus on practical problems first
and attend to doctrine later; a third, labeled "denominational ecumenists" felt that a Christian union for social purposes

without a union in faith or doctrine was a radically false
approach.

Soederblom who held the "union in service first, doctrine
later" position died in 1931; his sense of practical activities had dominated Life and Work; full theological considerations of organic union remained speculative and remote. Yet,
the underlying theological differences in denominations kept
surfacing. Denominational self-consciousness underwent a renewal. Some followed Luther; others held with Calvin.

> Life and Work increasingly recognized the
> importance of theological factors, and thus
> steered a course which gradually brought it
> into convergence with Faith and Order.[26]

The dilemma was the choice between a pragmatism which denied
denominational differences, or a policy position dominated
by one denomination. The first tendency would have L and W
acting like a secular body, the second would give L and W
the exclusiveness of the one denomination with a doctrinaire
Lutheran or Reformed Character. The path between and beyond
the dilemma of a non-church posture versus a one-denomination
thrust seemed, to the Protestant leadership, to be to emphasize the one Church of Christ, the *Una Sancta* invisibly em-
bedded in all the churches. Among those associated with
L&W there flourished the

> ...belief in the *Una Sancta,* a reality which
> operates in and through the diverse Churches,
> and which is the unifying center of their life
> and witness before the world. Consequently the
> goal of their actions must be not simply broader
> co-operation for social ends, but that the
> Churches in so cooperating may manifest and
> carry towards its fullness their common life in
> the one body of Christ.[27]

Thus, the belief in the *Una Sancta,* the one Holy Church of
Christ (a clear Faith and Order topic) surfaced as the path
through the dilemma of the opposing tendencies in Life and
Work. Such a theological topic held little attraction for
American and European social activists; it seemed rather to
belong to Eastern Orthodox or Anglican reflections except
that the *Una Sancta* that L and W referred to was an invisible
church, hidden by denominational facades. This emphasis on
the social nature of Christ's one church was a surprising
counterpoint also to the individualist view then flourishing.

> Large Protestant groups still centered their
> belief on individual salvation or on the

> immanent Kingdom of God. But by 1937 it had
> become clear that the Church and its nature
> was one of the central problems, perhaps *the*
> *central problem* to which at that date ecumeni-
> cal thinking must be directed.[28]

The theological problem of Christ's Church did, in fact,
move much closer toward the center of the L and W Council's
considerations. The recent research done in Sacred Scripture uncovered new interests and insights into the nature of
Christ's Church. The high level of biblical research produced so much agreement and common interpretation that a
commonly acceptable Bible was produced for the first time
since the Reformation. Further, the growing Nazi pressure
against both Catholic and Protestant churches and its effort
to set up a Nazi-dominated pseudo-church sharply centered attention on the transcendent, supra-national character of
Christ's Church.

Such factors led Life and Work to focus its next world meeting on the Church and its international implications. The
meeting was held at Oxford in 1937. Dr. J. H. Oldham, chairman of the preparation committee, emerged as the leading de-
signer of its program, entitled "Church, Community and
State."[29] Thus, Oldham became for Oxford what Soederblom
had been for Stockholm.

Over a third of the more than 800 in attendance were official
delegates of about 120 denominational churches. The Nazi
government barred the German delegation from the meeting,
whose overall character was Anglo-American Protestant. The
familiar name of Dr. John R. Mott appeared as principal conference chairman. The names of William Temple, Anglican
Archbishop of York (and later of Canterbury) and Willem A.
Visser't Hooft came into prominence here.

> The most distinctive feature of the Oxford
> ecclesiology however, was its bold declara-
> tion of the independence of the Church over
> against mundane counter churches of any and
> every kind.[30]

"Let the Church be the Church" or "The Church must be the
Church" became a slogan to encourage the christians of Germany,
Poland, Russia and China as their churches confronted the
furious storms of hostile secular and pagan governments.

Convergence of work topics and viewpoints, overlapping of
leadership personnel, and rising costs convinced the Oxford
delegates that a resolution proposed by Faith and Order to
merge their organized movements was highly acceptable. The

vote for merger was almost unanimous. The following year
(May 1938), Life and Work ceased to exist as a *separate* ecumenical movement.[31]

Faith and Order: Charles H. Brent

As Life and Work had advanced from concept to organization to
immersion of its influence into the forming of the World
Council of Churches, so Faith and Order went from vision to
organization to the work of framing the World Council of
Churches.

The leading spirit of the Faith and Order Movement was Charles
H. Brent, Protestant Episcopal Bishop of the Philippines and
later of Rockville Centre, New York; layman Robert H. Gardiner
was the tireless secretary of the formation commission. Other
unitive organizations and movements had carefully and explicitly excluded questions of faith and order; Brent was convinced that no true union of churches was achievable except
in and through faith and order. His aim was to form a World
Conference on Faith and Order. The expression implies the
inclusion of doctrinal beliefs, worship, moral questions as
well as questions on the church with its ministry, discipline
and authority.

> There was no doubt in the minds of those re-
> sponsible from the start for the leadership of
> the movement that participation in the confer-
> ence by representatives of the whole Christian
> world, Roman Catholic, Orthodox, and Protestant
> should be sought.[32]

In 1913 commissions from fifteen United States Protestant denominations convened in a preparatory meeting to formulate
principles for the World Conference. The preparatory group
agreed: that all Christian churches should be invited to discuss points of difference, agreement, and values of the various positions; that *organic unity* is the ultimate reality,
but the business of the World Conference is discussion and
prayer *without pressure or threat* of conference resolutions
troublesome toward any denomination; that this very preparation meeting was like an ecumenical council. An invited
Russian Orthodox guest favorable to the World Conference idea
nevertheless rejoined that the preparatory meeting was hardly
ecumenical with neither the Eastern Orthodox Church or Roman
Catholic Church present. He felt that Protestants should
first reconcile their own differences.[33]

Well before the start of World War I, Secretary Gardiner had
sent a letter (not an invitation) concerning the proposed
World Conference on Faith and Order to the leaders of all the

World's Christian Churches. This included also all Roman
Catholic cardinals and bishops. Incredibly, Gardiner managed
to mail about 100,000 letters.

Gardiner formulated a special letter in Latin to Cardinal
Gasparri to inform Pope Benedict XV. The Cardinal replied,
conveying the Pope's prayers and hopes for so worthy a project. The Pope prayed that the voice of Christ, which he
himself followed,would lead the Conference to find the *rock*
of unity which Jesus Christ Himself had established. The
Pope expressed affection for one who joined him in his own
constant care and labor for the unity of the Mystical Body
of Christ. The letter closed on a note of gratitude.[34]

Benedict XV, in gentle terms, left no doubt that he favored a
serious and sincere inquiry into the essential nature of the
Church, but also, that there was no uncertainty in Roman
Catholic belief where the unity of Christ's Church was to be
found. Other formulations in similar vein were given in response to Gardiner's proposal letter.

World War I terminated the international communications;
Americans led by the Brent-Gardiner team continued the planning. Actually, the Protestant Episcopal Church almost alone
carried the whole work forward for a decade or more. The
idea, the world-wide promotion, and the money came from Protestant Episcopal sources.[35]

In 1919, as soon as feasible after the war, deputations were
sent to invite the Church leaders in Europe and the Near East
to the World Conference. For the most part, the deputations
received affirmative answers. The German and other continental Protestant churches, however, were suspicious of this
movement,which came from an Anglo-American source. With a
strong feeling that it was an Anglican imperialist move, the
German churches refused the invitation.

Pope Benedict XV received the deputation most cordially but
definitely declined the invitation to the Conference *as proposed*. A written statement prepared for the occasion indicated that Roman Catholic teaching on the unity of Christ's
visible Church was universally known. It also pointed out
that the unity of Christ's Church required reunion with the
visible head of the Church, the Vicar of Christ, the successor of St. Peter.[36]

Not all members of the inviting deputation were sufficiently
prepared to have the invitation declined. Without consultation or much homework on the question, the pre-war committee
designing the world-wide Faith and Order organization had
voted that *all* Christian churches should and would be invited.

The struggle had been to achieve the *all* against the position
of those who felt that pan-Protestantism should be the objective.

The question had not been plumbed whether all those invited
could join an organization whose basic presupposition held
that the Church of Jesus Christ had lost its unity. The
Vatican's oft-repeated claim that Christ's gift of unity to
His Church flourished in the Roman Catholic Church precluded
that Church's joining an organization whose search for the
"lost unity" implicitly denied that claim. Thus, the deputation left the presence of Pope Benedict with its invitation
declined.

> Some of the deputation had hoped for another
> result, and it is reported that when they were
> returning from their visit the Anglo-Catholic mem-
> ber of it . . . raised his fist to heaven and
> expressed his judgement on the Bishop of Rome
> in terms more forceful than complimentary.[37]

The deep disparity of faith-positions surfaced sharply in the
rejection of the 1919 invitation to share in establishing a
World Organization of Faith and Order. Benedict XV had acted
in line with Pio Nono (1846-1878), Leo XIII (1878-1903) and
Pius X (1903-1914) who had preceded him; Pius XI (1922-1939)
and Pius XII (1939-1958) who followed him would address themselves more explicitly to the new movement emerging mainly in
the Protestant world.

As the focus of the developing movement shifted from Christian Social Action (avoiding doctrine) to doctrinal questions,
the interest of the Vatican grew, but very cautiously. This
change from a definite *no* to a carefully modified and continuing *yes*, which covers the period from Leo XIII to Paul VI,
becomes clearer as the inner dynamic of Faith and Order and
Life and Work leads to their convergence. This "no" to a
"modified yes" will be examined subsequently.

Concerning the Pope's rejection of the Protestant deputation's
invitation, George Tavard writes:

> It would be unbecoming for the Sovereign Pontiff
> to participate in ecumenical conferences if he
> were to join Protestants in trying to find out
> what kind of unity Christ intended His Church to
> have. To the extent that this was intended by
> inviting Benedict XV, the Holy Father could not
> help but answer as he did. The Protestant world
> is under an illusion if it imagines that the
> Catholic Church can change her doctrine on unity.[38]

On the Protestant side, especially in those churches in which
the social side of Christianity had been emphasized, the
Vatican position appeared as an unyielding doctrinal intransi-
gence.

The inviting deputation continued on its way to such ancient
ecclesiastical centers as Alexandria, Jerusalem, Damascus,
etc., and on into central and northern Europe. Many churches
accepted the invitation, but not all. In 1919 Russia and
Germany were inaccessible to the deputation.

Further, the war's end was too recent for Anglo-American
initiatives to be free of suspicion.

> There was a strong feeling on the Continent as
> a whole, not only in Germany, that the Faith
> and Order Movement was an Anglican imperialist
> move, entirely ignoring Continental circumstances
> and the Continental point of view. The German
> Churches at this stage refused all invitations
> to take part in the World Conference.[39]

The commission of the Protestant Episcopal Church (USA) called
a meeting in Geneva in 1920 of all the churches (to be represented by three-person delegations) which had accepted the
invitation to establish a World Conference on Faith and Order.
From some forty nations, seventy churches, doctrinally trinitarian, sent delegations. The meeting established a critically important "Continuation Committee" to which the Protestant
Episcopal Church transferred the full responsibility of the
Faith and Order Movement, thus giving the movement an international character and scotching the charge of Anglican im-
perialism.

The Orthodox delegation, anxious about Protestant proselytizing efforts among their people, expressed doubt about the
movement as a whole. Protestant Episcopal Bishop Brent, who
personally symbolized the meaning and life of the Faith and
Order Movement, was elected chairman. Brent described the
movement as "a pilgrimage *in search of* unity."[40]

The Movement's Continuation Committee appointed a "Subjects
Committee" to explore the range of concord and discord among
the Christian churches and to draft in-depth theological
studies in preparation for a first world conference. A second meeting of the Continuation Committee in 1925 and a third
in 1926 completed the preparatory work for establishing the
World Conference on Faith and Order at *Lausanne,* Switzerland
in 1927. Brent was elected its first president.[41]

The Subjects Committee had its six years of behind-the-scene

study and work discolored by the rumor that its papers were
decision papers which pre-empted the freedom of the churches
coming to the meeting. After painful reconsideration, the
labor of six years was scrapped and mainly topic headings
were presented on the agenda, thus:

1.   The call to unity
2.   The Church's message to the world--the Gospel
3.   The nature of the Church
4.   The Church's common confession of faith
5.   The Church's ministry
6.   The Sacraments
7.   The unity of Christendom and the place of
      the differing churches in it.[42]

The topics immediately indicate that Faith and Order deliberations are explicitly in the heartland of theology as contrasted with Life and Work conference topics. Further, the four
topics of the Sacred Scripture, Confessions or Creeds, the
Church's ministry and Sacraments are reminiscent of the presentation of the same topics to the Protestant Episcopal General Convention (U.S.A.) in 1886; the combination of these
four topics became known by the title of the Chicago
Quadilateral.

William R. Huntington (1838-1918) had envisioned the combination of "Scripture-Creeds-Sacraments-Historic Episcopacy" as
the irreducible minimum required to effect a union of the
various denominations with his own Protestant Episcopal Church
and thus to form the "Catholic Church of America."[43] The convention softened Huntington's straightforward view but saw
the four elements cited as inherent parts of Christian faith,
and essential to every effort at Christian unity.[44]

Two years later at the third decennial conference of Anglican
bishops at Lambeth Palace, London, in 1888, the assembly accepted the Chicago Quadrilateral with some modifications, as
a basis toward what was titled "Home Reunion," i.e. as a basis for membership in the world-wide Anglican Ecclesiastical
family. The four elements of "Scriptures, Creeds, Sacraments,
Historic Episcopate" were stated thus:

a)   The Holy Scriptures of the Old and New
Testaments as 'containing all things necessary
to salvation,' and as being the rule and ultimate standard of faith.

b)   The Apostles' Creed, as the Baptismal
Symbol; and the Nicene Creed, as the sufficient
statement of the Christian Faith.

c)   The two Sacraments ordained by Christ

> Himself—Baptism and the Supper of the Lord—
> ministered with unfailing use of Christ's
> words of institution and of the elements
> ordained by Him.
>
> d) The Historic Episcopate, locally adapted
> in the methods of its administration to the
> varying needs of the nations and peoples called
> of God into the unity of His Church.[45]

This statement, now also known as the Lambeth Quadrilateral, can be seen as corresponding topic-wise with four points of the Lausanne Faith and Order agenda. Of the remaining three Lausanne topics, the first, the "call to union" is a scripturally-based introduction; the remaining two: "the church," "the place of the various churches in the One Church," brought to the fore theological problems which continue in prominence to the present time.

Originally, the Quadrilateral was held to be only a starting point for discussion with churches considering reunion. More recently, some within the Anglican Communion have viewed the Quadrilateral as a terminal point, the achievement of which would constitute the Christian unity to be sought.[46]

The Christian elements common to Anglican, Orthodox, Reformed, and Roman Catholic beliefs contained in the Quadrilateral and the Lausanne agenda are indeed significant. At the same time each group has serious reservations about understatement, interpretation, or in some cases, overstatement.

At the Lausanne F and O Conference, the Orthodox representatives felt constrained to withhold their agreement from most of the reports generated on the topics listed. They could vote for the report of Lausanne's second topic (called Section II), "The Church's Message to the World--the Gospel." However, concerning all the others, they found that the principles underlying them were irreconcilable with the principles of the Orthodox Church. Orthodox Archbishop Germanos spoke for the Patriarchates of Constantinople, Alexandria, Jerusalem, Serbia, Rumania and others when, near the close of the Lausanne Conference, he declared that the Orthodox would abstain from voting.

> The tensions among the Orthodox was considerable, and Archbishop Germanos, after he had read the declaration, returned to his seat with the tears streaming down his face.[47]

The reports on the different topics at Lausanne are sharply condensed statements of theological sameness and difference manifested among the delegates. For example, the report on

"The Ministry of the Church" (identified as Section V) consists of only fourteen paragraphs. The first paragraph,
using the generic word *ministry,* names, in terms acceptable
to all, the origin, purpose and function of ministry in any
Christian Church. Thereafter, differences are cited in general terms until the later paragraphs, wherein specific beliefs are addressed.

In Section V the only churches specifically identified were
the Orthodox. They are cited as regarding Christ Himself to
be the institutor of ministry in His Church. They believe
that the threefold form of the ministry (bishops, presbyters,
deacons) must be based on the unbroken line of succession
from the Apostles. They express regret that they cannot
agree with many of the churches at Lausanne.[48] The position
of those who hold for a presbyteral or congregational polity
was properly identified without reference to any specific
church.

Similarly, in the nine-paragraph report on "The Sacraments"
(Section VI), the Orthodox belief that there are seven Sacraments is identified, while the conviction of the remaining
delegates, without specific identification as to church, is
that only Baptism and the Lord's Supper are Sacraments, or
that Sacraments are not practically useful or necessary.

In an overview, Lausanne 1927 was remarkable. More Christian
groups were in dialogue on essential Christian theological
issues than at any time since the Reformation. No delegation
withdrew from the three-week conference. Theological sameness and differences were faced with candor and with restraint. It was a serious theological beginning. Bishop
Brent had achieved what many had termed "impossible."

Lausanne's agenda, from its primary generation in Anglican
circles, had received an "ecclesiological emphasis," rather
than a "justification emphasis" which might have characterized a Lutheran or Reformed genesis of Faith and Order.[49]
This ecclesiological frame of reference assisted the Orthodox
as they sought communication across cultural as well as
creedal boundaries.

The Conference appointed a large official Continuation Committee with Brent as its head to continue the work of the
conference by compiling and distributing the report, by analyzing church responses to the report, by seeking new members,
and by preparing for the next World Conference on Faith and
Order.

Many delegates present at Lausanne 1927 had also been present
at the Stockholm Meeting of Life and Work in 1925. Despite

the practical versus theological divergence in emphasis, much
similar ground was covered.

> Consequently Faith and Order appointed a small
> committee to confer with a similar committee
> on Life and Work on the subject of their mutual
> relationship. This was the first hint of the
> movement which was to grow until it brought the
> two bodies together in the World Council of
> Churches. [50]

Robert Gardiner, who had done such extraordinary work in service of Faith and Order, had died three years before the 1927
Lausanne Conference; Bishop Brent, the center of this movement, died two years after Lausanne. The Anglican Archbishop
of York, William Temple, who would later become the Archbishop of Canterbury, was elected as chairman to succeed Brent.
Under Temple the Continuation Committee appointed a "Theological Committee," composed of experts in Theology, to ana-
lize and synthesize the theological input of the churches re-
sponding to the Lausanne report. [51]

The financial crash of 1929 interrupted and delayed the committee work of Faith and Order. In 1934 three theological
commissions with specific areas of expertise in Scripture,
Ministry and Worship were appointed to divide and deepen the
work of the one original "Theological Committee." These commissions actually had too little time to prepare in depth
area studies for the opening of the second World Conference
on Faith and Order at Edinburgh, Scotland in August 1937. [52]

In the meantime, the seedling hint of a convergence of the
separate unitive movements which arose at Lausanne had
flowered into a committee. The multiplication of diverse
movements which were seeking Christian unity on the world
level was becoming an embarrassment to the cause of unity.
As Willem Visser't Hooft observes in his *Memoirs*, "In the
early thirties the ecumenical movement went through a period
of uncertainty and confusion." [53]

The deaths of Gardiner, Brent and Soederblom and the world
depression following the 1929 crisis contributed to the difficulties, but more significant were the facts that they were
different ecumenical movements, and no one of them was clearly the work and responsibility of the Christian *Churches as
Churches*. [54]

Some integration of viewpoint and effort was needed to prevent a futile dissipation of the labor already expended. The
delegates to the various movements were not the church personnel capable of moving the force of each whole church into

the Christian unifying movement or its world Christianizing
work. A synthesis was necessary.

> But this is easier said than done. For the
> four movements—International Missionary
> Council, Life and Work, Faith and Order and
> the World Alliance for Friendship through the
> Churches—had each worked out their own spe-
> cific ethos and objectives, and they had also
> their own *idées fixes* and their diehards.
> There had been misunderstandings. When Life
> and Work had used the slogan 'Doctrine divides,
> service unites' this could easily be taken as
> a negative judgment on the Faith and Order
> approach. On the other hand the opposition
> of a number of delegates at the Lausanne Con-
> ference of 1927 to Soederblom's report...
> seemed to imply an unfriendly attitude to
> Life and Work.[55]

William A. Brown of the F and O Movement in the U.S.A., perceiving that Faith and Order and Life and Work were precisely
the theological side and the practical side of the one coin,
suggested to Archbishop Temple in 1933 that the leaders of
the principal ecumenical organizations be brought together to
search for a synthesis of efforts. In response, Temple invited ten such leaders to his home in Bishopthorpe, England.
Leaders of the World Student Christian Federation and the
YMCA world office were included.

The informal brain-storming group, in a two-day session, saw
the problem but no easy solution. Each group was entrenched
and wanted no loss of autonomy. As friendship and mutual
confidence increased, the invited leaders agreed that further
pooling of their efforts should be examined. The Bishopthorpe meeting was judged as worthwhile.

Two years later, the informal Bishopthorpe "Group of Ten"
formalized itself and determined to widen its circle to
thirty-five church and church-organization leaders. The
"Group of Ten" also decided to suggest joint study and action
in proximate places and times for F and O and L and W. Thus,
1937 was chosen as the meeting year. L and W would convene
at Oxford; F and O at Edinburgh. The "Committee of Thirty-
five" would hold a prior preparatory three-day meeting at
Westfield College, London.[56]

The "Committee of Thirty-five" met at Westfield College to
suggest further combining of the separated studies and activities of the several independent "unity-seeking" Christian
movements. All the movements were Protestant in origin and

leadership, as were the "Bishopthorpe Committee of Ten" and
the "Westfield Committee of Thirty-five." At Westfield, ways
and means of cooperation seemed to be the high point of business. No one expected the breakthrough of a master idea. One
American committee member, William Cavert, wrote:

> But after reviewing the situation it became
> more and more clear to all at the Westfield
> consultation that Life and Work and Faith and
> Order were complimentary aspects of one quest
> for unity.[57]

The International Missionary Council (IMC) felt that its exclusive missionary purpose required its independence; the
World Alliance for International Friendship Through the Churches thought that it should not merge with the other organizations because it was non-ecclesiastical in character. The
Westfield Committee decided to propose a merger to the upcoming world conferences at Oxford and Edinburgh. The idea of
forming a new body evoked the problem of a new name. Cavert
recalls:

> When the question of a name was being discussed
> in a subcommittee, I queried—on the basis of
> the conciliar experience in America—'why not
> World Council of Churches?' Archbishop Temple
> broke the ensuing silence by remarking, 'That's
> what we really want, isn't it?' Although some
> misgiving was expressed whether so bold a pro-
> posal could command the support of the official
> bodies...the Westfield College group voted unani-
> mously to present the proposal...to the Oxford
> and Edinburgh Conferences.[58]

The new name implied a *membership of churches*, not of other
types of organizations or cross-denominational agencies which
enjoyed membership in Life and Work and Faith and Order. Thus,
Federal Councils of Churches would not be constituent members.
The churches would have to be asked did they want this new
World Council in place of the World Conferences already available to them. This inquiry would be a demanding and time-
consuming task.

On the morning after the unanimous, "master idea" decision,
the "Committee of Thirty-five" voted, again unanimously, to
ask thirty-six year old Willem A. Visser't Hooft, director of
the World Student Christian Federation, to head up the work
for the new World Council, if it were adopted in principle at
the Oxford and Edinburgh conferences. Westfield had voted
for a sketchily blue-printed concept; someone had to lead the
way in formulating and selling an explicit constitution for a

future World Council of Churches. Visser't Hooft agreed to
start the work but withheld judgment as to becoming the Council's "General Secretary," until the body's basis and defined
membership should be made clear.[59]

At Oxford, the Life and Work Conference of 425 delegates (300
of whom came from the United States and British Commonwealth)
affirmed, against only two negative votes, the proposed formation of a World Council of Churches. About nine and a half
months later, Life and Work terminated its separate existence.

> As a consequence, the Universal Christian
> Council for Life and Work, on 13 May 1938,
> at Utrecht, transferred its responsibilities
> and functions to the new Provisional Committee
> of the World Council of Churches in Process of
> Formation.[60]

Life and Work, in trying to focus the force of the Christian
World on the problems of war and peace, economic inequity,
and totalitarian violence, felt that its work would not die
but rather would be given greater force from the more elevated
platform of a World Council of Churches. Thus, ecumenist
Ehrenstrom could write:

> To say that Life and Work died in 1938 would be
> to give a wholly false impression of what hap-
> pened; the movement merely changed its name, to
> continue its work and witness with undiminished
> vitality within the wider embrace of the World
> Council of Churches.[61]

If the flow of Life and Work into a World Council seemed natural and advantageous, the same cannot be said for the Faith
and Order Conference at Edinburgh. When practical action and
theological reflection had been combined in one arena, the
ease of action-talk had overwhelmed the slow-moving analytic
reflection-talk.

In 1910 the World Mission Conference had ruled out doctrinal
discussion; in 1925 Life and Work's slogan "Doctrine divides,
service unites" had undermined doctrine's status. Thus,
Faith and Order feared that its loss of autonomous control
would frustrate rather than aid its constitutional goal of
recovering the unity of Christ's one Church. How could a
council of divided churches produce the one Church?   How
could a supra-national council favor the Lutheran "confessing
church" in Germany and lean against the Nazi-approved "Christian" Church, and yet hope to recover the unity of Christ's
one Church? Such arguments clouded the Faith and Order consideration of the proposal to create a World Council of Churche

However, William Temple, seconded by John R.
Mott and Mark Boegner [an ecumenical pioneer
of the Reformed Church in France], succeeded
in convincing the vast majority of the Edinburgh delegates that the World Council plan
would strengthen and not weaken the work for
church unity which was the concern of Faith
and Order. But the conference decided to
formulate a number of requirements to which
the constitution of the new council would
have to conform if Faith and Order was to
enter it.[62]

All the churches which had approached Faith and Order since
its first conception by Brent in 1910 had joined on the required faith-basis that they "accept our Lord Jesus Christ as
God and Savior." F and O was concerned that this critically
important basis be kept. Further, the F and O Conference was
anxious that its theological work, without which it thought
Christian church unity inconceivable, be given workable *identity* within the new structure.

Later, Faith and Order spelled out its *required guarantees*
more explicitly. It would only consent to the formation of a
World Council of Churches if:

1. Its own Continuation Committee became the
Faith and Order commission and department within
the proposed World Council.

2. The new department's work could concentrate
on studying the theological differences between
the churches and emphasize to the churches their
obligation of manifesting the essential unity of
the Church of Christ.

3. It could continue its presently authorized
work leading toward the next F & O World Conference.

4. The F & O commission and its executive committee kept primary control over its work, personnel and budget.[63]

Faith and Order would accept the marriage provided its identity and function were in no way compromised. Some thought
the demands were too great; history may judge them too small.

After accepting the Westfield concept of the World Council of
Churches in principle, the Oxford and Edinburgh assemblies
appointed seven members each to form a "Committee of Fourteen"
as a joint constitutional drafting and continuation committee.

William Visser't Hooft sought a four-point assurance that:

1. The World Council would consist only of
churches.

2. The basis would be Christian.

3. A department of practical interchurch aid
would be included.

4. F & O and L & W would come closer together
in policies and study.[64]

About nine months after Edinburgh, the "Committee of Fourteen"
met at Utrecht, accepted the Faith and Order and Visser't
Hooft's requirements, elected Visser't Hooft general secretary
and widened itself to become "The Provisional Committee of the
World Council of Churches in Process of Formation,"[65] more
conveniently referred to as the "Provisional Committee."

It took another three months for Faith and Order to quiet the
membership's objections of "absorption" and "super-church" to
"this new and unprecedented body."[66]

Only after that could the letters of full explanation and invitation to form the New World Council of Churches be sent to
the autonomous churches which would constitute its founding
membership. The objections already met, plus questions concerning autonomy, the meaning of "church" in the projected
constitution, authority, etc. continued to obstruct the path
forward.

Visser't Hooft hoped that the consenting churches could come
together to create the World Council of Churches (commonly
abbreviated W.C.C., and later WCC) by 1941. But World War II
shattered this hope. The Provisional Committee, reduced by
the war to a few leaders led by Visser't Hooft, struggled for
ten difficult years from its base in Geneva, Switzerland, before succeeding in assembling the Constitutional Assembly in
Amsterdam in the summer of 1948.

Within a year of the sending of the invitations, fifty member
churches of F and O and L and W had submitted their consent
to the formation of the New World Council. From 1939 to 1945
World War II restricted the work of the Provisional Committee.

Nevertheless, by the end of the war another fifty churches
had consented to join in the creation of the World Council.
Visser't Hooft estimated that the six war-years which had
blocked the processes of developing the World Council, had
nevertheless deepened the need for, and enhanced the spiritual value of, the conciliar adventure.

Thus the Council received in those years far
more than it lost. For the losses were merely

> in the realm of organization, but the gains
> were in the spiritual realm. It was not the
> work of men but of the Holy Spirit that the
> time of interruption of ecumenical contact
> became in fact the time of discovery of the
> oneness and interdependence of God's people....[67]

The Provisional Committee held its first post-war meeting in
Geneva in 1946. It joyfully noted the added fifty churches
which had joined the movement, approved the establishment of
an Ecumenical Institute in Geneva, decided to hold in Amsterdam the founding assembly of the World Council of Churches in
1948 and adopted a slate of five representative presidents to
form the presidium of the new body. Each president represented a formation-source of the WCC.

The archbishop of Canterbury reflected the work of Anglican
initiatives of Brent and Temple (died in 1943); the archbishop of Uppsala represented Lutheran Soederblom's pioneering
efforts; Archbishop Germanos was an Orthodox representative;
Pastor Marc Boegner represented the French Reformed tradition;
and pioneer John R. Mott symbolized the missionary origin and
the Methodist tradition.

Thus also, England, the Scandinavian countries, France, the
Orthodox East and the United States were geographically represented, reflecting the New World Council's intention of
seeking denominational and geographical universality and of
becoming a sign of the Church's unity and universality.[68]

This last phrase, which readily suggests that the W.C.C.
could be viewed as a sign of the Church's unity and universality or catholicity, sounded an alarm in the ears of those concerned about the absolute autonomy of their own churches.
Given the expressed conviction of the leadership that the
Holy Spirit, not man, was revealing the interdependence of
God's people, the concerned members, hesitant about the new
venture, could envision the reconstruction of Christ's Church
with the marks of unity, holiness of the Spirit and Catholicity. The part of the German State Church which supported
National Socialism (Nazi Party) publicly denounced all supra-
national church structures, whether Roman Catholic or World-
Protestant, as the politicizing of Christianity.[69]

On the other hand, those who feared annihilation by assimilation needed a statement by the Provisional Committee that the
World Council entertained no idea of becoming a *super-church*
ruling the other churches from a centralized seat of power in
Geneva.[70] The super-church idea and the politicizing would
require still further attention.

In the meanwhile, the Provisional Committee, to which Life
and Work had yielded its powers, resources and services, grew
through the accumulation of services of the kind which Life
and Work had made its own. With the Committee's approval,
its administrative arm (headed by Visser't Hooft) grew from
nine persons in 1940 to 142 in the period of preparation for
the Assembly at Amsterdam. A mere list of the L and W type
services suggests the amounts of energy, time and money which
the Provisional Committee expended on them. An official report listed headings such as:

> Prefabricated church and church repairs;
> Christian institutions; Aid to Pastors
> (salaries and re-equipment of homes);
> Holiday-Health; Christian Education; Theo-
> logical Scholarships; Youth Work; Litera-
> ture and Papers; Evangelization and Home
> Missions; Exchange of Christian Personnel;
> Christian Social Service; Refugee and Dis-
> placed Persons; Material Relief; Transport;
> Ecumenical Loan Fund and General Needs of
> Churches.[71]

This is an impressive record of accomplishments during and
after the war. Such work not infrequently crossed Protestant
denominational lines and thus contributed to a sense of
Christian unity deeper than the denominational differences.
At the same time, such proliferation of practical works tended to characterize the WCC as a further flowering of Life and
Work rather than of Faith and Order. Services were helping
to unite, but the doctrinal divisions did not go away.

At Oxford, Life and Work had focused its attention into five
"Sections" which dealt respectively with the themes:

> Church and Community; Church and State; Church,
> Community and State in relation to the Economic
> Order; Church, Community and State in relation to
> Education; the Universal Church and the World of nations.[72]

The conference did not examine "the church" which appeared in
each section project; rather, it probed into the practical aspects of community, state and nation as related to *any* Christian
church. Scripture and theology were used to resolve practical
questions but not to examine the ever-present core question: *The Chu*

At Edinburgh, Faith and Order had developed its thought on the
core questions. It divided its final inquiry into five sectior

> I.   The Grace of our Lord, Jesus Christ
> II.   The Church of Christ and the Word of God
> III. The Church of Christ: Ministry and Sacraments

> IV.   The Church's Unity in Life and Worship
> V.   The Communion of Saints.[73]

As the Conference confronted these truly theological questions, points of common agreement and other points of tenacious difference emerged. The Orthodox again found the reports being formulated uncongenial to their own faith understanding.[74] Faith and Order's Continuation Committee carried
on its post-Conference work, analyzing the reports and the
member churches' responses to the reports. Even without
these responses,

> ...one thing had become clear before the end
> of the Edinburgh Conference. This was that
> most of the disagreements which that Confer-
> ence brought to light and failed to reconcile
> had their roots in differing conceptions of
> the Church.[75]

Thus, the Continuation Committee in 1938 directed its attention to setting up commissions on "the Church" and the intimately related problems of "ways of worship" and "intercommunion." World War II disrupted the interchange of scholarly
communications. Despite this, the Commission on the Church
generated a report from doctrinal statements sent to it by
Congregational, Methodist, and Anglican churches, as well as
the Society of Friends. The commission chairman, Dr. Newton
Flew, of Cambridge, England, discerned in his 1946 report
that the most significant problem "...was that of reconciling
points of view which might be called 'protestant' and 'catholic' respectively."[76] Visser't Hooft added, "There can be
little doubt that he is right."[77]

In his own summary to the inaugural Assembly of the World
Council Visser't Hooft acknowledged that responsible post-war
Protestant scholarship from England

> ...maintained that historical research sup-
> ported the traditional catholic view that
> the episcopate derives its status and author-
> ity in the Church from the Apostles through a
> series of consecrations down through the ages,
> that this link through successive episcopal
> consecrations is necessary to any Church if it
> is to be one with the Church of the New Testament.[78]

Over against this view which was supported by Dr. K. E. Kirk,
Bishop of Oxford, and believed also by Orthodox and Roman
Catholics, stands the protestant emphasis. Dr. Visser't
Hooft affirms that the protestant emphasis rests

...on the view that the ground of the Church's
unity and continuity lies in the *invisible*
world. It is to be found in the unity and
continuity of the risen and ascended Lord,...
[groups of the faithful] need no other unity
and continuity than that which is deepest of
all, membership in the body of the One Christ.[79]

After citing these conflicting views, termed "catholic" and
"protestant" in the Faith and Order report, Visser't Hooft
continued:

The reunion of Christendom will require a
conciliation of these two views, and it must
be a reconciliation which gives due place to
the truths for which each stands, without
ignoring any of them or explaining them away.
This is at the center of the problems entrusted
for study to the [Faith and Order] Commission
on the Church.[80]

Thus, it appears that "the Church" established by Jesus
Christ is the *acknowledged core problem* area dividing the
churches; the center question of that problem area is whether
Christ added to His own invisible and ascended presence a
visible continuous succession of bishops or not.

The other Faith and Order Commissions on "worship" and "intercommunion" rather broadly confined themselves to the comparative description of the customs and rules flourishing in
member churches which reported.[81] "Intercommunion" appears
as a Protestant focus; the Orthodox indicate that the whole
indivisible "Liturgy" is in question, not merely a part.

Faith and Order incorporated this most basic divisive question on the nature of the Church and its Catholic (visible
episcopal continuity) versus Protestant (invisible continuity)
interpretation into the first section of the Amsterdam Assembly's agenda. The two years between the acknowledgment
(1946) of the nature of the Church as the core area and the
opening of Amsterdam (1948) did not allow enough time for a
thorough study of this question by experts and assimilation
of that study by delegates to a constitutional assembly.
Thus, this study continued to demand attention of the Faith
and Order Department of the WCC and its later assemblies.

Visser't Hooft reported to the Amsterdam Assembly that, in
1939, the Vatican had been sent courtesy information concerning the projected formation of the World Council. Under
Temple's chairmanship, the Provisional Committee indicated
its understanding that the Roman Catholic Church "would not

desire formal association" with the proposed World Council.
However, the Committee expressed the hope

> that there would be opportunities for the
> exchange of information and for unofficial
> consultation with Roman Catholic theologians
> and scholars. (An answer received through
> the Apostolic Delegate of Great Britain,
> stated that there was no obstacle in the
> way of consulting, confidentially, the
> Bishops or the Apostolic Delegate).[82]

The Provisional Committee's awareness that the Vatican would
not desire formal association certainly reflected the disposition manifested during the pontificate of Pope Pius XI.
However, the committee generally neglected to manifest an
equal awareness of its overwhelmingly Protestant composition
with no single voice able to represent that body's faith or
theology.[83]

Two years before this courteous information message, Archbishop Temple, the committee's chairman, had "stressed the
need for a body which would provide 'a voice for non-Roman
Christendom,'"[84] on the ground that it suggested a super-
church.

The question of identifying the new structure as the *World
Council of Churches* when half the Christians of the world
would not be represented by it apparently did not arise. The
title of Federal Council of Churches (FCC) which had suggested the parallel title, World Council of Churches (WCC), had
also been representative of only part of its world. As the
context and composition of the FCC had tended to define that
body in the public forum, so presumably would context and
composition help to limit the global sweep of the title,
World Council of Churches. Finally, it could be argued that
the universal title expressed what the New Council hoped to
become; however, the very small Orthodox presence in the massive Protestant body left the Orthodox with the uneasy feeling that they were in a Protestant Council of Churches.

CHAPTER FOUR

WORLD COUNCIL AND THE ORTHODOX

The World Council has had consistent difficulty in reflecting
or expressing the sense of the Orthodox. The Orthodox Churches of Constantinople, Antioch, Alexandria, Jerusalem,
Cyprus (all relatively small), and Greece had manifested interest in the Council before Amsterdam (1948); the larger
Orthodox churches of Russia, Rumania, Bulgaria, Yugoslavia
and Poland had kept aloof from the council. The Orthodox
felt that their continuity with the Apostolic Church, their
position in the Middle East, and their numerical size gave
them a greater significance than the World Council allowed.
But the leaders of the World Council

> found it practically impossible under the
> given circumstances to ensure that the voice
> of Orthodoxy should not be drowned by West-
> ern and mainly Protestant voices. [1]

The number of voices at a large assembly can be very significant in a voice vote on the passage of a report; the number
of votes in the vote-count of an assembly is decisive in de-
termining a slate of officers or an assembly policy. The
same disproportion enters committee actions. Thus, the Orthodox felt that their small voice was not representative of
their significance in the world.

Norman Goodall, a former Assistant General Secretary of the
WCC, in the interest of facing the question of representation,
arrived at the following estimates for the Roman Catholic,
Eastern Orthodox and Protestant Christian bodies for the New
Delhi Assembly (1961):

Roman Catholic	500,000,000
Eastern Orthodox	130,000,000
Protestant	210,000,000[2]

No one seriously proposes that any doctrinal question is to
be settled by majority vote, rather than by inquiry into divine revelation. However, an assembly which has hundreds of
delegates representing 210 million, but only tens of dele-

85

gates representing the position of 130 million can hardly
fail to favor the overwhelming majority. In the above listing by titles, the term *Protestant* represents hundreds of
churches, *Orthodox* represents only about fifteen fully independent (autocephalous) churches, with no radical difference
in doctrine, but separated by national boundaries, *Catholic,*
represents only one Church.

The distress of the Orthodox serves to highlight the disparity of representation in the World Council Assemblies on
grounds (used for choosing the five presidents) such as geographical distribution and/or denominational basis. This
representational disproportion alone could dissuade the
largest Christian Church from joining a group in whose cham-
bers its voice could conceivably be reduced to impotency.

> The distress of the Orthodox was aggravated
> also by the deep suspicion in the East that
> Western Christianity was a proselytizing force
> undermining their churches. And there was the
> Protestant irritation when it seemed that Or-
> thodox ecclesiology was no more tolerant than
> the traditional ecclesiology of Rome, with which
> Protestants were very familiar. [Thus, the
> General Secretary of the WCC] could not help
> wondering whether it would be possible to hold
> any Orthodox churches in the World Council.[3]

A careful statement about the nature of World Council, the
calm persuasion of Patriarch Athenagoras of Constantinople,
and assistance from the World Council to the Greek Orthodox
Church in time of trouble managed to hold the fragile union
of Orthodox and WCC together.[4] The magnitude of the World
Council's difficulty in multiplying contacts with the Orthodox churches is further manifested by the location of Orthodox Christians, of whom "more than eighty-five percent are
in communist countries."[5]

Oxford-educated Timothy Ware, who joined the Orthodox Church
and was ordained a priest eight years later at the age of 32,
points out that there are many Orthodox "who are anxious to
see their Church withdraw from the Movement."[6]

> The reason is that 'full participation in the
> Ecumenical Movement compromises the claim of
> the Orthodox Church to be the one true Church
> of Christ, and suggests that all 'churches' are
> alike.'[7]

Those Orthodox leaders who have joined their churches to the
WCC have countered that membership in the Council does not

imply a specific doctrine of the nature of Christ's Church or
the acknowledgement that other WCC members are true churches,
and thus, does not compromise their Orthodoxy. Further, the
joiners argue they should enter the World Council to bear
witness that the Orthodox Church is the true, holy, catholic,
apostolic Church.[8]

Ware notes the enormous discrepancy in size between the largest
and the smallest of the fully independent (i.e., autocephalous) churches. The Russian Orthodox Church, which before
1917 numbered about a hundred million, is in 1980 reduced to
an unknown size; Jerusalem numbers are about sixty thousand;
Sinai, which consists of Saint Catherine's Monastery in the
shadow of Mount Sinai, numbers less than 20 monks.

This "rarity" in the Sinai wilderness was recognized as autocephalous by a Synod in Constantinople in 1575 and by the
four ancient Eastern patriarchs in 1782. Its continuous existence since the sixth century bears witness to the sense of
continuity with early Christianity so precious and necessary
in the estimation of the Orthodox.[9] Most Orthodox have difficulty in understanding how any church which started abruptly in recent centuries without continuity from the Apostles
can identify itself as the Church of Christ.

Demetrios Constantelos, in a work approved by Archbishop
Iakavos, head of the Greek Orthodox churches of North and
South America, also insists that unbroken continuity identifies the original Christian Church.[10] Constantelos, still
heeding the 1920 call by the Patriarchate of Constantinople
for cooperation of all the churches of Christ, wherever they
may be, endorses a continuation of the work for the unity of
the Church and cooperation with the WCC. In his book, *The
Greek Orthodox Church,* however, Constantelos seems more concerned with Constantinople's relationship to the Roman Catholic Church than to the World Council.

Constantinople is traditionally identified as the primary
Patriarchate among the four Eastern Patriarchates of Constantinople, Antioch, Alexandria and Jerusalem.[11] Before the
schism of 1054, Rome, the fifth Patriarchate, was acknowledged as having the primacy among the five ancient Patriarchates, known as the Pentarchy. Archbishop Iakovos describes as accurate, "authoritative in its correct interpretation" and "most valuable,"[12] the book of Constantelos who
writes about a limiting factor of ecumenical dialogue:

> It should be emphasized that as long as the
> Roman Catholic Church teaches a supremacy of
> authority and power of the Bishop of Rome over
> all Christendom, there is little hope for

progress in the ecumenical dialogue for reunion of the Churches. In the matter of the
ecumenical dialogue the Orthodox Church would
have no hesitation to accept the Bishop of
Rome as the *primus inter pares*, the first
among equals. But she would yield no other
ground on this important subject.[13]

Interestingly, Constantelos writes as if he is stating an
agreed position of all the Orthodox churches, whereas it is
commonly known that the Orthodox Churches acknowledged a
fuller Roman primacy to consummate reunions at both the Ecumenical Council of Lyons (1274) and the Ecumenical Council of
Florence (1438). However, neither reunion lasted very long.
The union of Florence lasted until 1453 at which time the
Islamic Turkish forces overran the last of the four Eastern
Patriarchates. In that year,

In the early hours of 29 May the last Christian service was held in the great Church of
the Holy Wisdom. It was a *united service* of
Orthodox and Roman Catholics.[14]

The conquering Sultan saw to it that an anti-Roman Orthodox
monk was elevated to the Patriarchate as he reduced the Orthodox Church and people to a controlled position of "guaranteed
inferiority."[15] The Patriarch of Constantinople still suffers under the power of Islam and *Sancta Sophia* (the famous
Church of the Holy Wisdom) remains a Turkish Mosque.

Although under Turkish restraint for more than five hundred
years, the Patriarch of Constantinople, bearing the title
"Ecumenical Patriarch," is still held as *primus inter pares*
(first among equals) among the Eastern Orthodox churches.
Thus, Constantinople's call in 1920 to "all the Churches of
Christ wheresoever they be" and its increasing dialogue with
new ecumenical bodies and the Vatican, encouraged, but could
not require, a similar opening with the other totally independent Orthodox churches.

If the Pope, John Paul II, were to open the door to "shared
liturgy" it would be open, however reluctantly, in every Roman Catholic Church throughout the world; if the Ecumenical
Patriarch, Demetrios I, opened the door, it would be open
only in the very restricted limits of his patriarchate. The
World Council could encourage door-openings but each member
church would have to decide for itself.

In fact, some of the smaller independent Orthodox churches
did cautiously follow the lead of Constantinople; others withheld any contact throughout the first half of the twentieth

century.   Notable among the holdouts was the massive Russian
Orthodox Church (formerly over 75 percent of the Orthodox
World) which itself was struggling to stay alive under the
grinding heel of the Communist political authority that defined itself as atheistic.

Prior to the time of the modern ecumenical movement, the Orthodox Metropolitan of Moscow had named obstacles which prevented the unity sought by an Anglican group with the Orthodox
Church.   The former Orthodox Archbishop, Philaret of Moscow,
held to be the greatest theologian of the Russian Church in
modern times, stated positions which to the present day continue to surface in the modern ecumenical dialogue.[16]   Reunion projections must take into account the sense of the
general body of people being united.   Philaret judged it obvious for the Orthodox that

> reunion...could not be brought about simply by
> an act of the hierarchy, but presupposed some
> participation of the general body of believers.
> He had some difficulties concerning the validity
> of Anglican Orders.   Finally, he suggested five
> points for further study:
>
> 1.   The Thirty-Nine Articles and their doctrinal
>   poisiton.
> 2.   The *Filioque* clause and its place in the
>   Creed.
> 3.   Apostolic Succession.
> 4.   Holy Tradition.
> 5.   The doctrine of Sacraments, especially
>   Eucharistic doctrine.[17]

Some of these items constitute faith-obstacles which preclude
shared liturgy between the Orthodox and the Anglican churches,
but these problem areas did not prevent some Orthodox churches from seeking and maintaining membership in the World
Council of Churches.

Both Protestant and Orthodox sources see Orthodox inclusion
in the WCC as mutually beneficial.   Orthodox scholar T. Ware
evaluates the membership thus:

> Orthodox participation is a factor of cardinal
> importance for the Ecumenical Movement: it is
> mainly the presence of Orthodox which prevents
> the World Council of Churches from appearing to
> be simply a Pan-Protestant Alliance and nothing
> more.   But the Ecumenical Movement in turn is
> important for Orthodoxy: it has helped to force
> the various Orthodox Churches out of their

comparative isolation, making them meet one
another and enter into a living contract with
non-Orthodox Christians.[18]

Presbyterian Calian agrees with this assessment but notes
that "...Orthodoxy's presence has made deliberation and progress slow, with misunderstandings at times outweighing areas
of understanding." However, Calian estimates that the benefits gained outweigh the slow-downs suffered.[19]

Ernst Benz in his study of the Eastern Orthodox Church sees
the Protestant side gaining from the enrichment in doctrinal
and liturgical traditions; whereas the Orthodox will benefit
from the confrontation with alternate structures, doctrinal
expressions, and world views after centuries of repression
under anti-Christian forces.[20]

Visser't Hooft adds that the Orthodox have brought a sense of
history and of transcendent mystery into the World Council to
counteract the decline of these two values in the West. He
estimates that the Orthodox-Protestant dialogue has not advanced very far but that at last the doors between these
separated worlds of discourse are now open.[21]

Stephen Neill, Anglican Bishop and former Associate General
Secretary of the WCC, perceives that the lack of advance in
the Protestant-Orthodox dialogue within the World Council is
partly attributable to an element of uncertainty characterizing the relationship. After naming some of the principal
delegates to ecumenical bodies, Neill says:

> Yet there has always been present a certain
> factor of anxiety, and the Protestant churches
> have never been able to feel quite sure that
> they could count on their Orthodox brethren as
> being fully committed to the ecumenical cause
> ...at almost every...gathering the Orthodox have
> found it necessary to make a separate statement
> ...to safeguard themselves against any misunder-
> standing of their position.[22]

Neill cites as reasons for this sense of uncertainty the
Orthodox doctrine on the nature of the Church, their distrust
of Western evangelization in predominantly Orthodox countries,
and the fact that in the Greek Orthodox churches theological
proficiency is found mainly among laymen rather than among
the bishops who guide the Orthodox churches.[23]

To the Orthodox the word *mission* connotes principally the
idea of converting from Orthodoxy to Protestantism or Catholicism and thus, in Neill's words "has come to stink in the
nostrils of the Orthodox world."[24]

This proselytizing difficulty, which a change of evangelization practice can substantially diminish, is not so deep a
problem as that arising from the Orthodox conviction about
the nature of Christ's Church. In the understanding of all
Orthodox believers, Neill observes, "the Orthodox churches
together make up the church—there is no other."[25]

Orthodox scholar Ware confirms the positive part of this observation but modifies slightly the exclusivistic note. After
naming and giving the approximate membership count of the
autocephalous Orthodox churches, Ware says: "The Orthodox
Church is thus a family of self-governing churches." A bit
further on he says: "The Orthodox Church is a federation of
local, but not in every case *national,* Churches."[26]

To Ware, the Church is a family or a federation of totally
independent churches of Orthodox belief. Neill's reverse
phrasing that "the Orthodox churches together make up the
church" (of Christ understood) also fits Ware's understanding.[27] Ware characterizes this sense, even with its exclusive
element ("there is no other"), as the standard Orthodox position, but immediately goes on to say that there are Orthodox
theologians who do not hold this doctrine of the Church with
such a totally exclusive meaning.[28] Thus both sides see that
the ecumenical advance is hampered by differing doctrines
about Christ's *Church*.

Orthodox Scholar, Nicholas Zernov, former Spalding Lecturer
in Eastern Orthodox Culture at Oxford, acknowledges that different Orthodox bishops hold opposing positions concerning
the nature of the Church. Metropolitan Anthony Krapovitaski
of the Russian Church taught the exclusivist position in 1936,
whereas Alexis, the Patriarch of Russia, in 1948 identified
the Roman Catholic Church as "the Sister Church."[29]

It appears that the exclusivist interpretation is not a fixed
and unchangeable doctrine in the Orthodox Church as a whole.
Zernov notes that some Orthodox theologians are still searching for a doctrinal explanation of the discrepancy between
accepting some sacraments outside the Orthodox Church as valid (ex. Roman Catholic baptism) and yet affirming that the
Orthodox Church alone is the Church of Christ.[30]

Anglican Neill, after more than thirty-five years of experience in the ecumenical movement, affirms that the dominant
Orthodox doctrine holds that other Apostolic churches are in
heresy or schism, that Protestant bodies are voluntary groups
of devout laymen with no authentic ministry or sacraments,
that converts from Protestantism in some cases are to be re-
baptized, and if ordained are to be reordained.[31] Ware confirms the requirement of reordination of Anglican clergy who
join the Orthodox Church.[32]

Neill summarizes as practical corollaries of Orthodox ecclesial doctrine that:

1. Orthodox delegates come to ecumenical meetings *mainly* to *testify* to the full Christian truth they claim they alone possess.

2. Other churches must become Orthodox churches.

3. They cannot subscribe to any ecumenical statement which clouds or undercuts these claims.

In a one-sentence paragraph Neill trenchantly observes, "the Orthodox are hampered and perplexed by their own lack of unity."[33]

Neill's experiences further highlight the centrality of the doctrine on *the Church* as an obstacle to the advance of the modern ecumenical movement. His experiences also emphasize the difficulties inherent in establishing an organization such as the World Council of Churches. Further, the Orthodox-Protestant dialogue reveals some positions which characterize the Roman Catholic belief about the one Church contained in its Vatican II document on ecumenism.

Despite the theological unsettlement which hampered the Protestant-Orthodox dialogue in the F and O Movement and the L and W Movement, the Provisional Committee was able to advance toward the formation of a World Council of Churches which would retain some Orthodox members without necessarily compromising their ecclesiological claims.

The Provisional Committee urgently wanted the founding Assembly of the World Council of Churches to be as widely representative as possible of all the Christian churches in the world. Thus, it was a severe blow, when a month before the founding of the WCC at Amsterdam, the major section of the Orthodox world, the Russian Orthodox Church, whose Patriarchal center is Moscow, rejected the World Council.

The Moscow Patriarchate called on all-Orthodox Consultation in Moscow (July 1948). The Patriarch of Constantinople, whose prerogative it is to call such pan-Orthodox meetings, went to celebrate Moscow's 500th anniversary as an autocephalous church, but refused to attend the consultation. The meeting, dominated by the Russian Orthodox, considered and rejected: (1) a change of attitude toward the Vatican; (2) recognition of Anglican orders; and (3) membership in the World Council of Churches.[34]

The Moscow Consultation rejected the WCC on the grounds that

during the previous decade (the period of the Provisional
Committee) the question of the reunion of the churches on a
theological basis had ceased to be discussed. The Consultation contended that the WCC had concentrated on social and
political questions and had succumbed to the political temp-
tation rejected by Christ in the desert.[35]

It appears that no one at the meeting had firsthand acquain-
tance with the ecumenical movement and thus the position that
the WCC might become a new World Church and a center of political action faced no rebuttal.[36] It would take over a
dozen years to modify the Moscow position.

The World Council of Churches Established

Despite the Orthodox and similar rebuffs, the Provisional
Committee succeeded in bringing official delegates of 145
churches from 44 countries to meet in Amsterdam in August
1948. On Monday, August 23, the Anglican Archbishop of Canterbury chaired the first general meeting. Presbyterian Dr.
Samuel McCrea Cavert, arrangements director, explained this
unique Christian Assembly's program of worship,[37] work and
study. Dr. Marc Boegner (Reformed Church of France) arose
to present the Provisional Committee's resolution:

> That the first Assembly of the World Council
> of Churches be declared to be and is hereby
> constituted,....

The resolution passed unanimously and thus founded the World
Council of Churches.[38]

In retrospect, Cavert estimates that the principal American
contribution to the World Council was neither its money (80
percent from U.S. churches in prior decades) nor its personnel,
but rather its creative conciliar model developed in the FCC.

> The organizational structure of the World
> Council was essentially that which had been
> worked out on a national scale in the Federal
> Council of Churches of Christ in America.[39]

Dr. Marc Boegner in his book, *The Long Road to Unity*, asks
whether the Amsterdam Assembly was a really great event. He
answers no and yes. No, because it produced no creative out-
burst as the 1910 Edinburgh Mission Conference had. Yes, because it proclaimed the decision of the churches present to
respond to Christ's prayer, "that they may be one;" next, because Protestants, Anglicans and Orthodox dedicated their
churches to the service of unity "...in the face of the Roman
Catholic Church" and finally, because it was the starting

point of the new event which continued the prophetic stance
of the movement's pioneers.[40]

Boegner remarks that the Amsterdam Assembly, which crowned
thirty-eight years of ecumenical work, had its time heavily
taxed with the business of modifying and adopting its constitution and rules.[41] This constitution, as indeed all written
constitutions, deals with membership, purpose, basis, structure, amendments, etc. in much of which it is mainly of interest to its constituents. The fact which makes this WCC Constitution most interesting to Theology is that it explicitly
embodies transcendent Christian belief and specifies whether
or not the World Council is a super-church.

World Council Constitution

The Constitution adopted at Amsterdam has nine headings,
namely, I *Basis,* II *Membership,* III Functions, IV *Authority,*
V Organization, VI Appointment of Commissions, VII Other Ecumenical Christian Organizations, VIII Amendments, IX Rules
and Regulations.[42] Of these the three which theologically
attract attention are the headings: basis, membership, and
authority.

Art. 1. The *basis* consists of two sentences. The World
Council of Churches is a fellowship of Churches which accept
our Lord Jesus Christ as God and Savior. It is constituted
for the discharge of the functions set out below.[43] The basis is framed as a definition in which the "fellowship of
churches" is the classification; the belief clause is the
specific identifying factor. The simplicity and directness
of the belief clause is striking. The simple words contain
an affirmation of towering transcendence. They affirm the
acceptance of Jesus of Nazareth as God; they affirm that this
divine Person is the Savior.

This Christological formula was the basis on which the Faith
and Order movement had originated in 1910. Faith and Order
required that the WCC express a clear and definite Christological foundation otherwise it would have refused to help
form the new organization. An almost identical basis had
been used by the YMCA in 1855 at the establishment of its
World Alliance.[44]

Since the basis had brought and kept Christian churches together for almost four decades (1910-1948) the World Council
of Churches, despite objections that "it said too much" and
other objections which claimed "it said too little," adopted
the Christological formula in the first sentence of its constitution.

Some churches, which felt that their membership could no
longer affirm this belief formula, apparently interpreted it
as a functional expression of a general Christian tradition.
Boegner, President of the Union of Reformed Churches of
France for thirty-one years, notes that a considerable number
of its pastors and faithful felt it

> difficult...if not impossible, for their union
> of churches to accept a dogmatic statement which
> qualified Christ as God-Savior.[45]

Yet they joined!

On the other hand, the Orthodox felt that the basis should be
explicitly trinitarian. Others thought that the exclusive
mention of the Divinity smacked of docetism (that Jesus gave
only the appearance of humanity), and should explicitly affirm both his humanity and divinity.[46]

The majority of the examining committee decided that these
theological elements were implicit in the Faith and Order
formula and that they would not yet subject the infant organization to such a difficult theological confrontation. "The
fact that this formula had proved acceptable in practice influenced the decision more than considerations of its theological adequacy."[47]

Thus, the basis was accepted by the Amsterdam Assembly but
its members did not uniformly believe it. The Faith and Order Commission of the WCC held this basis as a norm for both
its commission members and staff, whereas the Life and Work
membership, whose "practical Christianity" tended to dominate
WCC activities, muted the formula somewhat in its activities
and hirings.

The second sentence of the World Council's *basis* addresses
itself to the question of *why* this new organization is being
founded. It was established to fulfill the specific functions which are enumerated in the third title. The first
function is to carry on the work of the movements whose confluence brought the World Council into existence, namely
Faith and Order, and Life and Work. The second, third and
fourth functions are to facilitate and promote common action,
common study and the development of common or ecumenical consciousness among all churches. Thus, the constitution accepted the given denominational separateness of the Christ-
believing bodies and proposed to *promote convergence* by common action, study and ecumenical consciousness. The nine-
article constitution nowhere says that the God-Savior, Christ,
of its basis founded only one church, and prayed that "all
may be one" (John 17:21). The remaining functions of article

three express the intention to establish relations with world
church bodies, to call world conferences (possibly an Ecumenical Council in the historic sense?) and to support the churches in their task of evangelism (implying the continuing
practices of supporting and propagating division).

The World Council defines itself as a "fellowship of Christian Churches;" thus of necessity, its constitution and also
its thirteen-article set of rules abound in expressions of
plurality.[48] Convergence is certainly sought in discharging
functions of common action, common study, and the promotion
of ecumenical consciousness. The Faith and Order Commission,
now constitutionally just one among many functions, addresses
its attention to the unity of Christ's Church; World Council
documents from time to time refer to some kind of a unity,
but denominational plurality, the *status quo,* appears now to
be constitutionally reinforced.[49] This sustaining of denominational dividedness may function to preserve what Faith and
Order was designed to diminish and even eliminate!

Art. 2. The second article of the Constitution identifies
the Churches eligible for membership. It asks that any such
ecclesial body express agreement with the basis of the World
Council as the primary requirement. The church seeking membership must also satisfy such other criteria as are enumerated in *the rules* and then be approved by a two-thirds vote
of the assembly. Each member church has one vote; this appears to favor splintering as against the concept of a single
beam, a unique church. More splinters mean more votes!

The first rule gives a practical, external sense to the word
church in the constitution when it says: "Under the word
churches are included such denominations as are composed of
local *autonomous* churches."[50] Apparently Kenneth Scott
Latourette of the Northern Baptist convention introduced this
characteristically Baptist concept of local *autonomy* into the
thinking which constructed the WCC rules.[51] Thus, plurality
is more deeply entrenched than unity, and the concept of a
final, visible authority for the one Church of Jesus Christ[52]
appears to be ruled out of court even before the newly founded WCC engages in further inquiry as to the *unity* Christ intends for his Church. Such a rule constitutes a presupposition as regards the theology of Christ's one Church. It presupposes a plurality which appears to be at variance with the
ecclesiology of the Petrine texts and other sections of the
New Testament.

After naming autonomy, the first rule goes on to select stability, size and relationship with other churches as the
other criteria to be met by churches seeking membership in
the World Council.[53] In general, these criteria are public

and visible; they measure self-rule, years of existence, number of members, and contacts with other ecclesial groups.
These criteria are primarily sociological. They may involve
a theological dimension, as in Christ's promise of continuity
(implying stability) of his Church until the end-time. But
the time-place-numbers criteria of the World Council's rules
appear generally in the sociological sense.

Assessments of the Church which remain too heavily sociological provoke such a question as Richard McBrien's *Do We Need
The Church?* Such a superficial reality should evoke neither
community nor personal allegiance.[54] This is not to say that
the one Church of Christ will be lacking all these characteristics, but rather to note that the sociological sense is
secondary and subordinate to the theological reality. Yet,
the World Council had to start somewhere, and in a non-threat-
ening way.

An *autonomous* church is defined in the rules as "one which,
while recognizing the essential interdependence of the churches, particularly those of the same confession, is responsible to no other church for the conduct of its own life...."[55]
This definition apparently rules out the Petrine function of
preserving the true faith among all the Apostles.

The criterion of *stability* requires evidence of continuity
recognizable to other churches and a going program of Christian life and mission. *Size* must be taken into account but
is not specified in the rules. *Relationship* with other churches must also be examined but is not specified as to "kind
of relationship" or "degrees of contact."[56]

Art. 4. The question of the autonomy of the member churches
and the *authority* of the World Council is met in the fourth
article of the Constitution. The primary thrust of this article is found in the one-sentence paragraph: "The World
Council *shall not legislate* for the churches; nor shall it
act for them in any manner except as indicated...or as may
hereafter be specified by the constituent churches."[57]

The indicated modes of action are offering counsel, providing
opportunities of acting together, acting for a member church
and calling regional and world conferences.   The explicit
"shall not legislate" expression was necessary to calm the
concerns of those who feared that the World Council was designed to become the One Church of Christ in the world.

The historic ecumenical councils had defined Christian doctrine and *had legislated* for the whole church. By representation, the whole church went into the Council and the whole
Church was bound by it. The fear was voiced that this new

World Council would do the same for its members. The "shall
not legislate" expression did not fully put this fear to
rest.

Art. 5. The question of authority emerged in the next constitutional article entitled "Organization," in which *the Assembly* (to meet usually every five years) was identified as the
"principal authority in the Council."[58] Between Assemblies
all WCC work, except changing the constitution or its own
composition, was to be done by a *Central Committee* of approximately 100 members. The Central Committee was ordinarily to
meet once a year. Between Central Committee meetings, an
Executive Committee appointed by it would conduct the World
Council's business from Geneva, Switzerland. Willem A.
Visser't Hooft, who had successfully headed the Provisional
Committee from 1938 to 1948, was appointed General Secretary
of the Executive Committee.

David Gaines in his extensive study of the World Council
noted that:

> The Central Committee, with its Executive
> Committee, was...in effect the World Council
> of Churches.[59]

Official documents are generated from the assemblies, from
the Central Committee or from the Executive Committee with
the approval of the president of the Central Committee. These
documents bear the name and carry the moral authority of the
World Council of Churches. They have been compared to the
papal encyclicals of the Roman Catholic Church.[60]

During wartime and in other emergencies, authoritative WCC
statements may be made in which only a few men have determined the content and timing of the document.[61] Thus a few
men would, as spokesmen, voice the witness of the churches,
or as is sometimes said, of the Church. For the most part,
however, the World Council's documents have been hammered
out through the stages of research, committee modification,
and final approval at Central Committee or Assembly level.

The Assemblies following Amsterdam (1948) were held in Evanston, Illinois (1954), New Delhi, India (1961), Uppsala,
Sweden (1969), and Nairobi, Kenya (1975). The Assemblies'
documents are commonly referred to simply as Amsterdam's message, New Delhi's declaration, Nairobi said—etc.

The Central Committee also has held its meetings in varying
places throughout the world, adhering closely to its one-
meeting-a-year plan. It held its first meeting in Amsterdam
immediately following the first assembly. Its seventh

meeting was in Evanston following the second assembly, its
fourteenth in New Delhi and so on. In off-assembly years, it
has met in Chichester, England; Toronto, Canada; the island
of Rhodes, etc. Thus, its documents are likewise commonly
referred to merely by the place of the meeting. The Executive Committee's documents generally emanate from Geneva.

Finally, Faith and Order, although now a subordinate part of
the WCC, continues to hold World Conferences as it did at
Lausanne (1927) and Edinburgh (1937). Faith and Order held a
third World Conference in Lund, Sweden (1952); a fourth in
Montreal, Canada (1963); a fifth in Bristol, England (1967);
and its golden-anniversary sixth in Lausanne (1977).

As the lists of World Council documents are studied, the
reader becomes aware of the disproportion between the large
numbers of documents which deal with Life and Work and the
small number of documents which treat explicitly of the more
difficult, but more critically ecumenical, Faith and Order
matters. As Douglas Horton, former dean of Harvard's Divinity School and observer delegate at Vatican II, has perceived
regarding Federal Councils and the World Council of Churches:

> The difficulty with most councils...is that
> they almost inevitably tend to settle down at
> the level of cooperation and go no further.
> The demand for cooperation is so immediate
> and so vast that remoter interests, even
> though more important, tend to be crowded out.
> One could desire an organization dedicated to
> unity, all of unity and nothing but unity.[62]

Life and Work had formulated an initial conviction that "doctrine divides; service unites." But service alone cannot resolve the theological differences to which the World Council
churches cling in tenacious division. Multiplication of
services may preempt the time and energy needed to penetrate
to doctrinal unity. History has begun to reverse the Life
and Work slogan to read "multiplied services preserve doctrinal divisions."

The theological input for World Council thinking has been almost exclusively Protestant with a small contribution on the
part of Greek Orthodoxy. Life and Work brought a medley of
Protestant voices to the fore, whereas Faith and Order contributed a dominant theme of Anglican ecclesiology which involved a traditionally structured church and an historic
episcopacy. The Orthodox voice reinforced this theme.

However, the union of the two movements in the Provisional
Committee and its move to Geneva with Visser't Hooft as

general secretary brought into dominance a new theological
note. Visser't Hooft who had the greatest influence in
shaping the World Council was greatly attracted to the theology of Karl Barth. Barth was probably the foremost Reformed
Theologian of this century. Anglican Stephen Neill comments:

> In twenty years the World Council of Churches
> has come to be deeply marked by its first
> general secretary, both in his strength and
> in his limitations.
>
> Every great man has his limitations. For
> instance in early years 't Hooft[63] came deeply
> under the influence of Karl Barth and his
> theology. Some have felt that this has made
> him less sympathetic than he might have been
> with points of view other than those of con-
> tinental theology.[64]

Although an ordained pastor of the Swiss Reformed Church,
Visser't Hooft had directed his energies into the student
federation movement and had not been engaged in the work of
the Church at parochial, diocesan, or national levels. Thus,
another frequent criticism of the World Council of Churches
in its early years declared that it was simply the World's
Student Christian Federation grown up.

Visser't Hooft points out that the theology of Barth has been
the dominating influence on the Protestant World Student
Christian Federation.[65] Further, Visser't Hooft indicates
that Barth has had a very significant influence on both his
own theology and on the movement centered in Geneva.

Barth, whose Calvinist vision was focused on the awesome
transcendence of God and the power of God's word, has been
openly critical of the world Council Movement he termed the
"ecumenical circus." Barth's pointed theological questioning
sharpened Visser't Hooft's sense of the Christian ground on
which he and the movement stood. However, Barth modified his
position to such an extent that, at Visser't Hooft's invitation, he was the principal theologian to address the inaugural Assembly at Amsterdam. In his *Memoirs* Visser't Hooft
writes:

> I have therefore said more than once that
> without Karl Barth the movement would not
> have had the spiritual substance which it
> did receive.[66]

Concept "Church" in World Council Expression

In the light of Barth's influence it appears that when
Visser't Hooft speaks of the concept, "church," his basic
meaning refers to the invisible church which lies beneath the
denominational differences. Christians are called to make
their unity visible. In a carefully studied declaration published against the Nazi effort to nationalize the German
Evangelical Church, Visser't Hooft formulated the World Council's statement praised by Barth:

> We believe in the One, Holy, Catholic, and
> Apostolic Church. The national organization
> of the Christian Church is not an essential
> element of its life. It has its blessings,
> but it also has its dangers. But the recog-
> nition of the spiritual unity of all those
> who are in Christ, irrespective of...nation
> ...belongs to the essence of the Church. The
> Church is called to give *clear and visible ex-*
> *pression to this unity.*[67]

Thus the unity is there, but it must be made visible. The
Church is the entity called to manifest this unity visibly.
Thus, the already existent, but invisible, Church has a job
to do. By "Church" Visser't Hooft must mean the *Una Sancta*
in some invisible way, or the fellowship of churches forming
the WCC. The latter would make the WCC a super-church with
himself as its spokesman. "The Unity-of-those-in-Christ"
sense of Church is spiritual and invisible and has yet to
have its unity expressed. The basic difficulty as to the
nature of the Church of Christ emerges in World Council documents and statements when the term church is used. The same
expression "One, Holy, Catholic and Apostolic Church" already
in use at the Council of Nicea (325) and continuously used by
the Roman Catholic Church scarcely squares with the above
World Council sense. But the meaning of ecumenism in both
the World Council's and Roman Catholic Church's documents depends on it. And the goal of ecumenism depends on Christ's
intention for "His Church."

During the ten-year Provisional Committee period and for the
World Council's birth and early years Karl Barth was "the
acknowledged theological mentor of the General Secretary."[68]
Barth and Visser't Hooft were also both pastors and shared
the spirit, atmosphere and ecclesial sense of the Reformed
Church of Switzerland. Thus, unless the contrary manifests
itself in some explicit way, it appears that the term, church,
is used with Barthian presuppositions in Visser't Hooft's use
of the word. The value of a brief look at this sense of
church is to note that the one-word, *church*, signifies

deeply different things to persons of different theological
convictions.

The Anglican sense of Church was indicated by Lambeth's acceptance and careful formulation of the Quadrilateral. Brent
and Temple kept this content, at least, present in Faith and
Order formulations. But as the World Council set its roots
in Geneva and men such as Boegner and Visser't Hooft of the
Reformed tradition came to the fore, a different ecclesiological conviction colored its documentation. It was the theology of Karl Barth.

Reformed churchman Johann Hoekendijk, Professor of Ecumenics
and former staff member of the World Council in Geneva, held
that Amsterdam marked a turning point away from the Anglican
ecclesiological influence to the influence of the Reformed
tradition. Hoekendijk's book, *The Church Inside Out*, reveals
the nonstructured, functional concept of church he has in
mind.[69] Barth was the principal theologian of this Reformed
Church influence.

Daniel Jenkins, Congregationalist Professor of Theology,
writes perhaps a bit overenthusiastically that, "Karl Barth
is considered by many students of theology to be the outstanding Protestant theologian of the twentieth century."[70]
Barth,following Calvin, emphasizes the transcendent sovereignty of God and predominantly, perhaps always, "takes a
from-God-down-to-man" point of view in his theological explanations. God's Word in the flesh (Christ) and in the Sacred Scripture is the norm of all else. "His theology is best
described as a theology of the Word of God."[71] Barth views
the "man-up-to-God" positions as futile and disastrous.

Briefly, God's sovereign Word intermittently calls the Church
into being when He will. God's Word effects belief in some
hearers; His Word calls these believers to worship. This
worshipping *congregation gathered by the Word* is *The Church*.
This gathering or congregation of the Word is *The Church*.
Jenkins qualifies Barth's thinking about the Church as congregational.[72] In emphasizing the sovereignty and exclusiveness
of God's Word (in Sacred Scripture), Barth seems to denigrate
ecclesial structure and continuity as if it were merely man's
word usurping the place of God's Word.

In one passage Barth sees "Scripture as always autonomous and
independent" but the man-dominated church as the attacker of
Scripture, rather than its preserver.[73] Barth views both
liberal Protestantism (stemming from Schleiermacher) and Roman Catholicism as man-centered and corrosive of the sovereignty of God and His Word.

Liberal Protestantism made man's experience (man's word) the
norm, while Roman Catholicism put church control, man-control
(man's word) over the Word of God. In Barth's view it is the
function of the Word of God (in Sacred Scripture) alone "to
reform and renew the whole church and bring it back from self-
government to obedience."[74]

It appears that the church exists *only* for the Gospel.[75] "It
must be only the community of the Gospel, content to be no
more."[76] "The Church is apostolic and therefore catholic
when it exists on the basis of Scripture and in conformity
with it,...when it looks *only* in the direction indicated by
...Scripture...."[77]

As commonly noted, Barth's writing is heavily homiletic and
his concepts emerge in his on-running reflections. Barth
does not pause to make a concise definition and explanation
of his concepts. Also, he tends at times to be absolute. It
appears that the church comes only from the Word, exists
only for the Word, and becomes a mere assembly of men, even
somehow opposed to God, when the Word is not spoken or is
absent.[78] Barth's "all or none" mode of expression seems to
exclude all intermediate degrees of the Word's presence.

Men of other Christian traditions, including Roman Catholic,
have found much to praise in Barth's writings, especially as
a corrective to the corrosive secularism affecting twentieth
century Christians. Thus, Barth himself acknowledged that
he had received more notice, positively as well as critically,
in Roman Catholic theological circles than any Protestant theologian since the Reformation.[79]

While holding Barth in high esteem, some theologians nevertheless noted that his sense of the Church as "community gathered
only by the Word," "for the Word," and existing only when "the
true Word is operative" leaves the Church rather unstable and
subject to invisibility. One Anglican theologian perceived
Barth's denigration of the human structure in the Church as
resulting in a church which consists of only a passing series
of events, or a succession of Divine calls convoking separated assemblies at a local or world level. Catholic theologian
Avery Dulles cites this Anglican analysis with approval:

> Bishop Lesslie Newbegin, of the Church of
> South India, has objected that in Barth's
> view the Church seems to dissolve into a
> series of totally disconnected happenings.[80]

This indeterminateness aside, Barth's position nevertheless
persuaded Visser't Hooft that the World Council's voice should
proclaim the prophetic word as occasion warranted. The World

Council's basis indicated that the body had been gathered by
the Word; the Word was common to all the member churches; the
gathered body (the Church?) had the obligation to speak the
Word to the world. Thus, the WCC gathered "by the Word,"
subject to the Word and viewed as "for the Word," readily
suggested that Barthian concept of the Church of Christ.

Barth's sense of the sovereignty and insistence of God's Word
seems to explain the urge and motive felt in Visser't Hooft
to have the WCC speak special messages to the world in times
of crisis. The Word of God is prophetic, The Word is normative. The Word from the Assembly (WCC) gathered by the Word
(Jesus Christ as Lord and Savior; WCC basis) appears as a
statement of the Church. With some such rationale Barth and
Visser't Hooft believed that Geneva should function as a sort
of "Watchman." In Visser't Hooft's words:

> Karl Barth was convinced that 'Geneva' should
> speak for the whole ecumenical community and
> speak with authority. In letters, conversa-
> tions and articles he put strong pressure on
> me to speak out, not only as a person, but as
> the mouthpiece of the World Council.
>
> I agreed with Barth that the ecumenical move-
> ment should have been able to fulfill this
> 'watchman's office.'[81]

Unfortunately, but probably as a necessary consequence of his
denigration of man's word as if it were an opponent of God's
Word, Barth saw the Roman Catholic Church as a whole in a
pejorative light.[82] Barth's influence and position as a
persona grata to the World Council, could not help but contribute to making the World Council something problematic to the
Roman Catholic hierarchy.

Between meetings of the Amsterdam Assembly, a special corres-
pondent of the Amsterdam Catholic weekly, De Linie, inter-
viewed Barth about his thoughts concerning the Roman Catholic
Church. In Barth's speech to the Constitutional Assembly, he
had identified the absence of Roman Catholics and Russian
Orthodox precisely as the absence of Rome and Moscow. The
interviewer, a Reverend J. Witte, noting that Barth was re-
freshingly forthright and sometimes even blunt, asked if
Barth intended to suggest communism by naming Moscow instead
of Russian Orthodox.

> 'Indeed, I did,' Barth said very frankly.
> 'For I see a link there. I always felt
> Catholicism to be in agreement with Commu-
> nism. Both are totalitarian, both claim

> the whole man. Both reason from a closed
> circle. Communism uses about the same
> methods of organizations; it learned them
> from the Jesuits. Both alike stress the
> visible. But for Protestantism the more
> dangerous of the two is Catholicism. Com-
> munism will pass; Catholicism will remain.'[83]

Witte, aware of Barth's dominant place at the Assembly, and
his influence with the Council's leaders, asked Barth if his
logic led him to hope that the World Council would "develop
into an anti-Catholic bloc." Barth smiled and said frankly
"Leider ist das nicht" ("I regret that it isn't").[84] Witte's
article was openly in praise of Barth's characteristics of
cordiality and forthright honesty, but expressed regret that
Barth was not more deeply acquainted with Catholic theology.

Barth's own conception of the Church according to Witte was
almost exclusively spiritual. The Church is "no more than
the place where two or more give actual testimony to Christ."[85]
Barth so emphasized the "actually spiritual," that any ecclesial body which failed to manifest actual testimony to
Christ patently, could be labeled "man-centered."[86]

In the documentary record of Barth's speech to the Assembly,
he identified the Kingdom of God as the person of Christ himself, already present and victorious. Barth insisted that
the Work of the Kingdom was all and only God's, that the
hearers' interventions were useless and even injurious. The
only basis of everything is Christ.

> ...we ought to give up, even on this first day
> of our deliberations, every thought that the
> care of the Church, the care of the world, is
> our care. Burdened with this thought,...we
> should only increase disorder in Church and
> world still more. For just this is the final
> root and ground of all human disorder; the
> dreadful, godless, ridiculous opinion that man
> is the Atlas who is destined to bear the dome
> of heaven on his shoulders.[87]

The Assembly's delegates, although deeply touched by Barth,
nevertheless evidenced a more optimistic view of man's cooperation with divine inspiration. They established the
World Council of Churches, hammered out its constitution and
rules, planned for the future, and perhaps as the major ac-
complishment joined their divided Christian churches in a new
history-making international fellowship with the commitment,
"We intend to stay together."[88]

Up until now, this inquiry into the equivalence of the meaning of ecumenism, and consequently the meaning of church, in
World Council and Vatican Council thought has been found
mainly in Protestant sources. These sources richly yield the
origin and progress of the modern ecumenical movement. Roman
Catholic positions were mostly seen as reactions to frankly
Protestant initiatives, mutual understandings, enormous work
and perseverance. Now the Roman Catholic position must be
examined.

Its position about the nature of the Church, and consequently
its view of church union or the *oikoumene*, was set long before
the 1910 start of the modern movement. However, an explicit
synthesis of the church's nature did not reach full flower
until the Second Vatican Council (1962-1965). Defensive
polemics characterized most of the post-reformation period.
Theologians spent much of their energy seeking to show how
Orthodox and Protestant theologies were in error, instead of
positively exploring the fuller meanings implicit in Divine
Revelation. The emphasis was already shifting when Vatican I
in 1870 was abruptly halted with the arrest of Pope Pius IX
by Garibaldi and Victor Emmanuel.

CHAPTER FIVE

FROM CHURCH TOWARD ECUMENISM

The modern ecumenical movement arose among those interested
in Protestant mission, mainly because church divisions were
defeating the work of the missions. The frustration of competing divisions precipitated a new examination of cooperation, and ultimately unity, across denominational barriers. In
this sense the modern movement in the Protestant tradition
proceeded in a relatively short time from deeply-entrenched
divisions and plurality toward a new kind of unity. The motion went from the many divisions *toward* the one.

In the Roman Catholic tradition the movement proceeded from
the opposite direction, namely, from the one *toward* the many.
Ecclesial unity was the starting point. From a conviction of
Christ-given unity the Roman Catholic Church in a century-
long effort examined the nature of Christ's Church, and cautiously moved toward a new subsidiarity and increased local
autonomy in some ecclesial elements. Reaction to the Protestant Reformation had produced among Roman Catholics a sharpened sense of everything which fostered unity in creedal language, liturgy, and church law. Unity in some way even became uniformity. Then the tide began to change. It came by
way of examination of the one Church's nature, not by way of
concentration on Church divisions.

Johann Adam Moehler (1796-1838) is generally given the cred-
it for initiating the tide-reversal in theological mood from
defensive theology to positive theological emphasis within
the Roman Catholic Church. Moehler, German patrologist and
historian, in two books, *Unity in the Church* and *Symbolism,*
focused attention on the Holy Spirit's work and especially
on the Incarnate Word (Christ) as the model according to
which the Church was patterned.[1]

Roman theologians Clement Schroeder and Jean Baptiste
Franzelin brought Moehler's insight and vision to Vatican
Council I (1870). There, they are credited with articulating
his vision in the conciliar committee which produced the
first report or schema on the Constitution of the Church
(*primum schema de Ecclesia*). Vatican I was abruptly

terminated before this schema reached the council floor for
modification or voting.[2]   A biblical model of the Church is
high-lighted in the theological report.

The schema describes the Church as the Mystical Body of
Christ, a true and visible society, and God's appointed means
of salvation.[3]

Vatican I was the first in the historic sequence of Councils,
that the Roman Cathoic Church identifies as ecumenical, in
which the subject of the Church's nature was explicitly addressed.   The Council had already overwhelmingly voted that
Christ had endowed his Church's teaching authority with the
gift of infallibility and was preparing to face the papal-
episcopal relationship when Italian military forces ended the
Council's deliberations.   This sudden intrusion of the Italian state and the Pope's new status as a prisoner in the
Vatican prevented Pius IX from giving much further attention
to the prepared, but never-voted, reports on the nature of
Church.

Pius IX and the Unity Movement

Pius IX, whose long pontificate extended from 1846 to 1878 (the
longest since Peter's),   had frequently confronted the problem termed *indifferentism* which holds radically that "one religion is as good as another," and more moderately that "one
church's teaching on Christianity is as good as another's."
The Vatican saw this teaching, called indifferentism, as an implicit denial of the divine establishment of the church and
therefore as a threat to the life and unity of the Roman
Catholic Church.

In the eleventh year of Pius IX (commonly called Pio Nono) a
mixed group of Protestant Christians in London had formed an
Association for the Promotion of Christian Unity (APCU).   To
the inquiry whether Roman Catholics could be members of this
society, the Vatican replied to the Bishops of England, in a
long letter citing the establishment and marks of the one
Church of Christ, that:

>   ...the faithful should especially shun this
>   London society because those sympathizing
>   with it favor indifferentism and engender
>   scandal.[4]

The indifferentism referred to was the so-called *Branch Theory* which held that the Anglican, Greek Orthodox and Roman
Catholic communions constituted the three essential constituent branches of the one Catholic Church founded by Christ.
This theory, which had been formulated in the Oxford Movement,

was the basic tenet of the APCU. Members of the Association
were called upon to pray for the tenet's realization and encouraged to implement it.

The Vatican document relied on Paul's letter to the Ephesians
to indicate that Christ's Body, the Church, was one single
body and not a three-branch affair. To similar questions regarding membership in religious societies formed by Protestant Christians, this response provided a handy model. This
protective model prevailed in principle down through the establishment of the World Council of Churches in 1948.

The "Liberty, Equality, Fraternity" of the French Revolution
had sparked a liberal flame which singed the doctrinal beliefs of many Christians. Concern about errors of liberalism
engendered in Pius IX "...supreme anxiety about the safety
and welfare of the Catholic Church and the whole flock of the
Lord divinely entrusted to him..."[5]

This papal "supreme anxiety" concerning the "whole flock...
divinely entrusted to him" reflects the pyramidal concept of
the Church operative at that time. As a concept it was contained in the definition of the Church formulated by theologian Robert Bellarmine after the Council of Trent.

Bellarmine (1543-1621), in the fourth book of his *Solida Christianae Fidei Demonstratio*, defines the only one and true
church as the

> congregation of men bound by the profession
> of the same Christian faith, and in the com-
> munion of the same sacraments, under the rule
> of legitimate pastors and especially of the
> one vicar of Christ on earth, the Roman
> Pontiff.[6]

The picture: many lay people, a smaller number of pasters, a
still smaller number of bishops, and finally one ruler on top,
suggests the pyramidal structure.

Bellarmine immediately indicates that his definition makes it
easy to determine which people belong to the Church and which
people do not. He proceeds to point out that the three elements specifying his congregation of men, namely same faith,
same sacraments and same papal authority, each function to
point out groups separated from the Church. Thus, the first
requirement of the *same faith* excludes people who deny
Christ's divinity and humanity; secondly, catechumens, and
the excommunicated do not share the same sacraments; and
thirdly, those who reject the legitimate hierarchical *authority* are in schism.[7]

Bellarmine argues that opponents (who claim that only those
are members of Christ's Church who personally possess the
interior virtues of Faith, Hope and Charity), are making the
Church an invisible reality, whereas the Church, as the congregation of men, is as visible and palpable as the Kingdom of
France or the Republic of Venice.[8]

Without question, Bellarmine is here striving for clarity of
concept and an easily applicable test for identifying membership in the Church immersed in the chaotic divisions of the
Reformation. His defining elements of creed (faith), cult
(sacraments) and code (rulership under legitimate and especially papal authority) provided, and continued to provide for
Roman Catholics, the criteria of distinguishing membership in
the Church down to the twentieth century.

Bellarmine's examples of visibility and palpability, namely
the Kingdoms of France and Venice, served as easy targets for
opponents and critics in declaring that Bellarmine's Church
was purely an external organization or society. But Bellarmine's first chapter is on the Word of God and his second is
entitled "*De Christo, capite totius Ecclesiae*" (On Christ, the
head of the whole Church).[9] In this context and given his
insistence on faith and divine grace, Bellarmine addressed
both the intrinsic and extrinsic dimensions of Christ's
Church.

Bellarmine's third chapter, "On the Roman Pontiff," affirmed
supreme papal authority in matters of faith and morals, but
insisted that this authority entered the secular sphere only
if that sphere on occasion interfered with the religious
rights of the faithful. For this limitation, his book was
banned for two years. In a short time, however, the ban was
lifted and Bellarmine's book flourished for a century.[10]

Some of its explanations and his definition of the Church prevailed down to the eve of Vatican II. An example of this occurred in the *Synopsis Theologiae Dogmaticae Fundamentalis* by
A. Tanquerey, used in many major Roman Catholic seminaries
until the 1950s. The present writer used the twenty-fourth
edition of this three-volume work as the assigned seminary
text. Bellarmine's definition, with slight modification, is
visible in *Tanquerey's*. The Church is:

> The society, instituted by Christ, of pilgrim
> people, who by profession of the same faith
> and participation of the same sacraments, are
> united under the authority of the Roman Pontiff
> for obtaining grace and salvation.[11]

The specifying elements of same faith profession, same

sacraments and same papal authority are readily noticeable;
the change in the generic part of the definition manifests
the shift of emphasis emerging among Europe's theologians.
And the starting point and purpose are now explicit.

Bellarmine's "faith-sacraments-papal authority" definition of
the Church stood in contradistinction to the definitions of
Martin Luther and John Calvin in all three elements to some
degree, but mainly in the third, namely, the identification
of authority in the Church of Christ by Bellarmine; this was
absent in the reformers' definitions.

The *Augsburg Confession,* translated from the German text, defines the Church as

> ...the assembly of all believers among whom
> the Gospel is preached in its purity and the
> holy sacraments are administered according to
> the Gospel.[12]

The Latin text in translation defines the Church essentially
the same way but a bit more succinctly, using such equivalents
as "saints" for "all believers" and "rightly" for "according
to the Gospel." Thus the Church is

> ...the assembly of saints in which the Gospel
> is taught purely and the sacraments are ad-
> ministered rightly.[13]

In many passages of the *Book of Concord,* it is pointed out
that the content of the believer's faith equals the Apostle's
Creed,[14] indicating that the believers of Luther's definition
were making the same profession of faith as the believers of
Bellarmine's definition. The teaching of each author indicated interior as well as exterior dimensions of faith, but
Luther, to show the deplorable condition of evil men, including ecclesiastics and popes, stressed interior faith and pure
teaching and right sacraments with expressions which suggested the Church was invisible because only God knew who had the
pure faith and right sacraments.

Luther's sacraments were three, namely Baptism, Eucharist,
and Penance, whereas Bellarmine held to the same seven which
still flourished among the Orthodox five centuries after the
split with Rome, thus antedating that division. But the overriding topic of difference and major base of the polemics was
the question of *authority* omitted in Luther's definition and
essential to Bellarmine's.

Bellarmine's same faith, same sacraments, offer encouraging
dialogue relationship to Luther's pure Gospel, and right

sacraments, whereas Bellarmine's papal authority constituent
meets no corresponding element in the Lutheran definition.
Christ's invisible headship of his Church is agreed upon universally; this, of itself, changed neither concept.

There is no intention here of entering into the detailed difference of Reform and Roman Catholic theology in the Reformation and Tridentine documents, but only to see briefly the
concepts of *Church* (in comparison to the Roman Catholic Concept) which became operative in the sixteenth century. As
almost any Roman Catholic examines Luther's small and large
catechisms and notes the outline: Commandments, Creed, Lord's
Prayer, Sacraments, Prayers and Duties, he is immediately
struck by the item-for-item correspondence with the catechisms
of his childhood and youth except, perhaps, for the order.

Very many of the explanations are sound theologically to Roman
Catholic understanding, and devotionally elevating. However,
when the absence of the sacraments of confirmation, matrimony,
holy orders and anointing of the sick is noticed and the polemics of the *Large Catechism* (manifestly absent in Luther's
Small Catechism) is encountered, the reader is abruptly returned to the Reformation period. It is now commonly accepted
that Luther, at first, intended merely to reform the Catholic
Church, and only later, took the steps which in fact established a new ecclesial entity.

From a papal point of view, oversimplified to gain a clear
view of the position, Father Martin Luther was a priest who
taught some erroneous doctrines which had to be corrected.
His pathway of return to communion was correction of his errors. If others followed him, their pathway was the same as
his.

Even if other matters needed reform, and some certainly did,
(as the then recently ended Fifth Lateran Council, 1512-1517,
had noted) nevertheless, the one Church could not sustain
contradictory teachings of Christ's doctrine. Luther's confrontation had to be met. The die had already been cast when
Calvin appeared.

In his famous *Institutes of the Christian Religion,* John Calvin, the second major leader of the Protestant Reformation,
defines the Church in the same two categories as Luther,
namely, Gospel and sacraments.

> ...wherever we find the word of God purely
> preached and heard and the sacraments adminis-
> tered according to the institution of Christ,
> there, it is not to be doubted, is a Church of
> God.[15]

Calvin is here speaking of the external, *visible* Church which
stands in distinction to the invisible body, namely

> ...all the elect of God...so connected with
> each other in Christ; that as they depend upon
> one head, so they grow-up together as into one
> body.[16]

This distinction, which a later generation will refer to as
the *invisible* church, suggests two churches. Calvin denies
that there can be two churches because that would divide
Christ, which is impossible,[17] yet his discounting of the already reprobate and his emphasis on "the elect" (those predestined to Glory) yields his definition of the true Church
of Christ as: "the assembly of *the elect* in which the Word is
purely preached and the sacraments rightly administered."

Calvin's diminution of the traditional sacraments to two,
namely baptism and eucharist, and his explanation of the
sacraments in a sense more symbolic than Luther's, definitely
separated the Reform position from the Lutheran teaching and
still further away from Roman Catholic understanding.

As Luther had done, so too Calvin denied that the centuries-
old papal authority was an essential element in the definition of the Church. All acknowledged the primacy of Christ's
headship. But this is invisible and must be complemented according to Christ's plan. As Luther had, so Calvin had, himself, personally supplied the visible headship of the separated group. Then, on the basis of his own analysis of some
Pauline texts, Calvin chose a synod-pastor-teacher-elder-dea-
con structure[18] to replace the pope-bishop-priest-deacon
structure in operation since antiquity.

Although it is generally affirmed that the original reformers
wished only to reform the Catholic Church (this appears to be
more true of Luther than of the later Calvin), it was not too
long before new structures were devised which, in fact, established ecclesial bodies distinctly different from the Roman Catholic Church and from each other. From such beginnings have grown the different Church-concepts represented by
the "united-but-divided" member churches of the World Council
of Churches.

From these definitions of the Church in the Lutheran and Reformed sources, it is also clear that the elements of Gospel
and sacraments have much which continued in common from the
Catholic origins into the Lutheran and Reformed traditions.
Many samenesses continued, but the growing differences fed
the Reformation fires. However, as the samenesses, which all

claimed were genuinely from Christ, passed through the generations, many of them became less recognizable in the hands of
later groups. The Vatican saw them drifting further away
from the *fullness* of Christian origins and saw the diluted
later forms of Christianity as injurious to Roman Catholics
influenced by them.

Thus, two centuries after the Reformation's Westminister Confession, Pius IX repeats his predecessors' call for all separated
Christians *to return* to the Catholic Church from which the departure had taken place. Accompanying this mind was a posture
of warning to Roman Catholics, as already noted in the case of
the APCU.

Leo XIII Encourages Return

Pius IX died in 1878. Pope Leo XIII, who served the Church
for twenty-five years (1878-1903), further analyzed the nature of Christ's Church, and its relation to separated Christians. Pope Leo modified the Church's posture. First, however, he directed his attention to the Orthodox.

Leo XIII continued the traditional Vatican stance of calling
for a *return* to the one true church. But instead of awaiting
a return as prior popes had, Leo moved out to *initiate* a home-
coming. Moreover, in official documents, he replaced the use
of *terms* implying deliberate error or division, such as here-
tic and schismatic, with the expression "those separated from
us."[19] Further, Pope Leo directed his invitation to *entire
groups* of Orthodox, indeed to the whole Orthodox body, in
place of the former attitude of expecting those returning to
reunite as individuals. Finally, he positively encouraged
the preservation of the ancient *Orthodox rites* instead of
asking that Latin be adopted as a policy of uniformity to
preserve unity. Unity and catholicity would both be better
enhanced by a diversity of valid traditions.[20]

Reunion with the Orthodox was more important to Leo than uniformity of rites and language (Latin). Faithful Orthodox
rites and language were to be preserved. This break with
long-standing policy led toward a new "pluralistic conception
of Catholic Unity."[21] Liturgical diversity could flourish in
the Church's unity.

More than thirty of Pope Leo's writings concern the nature of
the church's unity and those separated from unity. Three of
these are: (1) *Praeclara Gratulationis* (1894) which is identified as the first Papal document dedicated to ecumenism,[22]
(2) *Satis Cognitum* (1896), and (3) *Divinum Illud* (1897).

Invitation to Return

The first document, *Praeclara Gratulationis,* noting the
'splendid (*praeclara*) tokens of rejoicing (*gratulationis*)'
on the occasion of his episcopal jubilee, expresses Leo's
profound wish first for the return of the Orthodox, and
then, for those who have more recently separated from the
original unity.

The Pope identifies the Church's unity as mysterious and
then writes: ...

> we hope that the...Eastern Churches...will
> return to the fold they have abandoned...the
> distance separating them from Us is not so
> great.[23]

Leo acknowledges that the principal topic of separation is
papal primacy and asks the Orthodox to consider again the
promise to Peter and the fact that many of the immediate
successors to Peter came, as Peter did, from the East. Of
the first six successors to Peter in Rome, three were from
the Church in the East and were interspersed with three from
the West.

Leo recalls the agreement to the Primacy at the Councils of
Florence and II Lyons as constituting an invitation to reconciliation.[24]

Leo assures the Orthodox:

> It is not for any human motive...that We ad-
> vise the reconciliation and union with the
> Church of Rome;....The true union between
> Christians is that which Jesus Christ, the
> Author of the Church, instituted and desired,
> and which consists in a unity of faith and a
> unity of government.[25]

The Pope further assures the Orthodox that there is no reason to fear any loss of rights, Patriarchal privileges, or
the established rituals or primitive traditions of any of
their churches.[26] Speaking from the conviction that Christian unity is the will of Christ, his Master, whose vicar he
totally believes himself to be, Pope Leo next addresses himself to Christian *nations* more recently separated from Catholic unity.[27]

Briefly noting the occurring drifting away, the diminution
of belief, the tendency to deny the "Divine Nature of Jesus
Christ, Our Savior," and a loss of the sense of the divine

inspiration of Sacred Scripture, Pope Leo nevertheless com-
mends their concern about a union in mutual charity, while
indicating that, of itself, it is inadequate.[28]

> But how can hearts be united in perfect
> Charity where minds do not agree in Faith?
> [Many returning have] clearly understood
> that they could never...really acquire the
> true Christian Faith if they rejected the
> legitimate teaching confided to Peter and
> his successors.[29]

Affirming that expert historians have shown the continuity of
the Church of Rome from the Apostles, Leo addresses those
separated from him as "brothers" and asks that they permit
him to invite them to come to "the unity which has ever existed in the Catholic Church and can never fail."[30]

After describing the Church as a divinely founded society,
perfect in its kind, to lead men by Gospel and Christian virtue to the happiness of heaven, Pope Leo ends his encyclical
with the prayer that God will hasten the arrival of Christ's
promise of one fold and one shepherd.[31]

In this papal document, ecumenism means a *return* implying no
change on the part of the Roman Catholic Church. Leo sees
Orthodox peoples closer to reunion than Protestants; he acknowledges that reunion efforts will require much prayer,
time and energy.

The Church and Its Unity

Two years later *Satis Cognitum* (1896), probably the longest
papal teaching on the nature of the Church and its unity, was
published. "Sufficiently well known" (*Satis Cognitum*) was
his concern to invite back the sheep who had strayed. For
this purpose he described the exemplar, form and lines of the
Church, of which its *unity* was the most worthy. The Divine
Author made this unity a sign of its truth and strength.[32]

Pope Leo addressed the encyclical to Catholics but also those
who were separated from him through no fault of their own. He
pointed out that God could have saved us any way He chose; He
preferred in His loving care "to help men by the instrumental-
ity of men."[33]

The chief purpose of the Church is spiritual and invisible,
but God chose the visible Incarnation, visible Apostles,
visible signs of His gifts to bring all men, whose knowledge
comes through their senses, into His *visible* Church. Faith
and grace are internal but faith comes by hearing (Romans

10:17) and grace by the *external* means Christ chose.[34]

This encyclical, heavily documented from Sacred Scripture and
the ancient Fathers of East and West, insists again and again
that what Christ wanted, and what Christ actually did, is what
counts. Leo looks to Christ as the exemplar of His own Body,
the Church.

> As Christ, the Head and Exemplar, is not
> wholly in His visible human nature,...nor
> wholly in the invisible divine nature...
> but is one, from and in both natures, visi-
> ble and invisible...so...is the true Church.[35]

The nature of the Church's unity and the whole constitution
of the Church, the encyclical maintains,

> ...belongs to the class of things effected
> by Christ's free choice. For this reason
> ....We must...investigate,...how He who
> founded it, willed that it should be one.
>
> ...Christ...mentions only one Church, which
> He calls *His own*—'I will build My Church.'[36]

Seeing the unity of the Church in Pauline terms, Leo says
"the Son of God decreed that the Church should be His mystical body, with which He should be united as the Head,...."
Scattered and divided members cannot make a body, but many
members properly alive and joined make one body, "...so also
is Christ" as St. Paul teaches.[37]

Leo pursues the Pauline image to point out that members separated from the body die; further, the body without this one
Head cannot live as Christ planned.

> Another head like to Christ must be invented
> —that is another Christ—if beside the one
> Church, which is His body, men wish to set
> up another.[38]

Leo rests on St. Augustine (died 431) to say that a Christian
separated from the body is like a finger amputated from the
hand. St. Cyprian (ca. 251) identifies for Leo the division
as a separation from the faith of Christ.[39]

One Church: One Faith

Unity of faith is identified as the first of the bonds uniting
Christians since this leads to agreement of wills and proper
relationships in action. The Pope reads St. Paul's "one body,

one spirit, one Lord, one faith, one baptism" (Eph. 4:4f) as
requisite unity characteristics of the Church; Leo interprets
Christ's "that they may be one in us...that they may be made
perfect in one...as you Father in me and I in you" (John
17:20ff) as a quality of the persons who follow Him and manifest, as individuals and collectively, His special transcendent unity.[40]

The Pope observes that faith in revelation involves mysteries
and is so subject to differing and conflicting interpretations that the unity Christ wants can only be attained by
another principle in addition to Sacred Scripture as a principle. Scripture alone can't bring Christian unity.

He again insists that the principle Christ actually adopted
(not what He might have done but what He in fact did do) is
decisive for the unity of His Church. Leo identifies the
principle as the *teaching authority* which Christ actually
constructed into His Church. Resting on New Testament texts
showing that Christ chose and sent Apostles (John 20:21),
that He required belief in His teaching, and that He wanted
His teaching to reach all nations, Leo invokes the Matthean
"Great Commission" as the first support of the "other principle" Christ actually gave: "all power is given to me...teach
all nations...to observe...whatsoever I have commanded you."
(Matt. 28:18ff).[41]

The Matthean citation closes with Christ's assertion that He
will be with them "even to the consummation of the world."
Leo points to this as showing that Christ's intention goes
far beyond the Apostles' times because the commands given far
exceed what they could realize before death.

> It was, consequently, provided by God that
> the *Magisterium* instituted by Jesus Christ
> would not end with the life of the Apostles,
> but that it should be perpetuated....(2 Tim.
> 2:1ff).[42]

Leo quotes the letter of Pope Clement of Rome to the Corinthians (circa 80)[43] to show that the teaching authority line
in Corinth at that time consisted of "Christ-Apostles-bishops-
deacons." Recent scholarship estimates that the early titles
and functions of "bishop and deacon" bear some definite relationship, but not a one-to-one correspondence of functions
with these same titles in the modern Church.[44] The question
involved in studies such as Raymond E. Brown's *Priest and
Bishop* is not whether these titles connoted authority in the
early Church, but rather what authority and which functions
were identified with which title in an emerging, growing,
shifting and blending process.

Leo reasoned from the authority which Christ gave His chosen
Apostles (and thus His Church) to the nature of the Church as
a society unique in its beginning, end, and means. Started
by Christ, it is divine in its beginning, its end is the
transcendent, eternal, and thus divine, salvation, and the
means (prayer, grace, and sacraments) given by Christ are
proportionate to its end. Thus, Leo sees Christ's Church as
divine in its beginning, means and end.

Leo characterizes the Church also as human because the Incarnate Son composed it of His human followers. The same divine
Originator wanted one fold and one shepherd. His chosen
Apostle, Paul, was inspired to see the Church as one body
under one head.[45]

One Faith: One Final Authority

Resting on the unity required for such a society, such a Mystical Body, Pope Leo estimates the governing means for preserving such a divinely planned unity, are also supported by
divine right or authority.

> ...as the unity of the faith is of necessity
> required for the unity of the Church, inasmuch
> as the Church is the *body of the faithful,* so
> also for this same unity, inasmuch as the
> Church is a divinely constituted society,
> unity of government, which effects and involves
> *unity of communion,* is necessary *iure divino.*[46]

Leo returns to the will of Christ expressed in the New Testament to observe what means Christ actually took to start and
to preserve the unity He wanted. The Pope affirms that Christ
is certainly the Head of His Church forever, but before returning to His Father, He actually chose a *visible* vicar for
His visible body of faithful. Leo rests his case on the promise of Peter "thou art Peter [kepha], and upon this rock
[kepha] I will build My Church" (Matt. 16:18) and the command
to Peter in John's Gospel, "Feed my sheep" (John 21:17).[47]

The Matthean "Peter: rock: Church" text "has been among the
most controversial in the whole of the New Testament."[48] However, the great advance in Scriptural scholarship has led to
a common acceptance of the text as belonging where it is and
as having an authentic Aramaic (Simon-bar-Jonah, flesh and
blood, bind and loose, Kepha-kepha) underpinning.

Protestant scholar Howard Clark Kee, while acknowledging the
Aramaic (Christ's own spoken language) source, nevertheless
thinks that the use of the word Church here suggests a post-
resurrection milieu. Kee further objects that the identifi-

cation of Peter as the rock (kepha, Petros, Peter) "does not
view him as the first bishop of Rome and the founder of the
Roman hierarchy...."[49]

Another internationally-acknowledged Protestant scholar, Oscar Cullmann, in his study of the Petrine texts, *Peter: Disciple, Apostle, Martyr,* appears to end one phase of the four-
hundred-year old discussion and then to shift the problem involved to another focus. Cullmann finds that long-standing
effort to identify the meaning of the word rock (kepha) as
faith is faulty. The Peter: rock (kepha:kepha) citation is a
reference to *the person of Peter* as the rock on which Christ
will build His Church.

> ...all Protestant interpretations that seek
> in one way or another to explain away the
> reference to Peter seem to be unsatisfactory.
> No, the fact remains that when Jesus says that
> he will build his *ekklesia* upon this rock, he
> really means the person of Simon. Upon this
> disciple, who in the lifetime of Jesus pos-
> sessed the specific advantages and the speci-
> fic weaknesses of which the Gospels speak,
> upon him who was then their spokesman, their
> representative in good as well as in bad, and
> in this sense was the rock of the group of
> disciples,—upon him is to be founded the
> Church, which after the death of Jesus will
> continue his work upon earth.
>
> The Roman Catholic exegesis must be regarded
> as correct when it rejects those other at-
> tempts at explanation.[50]

After this acknowledgment, however, Cullmann argues that the
Matthean text applies only to Peter and not to his successors.[51]

On the Roman Catholic side, it must be acknowledged that
there is much more data available on Peter than there is on
the Church leaders listed as following him in Rome. The official catalogues of the bishops of Rome, resting on ancient
catalogues such as that of Irenaeus (c. 160-202) with partial
support from archaeological evidence, list Linus, Cletus, and
Clement, Evaristus, Anacetus, Sixtus, Telesphorus as the
lineal successors of Peter.[52] When Cullmann shifts the focus
of attention to Linus, or Cletus, he can easily ask questions
for which no answer can be given. On the other hand, there
is no other extant line claiming primacy that connects any
Christian Church with Christ.

Pope Leo, knowing this hard-to-demonstrate, but *only* existent,
line of succession, nevertheless holds that the Petrine authority of "binding and loosing," and exclusive possession of
"the keys" continues in the Church by the will of Christ. He
finds that "a primacy of honor and the shadow right of giving
advice" correspond neither to the Biblical expressions of
Christ nor the real needs of Christ's living and developing
Church. Leo cannot see how Peter or his successors can preserve Christ's Church "without the power of commanding, for-
bidding, and judging, which is properly called jurisdiction."[53]

In his *Satis Cognitum,* Leo holds that the unity Christ willed
contains His divine authority to endow His Church with the
continuous means, the necessary supreme authority, to preserve that unity.

> For this reason the Pontiffs who succeed
> Peter in the Roman Episcopate receive the
> supreme power in the Church, *iure divino.*[54]

Pope Leo starts his supporting quotes from the Council of
Florence, almost a century before the Reformation when Europe
was Catholic, and works back toward the primitive Church.
After quoting the Fourth Lateran (1215) Leo calls upon the
witness of Third Constantinople (680), Chalcedon (451) and
Ephesus (431) as sources, honored by the Orthodox testifying
to the authority residing in Peter's successor in Rome.[55]

Leo next affirms that "Bishops belong to the essential constitution of the Church" and briefly examines the relationships
existing between Peter (as the "head of the college" of
Apostles) and the Apostles as the divinely given *design* of
his own relationship with the other bishops. Leo sees the
unity between Peter and the Apostles (Pope and Bishops) as
critical and undeniable for the safety of the Church.[56]

In closing *Satis Cognitum,* Pope Leo cites his own unworthi-
ness for the office of Peter's successor and appeals in the
words of Christ to those who are "not of this fold."[57]

The Holy Spirit: Indwelling and Powerful

A year later, in 1897, Pope Leo addressed an encyclical
Divinum Illud (On the Indwelling and Power of the Holy Spirit) to all who would respond to Christ's appealing invitation,
"Come to me...I am the Life...I am the Good Shepherd." In
his introduction Leo confided that a serious purpose of his
twenty-year service as pontiff was:

> ...to promote the reunion of those who have
> fallen away from the Catholic Church...since

> it is most undoubtedly the Will of Christ
> that all should be united in one flock under
> one Shepherd.[58]

The earlier encyclicals emphasized *visible* unity; *Divinum
Illud* focused on the *invisible* work of the Holy Spirit in
sanctifying the members of Christ's Mystical Body both cor-
porately and individually.

The Pope discerns that as the Second Person of the Trinity
sanctified the individual human nature, born of Mary, He
[Christ] prefigured the Holy Spirit's sanctification of
Christ's mysterious corporate body, the Church. Christ's
total self-offering on the cross is viewed as the divinely-
planned birth of His Church. Its public ministry would start,
as His had, with a special manifestation of the Holy Spirit.

> The Church which, already conceived, came
> forth from the side of the second Adam in
> His sleep on the Cross, first showed herself
> before the eyes of men on the great day of
> Pentecost.[59]

This Holy Spirit, as promised by Christ, will teach the
Apostles and thus Christ's Church "all truth" (John 16:13),
bringing to the Apostles' minds things not then fully understood and guarding His Church "by His all-powerful help from
ever falling into error." This other Paraclete, this guard-
ian of truth, will be with them forever (John 14:16).[60]

Leo uses Augustine's insight to present the interior mysterious relationship of the Holy Spirit to the Church. As the
soul is to man's body, so the Holy Spirit is to the Church:
Christ is the Mystical Body's Head and the Holy Spirit her
soul.[61] Pope Leo would be the first to warn that Augustine's
insight (as Man's soul: body:: so Holy Spirit: Church) is not
a limited analogy as if it were merely a mathematical proportion. The Holy Spirit vivifies the Church, but is not confined within it.

The Holy Spirit's action in the Church, although analogous
to man's soul in his body as necessary and invisible, nevertheless transcends the soul's limitations of vision, generosity and confinement to one body. Briefly, the divine: human
analogy is viewed as containing a real insight, an element of
true comparison, but the differences in a "divine-human"
analogy far exceed the samenesses.

Leo turns from the Church as a whole to its individual members to note that here too the Holy Spirit sanctifies as
Christ promised, but in even more mysterious ways, only partly

grasped.

> The manner and extent of the action of the
> Holy Spirit in individual souls is...more
> difficult to understand, inasmuch as it is
> entirely invisible....Christ Himself...com-
> pares it to an overflowing river (John 7:30).[62]

This encyclical, which heavily stresses the nonvisible, interior life of the Church, is a seventeen-page compendium of New
Testament texts on the Holy Spirit. Leo does not fail to
mention the work of the Holy Spirit in the power to forgive
sins and in the mysterious personal indwelling of the Holy
Spirit proclaimed by St. Paul (1 Cor. 6:19).[63]

In *Satis Cognitum*, Leo had given more attention to Christ's
Church as a visible society with less notice of the Mystical
Body image, whereas in *Divinum Illud* he emphasized the interior, divinely-given life of the Church without the use of the
words "society," or "society perfected by Christ" and with
one identification of the Church as "His Mystical Body."[64]

The Pope ended *Divinum Illud* with a mandate that the Universal Church establish in every parish a novena of prayer "for
the Reunion of Christendom" before Pentecost, the feast of
the manifestation of the Church through the power of the Holy
Spirit.[65] This was thirteen years before the 1910 Edinburgh
Mission meeting which started the modern ecumenical movement.

Pope Leo's interest in Christian reunion and his interest in
the Church of England aroused hope among some Catholics that
he might reverse the long-standing judgment against the validity of Anglican Orders. Fearing lest this new hope would
falsify the attitude of prayer "for the reunion in truth" he
sought to engender, Leo commissioned another exhaustive inquiry into the whole Reformation matter of the Edwardine
Ordinal of the sixteenth century which changed and replaced
the Catholic rite of Ordination after the death of Henry VIII.
He ordered the commission to examine every pertinent document
in the Vatican archives since the Reformation.

The commission, composed of theologians of differing opinions,
concluded that the composers of the Edwardine Ordinal had deliberately changed the essence of the sacrament of priesthood.
Leo XIII then, in 1896, issued an encyclical, *Apostolicae
Curae,* in which he adhered strictly in this matter to his
predecessors' decree of the nullity of the essentially changed
orders. Leo renewed their decrees by his own authority.[66]

The Pope closed his encyclical with an appeal, especially to
ministers of religion, to be reconciled with the Church, their

Mother, who will receive them with the deepest joy. Convinced that no door remained open for Anglicans except courageous reconciliation and return, Leo wrote:

> And We Ourselves in every lawful way shall
> continue to promote their reconciliation with
> the Church....In the meantime, by the tender
> mercy of the Lord our God, We ask and beseech
> all to strive faithfully to follow in the open
> path of divine grace and truth.[67]

This document *still stands* as the "authoritative but not in-
fallible" teaching of the Roman Catholic Church; it dampened
any hopes of an easy or early reunion between the Anglican
and Roman Catholic communities. It dispelled any illusions
that doctrinal questions could be glossed over in the process
of coming together. A glossed-over reunion simply could not
effect the unity willed by Christ.

Despite this realistic reminder of difficulties in the path
of unity the pontificate of Leo XIII had modified the Vatican's stance with reference to Christian communities separated from it. Focus on the Will of Christ, the nature of
His Church, the importance of the whole community approach,
the value of legitimate diversity in worship, addressing other Christians as *brothers separated* from himself, had softened the brittle tones of a former era.

Leo XIII died in 1903. A year before his death this "spare,
frail, but tough, highly intellectual Pope"[68] issued a review
of his twenty-five year pontificate, entitled *Annum Ingressi*.
Leo expressed alarm at the broad drift toward a liberal and
divisive secularism. He found the Church attacked even more
harshly than at the time of the Reformation which "broke the
precious link of the ancient unity of faith and authority"
and introduced a "principle of disintegration...amongst all
ranks of Christians."[69] The disintegration of unity among
nations followed the disintegration of unity in faith.

> We do not, indeed, hereby pretend to affirm
> that from the beginning there was a set pur-
> pose of destroying the principle of Christian-
> ity in the heart of society; but by refusing
> ...to acknowledge the supremacy of the Holy
> See, the effective *cause and bond of unity*...
> the divine structure of faith was shaken to
> its deepest foundations and the way was
> opened...to doubts and denials of the most
> important things.[70]

An attack on the canon of Sacred Scripture, the unity of

faith, the unity of marriage,with consequent disruptions in
the social order, followed.[71] Leo estimates that "society in
its foolhardy effort to escape from God, has rejected the divine order and revelation."[72] Yet he is convinced that
Christ's Church, which Christianized barbarous and pagan peoples, can initiate a rechristianization.

>   But the return of Christianity will not be
>   efficacious and complete if it does not re-
>   store the world to a sincere love of the one
>   Holy Catholic and Apostolic Church.[73]

"Stripped of the temporal sovereignty and consequently of
that independence which is necessary to accomplish his universal and divine mission"[74] Leo noted that the Church suffered as Christ, its master, had suffered and that its Lord
and Master was sustaining it and would refresh it and enable
its truth to scatter the enshrouding mists.[75] In *Annum
Ingressi* the Pope withdrew from his earlier reunion optimism.
Shortly after Leo's death modernism disturbed the Church;
World War I exploded in Europe.

Pius X and Benedict XV

Pope Pius X (1903-1914) followed Leo. The new Pontiff concerned himself with the interior life of the Church and efforts to stop the teachings of the modern liberalism, cited
by Leo, from undermining the faith of Roman Catholics. Pius X
made no significant moves toward the Orthodox or Protestant
Christians. In the external order of the relations between
the Church and various states, Pius X, the continuing "Prisoner of the Vatican" suffered further losses of his traditional Church rights in countries such as Italy and France.[76]
Within the Church a movement termed Modernism,[77] which tended
toward a denial of the supernatural character of Sacred
Scripture and of the Church,dampened any enthusiasm for further ecumenical overtures. Pius X died shortly after his
great appeal for peace (August 1914) was spurned by the bel-
ligerents who started World War I.

The First World War largely occupied the energies of Benedict
XV (1914-1922). With the Church on both sides of the war
frontier, Benedict, tenaciously holding an impartial stance,
tried to get both sides to define their goals in order to
move toward settlement. In the meantime, relief work pushed
ecumenical considerations into the background.

As already noted, Benedict responded cordially, but negative-
ly, to the separate initiatives of Anglican Bishop Brent in
America and newly-elevated Lutheran Bishop Soederblom in
Sweden. These initiatives from *unknown* individuals and groups

appeared as good-willed but not very promising to the Vatican
concerned to stop the imminent explosion of war. Further,
the initiatives had not come through or with the local bishops who constituted direct contacts in most countries and
cities of the world.

Being unknown in no way minimizes the good faith of such
initiatives. However, isolated initiatives by persons unknown to the Vatican, which daily receives in person known
bishops and missionaries from all over the world, to say
nothing of prepared visits of heads of state, must be viewed
in context.

World peace and Christian reunion are two enormous realities,
but small, nonbelligerent Sweden hardly seemed the base for
the former, and America, the land of multiplying denominational divisions, gave small promise for the latter. Nevertheless, Benedict XV gave cordial but not very hopeful attention to both.

Robert Gardiner's letter in Latin to Benedict and the Faith
and Order focus on doctrine received the more careful consideration at the time. Nevertheless, in regard to Christians
separated from the Roman See, Benedict's own thoughts moved
principally toward the Orthodox.

In sixteen of his documents which touch the Constitution of
Christ's Church, Benedict XV refers to the Petrine texts as
Leo XIII had done, but in more instances he refers to the
relation of priests to bishops, in which he invokes the ancient post-apostolic principle, "he who is not with his bishop is not with the Church."[78] In his encyclical on *The Faith
of Peter,* Benedict directs his attention to the Orthodox by
quoting Ignatius of Antioch, and the celebrated Fathers of
the East, Athanasius, Basil the Great, and John Chrysostom, in
support of the unique Petrine and Roman Primacy in safeguarding doctrines of faith.[79]

Practically, Benedict sought to build a bridge to the Orthodox: (1) by establishing a Pontifical Oriental *Institute* in
Rome, (2) by encouraging the foundation for Russian refugees
named *Istina* in Lille, France, and (3) by creating a pro-
Russia *Commission* in Rome. The Communist revolution drove
many Orthodox to the West and it was hoped that they would
seek and welcome union with Rome.[80]

A move with reference to other Christians was made by Benedict in 1916 when he sent an "Apostolic Letter" of approba-
tion to the Society of the Atonement in New York. He noted
as his "own very particular concern, that *Christians* who have
separated themselves from the Catholic religion should return

to the Church as to a mother whom they have abandoned."[81] The
familiar "departed/return" historic overview is present, but
the "Christians separated" repeats the more heartening and
dignified identification of Leo XIII.

As Benedict had quoted Ancient Eastern Fathers to show to the
Orthodox recognition of Roman Primacy, so he quoted the
learned Dante's writing on his sixth centenary to show the
same common acceptance in Western Christendom.[82]

Shortly before the end of Benedict's time, the sixth decennial meeting of the Anglican Hierarchy at Lambeth Palace,
known as *Lambeth VI,* issued an appeal for Christian unity under the title, "An Appeal to All Christian People." Bishop
Brent undoubtedly influenced this London meeting in 1920. The
"appeal" for unity, coming on the heels of World War I, captured public attention.

The Anglican hierarchy expressed willingness to receive some
type of "being recognized or commissioned" by other Christian
bodies in the hope that the ministers of the other communions
would accept a "commissioning by episcopal ordination" from
them.[83]

The "Appeal" was an effort to gain a mutual ministry in which
all would effectively be episcopally ordained in the Anglican
sense. It was directed more toward the European Evangelicals
than toward Roman Catholics. It is not clear whether Pope
Leo's 1896 decision on Anglican Orders entered their discussions.

However, Cardinal Mercier of Malines in Belgium noticed the
Anglican offer, as also did Catholic Abbé Fernand Portal C.M.,
and Anglican Lord Halifax (Charles L. Wood). These three,
interested in the reunion question since the time of Leo XIII,
and seeing a possible pathway in some form of mutual regulari-
zation of sacramental orders, initiated the famous *Malines
Conversations.* There were five unofficial seminar-type conversations in all between 1921 and 1926.

Apparently Benedict XV did not disapprove Cardinal Mercier's
hosting of these Anglican-Roman Catholic dialogues. In any
event, he died shortly after the first three-day meeting in
1921. Pius XI succeeded Benedict as Pope.

CHAPTER SIX

PIUS XI AND THE ECUMENICAL MOVEMENT

Pius XI (1922-1939) positively encouraged Cardinal Mercier to continue his hosting of the finely-tuned theological Malines Conversations "on condition that the discussions maintain an unofficial character."[1] Only three to six highly qualified persons represented each side. All polemical controversy was rejected as each member, in turn, with complete frankness sought to reveal the theological basis of his Christian convictions. It was agreed that each member must try to understand the others' positions and reasons without falsifying his own. Portal had argued for this nonpolemical, personal conviction approach. Numerous publications were inspired by "this new method of discussion."[2] It was positive, explanatory and exploratory.

These high caliber theological conversations were designed to clear the air, to knock down prejudices, to get at the underlying truth of faith, but not to negotiate reunion. All the Anglicans were "high church"; thus, the Roman Catholic participants who felt that common doctrine was the primary prerequisite for unity found common ground with them.

Yet it was noted by Lord Halifax that "high church" doctrinal explanations represented only a limited part of the theological positions in the Anglican Communion. It was judged that "high church" belief was closer to Roman Catholic doctrine than it was to the teaching in some "low church" quarters. In any event, the key question was recognized to be the nature of Christ's *Church*.[3]

Toward the end of the Malines Conversations, Cardinal Mercier published the suggestion that the Anglican Communion (Lambeth as its world center), in the event of getting together with Roman Catholicism, should be "united not absorbed." He suggested that the historic Episcopal sees should be maintained and the recently (ca. 1855) re-established Catholic sees suppressed.[4] The continental suggestion had to sound like a disastrous sell-out to the re-established Catholic hierarchy, which had no representative at Malines.

These conversations established: (1) that nonpolemical theological dialogue was practicable, (2) that small qualified
groups can achieve a deeper level of theological common
ground, and (3) that overall church rapprochement might be
possible with an episcopally-structured local church.[5]

In 1925 the first World Conference of Christian Life and Work,
with its attendant slogan, "doctrine divides, service unites",
had been held in Stockholm; Lambeth had sent an official delegation. In 1926 Cardinal Mercier died; Fernand Portal followed a few months later. The Catholic lights had gone out.
They had produced only shadowy benefits. Theological and
doctrinal conversations made little sense in the face of the
Life and Work slogan. Pius XI's initial enthusiasm for the
Malines Conversations appeared to be misplaced.

> Pius XI then became more and more reserved
> and finally, after the death of Mercier in
> 1926 asked that the Conversations not be
> taken up again.[6]

Furthermore, Pius XI had reinforced Pope Benedict's work for
the Orthodox by having the Benedictine Community open an ecumenical center which settled at Chevetogne. The Vatican, so
to speak, had opened new doorways to return. Few if any,
came through them; Anglican leadership appeared to be looking
elsewhere, the Orthodox refugees from atheistic Communism
were sustaining survival and cultural-displacement problems.
From this period on "there was a change in the whole policy
of Pius XI with regard to union."[7] A doctrinal indifferentism and liberalism seemed to be blocking the road to reunion
in Christ's Church.

The Pope, who had started a whole positive movement of participation by the Catholic laity in the Apostolic work of the
hierarchy (known as "Catholic Action"),[8] had approved the local Catholic bishop's denial of participation in Stockholm
(1925),and had reversed the Malines participation involving
both hierarchy and qualified laity (1926). In 1927 a negative response was given to the question of Catholic participation in the Anglican-initiated World Conference on Faith
and Order in Lausanne, Switzerland. Pio Nono's refusal of
permission for Roman Catholics to join the Association for
the Promotion of Christian Unity had been invoked in principle by Benedict XV and was again used by Pius XI. Private,
unofficial communication alone was admissible.

After the negative reply to the Faith and Order Conference,
Pius XI issued his decisively positioned encyclical on *The
Promotion of True Religious Unity* (entitled, in Latin,
Mortalium Animos).[9] This major, church-unity document

assessed the diverse ecumenical streams arising formally
among doctrinally-incompatible Protestant groups. Pius XI
thus officially diverted Roman Catholic participation from
the young movement that was assuming the name "ecumenical";
this name signified the Catholic Church's actions to Roman
Catholic ears.

In *Mortalium Animos*, Pius XI had in mind a movement of individuals whose end would be the union of all Christians in
the Roman Catholic Church. He looked at the divisions among
Protestant theologies; he saw the deep rift between the Protestant positions and Roman Catholic Doctrine. He said that
no union was possible without prior union in the Christian
faith. This union in faith could be obtained only by personal *return* to the one Church of Christ, from which the original
departures had taken place.[10]

Pius XI saw that after the vicious divisions of World War I,
the will for unity had captured the "souls of mortal men"
(*Mortalium Animos*) as perhaps never before. A League of Nations based on natural reasons suggested a League of Churches
for the same reasons. But such Church unions which joined
nonbelievers and believers meant the approval of *indifferentism* and the abandonment of divinely revealed religion.[11]

Pius XI reported that some, despite different faiths, were
organizing and calling themselves "Pan-Christians."[12] The
Pope notes that these Pan-Christians profess Charity, but
true charity requires the true faith. Then he asks how can
the Charity be true charity if it harms Christian faith by
joining contradictory faiths in one organization. The Evan-
gelist John, the foremost promoter of Charity, warns against
corruption of faith.[13] The Pope then names some profound beliefs still dividing Christians: Christian tradition, ecclesiastical hierarchy, Mary, priesthood, Eucharist as sacrament
and sacrifice, saints, transsubstantiation.[14]

Pius XI resting on the New Testament and tradition asks, how
can those who name themselves Christian fail to believe that
Christ established for all men, for all time, only one, visible, unfailing Church.[15] The document on "True Religious
Unity" points out that proponents of this new "one body movement," this "confederation of Christian churches", claim that
"the Church" is, in fact, divided and that it has practically
never been one anyway, except perhaps in antiquity.[16] The
more general opinion among the new-confederation builders
is:

>   They contend that the unity of faith and
>   governance which is the sign of the true and
>   one Church of Christ, has almost never existed

> up to this time and does not exist today;
> it can be wished for and perhaps sometime
> it can be obtained through the common sub-
> mission of the will but meanwhile it must be
> considered a fiction.
>
> They say, moreover, that the Church by its
> very nature is divided into parts, that it
> consists of many churches or particular com-
> munities which are separated among themselves
> and although they have certain points of doc-
> trine in common differ in others; and that at
> most the Church was the one Church and only
> Church between the apostolic era and the
> First Ecumenical Council.[17]

"Unity of faith and governance" identified by Pius XI is the
same unity-bonding phrase used by Leo XIII. It appears that
the bond of "faith" includes the sacraments as specified in
the definitions of Luther, Calvin, and Bellarmine. In this
light Bellarmine's definition contained both "faith and governance" bonds, while the Reformers clearly eliminated the
governance bond from the definition of the Church and replaced the visible governance of Christ's Community with the
invisible governance of the glorified Christ.

Pius XI also finds that the "new-confederation" authors are
holding a position utterly unacceptable to Roman Catholics,
namely, that the Church of Christ is, in fact, and by its nature, divided even in doctrine. This position seems even to
undercut the concept of Church held by Luther and Calvin.

Moreover, these "new unity" authors wish the "new-confederation" to put aside doctrinal differences and with a sort of a
common denominator mentality to construct a unity of churches
for the sake of mission and peace. This appeared to Pius XI
to be *the more general opinion*.[18] In practice it becomes a
sort of "Least Common Denominator" thinking (an LCDism) which
reduces the common area of faith proportionately as differences emerge.

A *second* opinion held by the "New-Confederation's" authors
acknowledged that "Protestantism...has rejected very inad-
visedly certain articles of faith and certain rites of external worship that are fully acceptable and useful,..."[19]
but alleged that the Roman Church "has corrupted the early
religion by adding to it...chiefly...primacy of jurisdiction."[20]

A *third* opinion held by very few sounded positive; it conceded papal authority, but for a divergent reason. This

opinion acknowledged endowment of

> ...the Roman pontiff with a primacy of honor
> or a certain jurisdiction or power which,
> however, they think is derived not from di-
> vine right but in a certain manner from the
> consent of the faithful.[21]

A *final* opinion, undoubtedly rare, expresses the wish that
"the Pope himself,...preside over their multi-colored conferences."[22]

The Pope judged that none of the foregoing opinions admitted
Christ's own establishment of a vicar on earth to preserve
the faith, keep the keys, or feed His sheep. Thus, *Pius XI
concluded* that these and other nonnegotiable truths of divine
revelation rendered unacceptable the participation of the
Apostolic See and Catholics in the newly-formed world conferences which rejected these revealed truths. If Christ founded one Church, gave one faith, and sent the Holy Spirit to
abide with His Church for all time, how does the rejection of
these things avoid the character of blasphemy?[23]

Concerned, possibly because some Orthodox and Anglican leaders were supporting doctrinally-divided assemblies which appeared to relativize divine truth, Pius XI withdrew from the
more positive attitudes of Leo XIII. Instead, Pius XI emphasized the Catholic-Protestant differences very sharply.

The "True Religious Unity" document was addressed to the
Bishops. It confirmed their traditional position against
doctrinally-mixed assemblies, as was clear when the World
Council of Churches held its second assembly in Evanston,
Illinois (1954) in the diocese of Cardinal Stritch.

Growing doctrinal indifferentism apparently convinced Pius XI
that the only path to true religious unity for separated
Christians was *personal return* to "the Church of the living
God, the pillar and ground of truth" (1 Tim. 3:15).[24]

> The unity of Christians cannot be otherwise
> obtained than by securing the return of the
> separated to the one true Church of Christ
> from which they once unhappily withdrew.[25]

The Pope concluded his Unity-document by noting that Christ's
mystical body could not be divided, suggesting that separated
Christians return to it, asking God to call them back, and
saying that he desires that return with the heart of a father
yearning for the embrace of his separated children. He
wishes those separated from him to know that.[26]

This encyclical appears to be a modern low-point of Roman
Catholic-Protestant relations as Church bodies. The Papal
documents did not refer to the Protestant denominations as
churches.

The Malines Conversations had suggested that theologians
were like diplomats bargaining a point here or there for the
sake of peace and union. *Mortalium Animos* excoriated that
concept. There can be no bargaining with Divine Truth; all
of it must be accepted.

The document in English was entitled *positively* "The Promotion of True Religious Unity" or "True Religious Unity" because it identified true Christian unity as achievable only
"through one teaching authority, one sole law of belief and
one sole faith among Christians."[27] However, because it
spoke against the new "Confederation of Churches," with
scant notice of the good will manifested, the encyclical is
characterized *negatively* in Protestant circles.

Marc Boegner classified *Mortalium Animos* as a "grievous blow"
to the hopes of many in the ecumenical movement. But he acknowledges that his fears were not realized. Although he believed that ecumenical hopes would be destroyed, he was "surprised, and even amazed, when the contrary proved true."[28]
In an appendix, Boegner quotes four of the encyclical's of-
fensive paragraphs, one of which identifies "the Church as
the pillar and ground of truth." Did Boegner perhaps fail
to notice that this last expression is from the Pauline corpus of writings, rather than originally from Pius XI?[29]

In retrospect, Willem Visser't Hooft still identifies *Mortalium Animos* as a "very negative encyclical"[30] and recalls
that it was a "disconcerting document", reflecting a negative
assessment of Stockholm's "Life and Work" as being the result
of theological indifferentism, liberalism and "the general
failure of Protestantism."[31] The disconcerting feature for
Visser't Hooft was the document's failure to note the deep
Christian motives underlying the unity-movement.

> That the Roman Catholic Church, given *its
> conception of the Church,* felt obliged not
> to participate in ecumenical meetings was
> one thing, but that it should misinterpret
> the motives of the ecumenical leaders in
> such an irresponsible manner was another
> thing....Rome would surely not have felt the
> need for such a sharp warning, if the attempt
> to bring the churches together had not made a
> considerable stir among Roman Catholic theo-
> logians and laymen.[32]

It is true that *Mortalium Animos* found little to praise
among the leaders of the new "one-body movement," but its attention was glued to the distinction between "false religious
unity" versus *True Religious Unity,* as its title and content
indicate. Honey, rather than vinegar, would have made the
message more palatable to the Protestant ecumenical leaders,
but perhaps Catholics would have swarmed to the orchard before the season of maturity had arrived.

In any event, the encyclical largely kept Roman Catholics
away from the movement for the next twenty years. From the
"True Religious Unity" document in 1928 to the instruction,
Ecclesia Catholica in 1949, the Roman Catholic Church officially remained in the stance Pius XI set for it.

In 1927 Pius XI declared, concerning the Orthodox, that "detached fragments of a gold-bearing rock also contain the
precious ore,"[33] but the principle's obvious application to
the common "Christ elements" among Protestants was not quickly made. Yet the image prefigures the Vatican II turning
point.

These common elements or *vestigia ecclesiae* (elements or vestiges of the Church) were identified implicitly every time
the theological differences between Roman Catholics and Protestants were examined, but the attention remained fixed on
the differences, not on the common elements of the Christian
Patrimony. However, these very expressions, "fragments of
gold-bearing rock," *vestigia ecclesiae,* and "Christian Patrimony" contained the suggestion of another emphasis, namely,
an attentive examination of that which was common.

Also, the ecumenical movements tended to deepen themselves
during the thirties. Karl Barth, as well as Pius XI, inveighed against the naturalist thrust in the growing movements. Barth's voice was influential for the Protestant
leadership, especially for a leader of the reformed tradition, such as Visser't Hooft. Barth's influence encouraged
the deepening process in a biblical and theological direction.

Both Life and Work in preparation for Oxford (1937), and Faith
and Order in preparation for Edinburgh (1937), became more
clearly theological.[34] "This explains why...Pius XI, taking
into account the change that had taken place, allowed some
Catholics to attend in a private capacity" the 1937 conferences.[35] This rare authorization in no way implied that the
general prohibition against participating in such conferences
was lifted.

The stance of *True Religious Unity* was maintained: "individual return" to the Roman Catholic Church appeared in this

period to be the only passable road to unity.

In 1939 Pius XI died. On the first ballot Eugenio Pacelli
was elected his successor. Pacelli continued many of the
emphases of his predecessor, which his choice of name Pius
XII indicated.

Pius XII and the Ecumenical Movement

Pius XII (1939-1958) began his pontificate six months before
the start of the second World War. This ascetical-looking
and scholarly pontiff set himself the task of "doing the
truth in love" (Eph. 4:15).[36] The new Pope took this expression from the Pauline passages on the unity of Christ's members (His Body); St. Paul identifies the Church as one body,
having one faith, one baptism and one Lord. It is the one
Lord "who gave apostles, prophets, evangelists, pastors and
teachers in roles of service for the faithful to build up
the body of Christ" (Eph. 4:11f).

After his futile initiatives seeking to prevent uneasy "Christian" Europe from deepening its divisions by World War II,
Pius XII designed many of his later communications to enhance
unity in the Church and society. In one 400-item collection
of Papal documents (1740 to 1959) on the Church, 139 out of
400 are credited to Pius XII. His first encyclical was on
the *Unity of Human Society*, wherein he sees man's unity of
origin from God, the unity of man's end in God, and the unity
of men in faith and Christ's church as the basis of the
strongest union in which men can find salvation.[37] Warring
sons frustrate the unity intended by their Father.

Many of this Pope's communications on the Church reflected
his continuous consciousness of those who are related to the
Church but are outside its visible unity. In 1943, Pius XII
promulgated his famous encyclical *Mystici Corporis* (on the
Mystical Body of Christ) which deepened Roman Catholic pre-
ception and sense of awe at the mysterious union of Christ
and His Church. At the same time this document, which highlighted the Pauline body-image of the Church, made a statement which envisioned Protestant Christians in a precarious
state regarding salvation. He wrote in effect that salvation
was achieved in and through the Mysterious Body of Christ and
that the Church is that Mysterious Body of Christ.

From the context and an explicit reference in paragraph #91
which said "nothing nobler...can be imagined than to belong
to the Holy, Catholic, Apostolic and Roman Church, in which
we become members of one Body as venerable as it is unique,
..."[38] many deduced the equation that the Mystical Body of
Christ = the Roman Catholic Church. The comparative "nobler"

allows the opinion that it is noble to belong to any Christian Church, but the context and the uniqueness of Christ's
Body tend to preclude this interpretation.

Further, the paragraph (#22) on membership in the Church excludes those who are divided from the "one Body." It reads

> Actually only those are to be included as
> members of the Church who have been bap-
> tized and profess the true faith and who
> have not been so unfortunate as to separate
> themselves from the unity of the Body or been
> excluded by legitimate authority for grave
> faults committed. 'For in one spirit,' says
> the Apostle, 'were we all baptized into one
> Body, whether Jews or Gentiles, whether bond
> or free.' As therefore in the true Christian
> community there is only one Body, one Spirit,
> one Lord, and one Baptism, so there can be
> only one faith. And therefore if a man re-
> fuse to hear the Church let him be consid-
> ered—so the Lord commands—as a heathen
> and a publican. It follows that those who
> are divided in faith, or government cannot
> be living in the unity of such a Body, nor
> can they be living the life of the one di-
> vine spirit.[39]

Thus, Catholic theologians enumerated the elements of baptism, profession of true faith, and nonseparation from this
Church by self-exclusion or excommunication as the three
requisites of *membership*. The validly baptized persons who
in good faith had neither been excommunicated, nor excluded
themselves from the Roman Catholic Church have been held to
be "connected with" Christ's one Church in some definite way
which theologians found hard to formulate.

Pius XII had focused his attention on the positive sources
of theology, namely the Scriptures, the Fathers and the
Church's previous documents, to emphasize the interior, mysterious, transcendent meaning of the Church for deepening
the faith of those in communion with Rome.[40] He chose not
to examine the problem which the theologians found hard to
formulate. Rather, he expressed his ardent desire that:

> those *who do not belong* to the visible Body
> of the Catholic Church...may...enter into
> Catholic unity...with Us in the one, organic,
> Body of Jesus Christ,...Persevering in prayer
> to the Spirit of love and truth, We wait for
> them with open and outstretched arms to come

not to a stranger's house, but to their own,
their father's home.[41]

This authentic, but noninfallible teaching of Pius XII in
1943, dominated the seminary manuals up until the time of
Vatican II. The war had almost reduced the ecumenical movement to a mere hope and Pius XII attended more to the felt
needs of the Roman Catholic world in doctrine. The post-war
resurgence of Protestant ecumenical activity soon commanded
more of his attention.

The Provisional Committee for the founding of the World Council of Churches held its first post-war meeting in 1946. It
was the first full meeting since 1939.[42] In planning for the
constitutional meeting of the World Council at Amsterdam, uncertainty about the attendance of Roman Catholic observers
was felt.[43] On the advice of a Roman Catholic theologian, but
without Vatican approval, ten ecumenically-interested Roman
Catholics were invited as observers.[44] That meant a Roman
Catholic presence to, and in some sense a Catholic witness
and seeming approval of, Constituting an alternate Christian
World *Church* Assembly, at least in the public eye.

The Archbishop of Utrecht, whose responsibility includes Amsterdam, the site of the 1948 WCC Assembly, indicated some
months before the assembly that if Catholic observers were to
be present, they would be chosen by the Church for whom they
were observing rather than by the Protestant Secretariat of
the Assembly. While this interchange was in progress, the
Vatican issued a *Monitum* (a cautionary advisement) that all
Catholics were forbidden to take part in *mixed religious
gatherings* in which faith-questions are the agenda,—"without
previous permission of the Holy See."[45]

There is still more reason for observing such a prohibition
warned the *Monitum,* when there is question of conventions
(*quos "oecumenicos" vocant*) which are called "ecumenical."[46]

The reason for the prohibition was the safeguarding of Catholic faith and worship. It was known that Life and Work and
Faith and Order had set up intercommunion worship events
which, under the rubric of "communication in sacred rites",
(*communicatio in sacris*) were absolutely forbidden.[47]

A commentary on the *Code of Canon Law* gives the background of
canon 1325, which the *Monitum* cited by referring to its origin (under Pius IX) in 1864, its use in 1919 (by Benedict XV),
and the negative response made in 1927 (by Pius XI) concerning the Lausanne Constitutional Meeting for Faith and Order.[48]
Thus, Pius XII in 1948 invoked the same prohibition as his
predecessors; the warning regarding *communicatio in sacris*

in this context was new, because the public pressure to practice intercommunion in this new setting had arisen.

The World Council constituted itself and no Roman Catholics
were in attendance as official observers. However, some ob-
jection to the strictness of this position must have been
felt in the Vatican because a year or so after the World
Council Assembly in Amsterdam, a carefully worked-out *Instruction* concerning the ecumenical movement, *De Motione
Oecumenica,*[49] was issued by the Holy Office whose official
competence embraced matters of faith. The *Instruction* is
also commonly referred to by its opening words, *Ecclesia
Catholica*.

This eight-page document starts off on the negative note that,
"The Catholic Church takes no actual part in 'ecumenical'
conventions or other assemblies of a similar character,"[50]
but then proceeds immediately to enunciate the attitude and
principles according to which Catholic bishops, religious
superiors, priests and laity should be guided in ecumenical
activities. The document distinguishes between the Church
as a total entity and the local churches under the bishops in
whose dioceses mixed-belief gatherings, colloquies, and conventions might take place. In each diocese in the world, the
faith problem varied in kind and depth and the Universal
Church was not about to enter an arena of conflicting faith-
voices as one voice among many.

Thus, the situation was divided. The Church as a whole would
not join the various ecumenical movements (they were still
multiple in 1949), but each bishop was obligated to give the
local movements his serious attention and to appoint qualified and carefully-selected priests to become conversant with
the ecumenical roots. The involvement was to proceed most
carefully because faith was involved and *communicatio in
sacris* was forbidden except for the common recitation of the
Our Father and other approved prayers.[51]

The persons selected were to know the documents: *Satis
Cognitum, Mortalium Animos* and *Mystici Corporis,* and to alert
their respective bishops to the faith-problems encountered.
The bishops in turn were to notify the Vatican annually concerning the faith situation resulting from this new, cautious,
but definitely get-involved policy.[52]

The instruction, *Ecclesia Catholica* (On the Ecumenical Movement), in this way formulated a positive operational proced-
ure of a cautious contact with the various ecumenical movements at the local diocesan level. Thus, contact with the
movement's conventions were no longer forbidden outright, provided the competent ecclesiastical authority gave permission.

If the convention crossed diocesan boundaries or became national or international, then the consent of the Holy See
was required.[53]

Although the Catholic Church as such, according to the document, does not take an actual part in ecumenical conventions,
she pursues with the deepest concern and prayer every effort
to bring about a perfect unity in Christ. "Indeed she embraces with truly maternal affection all who return to her
as the only true Church of Christ."[54] Hence, efforts to assist those returning are fully encouraged.

The document clearly acknowledges that the growing desire for
a reunion "among all who believe in Christ the Lord" is to be
attributed to the "inspiring grace of God."[55]

Various efforts by nonqualified persons in different countries have sought to bring about a nontheological reconciliation with the Catholic Church. The manifest good intentions
have failed, according to the document, to safeguard "correct
principles." "The work of 'reunion' belongs, above all, to
the office and charge of the Church."[56]

Ecclesia Catholica warns against dangers inherent in mixed-
faith dialogues. Some participants stress agreed-upon doctrines while suppressing essential differences; others emphasize minor points while neglecting the main fact of defec-
tion from Catholic Faith. The document insists that the
whole Catholic truth must be presented.

The suppression of truths of faith for the sake of reunion is
named *irenicism*. Neither silence nor ambiguity must be allowed to smother the realities of Christ's Church. Justification, the nature of Christ's Church, Petrine, and consequently papal, primacy must be faced. "Outside of the truth no
true union can ever be attained."[57]

This document was called at the time "the official charter...
of Catholic ecumenism."[58] It praised the ongoing movement as
resulting from God's Grace and worthy of attention and prayer,
while cautioning sharply against its inherent pitfalls. Irenicism became an identifying term for false ecumenism. The
expression "reunion belongs to the Church" reminded Roman
Catholics of the source of norms and practical ways of doing
ecumenism different from the World Council, and consequently,
encouraged the distinction between World Council and Roman
Catholic ecumenical movements. The document repeatedly used
the expression "return" but in no way addressed itself to
"group return" or "church reunion" and thus, could perhaps be
accused of fishing for large-scale individual conversions in
ecumenical waters. However, a responsible leader of the

newly-emerged World Council did not give the document such a
restricted reading.

Willem Visser't Hooft, the World Council's general secretary,
read the document as an official acknowledgment of the Roman
Catholic Church that the already existent ecumenical movement
was influencing its members, both clerical and lay. He noted
positively that some common prayers and common social action
could occur. He disliked the document's emphasis on "return"
and interpreted this emphasis as a form of seeking ecclesiastical victory in line with secular models.

> The churches in the World Council have a dif-
> ferent conception of true unity, namely that
> (in the words of the Amsterdam Assembly) they
> are to be bound closer to Christ and therefore
> closer to one another.[59]

Visser't Hooft concluded his published statement with the remark that other Christians "should continue to pray that the
Roman Catholic Church may be led to a wider and deeper conception of Christian unity."[60]

Less than a year after the Holy Office published its instruction, Pius XII promulgated the encyclical *Humani Generis,* in
which he warned the Church and its leaders about some false
opinions which threatened "to undermine the foundations of
Catholic doctrine."[61] Although directed to all those in
"communion with the Holy See," its seventeen-page content
was also pointed toward those responsible for teaching Christian doctrine.

Humani Generis reminded theologians that truths about God
and His relations with man "completely surpass the sensible
order," and that straining human intellects impeded in their
probing of divine realities easily "persuade themselves...
that what they do not wish to believe is false or at least
doubtful."[62]

In this document, Pius XII insisted on the moral necessity
of divine revelation, and the further necessity of the living
"teaching authority" with which Christ fortified his Church
to preserve and authentically interpret his revelation.[63] He
warned again of an "eirenism"[64] which overlooked real obstacles to reunion, or identified as obstacles "things founded on the laws and principles given by Christ and likewise
on institutions founded by Him."[65] The Pope warned theologians against any reduction of Catholic doctrine for the sake
of "a mutual assimilation of Catholic dogma with the tenets
of the dissidents."[66]

Humani Generis maintained that the doctrine on the Church of
Christ, as expounded by the Holy See, "is deliberately and
habitually neglected by some with the idea of giving force
to a certain vague notion [of the Church]..."[67]

Pius XII closes this document by reminding teachers in ecclesiastical institutions that "if the whole truth found in
the Church is not sincerely taught to all without corruption
or diminution", they will be engaging in an "*eirenism*" which
will not produce reunion.[68]

Visser't Hooft felt that *Humani Generis*, and Rome's promulgation in that same year of the doctrine of Mary's bodily assumption into heaven, seemed to place new obstacles in the
path of ecumenical dialogue.[69]

Lukas Vischer, a Swiss Reformed Minister and director of the
Faith and Order Secretariat of the WCC, estimated that *Humani
Generis* was even more of an obstacle to dialogue with Roman
Catholics than the instruction *On The Ecumenical Movement* had
been. He felt the documents signified a total lack of inter-
est in unity on the part of the Roman Catholic Church.

Vischer sensed the position as an embarrassment to the WCC
membership which, on principle, had to keep itself open to
all Christian Churches including the Roman Catholic Church.
The World Council adopted a generally "waiting attitude and
avoided controversy as well as any special cultivation of
contacts with the Roman Catholic Church."[70]

On the other hand, Roman Catholics who saw the positive but
cautious opening to the ecumenical movement created by the
1949 *Instruction,* recognized among the admonitions of *Humani
Generis* a specification of cautions already given in principle.

During the remainder of his pontificate, Pius XII continued
to recall the ecclesial dimensions of *Mystici Corporis* and
from time to time alluded to the prescriptions of *Humani
Generis*. Thus, in 1956, he reminded Roman Catholic theologians of the necessity of sound research as against the shal-
low and corrosive influence of the so-called "New Theology."
He warned of the dangers of faulty scriptural exegesis and
secularism's denial of divine, supernatural realities. He
stressed "the 'jure divino' basis for the teaching authority
of the Pope and of Bishops."[71]

Finally, a short time before his death in October of 1958,
Pius XII again emphasized the unity of the Mystical Body of
Christ. Despite physical persecutions which liken the Church
to its thorn-crowned Head, "the unity of the organism is not

divided."[72] A severed branch will die; a cut-off rivulet
must dry. But the unity of the suffering local Church with
its petrine trunk and well-spring remains firm. The Pontiff
quotes the martyred Bishops, Cyprian and Ignatius of Antioch,
whose suffering in no way separated them from the Holy See,
to support the imprisoned bishops of Middle Europe and
China.[73]

CHAPTER SEVEN

JOHN XXIII AND CHRISTIAN UNITY

Angelo Cardinal Roncalli, elderly enough to be held merely as a compromise, caretaker pontiff, was elected the next pope.

In short order Pope John XXIII (1958-1963), through his disarming manner and personal warmth, added an attractive glow to the whole ecumenical horizon. His manifest conviction of brotherhood was contagious. His humble and trusting spirit caught the media's attention; his down-play of protocol, his visits to hospitals and prisons, his joy at greeting his unpretentious relatives delighted newsmen.

This good-natured, grandfatherly Pope electrified the ecclesiastical and theological world by unexpectedly announcing (January 25, 1959), in the third month of his pontificate, his intention to hold an Ecumenical Council. The year following, Pope John set up a Secretariat for the Promotion of Christian Unity (SPCU).

A World Council commentator wrote of John XXIII, "Within a few months it became clear that his election would mark the beginning of a new era...for the ecumenical movement."[1] It is thus surprising to discover how explicitly traditional this Pontiff's emphases were.

Pope John identified himself on November 4, 1958, as the "Vicar of Christ and his personal representative on earth," made his own the directives of Pius XII, and declared that Christ's flock should be one, with only one shepherd.[2]

In December, the new Pontiff used such self-identifications as "the Pastor of all Christians" and the "one authority... of the Sovereign Pontiff, which the Divine Redeemer Himself established as the immovable rock and the foundation of the entire Church."[3] His public image perhaps suggested bedrock and familiar foundation rather than distant Vatican authority. The petrine image is a foundation rock. His predecessor's emphases were still there but Pope John's public figure apparently made them more acceptable.

In his first Christmas message, Pope John focused on the unity
of Christ's Church and asked that this unity "be turned toward
the reconciliation of different races and nations."[4] He noted
some efforts of the Orthodox which had tended toward "the unity
of all Christians under one Pastor, the Vicar of Christ." He
referred to the Orthodox as "Our dear separated brethren, who
also bear on their foreheads the name of Christ."

John cited his five immediate predecessors as "Pontiffs—who
from this Chair of Peter have sent forth the invitation to
unity." The new Pope himself intended to pursue this same task
that "there shall be one fold and one shepherd" (John 10:16).[5]

On the feast of the conversion of Paul, January 25, 1959, on
which he projected the second Vatican Council, Pope John
identified himself as the Successor of St. Peter and Sovereign Pontiff. He emphasized the unity of Peter and Paul, as
contrasted with their falsely assumed opposition, to highlight the unity Christians are called to in the one, holy,
catholic, apostolic Church of Jesus Christ. St. John's "One
fold and one shepherd" appears to be a favored expression.[6]

The following March, Pope John, on returning to St. Marks in
Venice, again proclaimed the Church's unity:

> Jesus did not found several Churches, but one
> single Church, which is not a Gallican, or a
> Greek, or a Slavic Church,...but an Apostolic
> and Universal Church.

In this speech he paralleled St. Ambrose's expression, "Where
Peter is, there is the Church," by saying "Where Mark is, there
is Peter," in order to capture the universality also of the
local Church of St. Mark, Peter's "disciple and son."[7]

Pope John's spirit and acts contributed even more than his
words to the ecumenical movement. Of his acts, the holding of
Vatican II was the most significant. It changed the centuries
old posture of the Roman Catholic Church to all other Christians. The emphasis on difference, with muted acknowledgment
of sameness, was shifted to an emphasis on sameness, with acknowledgment of difference mentioned afterward, but not
polemically. The magnitude of the divinely-based sameness was
evaluated as greater than the magnitude of the differences,
some of which were due merely to natural diversity.

Roman Catholics were challenged by their own Church to note
and acknowledge the precious Christian elements in the lives
of other Christians. The experience was traumatic! Nothing
since the Reformation has so shaken the Roman Catholic Church!

The tremors continue into the second decade after the Council.

World Council leader, Lukas Vischer, wrote that Pope John's announcement came "to the surprise of the entire world." Its suddenness and general terms "stirred the imagination." Vischer refers to it as a "Charismatic decision." Yet, he notes that John's "own understanding of unity did not greatly differ from the traditional view. Like his predecessors he often spoke of return as the only way to unity."[8]

Although the Pope's speeches "seemed to herald no decisive changes, the opening announcement nevertheless continued to exercise great influence" continues Vischer. "The dam erected by *Humani Generis* began to collapse."[9]

Specifically, the "Secretariat for the Promotion of Christian Unity" became the actual conduit for an immediate, practical two-way exchange with the World Council and all post-reformation Christians. Scripture scholar and linguist Augustin Cardinal Bea, in his late seventies, was named its first president. He chose a young Dutch priest, Jan Willebrands, whom he had earlier encouraged to form a "Catholic Conference for Ecumenical Problems" in Fribourg, to be his executive secretary.

Willebrands already knew Visser't Hooft, general secretary of the WCC; they came from the same part of Holland. Bea sent Willebrands to tell Visser't Hooft about the new Unity Secretariat; "the Cardinal wanted me to be directly informed about this before the public announcement was made."[10]

Willebrands had a second message for Visser't Hooft. Bea said he would be pleased to have a "private personal rapport and overall-understanding meeting" with him in the near future. Visser't Hooft accepted at once.[11] To avoid "Geneva goes to Rome," or "Rome goes to Geneva" press play with its corresponding speculation and premature intrusion, Bea set up the meeting in Milan. In September, Bea, Visser't Hooft, and Willebrands met in a Milanese convent. Visser't Hooft appreciated that a "common wavelength was not difficult to find."[12]

The Central Committee of the World Council had recently met in St. Andrews in Scotland; the year before it had met on the Island of Rhodes. The World Council was in the process of preparing for its third World Assembly to be held in New Delhi, India in 1961, even as Rome was preparing for Vatican II.

The Bea-Visser't Hooft meeting in Milan smoothed out some wrinkled understandings and affirmed a basic common theological ground. Some working relationships for communication and

the possible presence of observers at New Delhi and Vatican
II were taken up. Bea indicated that:

> ...the Vatican no longer considered the ecu-
> menical movement as tending to 'indifferentism'
> or 'relativism' and believed that the Holy
> Spirit was at work in it.[13]

This sentence and the consequent actions of the Secretariat
and Pope John, which brought 150 delegates from Orthodox and
Protestant churches as observers to Vatican II, appear to pin-
point the enormous attitude turn-about with which the Roman
Catholic Church views Protestant communities. It signified
the end of a fortress-Church mentality.

Visser't Hooft noted immediately that the change taking place
was "a change in procedures and climate and did not mean that
the fundamental indifferences which existed between the Roman
Catholic Church and the churches in the World Council had
been solved."[14] Thus, common ground for further cultivation
was affirmed, while differences were clearly acknowledged.

Cardinal Bea's constant affirmation of, and stress on, the
transcendent effects of Christian baptism appear to be the
special emphasis he brought to the dialogue. Christ and his
gifts of Himself and his life bind Christians together at a
level which exceeds human telling. The sharing in his divine
life which Christ gives germinally in baptism binds Christians in a unity which exceeds all their differences.

Bea deeply loved St. Paul's insight that baptism incorporates
a person into the mysterious Body of Christ. Thus, through
baptism a union already exists among all Christians; this
union needs development to its intended completion.[15]

In the introduction to the collection of Bea's published
statements, Apostolic Delegate Gerald O'Hara notes that Bea's
words are "supremely valuable as being the expression of the
mind in closest contact with Pope John XXIII."[16] Bea had also been the Father Confessor for Pius XII. For Bea, the
words "brother in Christ" expressed a theological reality,
not merely a pious greeting. The words "separated brothers"
required emphasis on the second word in contrast to the post-
reformation emphasis on the first.

On the occasion of the visit of Dr. Goeffrey Fisher, Anglican
Archbishop of Canterbury, to Pope John XXIII, Bea wrote that
a clear understanding of theological principles should illum-
inate and govern such contacts. The *first* principle is integrity in safeguarding the *full truth* of Jesus Christ; such
integrity reflects not inflexibility but rather love and

fidelity to the Person of Christ.[17] "The *second* principle,
equally essential, is that of Charity."[18] It dictates love
of brothers, even though separated. As Pope John chose to
express it, the principle is love "towards 'our brothers' for
they are our brothers even though separated from the Catholic
faith."[19]

Bea went on to quote *Mediator Dei* (1947) and Canon 87 of the
Code of Canon Law to point to the Pauline teaching that "a
person, validly baptized, becomes a member of the Church of
Christ, with all the rights and duties of a Christian, save
only in those cases where an obstacle prevents a person enjoying the use of these rights."[20]

To Bea, the tension present is that between two loves: first,
love for Christ, with all that means for holding his full
teaching; second, love for our brother, with the suffering
implied because of a deep difference in faith and order. It
is a tension of two principles, two loves. Bea continued by
saying that the Church, whose baptism mothered Christians,
cannot forget her children even though separated from her, as
a mother cannot forget her separated child.[21]

> These two essential principles...enable us to
> understand how delicate a situation arises for
> those responsible for the welfare of the church
> on the occasion of a visit of the head of a
> separated communion.[22]

Pope John said he prepared by earnest prayer for the meeting
with the Anglican Archbishop.[23] The Church's motherhood is
of supernatural origin. She is Christ's spouse, Christ's
Church; consequently love and loyalty to the person of Christ
must govern such a meeting. Such a delicate meeting cannot
take place in the marketplace. Even the model of diplomatic
negotiations is essentially inadequate. Among believing
Christians, divine and theological realities are involved,
and only one Bride has mothered the separated children.

Bea, whose thought corresponded so closely with Pope John's,
continued, "we are well aware of this mother's firm faith
that she is the only true Church of Christ, and of the duty
of all her children to follow her."[24] This meeting, inconceivable so short a time ago, "reveals and symbolizes: a new
atmosphere now shared by the Roman Catholic Church and An-
glicanism."[25]

In retrospect, the meeting of Bea with the general secretary
of the WCC suggests a meeting of *agencies* for cooperation,
whereas the meeting of Pope John and Archbishop Fisher indicates a communication between churches, although of differing

universality. The first meeting can aid toward reunion, the
second meeting appears to be the place where reunion can be
effected.

If division took place at the top, so to speak, it appears
that reunion must take place there also. "The top" is probably a poor image because of its secular orientation, but it
does easily connote the persons who represent the communions.
Perhaps a foundation image, hidden bedrock, piece of the rock,
would suggest new cognitive orientations. In any event, of
the two meetings mentioned, the Archbishop Fisher-Pope John
type meeting can reach a goal which the other type meeting
cannot.

Both in speech and writings Cardinal Bea cultivated the ecumenical ground in Italy, Germany, France, England, the United
States and elsewhere. He emphasized the transcendent, commonly shared life received in baptism, the many common elements variously binding Roman Catholic and Protestant communions, the deeply supernatural character of the ecumenical
enterprise, and the vision of the final goal as a unity in
faith, sacraments and governance as principles of "Catholic
Ecumenism."[26]

The use of the expression, "Catholic Ecumenism" as late as
1961, suggested that there were at least two kinds of ecumenism, a "Catholic one Church" type and a World Council, federation, or "fellowship of divided-churches" type. In the Secretariat, Bea and his coworkers picked up this implication.
They transposed the term "Catholic" to a different word to
read "Catholic principles of Ecumenism," thus signifying the
over all unity of the modern ecumenical movement in the decree which Vatican II made its own.

Bea, despite his age, energetically emphasized the Christ-
given life shared with all the baptized as a starting point.
Baptism initiated the life intended to grow toward full unity
under the Holy Spirit. The end of this new life was to be,
as Christ said, that his followers may be one as He and His
father are one (John 17:21). Thus Bea, with an insight reflecting Pope John's, envisioned the beginning, middle and
end of the divine plan for Christian unity.

The Unity Secretariat, although started as a hospitality go-
between for other Christians and Vatican II, took on a deeper
significance as it embodied Bea's vision. At the start of
the Council, Pope John reinforced Bea's influence by elevating the Unity Secretariat to the status of a "Commission of
the Council" on an equal level with the other ten Conciliar
Commissions.[27]

Pope John himself titled his address for the Council's opening day (October 11, 1962), *Toward Christian Unity*. This
opening speech, heard by approximately 2,400 voting bishops,
characterized the divine and human Church of Christ as *Mater
Ecclesia* (Mother Church).[28] In a startling paragraph, Pope
John classified some of his regular advisors, who see nothing
but ruin, as gloomy prophets.

> We feel we must disagree with these prophets
> of doom who are always forecasting disaster,
> as though the end of the world were at hand.
>
> In the present order of things, Divine Provi-
> dence is leading us to a new order of human
> relations which...are directed toward the ful-
> fillment of God's superior and inscrutable
> designs.[29]

The Pope strengthened his happy prophecy by citing the freedom from undue civil interference of the present historic as
sembly. The Council's greatest concern is that "the sacred
deposit of Christian doctrine should be guarded and taught
more efficaciously."[30]

As if to quiet the worries of his "prophets of doom," John
affirmed the continuity of this twenty-first Council with the
preceding twenty and declared Christ's Church should never
depart from its "sacred patrimony of truth."

> But at the same time she must ever look to the
> present, to the new conditions and forms of
> life introduced into the modern world which
> have opened new avenues to the Catholic Apos-
> tolate.[31]

The Church must proclaim its patrimony, which belongs to all
men, in the modern world. The Church does not need this
council to decide a great doctrinal problem. It needs a
council for pastoral reasons, to bring Christ's doctrine forward into modern consciousness in the modes of modern thought.
Persons of universal and apostolic spirit expect

> ...a step forward toward a doctrinal penetra-
> tion and formation of consciences in faithful
> and perfect conformity to the authentic doc-
> trine which, however, should be studied and
> expounded through the methods of research and
> through the literary forms of modern thought.
> The substance of the ancient doctrine of the
> Deposit of Faith is one thing, the way in which
> it is presented is another.[32]

This affirmation strongly reinforced the bishops engaged in
the biblical, liturgical and ecumenical *aggiornamento* which
the "prophets of gloom" had restrained. Forward rather than
backward, pastoral rather than speculative, kindness rather
than condemnations of erroneous doctrine were the emphases
which brought joy to the majority of bishops in the Council.

Rejecting a gloomy, siege mentality, the warm and genial Pontiff himself appeared to be the model of the attitude he
wished the Church to take.

> The Catholic Church...desires to show herself
> to be the loving mother of all, benign, patient,
> full of mercy and goodness toward the children
> separated from her...to distribute the goods of
> divine grace...raising men to the dignity of
> the sons of God.[33]

Possibly taking his cue from third-century Cyprian's image of
light rays, Pope John sees a relationship of Catholics, other
Christians and non-Christians as concentric circles of light
with the center circle signifying the "unity of Catholics
among themselves," the next circle as Christians separated,
but united in prayer and desire, and the outer circle as non-
Christian religious peoples united with him in esteem and
respect.[34]

John's vision of the divine plan embraced the unity of mankind in peace and justice, but he saw the central unity of
Christians as the prerequisite of a world-wide unity. Describing himself as seated near the tomb of Peter, Pope John
invoked the same Holy Spirit who aided the Apostles and Peter
around whose tomb as golden candelabra (churches) his Brothers in the episcopate were gathered.[35]

From Juridical to Pastoral Emphasis

The Council's preparatory commissions had produced seventy-
three reports or schemata from the mountain of interventions
sent to Rome by the bishops, universities and others consult-
ed. Seven of the schemata had been forwarded to the bishops
in July of 1962. The preparatory commissions, largely
staffed by personnel approved by the Vatican Curia, expected
the assembled Fathers to appoint them to be the Council's official commissions.

An unexpected bombshell in line with Pope John's surprising
reference to "prophets of doom," shattered the general expectations of the first General Congregation.* Two bishops

---

*Each day's Council meeting was termed a "General Congregation";
the sum of the meetings from October to December was identified as a
session.

called for the replacement of the *whole* Curia-prepared *slate*
of commission personnel. The commissions were merely committees serving the Council, not the reverse! Vigorous applause
revealed the overwhelming sentiment of the Council Fathers and
the impending clash between some Cardinals who headed the
Curia and the majority present.[36]

Cardinals Ottavianni, Ruffini, Parente, and Siri frequently
expressed a very conservative and academic Curial position,
whereas Cardinals Bea, Lienart, Frings, and Montini generally
expressed a more pastoral and forward-looking position more
in line with Pope John's opening guideline.

The first position emphasized academic scholasticism, Canon
Law and Latin; the opposing trend emphasized pastoral and
scriptural explanations, vernacular (replacing Latin) for
better understanding, and less use of legal norms.

The foregoing somewhat simplified characterizations may assist in gaining a perspective on a de facto clash of serious-
ly-held positions. The Latin-language proponents focused on
the continuity of the Church and against many changes. The
Vernacular proponents centered on the changes needed to update the continuing Church to the world's changing needs.

The schema on the *Liturgy* was the first chosen for the full
assembly's consideration. Although all acknowledged its general soundness, it was returned to the newly-formed commission for reworking after three weeks of discussion. The move
from 1600 years of liturgical Latin to the vernacular, as
more pastoral and ecumenical, symbolizes the trend emerging
in the Council's struggle and the subsequent change that
touched every practicing Roman Catholic throughout the world.

Key concepts which touch the ecumenical problem in the final
document on the Liturgy concern the insight that the Church's
liturgy is prior to its service (*diakonia*) to the world, and
the concept that the Church itself is a kind of sacrament,—a
sacrament whose very existence is prior even to the seven
sacraments. The World Council of Churches is tending to make
diakonia primary. Some WCC members view even the visible
church itself as a merely sociological entity, or an adiaphoron (i.e., a theologically indifferent reality).

The final document on the Liturgy (as all sixteen final documents of Vatican II) is divided into chapters and articles.
The articles are generally a paragraph or a couple of paragraphs, and are numbered sequentially for ease of reference.

Since liturgy is so important a work of the Church, and the
Church in the Council's belief comes from Christ, the document

on the liturgy starts with Christ as the unique mediator; it
then proceeds to the Church and the significance of her worship. During Christ's public ministry, he had, so to say,
constructed the *material* ensemble of his church in primitive
form; after this he gave this new reality, this new apostolic
structure, its unique divine quality or effective form from
his sacrificial death. The document expresses this theological belief thus:

> For it was from the side of Christ as He slept
> the sleep of death upon the cross that there
> came forth the wonderous *sacrament* which is
> the whole Church.[37]

This identification of the Church as a sacrament is new in
Conciliar documents. It identifies the Church as the "sacred
entity," rather than as a merely sociological entity, or an
adiaphoron (i.e., a theologically indifferent matter).

A sacrament is basically a visible sign of an invisible divine reality. Thus, the document is indicating that the
Church is the visible sign of the new invisible divine reality which Paul identifies as the Body of Christ and the document refers to as the Mystical Body of Christ. Significantly,
the document is emphasizing that the Church is essentially a
divine-human reality, and not merely a human organization or
society totally amenable to man's restructuring. Theologians
use the term primordial of this sacrament to distinguish the
Church from the other sacraments.

The word primordial (an English equivalent of the German
Ursakrament) indicates the Church's primacy for and difference from other sacraments.[38] Thus, as Christ is the visible
sign of God his invisible Father, so the Church, the visible
body, is the sign of the ascended and now invisible Redeemer.
Thus, the Church is the originating source (after Christ) for
the other sacraments, which are seen as her particular acts or
actions. As a human person acts by talking or laughing, so
the Church analogously acts or "sacramentates" by baptizing
or anointing. This perception, highly regarded by some theologians,[39] aids in perceiving the other insight previously
mentioned, namely that the liturgy as value surpasses the
value of the Church's service (diakonia) for the world.

> ...every liturgical celebration, because it
> is an action of Christ the priest and of His
> Body the Church, is a sacred action surpassing
> all others. No other action of the Church can
> match its claim to efficacy, nor equal the de-
> gree of it.[40]

Thus, the Council Fathers judge that the Church expresses
herself more surpassingly in liturgy than in service to the
world. This in no way denies the great value of service to
the world, but it does clearly spell out the priorities among
the Church's works. The document goes on to express the relationship of the liturgy to her other saving powers.

> ...The liturgy is the summit toward which the
> activity of the Church is directed; at the
> same time it is the fountain from which all
> her power flows. For the goal of apostolic
> works is that all who are made sons of God by
> faith and baptism should come together to
> praise God in the midst of His Church, to
> take part in her sacrifice, and to eat the
> Lord's supper.[41]

This is the heart of the Church's official teaching about her
principal acts. Without this orientation to its liturgy, the
Church would cease to be the Church. If the Church is reduced to an organization which only or primarily does service
(diakonia) for the world, it would cease to be Christ's
Church in the belief of the Council Fathers. If the final
goal of ecumenism is the realization of the one Church of
Christ, then liturgy is its summit act.

These texts of Vatican II indicate that the Council's sense
of ecumenism is substantially a religious reality involving
the final one Church in a single commonly acceptable liturgy.
The World Council of Churches, because of radically different
faith expressions, has had to realize its major expressions
in service (diakonia) to the world. This latter is without
question very valuable but appears to be secondary and sometimes so removed from the unity of the Una Sancta that the
activities are not readily distinguishable from the acts of
secular organizations, or even political states.

The Second Vatican Council struggled on in its effort to
formulate its theological expression concerning liturgy, revelation, communications media, unity with the Orthodox, and
Christ's concept of the Church.[42] A "hold things as they
were" versus "update everything" struggle continued throughout the Council.

Some bishops of the Vatican Curia maintained the first position; while many council fathers spearheaded by French and
German spokesmen variously stressed the updating process
initiated by Pope John. With refreshing freedom, the speakers covered the spectrum of debatable opinions from full
agreement to outright contradiction.

After the document, *The Sources of Revelation,* was returned
to the Theological Commission for major revisions, the schema on "Unity with the Orthodox" (*Ut Unum Sint:* That They May
Be One), conservatively formulated by the Preparatory Commission for the Oriental Churches, was presented to the Council.
For many reasons, including emphasis on "return," failure to
acknowledge fault, sense of domination instead of service,
Latinizing tendency, failure to integrate the problem with
the study on the Church as well as with the work of the Unity
Secretariat, the schema, as written, was rejected by a vote
of 2,086 to 36.[43]

On December 1, Cardinal Ottaviani, Chairman of the Theological Commission, opened the topic of his commission's schema,
"On the Church" (*De Ecclesia*). It consisted of *eleven chapters* whose topics were: 1. Church Militant; 2. Membership;
3. Episcopacy; 4. Residential Bishops; 5. States of Perfection; 6. Laity; 7. Magisterium; 8. Authority and Obedience;
9. Church and State; 10. Church Needed for Mission; 11. *Ecumenism.*

This eighty-page schema (or report) was immediately attacked
for its exclusive identification of the Mystical Body of
Christ with the Roman Catholic Church. On the other hand,
the schema was defended as written with equal spirit. The
"let us progress" versus "let us change nothing" foci in the
Council's attitudes were clearly manifest in the speeches of
the various cardinals and bishops. On the very first day of
the six-day debate, the speech by Bishop Emile De Smedt of
Bruges, Belgium, struck the death knell of the schema as
written. De Smedt, who worked in Cardinal Bea's Secretariat,
described the document as characterized by "triumphalism,
clericalism and legalism."[44] It was argued that the divine
element in the Church is mysterious as *Mystici Corporis*
(1943) had pointed out, that the Church is much more than a
pyramid of ruler over ruled, that the Church is a dynamic
body moving through history,—not a static, legally-contain-
able organization. The schema was returned to the Thelogi-
cal Commission for total revision. Pope John added Bea's
Secretariat, which had stressed the spiritual and dynamic
character of the Church, to the Theological Commission for
the revising of the schema.

A comparison of the chapter headings of the original schema,
the first revised schema and the final approved draft, entitled *Lumen Gentium,* reveal the emphasis shift which took
place.[45]

1st Schema	2nd Schema	Final Document
1. Church Militant	1. Mystery of the Church	1. Mystery of the Church
2. Membership		2. People of God
3. Episcopacy	2. Hierarchical Constitution (esp. episcopal)	3. Hierarchy (esp. episcopacy)
4. Residential Bishops		4. Laity
5. States of Perfection		5. Call to holiness
6. Laity	3. The people of God and the laity in particular	6. Religious
7. Magisterium		7. Pilgrim Church (eschatological)
8. Authority and Obedience		8. Mary's role
9. Church and State	4. The call to holiness	
10. Church needed for mission		
11. Ecumenism		

The first schema rested on the "faith, sacraments, pyramid-ally-structured" *visible organization* picture with the iden-tifiable "Baptism, faith, non-separated" membership criteria of *Mystici Corporis*. It also identified absolutely and to-tally the Church of Christ as the Roman Catholic Church. The later schemata gave initial attention to the *invisible* divine character of Christ's Church.

The first schema heavily emphasized the ruling element as a dominant theme, the later schemata, while clearly affirming the divinely given authority in the Church, pushed it back to a position of service for the whole pilgrim "People of God."

The first schema tended to define the relationships in the Church in a static way, the later schemata focused on the dynamism of changing relationships as the whole Community-of-God People moved on its pilgrimage through history to the end (*eschaton*) intended by God.

The model shifted from a pyramidal structure to a great cir-cle of pilgrim people at whose core was a college of apostol-ic bishops whose foundation-center was the Pope. *Ecumenism* was deleted as a chapter to become an independent decree in its own right.

The dominance of a pilgrim-people concept countered the tri-umphant character, the emphasis on the invisible divine ele-ment as primary countered the legalist character, and the primacy of the whole people of God as the Church countered the dominating clericalist character of the first schema.

The shift of emphasis from schema to schema was a serious
theological struggle. The shift in emphasis in the lives of
Roman Catholics, involving radical reorientation, continues
toward century's end. Generations rather than decades now
appear to be the time-units by which to measure the implementation of *Lumen Gentium*.

The Council Fathers believe that the Church which came from
Christ is a divine-human reality. It is believed *divine* because its founder is believed divine, because the sacraments
are believed to be efficacious divine sign-actions, because
its invisible guiding power is believed to be the divine person of the Holy Spirit. It is simultaneously a *human* reality
because the incarnate Christ started it with visible human
beings; it continued and continues with them.

The Mystical Body image highlights the *divine* constituent,
implies transcendence, suggests the sinless, spotless Bride
of Christ. The People of God image emphasizes the *human*
constituent of the one ecclesial reality. The latter image
implies the dynamism of people, all kinds of people, saints,
undecided and sinners, people of all times and places.

The combination of the two elements, divine and human, constitutes an essential unity which corresponds to the believed "divine/human" duality of natures in its founder,
Jesus Christ.[46] Overemphasis of his divinity led to a rejected distortion; over-emphasis of his humanity led to a
rejected distortion; denial of his unity led to a plurality
which was rejected. The Church itself, as an object of belief (Nicene Creed: Credo...in unam...ecclesiam), suffers in
various times from similar distortions: overhumanizing begets a purely human construct, overdivinizing begets a sinless, transcendent construct alien to human experience.
Within these limits Vatican II hammered out *Lumen Gentium*,
the first, full scale conciliar conceptualizing of the
Church's nature since its founding.

The Council struggled with the equation: The Mystical Body
of Christ = the Roman Catholic Church. Cardinal Ruffini
proposed it; Cardinal Lercaro could not accept it because
valid baptism makes one a member of the Mystical Body of
Christ, and many of the baptized are not in the Roman Catholic Church. Cardinal Frings suggested that the time was not
ripe for a definitive solution of this question.

Thus, the council searched for a different way of defining
the relationship between the Church Christ founded and today's Roman Catholic Church. It chose the word "subsists,"
meaning "exists," "has existence," "abides," "is maintained."
Thus speaking of *the Church founded by Christ,* the Council

affirmed:

> *This Church,* constituted and organized in
> the world as a society *subsists in the Catho-*
> *lic Church,* which is governed by the succes-
> sor of Peter and by the bishops in union
> with that successor, although *many elements*
> of sanctification and of truth can be found
> *outside* of her visible structure. The ele-
> ments, however, as gifts properly belonging
> to the Church of Christ, *possess an inner*
> *dynamism toward Catholic Unity.*[47]

This paragraph (Article 8) of the *Dogmatic Constitution On*
the Church, known by the shorter Latin title *Lumen Gentium*
(Light of the Nations), presents the key formulation of the
Roman Catholic Church's relation to the Apostolic Church; it
also points up the basic principle (elements...outside...
dynamism toward Catholic unity) on which she is judging her
relationship ecumenically to the Christian Communities separated from her.

The expression, "the Church [of Christ] subsists in the
[Roman] Catholic Church" contains the belief that the Apostolic Church founded by Christ continues essentially in the
ecclesial community known as the Roman Catholic Church. The
expression leaves open the position that the Church of Christ
may subsist *in some way* elsewhere. The expression denies the
position which holds that the one Church of Christ no longer
exists in the world, or can no longer be determined.

The "elements" term carries forward the idea contained in
such previously used expressions as "a piece of the gold-
bearing rock," "*vestigia ecclesiae,*" and "part of the patrimony." These elements, such as baptism and the Word of God,
are essential to the Church of Christ, so they are known as
"ecclesial elements." These elements from Christ are believed to possess an inner power inclining their proper
users toward the one Church founded by and intended by
Christ. Thus these elements are motive-forces, internally
moving their proper users toward ecumenism—toward ecclesial
unity.

The original schema on the Church contained a final chapter
on ecumenism. As the Council progressed, the awareness of
"ecclesial elements" as the positive theological basis of
ecumenism grew and displaced the negative juridical position
with which the Council Fathers were familiar. Pope John's
intention that Vatican II be a Council of renewal and unity,
plus the new insights in the Council, magnified the importance
of the "ecclesial elements" so that the chapter of the

original schema was expanded by Cardinal Bea's Unity Secretariat to become an independent document titled, *Decree on
Ecumenism*.

CHAPTER EIGHT

POPE PAUL VI AND VATICAN II

Between the first and second sessions of the Council, as such documents were being developed, Pope John XXIII died. About three weeks later Cardinal John Montini of Milan was elected pope. Inspired by the vision of St. Paul's apostolate to the Gentiles, Cardinal Montini took the name of Paul VI. In his first public address he announced his intention of continuing Vatican II on the course his predecessor had set for it.

During this same period, octogenarian Cardinal Bea developed, with an energy beyond his years, the work of the Unity Secretariat and the work of ecumenism. In a speech at Harvard University he focused attention on the theological basis of ecumenism. He said that Christians must seriously accept the New Testament teaching on baptism and its consequences.

> Each baptism validly conferred, makes one a member of the Mystical Body of Christ. It therefore effects an organic union with Christ and an intimate relationship with all the other baptized...the baptized form the one, unique Family of God....The degree of unity that is to be reached is nothing less than the unity of the Father and the Son in the Blessed Trinity: 'That they may be one, *as Thou Father, in me, and I in Thee*' (John 17:21).[1]

Bea's positive emphasis on the organic union with Christ as the beginning, middle and end of the divine plan for Christian Community provided the frame of reference for his Secretariat's formulation of the Council's Decree on Ecumenism, titled *Unitatis Redintegratio* (The Restoration of Unity).

Another position which Cardinal Bea perceived clearly was the relationship between truth and personal freedom. He very calmly insisted that all in the ecumenical dialogue were bound to the truth, yet each person and group must arrive at the truth, even the divinely-given truth, freely.

161

Too often had the position been invoked that "error has no
rights." When Bea spoke of liberty of conscience, he pointed out that rights belong to neither truth nor error, but
only to persons. Rather sharply, Bea referred to this negative proposition as "sheer nonsense." Xavier Rynne summarizes Bea's thought in the sentence, "it is persons who have
rights, and even when they are in error their right to freedom of conscience is absolute."[2]

In the Secretariat, Bea kept liberty as a highly prized characteristic of the dialogues with the observer-delegates of
Vatican II; the end always to be sought by the theological
dialogue is divinely-revealed truth.

Ecclesiam Suam (His Church)

Similar emphases appear in the first encyclical letter of
Pope Paul VI. The new Pontiff, elected between the first
and second sessions of Vatican II, waited for a bit more
than a year before publishing it in August of 1964. It was
titled *Ecclesiam Suam* (His Church).[3]

Three parts comprised the encyclical's work, namely, the nature of the Church, its renewal, and finally, its dialogue
with the world. In this last part, responsible freedom is
affirmed. In both the first and third parts, the critical
importance of Christian baptism is emphasized.

Pope Paul stresses the mysterious spiritual side of the
Church without neglecting its visible side. He emphasizes
that Baptism incorporates a person into the Mystical Body of
Christ; he also recalls the image "suggested by Christ Himself, that of the edifice for which He is the architect and
the Builder, an edifice indeed founded on a man...."[4]

The Pope cited *Satis Cognitum* of Leo XIII and liberally used
the insights and supernatural emphasis expressed in *Mystici
Corporis*. Without doubt, Pope Paul's explicit highlighting
of the Church as a mystery[5] contributed toward the selection
of this insight, i.e., "that the church is a mystery," as
the revised first chapter of *Lumen Gentium*.

As Pope John had pictured the Church's relationship to the
world with the image of concentric rays of heavenly light
leaving concentric circles of light on the world, so Pope
Paul viewed the relationship of the Church's dialogue with
the world by means of four concentric circles.[6] In the
outermost ring, bounded by the horizon and most distant from
the *center* circle (the Church), he envisioned those who profess no religion. In the *next* circle he saw nonchristian
monotheists, Hebrew and Moslem peoples, who worship the one

true God. In the circle *closest* to the Church, the circle
of Christianity, the Pope saw separated brothers with whom
the Church could engage in the most meaningful dialogue.

Sharing Cardinal Bea's conviction, Paul VI wrote:

> Let us stress what we have in common rather
> than what divides us.[7]

He insisted that the Church, despite setbacks, misunderstandings, or slowness of achievement, will not cease the prayers,
penance, or work necessary for this much-desired reconciliation.[8] Yet he cautioned that

> it is not in our power to compromise with the
> integrity of the faith.[9]

Distressing to Paul VI was the recognition that, despite his
very serious hope of reunion, he, as Pope, was viewed by many
of his other Christian brothers as being reunion's "stumbling
block, because of the primacy of honor and jurisdiction which
Christ bestowed upon the Apostle Peter, and which we have inherited from him."[10] Pope Paul pointed out that elimination
of the Papacy would not facilitate a real reunion.

> We beg the separated brethren to consider the
> inconsistency of this position, not only in
> that, without the Pope the Catholic Church
> would no longer be Catholic, but also because,
> without the supreme, efficacious and decisive
> pastoral office of Peter the unity of the
> Church of Christ would utterly collapse.[11]

Since Christ Himself had placed the unity-principle in his
Church, Pope Paul felt that it would be vain to search for
some other principle. However, he affirmed that this unity-
principle should be one of service, not pride. It should be
a ministry of love and truth, not domination.[12]

Finally, Paul VI identified the persons of the inner-most
circle, "the children of...the one, holy, catholic, and
apostolic Church, of which this Roman Church is 'Mother and
head.'"[13] With this group he stressed first the essential
character of charity while also noting the hierarchic constitution of the Church and its authority instituted by Christ.[14]

The Pope affirmed that "the Church...is the *principal* object
of attention of the Second Ecumenical Vatican Council."[15] He
warned that renewal could not come from reducing the Church
to some unreal minimum, or whimsically condensing the Church
to one charism or conforming the divine-human reality of the

the Church to the secular world. Such reductionism, arbi-
trariness, or world comformity could not produce a renewal
of divine life in the Church, nor could watering down of her
doctrine. The secret of *aggiornamento,* or renewal, was an
interior assimilation to Christ.[16]

One Protestant source interpreted *Ecclesiam Suam* as a disap-
pointment for official Protestant circles in Geneva and the
Orthodox in Istanbul and Moscow.[17] Visser't Hooft felt that
it reduced the goal of ecumenism to "better relationships"
rather than "full union." The importance of papal primacy
in *Ecclesiam Suam* seemed to him to require this reduction.[18]

In his *Ecclesiam Suam,* Paul VI manifested his mind to the
Council, the Church, and the Observer Delegates. His encyclical supported the position of those who moved toward the
new schema on the Church. His affirmation of defined positions and warnings against structural demolition partially
allayed the fears of the bishops wedded to a total conserva-
tism.[19] His encyclical spurred the transition from the
Mortalium Animos of Pius XI and the extreme care manifested
at that time. As one Catholic theologian observes: "how
things have changed in the Church since the 1928 encyclical
of Pius XI, *Mortalium Animos*! In this document ecumenists
are called 'pan-Christians' and Catholics are strictly forbidden to take part in the movement...."[20]

The Council assimilated the thought of *Ecclesiam Suam* but
moved from the image of the Mystical Body to emphasis on the
broader image of the "People of God." The Council affirmed
both scriptural *images* as different facets of the same
diamond.

Lumen Gentium (Light of the Nations)

This retention of both scriptural images, i.e. the "Mystical
Body" and "People of God," is viewed by one theologian as an
ambivalence[21] and by another as a deliberate shift in para-
digms (or dominant operative images).[22] Both theologians
point out that the Council's Dogmatic Constitution on the
Church, *Lumen Gentium,* had definitely shifted the conceptual
emphasis from the Church as primarily its hierarchy to the
Church as primarily its whole people.

In *Lumen Gentium* the Council significantly placed the topic
on the People of God (ch. 2) ahead of the topics on the distinction among the People of God, namely the Hierarchy (ch.
3) and the Laity (ch. 4). That which is common to all in
the ecclesial reality is to be explained before that which
is a special service within the Church.

Although Vatican II made ample use of other models of the
Church, such as Body of Christ, Sacrament, Bride of Christ,
its paradigm or "dominant model was rather that of the People
of God."[23] It was felt that this scriptural paradigm brings
out the "all-kinds-of-people" dimension, the historical dynamism and "dignity-of-all" dimensions better than other images.[24] Also, this paradigm, while not denying the validity
of the other scriptural models, opens more avenues of ecumenical dialogue with other Christians because of its personal
rather than institutional emphasis, and its openness to the
eschatological "not yet", which *Lumen Gentium's* seventh chapter
covers.[25]

In line with the emphasis suggested by Pope Paul, *Lumen Gentium*
first proclaims (ch. 1) the work of *God* in freely *calling* alie-
nated humanity to salvation. The Latin word for calling together (*convocatio = ecclesia*) is the equivalent to the Greek
New Testament word for Church. Thus, buried in the language-
changes, the emphasis on God's primacy (in calling the Church
into being) is contained. The free act of God (radically
mysterious to man) calls together a people to form a New
Covenant through Christ. All people are invited to respond
to this call. The Apostle Paul saw revelation here, namely,
in God's plan to make both Jew (his own people) and Gentile
a single people.

Chapter two of *Lumen Gentium* focuses on this called-together
people, this convoked assembly, this ecclesial body, this
Church. It notes that this People of God is made one by a new
baptism instituted by Christ. This people takes on the character of Christ, is vicariously immersed in his death, and
brought to a new state, a new birth, a new life in his resurrection. This chapter further points out the priestly and
prophetic character of this Christened people. It enumerates
the historic sacraments and necessity of going to the Father
through Christ, "the way." Full belief that God is acting through
Christ and the Holy Spirit is the over-arching point of view.

Only after these theologically-packed sentences, for which
Scripture and prior councils were adduced in support, does
the Council turn to the special character of groups within
the whole people of God. They are basically two: the hierarchy (ch. 3), consisting of the scriptural triad: bishop,
priest, and deacon, and the laity (ch. 4).

Chapter five presents the holiness to which all members in
the Church are called by God; chapter six deals with the
state of those persons living lives vowed to God in religious communities.

God's plan to bring his pilgrim people, his Church, to its

full flower in the end-time (eschaton), an event whose moment
and detail are hidden from Christians, takes up chapter sev-
en. The final chapter (ch. 8) deals with God's choice of
Mary as the specially chosen one through whose free cooperation he mysteriously sent his Son.

This condensed overview manifests that Vatican II kept its
vision fixed on God's plan and the providential unfolding of
that plan in its belief. To one accustomed to Roman Catholic
teaching, the familiar doctrines are there. The emphases
have shifted: from the static to the dynamic, from a people
supported with its rules and set ways to a pilgrim people encouraged to move from principle rather than explicit law;
from a secure defensive stand to a movement troubled with
the insecurities of a pilgrimage; from a people quietly heeding its leaders to a people seeking a dialogue-balance between servile obedience and nonresponse to its hierarchical
and other religious leaders.

The consequences of this emphasis on the "whole people" "will
be discovered only with the passing of time. [Congar's]
opinion is that they will be considerable."[26]

Within *Lumen Gentium,* the Council Fathers strongly reaffirmed
the belief of Vatican I that Christ had set up offices in his
Church to which he attached *sacred power* for the sake of salvation.

> This sacred synod, following in the steps of
> the First Vatican Council teaches and declares
> with it that Jesus Christ, the eternal pastor,
> set up the holy Church by entrusting the Apostles
> with their mission as he himself had been sent
> by the Father (cf. Jn. 20:20). He willed that
> their successors, the bishops namely, should be
> the shepherds of his Church until the end of the
> world. In order that the episcopate itself,
> however, might be one and undivided he put Peter
> at the head of the other apostles and in him he
> set up a lasting and visible source and founda-
> tion of the unity both of faith and communion.
> This teaching concerning the institution, the
> permanence, the nature, and import of the sacred
> primacy of the Roman Pontiff and his infallible
> teaching office, the sacred synod proposes anew
> to be firmly believed by all the faithful.[27]

Practically all the member-churches in the World Council reject this belief of the Roman Catholic Church. Whenever Vatican II speaks of ecumenism, this belief is inextricably incorporated into the goal sought. On the other hand, the World

Council looks to an ecumenical goal which bypasses or rejects
this belief in the continuance of the petrine primacy until
the end-time.

The passage quoted suggests the continuation of the pyramidal
concept of the Church. However, immediately following this
reaffirmation of Vatican I teaching on the papacy, Vatican II
completes the former doctrine by situating Peter in the midst
of the other apostles, and the Pope, the bishop of Rome, in
the center of the other bishops.[28] Peter as center of the
apostolic college and the pope as center of the college of
bishops suggests a wheel and its hub as an image replacing
the pyramidal picture.

The function of the hub as orienting the spokes and holding
them in a unity suggests the Petrine functions of maintaining
the faith orientation and faith-unity (Luke 22:32) of the
Apostolic College and the whole church around the college.
This analogy also admits of the interchange between hub and
spokes and vice versa.

The documents have not used such nonscriptural pictures as
pyramid and wheel; rather they define the relationships implied in the apostolic directives. Thus, *Lumen Gentium* cites
the texts which show Christ choosing his apostles and constituting them "in the form of a *college* or permanent assembly,
at the head of which he placed Peter, chosen from amongst
them (Jn. 21:15)."[29]

While the wheel, lying horizontally, or as a diagram on paper,
suggests a more democratic picture of the "People of God"
than the pyramid does, it is not intended to diminish the authority of the ecclesial center. The texts demand that the
relationships of the collegiate character be seen as an
organic unity in which the center is necessary for the collegiate structure. Thus, *Lumen Gentium* continues:

> The college or body of bishops has no author-
> ity unless united with the Roman Pontiff,
> Peter's successor, as its head, whose prima-
> tial authority, let it be added, over all,
> whether pastors or faithful, remains in its
> integrity. For the Roman Pontiff, by reason
> of his office as Vicar of Christ, namely and
> as pastor of the entire Church, has full,
> supreme and universal power over the whole
> Church, a power which he can always exercise
> unhindered. The order of bishops is the suc-
> cessor to the college of apostles in their
> role as teachers and pastors, and in the
> apostolic college is perpetuated. Together

with their head, the Supreme Pontiff, and
never apart from him, they have supreme and
full authority over the universal church.[30]

At this point the wheel analogy fails to match the teaching,
because the spokes need the hub whereas the hub has authority
over the rim without the intervening spokes. Vatican II
points out that Peter alone was made the rock of Christ's
Church (Matt. 16:18f), Peter alone was made holder of the
keys; Christ made Peter alone the shepherd of his whole
flock (John 21:15ff).[31]

Regarding "binding and loosing" however, Peter's commission
is received once alone (Mt. 16:19), and later as an apostle
in the college of apostles (Mt. 28:16ff).[32]

No one picture or image adequately portrays the complexity
of the relationships represented by the scriptural texts.
Nevertheless, at different stages of the Church's life, one
or other image of the Church dominates or is uppermost (para-
digmatic) in the consciousness of the people who are the
church. Peter in the center of the Apostles and the Apostles
in the center of the People of God evokes more the image of
the great circle of people than of the pyramid.

It takes time for one paradigm to be replaced by another one.
To become operative, any image must also manifest an adequate
correspondence with the scriptural and experiential sense of
the faithful.[33] At any event, the core of the Vatican II
theology seeking expression in a new structural paradigm is
Peter in the college of apostles continuing in unbroken succession[34] into the present Bishop of Rome centered in the
college of bishops.

The Orthodox, Anglican, and some Lutheran members of the
World Council of Churches also hold the necessity of an unbroken succession of bishops stemming from the Apostles,
whereas many other WCC members reject this requirement as a
constituent of the ecumenical goal. Roman Catholics see
this relationship of Peter and the Apostolic College and its
continuance as critically essential for the one Church of
Christ and consequently of the goal of ecumenism.

Peter (chief shepherd, key-keeper and foundation), in the
center of the apostolic college, which in turn is the center
of the whole People of God, is believed by Vatican II to continue in unbroken succession into Pope, episcopal college,
and whole people of God. This cone-shaped pipe-line (composed of each era's concentric-circle from Christ to the
present), safeguarding the unicity of the center, appears to
be the emerging image of the universal church underlying the

newer ecclesial expression, *People of God*.

Then each residential bishop is viewed as the head and center of a particular, diocesan church in union with Peter's
successor. Thus, the universal church can be viewed as a
single community of particular churches (i.e., dioceses) in
union with the centermost Petrine Church and with all other
particular churches. The pictured structural unity would be
a visible corporate aspect of the underlying, less obvious
unity of faith profession, sacramental life and essentially
common evangelical moral obedience.

On this view, the bishop of a dissident church which already
professed the same faith, sacraments and evangelical code
would, with his people's approval, become reunited to the
universal church by joining the college of bishops in union
with the center.

The foregoing picture is evoked by *Lumen Gentium* when it
specifies the collegiate relationship between the Pontiff
and the bishops.

> Collegiate unity is also apparent in the mutual
> relations of each bishop in individual dioceses
> and with the universal Church. The Roman Pon-
> tiff, as the successor of Peter, is the perpet-
> ual and *visible source and foundation* of the
> unity both of the bishops and of the whole com-
> pany of the faithful. The individual bishops
> are the *visible source and foundation* of unity
> in their own particular Churches, which are
> constituted after the model of the universal
> Church; it is in these and formed out of them
> that the one and unique Catholic Church exists.
> And for that reason precisely each bishop repre-
> sents his own Church, whereas all, together
> with the Pope, represent the whole Church in a
> bond of peace, love and unity. [35]

As an individual, each residential bishop is pastorally responsible for a particular assembly of Christians assigned
to him, but in collegiate action with the successor of Peter
he is responsible for the faith, worship and discipline of
the universal Church. [36] This relationship is implied in expressions such as 'particular churches are "portions of the
universal Church."'   The Mystical Body from this view can also
be seen as "a corporate body of Churches." [37]

These organically united particular Churches providentially
clothed themselves in the diverse languages and customs germane to the peoples baptized. Thus the one faith, worship,

and code moved into diverse languages and cultures. Diverse
liturgical usage, theological expression and particular response to local moral problems characterized the one Church
of Christ with the dispersion of the original Apostles and
their co-workers.

The Pastoral epistles to Timothy and Titus manifest the unity
of faith and communion preserved as the one Church of Christ
moved into diverse circumstances. Unity in an ever-widening
linguistic and cultural diversity marked Christ's Church.

The seven extant letters of the Bishop Ignatius of Antioch
(martyred about 110 AD), to the different regions between
Syrian Antioch and Rome testify to the unified sense of
faith, worship and authority in the post-Apostolic era.[38]
The multiplicity of particular episcopal churches did not
fragment the deeper unity. *Lumen Gentium* views such diversity as a reflection of the Church's universality. "This multiplicity of local Churches...shows all the more resplend-
ently the catholicity of the undivided Church."[39]

Gathered about its bishop, such a particular church united
with its Petrine center and the other particular Churches
(dioceses of New York, London, Athens, etc., would exemplify
particular churches) are held by *Lumen Gentium* to embody and
be constitutive of "the One, Holy, Catholic and Apostolic
Church."[40]

In theory, if a particular church led by its bishop were to
depart from the corporate union of Churches attached to their
necessary center, it would cease to belong to the one Apostolic Church. Similarly, if it returned to corporate unity
it would again be a particular instance of the one, Apostolic Church. In this view the consecrated bishop is seen as a
church-maker, as the representative who embodies the particular church, as the one who keeps the local or particular
church incorporated in the collegiate body of churches gathered about its Petrine center. Consecration as bishop, communion with the College of Bishops and identification with a
particular assembly of faithful constitute him as representative of a particular church.

This explains the anxiety among the other churches and especially the center when a particular bishop manifests inexpli-
cable doctrine or practice. Such relationships seem to present a model, or part of a model, for achieving a fuller unity
of Christians without denying (as Faith and Order search for
the lost unity implied) the *continuity of Christ's gift* of
unity from the Apostles to the present.

Another structural element, newly-developed and influential

at Vatican II, is the National or Regional Conference of
Bishops with continuing secretariats.[41] The National Conference of Catholic Bishops (NCCB) in the United States, whose
history dates from World War I, is one such conference. Some
countries have similar episcopal conferences, others do not
as yet. As a structural element it is analogous to the
structure of practically all the autocephalous Orthodox Churches, which, until recently, were each identified with particular countries.

This new type of episcopal structure, useful for the bishops
to respond more capably and promptly to changing positions
and attitudes within nations,[42] will perhaps provide a model
in which other episcopal churches can see a possible construct of the Universal Church of Christ. Its danger is
that nationalism can cloud its world-Christian vision. The
Apostolic Church quickly transcended the cultural nationalism
of its Jewish matrix.

However, Vatican II is clearly convinced that Christ had provided only one structural center for his Church, namely
Peter in the Apostolic College, and that this structural center continues uninterruptedly to the present day.[43]

This Roman center has moved into the modern ecumenical movement in a positive and determined way only after the movement
had, with great effort, established a center in Geneva, namely
the World Council of Churches. The World Council, for fifteen years, has been the principal center of the movement.
Lumen Gentium views the see of Peter as the center of the
Church rather than of this modern movement. But with Rome's
official entrance into the movement, another center of theo-
logically-oriented ecumenism has developed.

At the opening of the Vatican Council's third session, while
encouraging the sense of collegiality among his brothers[44]
(not his sons) in the episcopate, Paul VI nevertheless emphasized that the unity of the Church required centralization, even an increased centralization in the times ahead.
After indicating that Papal authority is obliged at times to
restrict, regulate, prescribe episcopal modes of action, Pope
Paul pointed out that such actions were done

> ...for the good of the entire Church, for the
> unity of that Church which has proportionately
> greater need of centralized leadership as its
> worldwide extension becomes more complete, as
> more serious dangers and more pressing needs
> threaten the Christian people in the varying
> circumstances of history and, we may add, as
> more rapid means of communication become

operative in modern times.[45]

The Pope saw this centrality as a safeguard of the divinely-
given unity of the Church, as a more sure way of preserving
the Christ-given treasures of grace and faith, and as support
for the bishops scattered throughout the world. Paul continued:

> For your part, dispersed as you are all over
> the world, if you are to give shape and sub-
> stance to the true Catholicity of the Church,
> you have a need of a *center*, a principle of
> unity in faith and communion, a unifying power,
> such as, in fact, you find in this Chair of
> Peter. Similarly, we need to have you always
> nearby...[46]

Center(s) of Church, Ecumenism, Unity?

At the end of this address, Paul VI identified the tomb of
Peter in Rome as the keystone[47] or center[48] of unity. Shortly before this, his first encyclical, *Ecclesiam Suam,* had affirmed that the unitive activity begun by Pope John and the
Council would not falter as it sought to combine uncompro-
mising integrity with efforts at reuniting all Christians.

> ...it is not in our power to compromise with
> the integrity of the faith or the requirements
> of Charity. We foresee that this will cause
> misgiving and opposition, but now that the
> Catholic Church *has taken the initiative* in
> restoring the unity of Christ's fold, it will
> not cease to go forward with all patience and
> consideration.[49]

Some Reformed ecumenical circles viewed the foregoing conception as "Romano-centric"[50] and as a disappointing reaffirmation that "the See of Rome is the center of everything."[51]
As that Church moved from critic of the ecumenical movement
to tentative participant, and then to active participant in
the modern movement, Visser't Hooft expressed concern lest
the public conclude that *the center* of the movement had
shifted from Geneva to Rome and that the real ecumenical
movement had only then begun. Visser't Hooft wrote:

> I was of course especially concerned about
> the consequences of this development for the
> life of the World Council of Churches and
> made a number of addresses on the abiding
> task of the World Council as a body in which
> no church is 'more equal than the others' and

all seek together to advance towards unity.[52]

This expression appears to imply that even the one Church of
Christ, if extant, is merely the equal of the many profess-
edly man-made "churches" which continue to proliferate.
Moreover, it intimates that the one Church of Christ is no
longer visible in existence and must be sought out or constructed anew. It perhaps suggests that all the presently
extant churches are fragments or parts of the one former
Church of Christ which, when brought together, like pieces of
a very difficult jigsaw puzzle, will once again manifest
Christ's one visible Church.

Perhaps such imagery is too commonplace. Visser't Hooft
cites, with restrained approval, however, what he terms
Soederblom's "ecumenical geometry." Archbishop Soederblom
had projected the construct of a circle of which Christ is
the center; all Christian churches are in a circumferential
position variously distanced from the center toward which
they are moving at different speeds.[53] The invisibility of
the center seems to evoke a return to the concept of the
"invisible Church." Visser't Hooft retains the invisible
center but prefers many-sidedness to circularity.

> The truth is that the center of the ecumenical
> movement cannot shift because it has no earth-
> ly center. Its earthly expression is multi-
> lateral. The one center of the ecumenical
> movement is our common Lord.[54]

This affirmation of the centrality of Christ is indeed necessary; Vatican II expresses this same belief many times, as
when it speaks of God's inviting all persons into special renewal in Christ, "For it is in him that it pleased the Father
to restore all things" (Eph. 1:4ff).[55] The Council Fathers
named their document on the Church from the image of Christ
as the light of nations, *Lumen Gentium*. Furthermore, the
Council paraphrased the Christological focus of the Church
expressed by Pope Paul "Christ our life and guide, Christ
our hope and our end"[56] in *Lumen Gentium's* opening article:
Christ, missioned from the Father, became the way for all to
enter a profound ecclesial union with him. "All men are
called to this union with Christ, who is the light of the
world, from whom we go forth, through whom we live, and towards whom our whole life is directed."[57]

These citations identify the Christo-centrism of Vatican II.
Thus, Visser't Hooft's maxim, "Christ is the one center of
the ecumenical movement," is not what distinguishes his World
Council position from that of the Council Fathers.

It is rather Visser't Hooft's "it has no earthly center."
This implies that the visible incarnate Christ left no visible reality which could serve as center for his newly-cov-
venanted people, or that the center he left is lost.   The
Conciliar understanding of "on this rock I will build my
Church" (Mt. 16:18)[58] supplies Christ's continuing center
for Vatican II.

The Roman Catholic belief that Christ established this visible petrine centerpiece in the midst of his chosen Apostles
as constitutive of the Church (mysteriously his body), is repeatedly imbedded in the Vatican documents.   One decree
alone (Pastoral Office of Bishops), refers to this belief no
less than twenty times.[59]

Although Vatican II addressed itself to the elimination of
qualities that had been named by Bishop De Smedt as "triumphalism, legalism and clericalism," it in no way sought to
dislodge what it believed to be the Christ-intended visible
center.

The Council replaced a pyramidal monarchical image with a
concentric-circle image, but not a single council voice
sought to resituate or eliminate the petrine center.   This
center has become the source of numerous and extensive Roman
Catholic initiatives in the work of reuniting separated
Christians.

All can clearly agree that the invisible center of unity in
the ecumenical movement is the risen Christ.   But as far as
the visible center goes there is, at worst, disagreement, and
at best, ambiguity.   Rome believes itself to be that continuing visible center of Christ's Church; and the center of
ecumenism cannot readily be kept separate from the center of
Christ's Church.   Geneva believes otherwise.

Outsiders see two visible centers of ecumenical initiatives.
Better perhaps, they see two major foci (and many lesser
ones) in the one great magnetically unitive movement among
Christians in the last two decades of the twentieth century.

To the framers of Lumen Gentium the end-product, or goal, of
the ecumenical movement appears inconceivable without the
petrine center and the collegiate episcopal core of the people of God.   Christ, in his roles of priest, teacher and king,
is believed to continue his work in the Pope, the episcopal
college, and his body of people.   These constituents of his
Church are held to be of divine institution,[60] and thus ir-
reformable.   One passage of Lumen Gentium mentions the three
roles cited as the representative sense of Christ's instruction: "Who hears you, hears me" (Luke 10:16).

> ...episcopal consecration confers, together
> with the office of sanctifying, the duty also
> of teaching and ruling, which, however, of
> their very nature can be exercised only in
> hierarchical communion with the head and members
> of the college. In fact, from tradition...of
> both the Eastern and Western Church, it is
> abundantly clear that by the imposition of
> hands and through the words of the consecra-
> tion, the grace of the Holy Spirit is given,
> and a sacred character is impressed in such
> wise that bishops...take the place of Christ
> himself, teacher, shepherd and priest and act
> as his representatives (*in eius persona*).[61]

After the close of Vatican II, Pope Paul identified the Dogmatic Constitution of the Church (*Lumen Gentium*) as the central work and preeminent achievement of the Council.[62]   Addressing the very question: "Which is the key work of all
the documents that constitute the great volume of the Council?", he replied, "...it is a certainty that among all these
there stands preeminently the doctrine on the Church, her
mystery, her framework, her mission."[63]   After the Council,
one of the Cardinals characterized the Dogmatic Constitution
on the Church as "the Council's master and pivotal document."[64]

Thus, the structural 'college of Apostles around and under
Peter continuing into the college of bishops around and under the Pope' appears to be an essential constituent of foreseeable Roman Catholic ecumenical thought. The Council
Fathers believe that this structure is divinely given and
preserved; consequently, in their thought, the truth and
fact of it cannot ultimately be an obstacle to ecumenism.

Variations, maintaining some form of this essential constituent, may emerge,but the remodeling of tomorrow's one Church
of Christ must conform to the intent of the Primary Architect.   Under the influence of this conviction, Paul VI,
after the Council, sought to discourage thoughts of arbitrary innovations with the declaration: "We must be profoundly convinced that we cannot demolish the Church of yesterday
to construct a new one today."[65]

Rejecting the position of those who would substitute modern
worldly opinions and norms in place of the primary requirements of the word of God and continuous traditional conviction, Pope Paul said:

> We must instead continue the construction of
> the Church by conforming its new additions to

> the design pre-established by Christ and by
> building with trust and loyalty on the struc-
> ture already in existence.
>
> It is this positive psychology which must
> guide the constructive work of the Church in
> the aftermath of the Second Vatican Council.
>
> ...The work of the bishops' conferences, for
> example, introduces and inaugurates a new
> and fruitful period of the history of the
> Church.[66]

Although visible structural elements of the Church are more
easily addressed, nevertheless the invisible divine element
of the interlocked divine-human reality of Christ's Church
is identified as primary. At times the divine, supernatural factor is referred to as the vertical element, while the
interlocked human dimension is called horizontal. The ecclesiology of *Lumen Gentium* is rooted in the plan and action
of the Trinity.[67] Reflecting on this faith mind-set of the
Council, Pope Paul noted:

> Some read in the Council the Church's orienta-
> tion in, so to speak, a horizontal sense: to-
> ward the human community that makes up the
> Church itself; toward the brethren still
> separated from us,...toward the surrounding
> world...
>
> All this is very true and marvelous but we
> must not forget, may we say, the vertical
> orientation, which the Council has reaffirmed
> as being primary for interpreting the design
> of God on the destiny of mankind...
>
> God...always retains first place. Christ,
> mediator between man and God is the necessary
> Redeemer...The Spirit, who makes us Christians
> and raises us to supernatural life, is the true
> intimate principle of our interior life...[68]

The primacy of the vertical (God-oriented) component over
the horizontal component is manifested also in the overall
output of the Second Vatican Council. Because the Church is
held to be ontologically a divine-human interlocked reality,
the two components are thought to be never totally separable
on earth.

The body-soul inseparability of man on earth was thought a
useful analogue, but the human-divine natures in the One

Person of the Christ who founded "his Church" was preferred
by the Council.[69] Thus, all the conciliar documents deal
necessarily with both interlocked components; the Council's
sixteen documents disclose the predominant emphasis on the
divine and religious element.

The Council itself identified the order of importance of its
documents with the titles: constitutions (of which there are
four), decrees (nine) and lastly declarations (three). *Constitutions* deal with the most weighty and permanent matters
of belief and practice; *decrees* are in closer contact with
doctrinal positions or practices; *declarations* with the more
transient positions, or positions less deeply probed, or
more remote from doctrinal positions.

The extraordinary nature and authority of an ecumenical council gives all its documents special importance, but that importance is graduated hierarchically as indicated.

Furthermore, both Popes John and Paul specified that the
Council's thrust was to be pastoral rather than focused
on definitions and condemnations of contradictory positions. As the council progressed through the four years
(four sessions) of work, the shift of emphasis seemed to
proceed from the definitive and juridical past to the
perceptively religious and pastoral, until all the documents began to fall into an order relating to the Church
as a center. Most of the documents deal with the groupings *within* the Church and her Christocentric activities,
or with her relations to the world outside her boundaries
in the light of her salvific obligations toward them.

Inner-oriented documents: Starting with *Lumen Gentium* as the
central constitution, six other documents expand its articles, namely the decrees: on the *Episcopacy,* those on the
Priesthood and *Formation of Priests,* one on the *Life of Religious Communities,* that on the *Laity* and the declaration
on *Catholic Education.* The decree on *Eastern Catholic
Churches* is an expression on particular churches. The
Church's work of worship and sanctifying is contained in the
Constitution on the *Liturgy;* the Constitution on the *Word of
God* further articulates her concept of Divine Revelation and
teaching functions.

Outward-Oriented documents: Pope Paul's image of the great
circles of persons around the Church seems to indicate the
relation of the remaining six documents to the activity of
the Church. The decree on *Ecumenism* defines the relationship between other Christians who are believed to be linked
to the Roman Catholic Church by divine "elements". The next

great circle, consisting of those who are believing monotheists, is considered in the declaration on *Non-Christian Religions*. For the final circle, the decree on *Missions* is an
expression of the Church's outreach to all non-Christians.
The declaration on *Religious Liberty* expresses the right and
responsibility of every human, while the decree on *Instruments of Social Communication* is a conciliar effort to express the rights and responsibilities of communications
media. Finally, the *Pastoral Constitution on the Church in
the Modern World* embraces reflection on the Church's relationship to all of mankind including the indifferent, the
totally nonreligious and those hostile even to God.* The
viewing is centrifugal, from the center of the Church out to
the final horizon; the pastoral spirit, the offering of
Christ's revealed truth, and attraction of love is intended
to be centripetal.

---

*For clarity the Council documents are listed below:

Constitutions	Decrees	Declarations
1. The Church *Lumen Gentium*	1. Instruments of Social Communication *Inter Mirifica*	1. Christian Education *Gravissimum Educationis*
2. Divine Revelation *Dei Verbum*	2. Ecumenism *Unitatis Redintegratio*	
	3. Eastern Catholic Churches *Orientalium Ecclesiarum*	2. The Relationship of the Church to non-Christian
3. Sacred Liturgy *Sacrosanctum Concilium*	4. The Bishops' Pastoral Office *Christus Dominus*	Religions *Nostra Aetate*
	5. Priestly Formation *Optatam Totius*	
4. Church in the Modern World *Gaudium et Spes*	6. Appropriate Renewal of Religious Life *Perfectae Caritatis*	3. Religious Freedom *Dignitatis Humanae*
	7. Apostolate of the Laity *Apostolicam Actuositatem*	
	8. The Ministry and Life of Priests *Presbyterorum Ordinis*	
	9. The Church's Missionary Activity *Ad Gentes*	

The centrality of the document on Christ's Church illustrates
the priority of the spiritual thrust over the secular in the
Council's four years of work. The vertical component is
prior in importance to the horizontal. Both are necessary.
But in doctrine, if not always in practice, the Will of God
manifested in Christ characterizes and terminates their
final positions.

This overview is significant when comparing it with the overview of the World Council's work as produced in its assemblies. The goal of Roman Catholic ecumenism is theological;
it is the One Church of Christ. The thrust and focus of the
World Council's ecumenism seems to be mainly sociological;
the WCC works chiefly on social problems of Christians and
non-Christians alike (generally for Christian motives).
These problems are important; they unendingly call for sympathetic initiatives, but the practical identification of
such problems with ecumenism changes the goal of ecumenism
from the reuniting of Christians in Christ's one Church to
a cooperative effort of divided Christians for the solution
of problems more secular than religious.

CHAPTER NINE

DECREE ON ECUMENISM

From the central constitution *Lumen Gentium* comes the theological starting points of most of the remaining documents of Vatican II. Such is the case for the decree on ecumenism (*Unitatis Redintegratio*: The Restoration of Unity) which had been placed as the last chapter in the original schema on the Church as proposed by the Council's Theological Commission. When the Council Fathers saw that the Commission on the Oriental churches and the Secretariat for the Promotion of Christian Unity were also sources of variant positions on ecumenism, they voted overwhelmingly for a single document expressing the Council's theological position on the restoration of unity among Christians.[1]

Encouraged by this vote of the Council, the Pope made some adjustments in the membership of the conciliar commissions, so that the static position of those who held a "let them return" attitude would be confronted by Cardinal Bea's insistence, shared by many, that "quite a few elements already unite the Orthodox and Protestants to us." Dialogue and reaching-out were the pastoral attitudes to be sought, not a repetition of confrontation and former condemnations.

Cardinal Bea's Secretariat formulated the new schema on ecumenism; it was accepted as the basis of discussion in the Council's second session. Over a thousand suggestions for improvement or *modi*fication (termed *modi*) of the new schema were presented to the Secretariat by Council Fathers. Pope Paul himself suggested a number of changes. After the proper commission had processed and incorporated the interventions, the decree was brought to a vote at the end of the third session. The Council voted to engage positively in the modern ecumenical movement by an overwhelming majority; 2,137 voted for the doctrinal and pastoral decree; only eleven registered their dissent.[2]

The *Decree of Ecumenism* flows from and follows after the constitution on the Church.[3] At the same time it throws the briefly stated principles on separated Christians of *Lumen Gentium* into a fuller and more explicit light.[4]

The *Decree on Ecumenism* is written with a brief introduction
and three chapters; in all it numbers twenty-four articles.
The first chapter identifies the Catholic principles of ecumenism; the second spells out the Church's practice of ecumenism in the light of the principles; and the third notes
the different elements which positively unite the Roman
Catholic Church to the East and to the West.[5]

Introduction: Echoing Popes John and Paul, the decree's
introduction declares "the restoration of unity among all
Christians is one of the principal concerns of the Second
Vatican Council."[6] It affirms three significant preliminary
facts: that Christ founded "one Church and one Church only,"[7]
that Christians (it does not say the Church) are divided,
and that a growing movement for the restoration of unity
among believers in Christ and the Trinity is "fostered by
the Holy Spirit."[8]

1. Principles - The decree's first chapter rests on the
revealed knowledge that the Father sent the Son to give the
human race new life and make it one. His Church, already
considered in *Lumen Gentium,* would have its unity signified
and deepened by the Eucharist, by its response to his command of love and the presence of the Holy Spirit.[9] The decree first enunciates the *invisible* mysterious unity produced by baptism in Christ (Gal. 3:27f); it then turns to
the *visible* unity of the College of Apostles,with Peter receiving his appointed place in their midst. Reference is
made to the Scriptural passages which indicate that Christ
named Peter alone "rock," gave him "the keys," confirmed his
faith and commanded him "to feed his sheep."

The College of Apostles flows in time into their selected
successors, "the bishops with Peter's successor at their
head."[10] Thus, through their unity in faith, worship, and
governance in love, Christ wishes his Church "to increase
under the action of the Holy Spirit, and He perfects its
fellowship in unity."[11] The decree declares that this ecclesial unity *transcends earthly models* of unity in some essential and mysterious respect.

> This is the sacred mystery of the unity of
> the Church, in Christ and through Christ,
> with the Holy Spirit energizing its various
> functions. The highest exemplar and source
> of this mystery is the unity, in the Trinity
> of Persons, of One God, the Father and the
> Son in the Holy Spirit.[12]

After citing the divine life of the Trinity as the source
and exemplar of the Church's unity, the decree notes

instances in the New Testament pointing to human rifts which
nevertheless nagged the infant Church. But in later centuries, large groups of people in worse dissensions "became
separated from *full communion* with the Catholic Church—for
which, often enough, men of both sides were to blame."[12a]

Thus, in an official document of the highest authority, the
Church acknowledges faults of some of its own members. It
avoids imputing sins or faults to the Church made "holy and
immaculate, without stain" (Eph. 5:26f) by Christ. Moreover,
the sins which contributed to the original divisions among
Christians are not to be imputed to those born into the divided communities.

> ...one cannot charge with the sins of separa-
> tion those who at present are born into these
> communities and in them are brought up in the
> faith of Christ, and the Catholic Church ac-
> cepts them with respect and affection as
> brothers. For men who believe in Christ and
> have been properly baptized are brought into
> *certain, though imperfect, communion* with the
> Catholic Church.[13]

There nevertheless remain barriers to the achievement of full
or perfect communion. Some barriers pertain to doctrine,
others to ecclesial life and structure.

> But even in spite of them it remains true that
> all who have been justified by faith in bap-
> tism are incorporated into Christ...they there-
> fore have a right to be called Christians, and
> with good reason are accepted as brothers by
> the children of the Catholic Church....[14]

The document proceeds to invoke the insight already acknowledged in *Lumen Gentium,* that many of Christ's church-forming
and life-giving "elements" can also exist outside the visible
boundaries of the Catholic Church.[15] These elements, some
invisible such as the life of grace, and others visible such
as sacred scripture and valid, continuous episcopacy, belong
to Christ's one Church and lead back to him and to it.[16]

Because *communities* of people use these Christ-given elements,
these communities certainly cultivate a life of grace and
"can aptly give access to the communion of salvation."[17] The
document next identifies such separated communities as churches without explicitly distinguishing between Orthodox, Anglican and Protestant communities.

The term church, in the sense of separated particular church,

had previously been applied to Orthodox churches in official
Vatican documents, but not to a Protestant Community.[18]   In
the New Testament the term applies to the one universal
Church of Christ or to its local particular embodiments, as
the Church at Corinth or at Thessalonika, but the term is
never applied to those separated from Christ's one community.
However, Vatican II, following its recognition that separated
communities are using some valid ecclesial elements which be-
get Christian community, refers to such communities as churches, thus:

> It follows that the separated Churches...
> and Communities as such, though we believe
> they suffer from defects...have been by no
> means deprived of significance and importance
> in the mystery of salvation. For the Spirit
> of Christ has not refrained from using them
> as means of salvation which derive their ef-
> ficacy from the very fullness of grace and
> truth entrusted to the Catholic Church.[19]

Thus, the Council Fathers affirm their belief that other
Christian churches "as means of Salvation" are really but
not totally united with the Roman Catholic Church. There is
a "certain though imperfect communion with the Catholic
Church."[20]

The Council Fathers believe that "our separated brethren...
are not blessed with that unity which Jesus Christ wished...
that unity which the Holy Scriptures and the ancient Tradition of the Church proclaim."[21]   In this article the Council
professes its faith that the *fullness of means* of salvation,
given exclusively to the Apostolic College with Peter at its
head, can be found only in the Catholic Church.[22]

Vatican II believes it to be the will of Christ that all
Christians should be incorporated into the one visible body
enjoying the fullness of the means of salvation. This is
the fullness of unity at which the ecumenical movement aims.
This is the unity toward which renewal, dialogue, cooperation, and common prayer should proceed. The Council professes that this fullness of means constitutes an essential
unity with which Christ endowed his Church and which can
never be lost.[23]

The ecclesial "elements" used by all believing Christians
have in them a divinely given dynamism toward unity. Renewal
and extension of ecclesial elements should slowly overcome
the obstacles to unity. Thus, Vatican II combines its hope
and belief in one passage:

> The result will be that, little by little, as
> the obstacles to perfect ecclesiastical com-
> munion are overcome, all Christians will be
> gathered, in a common celebration of the Eu-
> charist, into the unity of the one and only
> Church, which unity Christ bestowed on His
> Church from the beginning. This unity we be-
> lieve, subsists in the Catholic Church as
> something she can never lose, and we hope
> that it will continue to increase until the
> end of time.[24]

After stressing the requirement of unity in essentials, the
Council quickly pointed out that *diversity* of forms and variety of rites and even of theological explanations need not
destroy the critical unity. Christ's superabundant gifts
should encourage a richness of expression. Thus Vatican II
affirms a *diversity in unity* within Christ's one Church.
Church leaders, while safeguarding unity in essentials, are
instructed by the document to

> ...preserve a proper freedom in the various
> forms of spiritual life and discipline, in
> the variety of liturgical rites, and even in
> the theological elaborations of revealed
> truth.[25]

In closing the first chapter of the *Decree* the Council acknowledges that Christians "joined to the Church yet separated from full communion", prevent the realization of the
"fullness of Catholicity,"[26] in her witness before the world.

2. Practice - The eight articles of the second chapter deal
with the practice of ecumenism. After indicating that
ecumenism is, in varying degrees, the concern of all members
of the Church, the document insists in three articles (Numbers 6, 7, and 8) that spiritual renewal is an essential
precondition of ecumenism. No renewal, no interior conversion, means no true ecumenism.[27]

The Council, in a notable expression, suggestive of a Reformation theme, acknowledges the need for reform, reaching perhaps even to the timing and way church teaching has been expressed.

> Christ summons the Church, as she goes her
> pilgrim way, to that continual reformation of
> which she always has need, insofar as she is
> an institution of men here on earth. Conse-
> quently, if, in various times and circumstances,
> there have been deficiencies in moral conduct

> or in church discipline, or even in the way
> that church teaching has been formulated—
> to be carefully distinguished from the de-
> posit of faith itself—these should be set
> right at the opportune moment and in the
> proper way.[28]

Such conciliar expressions of "deficiency in the mode of some
past teaching formulations" and an admission of "needed reformation" are rare in official and authoritative ecclesial
documents of the last four centuries. Strong opposition attended their initial presentations in the Council. Papal
authority was needed to overcome the reluctance to make such
acknowledgements.

Pope John's distinction, "the substance of the ancient doctrine of the Deposit of Faith is one thing, and the way in
which it is presented is another,"[29] gave the necessary impetus and support to the reformulation-of-teaching theme.
Pope Paul's expression of the need for the reform of institutions in the Church, even of the Vatican Curia,[30] gave a
base for the Council's affirmation of the need for reform
of the Church composed of very human disciples of Christ.

Moved by the declaration in the Johannine writings that one
who says he has not sinned falsifies the Word of God, the
Council Fathers made an even more explicit acknowledgment of
fault in an ecumenical context.

> St. John has testified: 'If we say we have not
> sinned, we make Him a liar, and His Word is not
> in us (1 Jn. 1, 10). This holds good for sins
> against unity. Thus in humble prayer we beg
> pardon of God and of our separated brethren,
> just as we forgive them that trespass against
> us.[31]

This simple confession of guilt and petition of pardon added
a deeper dimension to the Council's insistence that "spiritual ecumenism" is the driving force or "the soul of the
whole ecumenical movement."[32] The Council called for a
change of attitude and encouraged prayer in common with
Christians separated from the Roman Catholic Church, but issued a caution with reference to any indiscriminate mixing
in worship. This concept, commonly expressed with the Latin
phrase *communicatio in sacris,** refers to sharing in such

---

*Communication or intermingling in sacred or sacra-
mental things.

activities as the sacraments, particularly Mass and the
Eucharist.

> ...worship in common (*communicatio in sacris*)
> is not to be considered as a means to be used
> indiscriminately for the restoration of unity
> among Christians. [33]

The churches and ecclesial bodies separated from the Roman
See differ greatly among themselves as regards the Apostolic
episcopacy, the distinct sacrament of holy orders, and the
eucharistic liturgy. Thus, indiscriminate or fully-opened
sharing in worship was withheld. A simple solution fails
to solve the complex situation. The bishop in Orthodox
countries must solve it one way; the Roman Catholic bishop, in communication with groups which deny holy orders or
which regard the eucharist merely as a symbol, must solve
it another way.

The second chapter's last four articles (9-12) share an intellectual theme. Study, fidelity to Christ's teaching,
"equal-footing" conversations, nonpolemic, yet not falsely-
irenic, theology were the emphases given as Vatican II instructed Roman Catholics to seek first the bonds already
present, while not failing to face the continuing differences, in dialogue with separated brothers. [34]

One remarkable breakthrough here was the expressed concept
that not all the truths of Catholic doctrine are of the same
value, even though they may be equally true. Thus, the Incarnation and Purgatory as doctrinal truths are of enormously different value.

Most theologians would name God, the Trinity, and the Incarnation as most basic to any beginning enumeration of essential Christian doctrines, and thus, implicitly, the concept
of scale of truths has existed for centuries. But the concept was neither named as such nor was it developed. Vatican
II named it but left its development for later theological
exploration.

The Council directed Catholic theologians to hold fast to defined doctrine while humbly probing the unmined riches of
Christian truth with their separated brothers.

> When comparing doctrines with one another,
> they should remember that in Catholic doc-
> trine there exists an order or 'hierarchy'
> of truths, since they vary in their relation
> to the foundation of the christian faith.
> Thus the way will be opened whereby this

> kind of 'fraternal rivalry' will incite all
> to a deeper realization of the unfathomable
> riches of Christ.[35]

This seems to open up the possibility that unity may be
achieved between ecclesial communities which agree on all
the essential foundational truths,while not yet having
reached agreement on some more remotely derived truths.
Small and remote differences ought not to divide whole communities of Christians.

The Council did not address itself to the more difficult
question of distinguishing the truths immediately connected
to the foundation and those which are only remotely connected. It is already visible,however, that even relatively
smaller matters of practice, as for example receiving Holy
Communion under both species (i.e., under the forms of bread
and of wine),or receiving communion in the hand, take patient
instruction and different amounts of time to extend to the
whole, massive, diversely-situated Roman Catholic world.

Such a return, even though modified, to Apostolic practices
also assisted in the approach to Orthodox and Protestant
practice, while differences of practice still remain with
the Orthodox and differences of doctrine with very many
Protestant communities.

3.   Unitive Elements - The third chapter of the *Decree
on Ecumenism* concerns Roman Catholic practical vision in ap-
proaching the historic divisions among Christians,which have
continued in the Orthodox East from the fifth, sixth, and
eleventh centuries,and in the West from the sixteenth (Reformation) century.[36]

The chapter title of the document's first schema read "Christians separated from the Catholic Church"; the title, finally accepted, reads "Churches and Ecclesial communities separated from the Roman See." The changes are significant. The
perspective was changed from that of single individuals to
that of entire assemblies of peoples; also the separation is
viewed as being from an element or elements of the Catholic
Church rather than from its totality as if there were no
bonds uniting separated Christians.

Since the Council believed that Christ founded "one and only
one" Church and that "His Church subsists in the Catholic
Church," it had to find an expression which safeguarded its
belief in the Church's unity,while affirming the unitive
"elements" found among Christians separated from unity. Fullness
and the lesser degrees of fullness emerged as the terminolo-
gy acceptable to the Council.

Thus, full and partial, all and some, complete and incomplete, perfect in essentials and imperfect, integral and deficient, surfaced throughout the documents as Vatican II considered the relationship between its own Church, as having
all the essentials Christ willed, and other Christian churches, as wanting in one or more of the essential elements.[37]

The binding *elements* are real; they are Christ-given, thus
transcendent and supernatural, as faith in Christ and his baptism; but not all of Christ's given elements are found in
the separated or dissident communions in the Council's belief.

> Thus, there must be a real relationship of
> these dissident Communions to the Church.
> They are separated from 'full communion'
> with the Catholic Church; this implies that
> there still remain degrees of communion,
> though imperfect. It seems that the rela-
> tionship should be based on the degree to
> which a dissident communion resembles local
> or particular Churches.[38]

Particular churches, such as the dioceses of New York, Athens
or London, are believed to express the fullness of the Universal Church in their profession of faith, their liturgy
and their discipline, provided the particular episcopal Church
remains in communion with all the other churches in union
with the See of Peter. The unity exists in creed, cult, code,
and ecclesial communion.

A separating bishop, followed by his people, makes his particular church a separated or dissident church in the Council's view. If the separated bishop discards other Christ-
given ecclesial *elements*, such as the sacraments of eucharistic sacrifice or penance, the Council sees this as a further
sliding away or losing of the full elements essential to
Christ's one Church. Yet the bonds of baptism and sacred
scripture remain.

Thus, a norm or judgment-scale of elements is implicit in
the Council's order of naming: first the Orthodox Patriarchal
churches, then Anglican, and finally other Reformation Communions.[39]

> The Decree of Ecumenism seems to evaluate the
> churches separated from Rome according to a
> sliding scale of institutional elements which
> they share with the Catholic Church. There
> are numerous elements which they share with
> the Catholic Church, and they are found in

varying numbers in the non-Roman Churches.[40]

These visible institutional elements, while definitely and
explicitly secondary to the invisible transcendent bonds
which unite believing baptized Christians, are nevertheless
believed to be necessary for the One Church as Christ intended it. Consequently, the Council affirmed that nothing
more than elements held to be necessary should be considered
in encouraging the restoration of unity among Christians.[41]
This was the norm used in the Apostolic Meeting in Jerusalem
and sent by messenger to the local Church at Antioch. "'It
is the decision of the Holy Spirit, and ours too, not to lay
on you any burden beyond that which is strictly necessary,...'" (Acts 15:28).

After its overall introduction of the historic divisions
separating Christians in the East and in the West (Art. 13),
the *Decree on Ecumenism* directs its next five articles (14-
18) to considerations regarding the Orthodox, as if they were
particular or local churches lacking mainly episcopal communion in the full college of bishops in union with the successor of Peter. The great Patriarchal churches, some of
which are apostolic foundations, still hold a privileged
place among particular churches.

> This Council gladly reminds everyone of one
> highly significant fact among others: In the
> East there flourish many particular or local
> churches; among them the Patriarchal Churches
> hold first place,...[42]

The document praises the treasures of Eastern spirituality
and liturgy, of jurisprudence and dogmatic formulations of
the early Councils, which have defined the trinitarian and
christological faith of both East and West.[43]

The document examines acceptable diversity in unity in matters of cult (article 15), code or discipline (article 16)
and theological expressions of creed (article 17).

Orthodox love of liturgy and sense of divine sharing, which
they commonly term "theosis," is highly praised. Love of
Mary, fidelity to the Eastern Fathers, preservation of continuous sacred orders and true sacraments are cited as precious bonds, whereby these Churches

> are still joined to us in closest intimacy.
> Therefore some worship in common (*communicatio
> in sacris*), given suitable circumstances and
> the approval of church authority, is not mere-
> ly possible but is encouraged.[44]

It was noted with approval that the Orthodox Churches show
forth their own unity by means of concelebration. The Council's approval suggests the sign by which reunion between
the Patriarchs of East and West will, in the undetermined
future, be again manifested.*

The Council "solemnly declared"[45] that the Eastern Churches
have the power of regulating their own discipline, customs
and observances, as long as such norms do not violate the
unity of the Church as a whole.[46]

Even the conciliar thoughts concerning the creed of the Orthodox reflect the awareness of diversity. The document
identifies the diversity not as any kind of pluralism but as
"legitimate variety...in theological expressions of doctrine."[47] It notes that differences of method and perspective yield diverse insights and consequently different expressions of the divine mysteries.

Such insights flowing from Sacred Scripture and nurtured by
the Apostolic traditions are "more complementary than conflicting"[48] when seen in the light of the total Christian
perspective. Complimentary insights flow from the full
Catholicity of the Apostolic tradition, while no one insight
can exhaust the wealth of the divine mysteries. The East-
West religious complementarity already exists in the many
Eastern-rite Catholics in full communion with their Western
brothers.[49]

When the *Decree on Ecumenism* moves from the Orthodox World
to the post-Reformation World in the West in its next five
articles (19-23), it maintains the perspective of citing the
bonds which unite while also pointing out the differences
which divide. The bonds are real but less visible and full;
the differences are deeper and not merely legitimate diversity. Thus, for example, the seven Sacraments unite the Orthodox churches to the theological belief of Vatican II,
whereas mainly one sacrament, baptism, unequivocally unites
the evangelical communities to the Council's belief.

The centuries of ecclesial communion bind Reformation communities "to the Catholic Church by a specially close relationship"[50] whereas the Orthodox had been as "joined to us
in closest intimacy"[51] by the true sacraments and apostolic
succession.

---

*Pope John Paul II attended an Orthodox Mass with
Patriarch Dimitrios I in Istanbul on November 30, 1979. He
was the first pope to do this in one thousand years. This
was *not yet* a concelebration.

The legitimate and praiseworthy diversities describing the
Orthodox-Roman Catholic relationships in cult, disciplinary
code, and creedal expression have become in relation to the
post-reformation "churches and ecclesial communities...very
weighty differences...especially in the interpretation of revealed truth."[52]   The bonds are real and vital, but the Reformation wounds are deeper. Despite this, the bonds are divinely given gifts and thus more important than the wounds
which resulted from human failings.

Finally, the Orthodox-Roman Catholic relationships were analyzed from an overview of cult, code and creed, whereas the
Reformation-Roman Catholic relationships are recognized as
considerably more variable and consequently sharing fewer
common elements. However, the elements believed and shared
remain highly significant. They are: open belief in Christ
as God and Lord (article 20), reverence for Holy Scripture
(article 21), preservation of the sacrament of baptism (article 22) and the cultivation of a Christian way of life.

The Council Fathers were pleased to concern themselves with
those Christians who openly profess *Christ* as God and Lord.
They noted that differences arose when questions of mystery
and ministry of Christ's Church were posed, but they expressed joy

> ...that our separated brethren look to Christ
> as the source and center of ecclesiastical com-
> munion. Their longing for union with Christ
> impels them ever more to seek unity, also to
> bear witness to their faith among peoples of
> the earth.[53]

This acknowledgment reflects the original constitutional basis of the World Council of Churches adopted at Amsterdam.
Vatican II saw this belief as the necessary foundation for
dialogue among Christians.

The love of *sacred scripture* among the separated Christians
is praised, but the difference in the relation between scripture and the Church is immediately noted. The authentic
teaching office or magisterium in the Church is cited as an
element of Roman Catholic belief whereas other Christian
bodies hold variously different positions.[54] Despite this,
the Word of God holds a very special position in any dialogue concerning unity.

Baptism, given as Christ willed, incorporates a person mysteriously into a unique union with Christ; the person "is
reborn to a sharing of the divine life."[55] The Council
states its belief in this new birth, this new ontological

relationship with Christ through baptism simply and directly.
This is the profound belief that the real, transcendent relationship is a bond which, in fact, if not in acknowledgment
of all the baptized, unites all Christians.

> Baptism, therefore, constitutes the sacra-
> mental bond of unity existing among all who
> through it are reborn.[56]

However, as infant life is just a beginning which looks toward future development and a still later full maturation,
so baptism gives this new life in a germinal way which tends
toward a fuller union with Christ. This divine reality accepted in faith gives rise to the Christian sense of union
with God and each other in Christ. In more general terms,
the Vatican II continues

> But baptism, of itself is only a beginning,
> a point of departure, for it is wholly di-
> rected toward the acquiring of fullness of
> life in Christ. Baptism is thus ordained
> toward a complete profession of faith, a
> complete incorporation into the system of
> salvation such as Christ Himself willed it
> to be, and finally, toward a complete inte-
> gration into eucharistic communion.[57]

Here, the document expressed the Council's basic outline of
the beginning, middle and end of the envisioned ecumenical
program. Vatican II envisions the beginning of a divinely
given life in baptism, the growth of the baptized toward maturity and unity in community, and a fulfillment, *not* in inter communions of discordantly-believing Christians, but in
a single communion which truly signifies an achieved unity
in faith.

The vision expressed by Cardinal Bea in the early stages of
the Council had, despite difficulties and forthright opposition, become the almost unanimous conviction of the Council,
and thus the authentic teaching of the Roman Catholic Church.

If polemic emphasis on differences had characterized the program of the Church for over four centuries, the emphasis had
clearly shifted to a primary focus on the gifts given by
Christ. The program of the Catholic Church with regard to
separated Christians was set for the foreseeable future.

After acknowledging the Christian values flourishing in the
way of life of the separated brethren, namely: faith, baptism, the Word of God, private prayer and meditation, common
worship and also organizations for Christian education,

social action and peace, the Council judged that the goal of
ecclesial unity exceeds human powers.

> Further, this Council declares that it real-
> izes that this holy objective—the reconcili-
> ation of all Christians in the unity of the
> one and only Church of Christ—transcends
> human powers and gifts.[58]

The Council concluded its decree by expressing its entire
hope in Christ's prayer for his Church and the love and power
of the Father and the Holy Spirit. The signatures of Pope
Paul VI and the Council Fathers terminate the document.[59]

The *Decree on Ecumenism* extended the teaching of the *Dogmatic
Constitution on the Church* from a naming of elements uniting
separated Christians to the Roman Catholic Church to a fuller
consideration of the assemblies of people thus united. The
expression, "Churches and ecclesial assemblies," was used in
both documents for these communions. The term Church was
clearly applied as a reference to the Orthodox; its sense
was that of particular or local church.

With regard to the post-Reformation communions, the same expression "Churches and ecclesial communities" was also used;
but it was noted that these bodies vary greatly in many ways.
The Council chose to use the expression only in a general
way without specific identifications. However, because of a
continuation of particular "Catholic traditions and institutions, the Anglican Communion occupies a special place."[60]
Thus, as already noted, the implicit criterion or scale of
judgment of ecclesial assemblies or churches appears as:
Catholic, Orthodox, Anglican, Evangelical and other.

A Lutheran scholar and official observer at Vatican II, Edmund Schlink, takes exception to this criterion. He perceives that in evaluating the rest of Christendom the Council's "first criterion is the Roman Catholic Church itself."[61] Schlink assesses this as an ecclesiological yardstick which corresponds to the magisterial office and thinking in the Church. He surmises that use of such a yardstick
generated a quantitative judgment regarding the number of
elements which link the separated churches with the Council's
Church. Thus Schlink affirms:

> This quantified thinking determines the order
> of precedence of non-Roman churches. In this
> connection the presence of hierarchical order
> in the apostolic succession of ordination plays
> a special role.[62]

This last observation suggests that the elements are not of
equal weight, and that perhaps priority of nature should be
presupposed in the Council's thought rather than mere quantity of common elements.

In any event, Schlink observed that the Will of Christ and
the action of the Holy Spirit provided other yardsticks within the Council and its documents. He preferred these so-
called Christological and pneumatological criteria because
he felt them equivalent to "the biblical yardstick common to
all churches", which teaches from the perspective of the experience of mysterious oneness in Christ.[63] Schlink felt
that a mutual ecumenical understanding could begin only from
the biblical and not from the ecclesiological yardstick.

Further, Schlink judged that dogmas believed and reaffirmed
by The Council Fathers, especially supreme and universal
papal primacy and also the Council's failure to consider the
World Council of Churches, limited the value of the *Decree
on Ecumenism*. Despite some acknowledged benefits of renewal
and updating, the bottom line of Schlink's analyses is that
the ecumenical decree is a rather narrow in-house ecumenism.
"The net result of these analyses is that the ecumenism of
the decree is a specifically Roman ecumenism."[64]

If, as a pastor in the Reformed Church and Secretary General
of the World Council of Churches, Willem Visser't Hooft
shared Schlink's sentiments concerning the *Decree on Ecumenism*, he did not express them in his *Memoirs*. His acknowledgment was understandably restrained; the end of ecumenism
was beyond the horizon. However, "the fact remained that
the new decree represented a decisively important new development in the attitude of the Roman Catholic Church to other
Churches."[65] Furthermore, the Council had dealt with World
Council agenda topics; what happened in St. Peter's "had
profound and far-reaching significance for the whole ecumenical movement."[66]

CHAPTER TEN

POST-CONCILIAR DIRECTIONS

The judgment that the Vatican Council Agenda had overlapped the WCC Agenda received public support in the almost immediate formation of a "Joint Working Group" (abbreviated as JWG), consisting of eight World Council members and six Roman Catholic members, to explore the avenues of dialogue and collaboration between the World Council and the Roman Catholic Church. Six months after the ecumenical decree's publication in November 1964, the Joint Working Group (JWG) met in Geneva.[1]

The *Decree on Ecumenism* had enunciated Roman Catholic principles and practices of ecumenism in relationship with the separated Christian churches of both East and West. Its impact on the Roman Catholic World continues to be enormous and expectedly uneven. Vatican directives are interpreting, in a practical way, the Council's document.

Ecumenical Directory: Part I

In May of 1967 Pope Paul confirmed and ordered to be published the *Ecumenical Directory: Part I*[2], developed by the Secretariat for Promoting Christian Unity (SPCU), for the purpose of implementing and precisioning the Conciliar decree on ecumenism throughout the Roman Catholic world. This official document (24 pages) gives directives for setting up ecumenical commissions or local secretariats in Roman Catholic dioceses throughout the world; it further considers the question of doubtful baptism, the fostering of "Spiritual Ecumenism," and "the sharing of spiritual activity and resources with our separated brethren."[3]

The *Directory* rests fully on the *Decree on Ecumenism*. It manifests concern lest ecumenism be seen as a watering down of Catholicism. "'Ecumenical activity cannot be other than fully and sincerely Catholic,....'"[4]

The *Directory* reminds ecumenists that ecumenical policy decisions belong to the Apostolic See and the bishops, and further, that the extremes of "false irenicism or indifferentism"

will injure both the movement and the faithful while, on the
opposite side, fear of engaging in proper activity will prevent the renewal adjustments required by the Council.[5] The
modern ecumenical movement initiated by the Holy Spirit requires the renewal and growth of the faithful in the gifts
of Christ; blocking the work of the decree appears equivalent
to obstructing the plan of God.[6]

Mutual recognition of the sacrament of Baptism is sought by
the *Directory*, unless reasonable doubt concerning the cleans-
ing with water while using the Trinitarian formula hinders
such recognition.[7]

This only-once-to-be-conferred baptism, needed for salvation
by the will of Christ, links other Christians to the Roman
Catholic Church even though they neither hold the faith in
its entirety nor recognize the need of "'unity of communion
with the successor of Peter.'"[8]

This bond resulting from baptism is real, even though it is
less than full and perfect. The Roman Catholic Church has
no question about the fact that the baptism which incorporates a person into Christ also certainly initiates communion
with her by means of a transcendent and invisible connecting
link.

Those truly baptized are brothers and sisters in Christ.
When they go separate ecclesial ways, they are separated
Christians. Reaffirming the theological insight of the Coun-
cil's documents, the *Directory* insists

> Baptism is, then, the sacramental bond of
> unity, indeed the foundation of communion
> among all Christians. Hence its dignity and
> manner of administering it are matters of
> great importance to all Christ's disciples.[9]

The *Directory* instructs ecumenists to bring up in dialogue
the whole matter of baptism's theology and administration by
which persons are initiated into Christ's new covenant. The
dialogue which deals not only with the externals of the "sacramental sign," but also probes the meaning of the "reality
signified" will deepen the appreciation of the bond between
the Catholic Church and the other separated churches and
communities.[10]

In calling for *metanoia* (renewal in holiness and prayer for
the unity of Christians), the *Directory* repeats the call of
the ecumenical decree and suggests that these spiritual means
which are regarded as "'the soul of the whole ecumenical
movement'"[11] should be used also on appropriate occasions

added to the "Week of Prayer for Christian Unity."

In the matter of sharing spiritual activity with separated
brethren, the *Directory* introduces a new expression to distinguish the activities which may be shared between Christians linked with differing degrees of unity.   The new expression, *communicatio in spiritualibus* (sharing in spiritual
things), is distinguished from *communicatio in sacris* (sharing
in sacred things); this latter expression, which is primarily
focused on the sacraments, and especially the eucharist, has a
centuries-old cautionary connotation.   The former expression
is directed to the sharing of prayer, the liturgy of the
word, and sacred places.

The distinction aims at the degree of authentic sharing
which can take place without compromising the belief position of the "united yet divided" Christians.   The *principle*
presupposed appears to be: what is honestly and fully believed in common may become the basis of a genuine, shared
religious activity.

Belief in Christ's baptism can yield a shared baptismal liturgy and mutual acceptance of each other's baptism; common
belief in sacred scripture can yield a shared scriptural
liturgy; shared belief in the apostolic and priestly episcopacy and eucharist may *sometimes* yield a shared eucharist
which preserves Christian integrity;* a common belief in
Christ's establishment of the petrine principle would manifest to all Christ's one and unique Church.

A shared liturgy in which half the people coming together
denied the faith basis of the liturgy would be a false affirmation.   It would be a public act, as of a faith-community,
by a group which in fact was not a community of faith. Christian unity without a shared faith is a false unity which
cannot last.   Thus, a shared eucharistic liturgy (frequently
identified merely as intercommunion) should not precede the
belief-unity of the participants.   Those who deny Christian
episcopacy and priesthood cannot be a single faith-community
with those who believe them necessary for a valid and full
eucharist.

A lack of shared belief also precludes reciprocity in practice.   Even when a critical Christian belief is shared, as
belief in the seven sacraments is shared by Orthodox and
Roman Catholics, one party is not to intrude into the other's
liturgy without permission.   Such intrusion forestalls the

---

*Caution must be observed here because shared eu-
charist is the *proper sign* of fully achieved unity.

progress of ecumenism. The *Directory* reminds bishops that
"in granting permission for sharing in the sacraments it is
fitting that the greatest possible attention be given to reciprocity."[12]

The sacraments are actions of the ecclesial community performed inside the community. They signify the unity "in
faith, worship and life of the community."[13] Where this unity in faith in the sacraments is lacking, the *Directory* says
that "participation..., especially in the sacraments of the
Eucharist, Penance and Anointing of the Sick, is forbidden."[14]

Yet the prohibition is not absolute. If in urgent need and
away from his own minister, a separated Christian manifesting
true belief and right disposition freely seeks these sacraments, a priest may give them to him. A Catholic in a reciprocal case "may not ask for these sacraments except from a
minister who has been validly ordained."[15] Thus, the easily-
applied principle of reciprocity, which many people take as a
final test, must cede to theological principle of sacramental
validity. The final test must be Christian truth rather than
reciprocal ease.

A year and a half after the promulgation of the *Directory*,
cautionary "notes" were issued by the Secretariat for Promoting Christian Unity. This official publication (Cardinal
Bea's last) pointed out that the norms for the admission of
separated Protestant brothers to the Eucharist were being
violated. Only spiritual disposition and the person's own
request were being taken into account; nonavailability of the
person's own-faith minister in the urgent necessity and sacramental faith in harmony with the Church's faith were again explicitly identified as requirements.[16] Urgent necessity has
generally been specified in this case as imprisonment, persecution or danger of death; the local bishop may judge that
other cases share the necessary urgency.[17]

Ecumenical Directory: Part II

Two years later, over the name of John Cardinal Willebrands,
who had replaced the deceased Bea, the Secretariat for Promoting Christian Unity issued the *Ecumenical Directory: Part
II*. Pope Paul VI approved it and ordered it published. Thus,
these directories are normative documents endowed with the
highest approval.

The *Ecumenical Directory: Part II* focuses its attention exclusively on ecumenism in higher education. It appears to be
more of a prodding and suggesting document, designed to implement seriously and universally the production of an ecumenical mind among Catholics at the seminary and university levels

of education. The document implies a determined stance for
the long haul until the ecumenical goal is reached. As
identified in the *Decree on Ecumenism,* the goal is still
the unity of all Christians as Christ's single people of one
faith and celebrating the same eucharistic mystery.[18]

Spiritual and theological formation is a necessary preparation, after which dialogue and cooperation, even at the institutional and seminary levels, is forthrightly encouraged.
Seminary subjects are to be characterized by an ecumenical
frame of mind. Scripture is significantly specified as "the
common source of the faith of all Christians"; canon lawyers
are cautioned to distinguish carefully the elements of the
divine law from those of "merely ecclesiastical law."[19]
Minted into common coinage is Pope John's distinction between "the deposit of faith itself" and the "varying ways of
expressing it," "often complementary rather than contradictory."[20]

The *Directory: Part II* reinforces the evaluative norm that
among Catholic doctrines, which "all demand a due assent of
faith," there still exists a hierarchy in order based on
"their relationship to the foundation of the Christian
faith."[21]

Theologian Thomas Stransky succinctly illuminates this concept of "hierarchy of truths" with a series of examples.

> Grace has more importance than sin, sancti-
> fying grace more than actual grace, the Holy
> Spirit more than Our Lady, the resurrection
> of Christ more than His childhood, the mysti-
> cal aspect of the Church more than its juri-
> dical, the Church's liturgy more than private
> devotions: baptism more than penance, the
> Eucharist more than the anointing of the
> sick.[22]

The *Directory: Part II* strongly supports the outreach of the
prior ecumenical documents and provides an outline of inquiry
and activity for the diocesan secretariats mandated three
years earlier.

Declaration on Shared Eucharist

In the same year as the publication of the *Directory: Part II*
(1970), the Vatican Secretariat for Promoting Christian Unity
(SPCU) issued a sharp declaration with negative overtones on
the matter of the "eucharist in common" among Roman Catholics,
Anglicans, and Protestants. The document is entitled *Declaration on the Position of the Catholic Church on the Celebration*

*of the Eucharist in Common by Christians of Different Confes-
sions.*[23]

This document, more briefly referred to as the *Declaration on
Shared Eucharist,* brings no new norms or rules to the fore;
it rather quotes verbatim for emphasis the instructions of
the original conciliar *Decree,* the *Directory I,* and Bea's
cautionary *Note.* Apparently Roman Catholic-Anglican-Protes-
tant eucharistic interchanges were proceeding without regard
to the real theological relation between ecclesial and eucharistic communion.[24] The eucharist was being used as a
means rather than as the crowning act of a community fully
united as Church.

The *Declaration on Shared Eucharist* recalled again the Orthodox preservation of apostolic succession, priesthood, and eucharist as distinguishing the Eastern churches from the churches and the ecclesial communities of the West. With the
Orthodox, shared eucharistic worship is cautiously recommend-
ed under appropriate conditions; with the Western churches
and ecclesial assemblies it is *generally ruled out.*[25] This
general norm yields to the special cases of persons in such
urgent necessity as danger of death, imprisonment or persecution; here too, full faith, own minister lacking, own request,
and right dispositions are again required.[26]

The *Declaration* relates the doctrine of *full* sacramental life
to the appeal for dialogue, noting that ministerial priesthood is a requirement in Roman Catholic belief.

> ...the Catholic Church attaches a *decisive*
> importance to the traditional teaching about
> the necessity of the ministerial priesthood
> connected with Apostolic succession...[27]

Since the 1970 *Declaration* is restating the eucharistic norms
of the *Ecumenical Directory,* the Secretariat included Pope
Paul's affirmation on the *Directory's* authenticity in an address to the Cardinal and bishops of the Secretariat.

> We need not tell you that, to promote ecumen-
> ism in an efficacious way, one must also guide
> it, submit it to the rules that are quite pre-
> cise. We regard the Ecumenical Directory not
> as a collection of advisory principles which
> one can freely accept or ignore, but as an
> authentic instruction, an exposition of the
> discipline to which all those who wish truly
> to serve ecumenism should submit themselves.[28]

The Secretariat noted that it was giving continuing attention

to this question which frequently surfaced in ecumenical dialogues. However, "these dialogues have not yet produced results which can be adopted on both sides by those who have
responsibility in the churches and ecclesial communities involved."[29]

The Secretariat closed its *Declaration on Shared Eucharist* by
praising the desire for a shared eucharist as a powerful spur
to the drive toward the full ecclesial unity intended by
Christ, even though the warning against indiscriminate use
was the reason for the document.[30]

Dialogue Guide

In August of the same year (1970), the Secretariat for promoting Christian Unity issued a working instrument on the modern phenomenon of ecumenical dialogue among separated Christians. In plenary session the forty bishop-members of the
Secretariat declined to make the dialogue guide a part of the
official, juridical *Directory,* but preferred that it be sent
as an aid, resting on the value of its own insights, to the
Roman Catholic bishops of the world. The Joint Working Group
(JWG) between the World Council and the Roman Catholic Church
had already done a study on ecumenical dialogue, and undoubtedly some of the experience and insights of the JWG flowed
into the Secretariat's dialogue guide.[31]

The 1970 *Dialogue Guide* (22 pages) rests solidly (over thirty
references) on the 1964 Conciliar *Decree on Ecumenism.*
Stressed again are fidelity to apostolic, patristic and ecclesial truth, fullness of Christ's means in the Catholic
Church, and elements elsewhere, emphasis on scripture, hierarchy of truths, and equal-basis ('*par cum pari*') dialogue.

The *Dialogue Guide* (called the *Guide*) adds a distinction to
the *Decree's* affirmation that "the *unity* of Christ's one and
only Church dwells in the Catholic Church" by indicating that
the "*fullness* of this unity" remains open to the future "as
the great gift that God alone will bestow, in the way and at
the time that He wishes."[32]

The *Guide* takes care to point out that the equality, which it
calls for, pertains to the dialogue participants as to their
mutual openness, sympathy, receptivity, level of competency,
and commitment, but *not* to an assumption that the ecclesial
communities represented are equal fulfillments of the one
Church of Christ.

> In ecumenical dialogue, those who take part
> recognize honestly that because of existing
> differences there is an inequality

between the different Christian Communions.
Hence they reject on the one hand that doctrinal indifferentism which would claim that,
before the mystery of Christ and the Church,
all positions are equivalent. On the other
they do not pass any judgment regarding the
willingness of one side or the other to be
faithful to the Gospel.[33]

The *Dialogue Guide* cautions that dialogue is never a debate
whose end is victory, but rather a mutually sympathetic probing of the unfathomable riches of Christ to find common
ground and a healing reconciliation of differences. The Roman Catholic participant is reminded that his work is to express

his Church's faith, without either over-
stating it or minimizing it, remembering
that ecumenical encounter is not merely an
individual work, but also the task of the
Church, which takes precedence over all
individual opinions.[34]

The document, which strictly confines itself to dialogue
specifically among Christians, assumes that each participant
will express the doctrine of his own ecclesial body and suggests that this be done in a positive, constructive way rather than by negatively caricaturing the position of the other.
Constructive synthesis is to be sought, while recognizing
that dialogue alone cannot eliminate all differences. Some
differences will at the time be seen as irreducible.[25]

In defining that any real-life Christian-faith subject is
proper matter for dialogue, the *Guide* affirms the special
value of subjects such as scripture, the sacraments and liturgical life. The *Guide* significantly calls attention to
the documents of the World Council of Churches as well as to
those of Vatican II.[36] Since this working guide confined
itself to dialogue, it did not explicitly bring up the activity of *communicatio in sacris* (or intercommunion), which
topic, nevertheless, continued to demand the *Secretariat's*
attention.

Already mentioned were the three cautions against intercommunion of '67, '68, and '70. An apparent slowness in honoring the norms evoked two more official statements from the
Secretariat, in 1972 and in 1973. Neither document backed
down from the position taken; both showed concern lest intru-
sive intercommunion destroy the very unity it professed to
seek. Intercommunion of contradictory faiths makes unity a
charade whose doctrinal basis is privately and in conscience

denied. The warning documents explained the theological doctrine underlying the *Decree on Ecumenism,* not a diminution of
its norms.

Instruction: On Admitting to Communion

The 1972 document, *On Admitting Other Christians to Eucharistic Communion In the Catholic Church,*[37] referred to as *Instruction: On Admitting to Communion,* insisted on the intimate connection which is the Church and the Body of Christ
which is the eucharist.[38]

The document used expressions such as "close link," "simultaneously and inseparably," "strict relationship," and "essential relation" to describe the connection between ecclesial and eucharistic communion.[39]

The Church expresses its fullness in its eucharistic liturgy,
and the eucharist is the flowering of the Church's realized
unity. The eucharist is an expression of unity which rests
on apostolic episcopal succession, the oneness of ministry
from Christ, and the full faith of the Church. The document
spells out these three elements as presupposed and inclusive-
ly carried in its eucharistic liturgy.

> The Eucharist really contains what is the very
> foundation of the being and Unity of the Church:
> ...the sacrament...of its nature carries with it:
> a) the *ministerial* power which Christ gave to
> his apostles and to their successors, the bishops
> along with the priests, to make effective sacra-
> mentally his own priestly act—that act by which
> once and forever he offered himself to the Father
> in the Holy Spirit and gave himself to his faith-
> ful that they might be one in him;
> b) the *unity of the ministry,* which is to be
> exercised in the name of Christ, Head of the
> Church, and hence in the hierarchial communion
> of ministers;
> c) the *faith of the Church,* which is expressed
> in the Eucharistic action, itself—the faith by
> which she responds to Christ's gift in its true
> meaning.[40]

The Roman Catholic teaching authority believes that much more
is involved in what some have underestimatingly termed "intercommunion" than the mere courteous reciprocity of a religious act between divided Christian communities. The eucharistic liturgy is the summit toward which the other sacraments
and beliefs are ordered. Its celebration "is the center of
the whole Christian life, for the Universal Church as for the

local Church and for each Christian."[41]

In this summit mystery the Church most fully realizes her own
identity as the Body of Christ. The sacramental communion inherently expresses the realized communion of faith and order
from Christ. "...in the Mass, the Church celebrates her own
mystery and manifests concretely her unity."[42]

It is on the basis of this intimate connection between ecclesial and eucharistic communion that the 1972 document,
Instruction: On Admitting to Communion, repeats its clear reserve on the matter of "intercommunion."

In the following year the Secretariat issued another publication to prevent any inaccurate interpretations or misapplica-
tions of the instruction. This 1973 publication is identified as a *Note* (or the 1973 *Note*), interpreting the previous
instruction.[43] Ecumenical contacts were multiplying rapidly.
Local, regional and international meetings were increasing;
many of them prepare common prayer sessions. The World Council of Churches always includes common worship at its assemblies. There is increasing pressure to practice "intercommunion."

For many Protestant Christians interchange of worship presents no problem; for others, as well as for Orthodox and Roman Catholics, such interchange presents a significant doctrinal problem. The pressure for full common worship is a wish
for full ecclesial unity, and thus, a blessing. But the summit cannot exist unless the necessary faith-foundation supports it. Thus, again, the Secretariat addressed this problem.

The 1973 *Note* added nothing new to the previous documents by
way of norm or rule. It expressed some prior data more con-
cisely. Thus, the connection between the mysteries of ecclesial and eucharistic communions were identified as an *indissoluble link;* also, the admission-to-communion norm was
specified as a discipline which "derives from the requirements of the faith and so retains its full vigor."[44]

This ecclesial/eucharistic bond, generally indivisible in the
thought of the Vatican documents, appears to be the doctrinal
key governing the practice of Roman Catholic bishops throughout the world.

Where communion of apostolic episcopacy and sacramental
priesthood exist (constituents of a local church), eucharistic communion may be reciprocally granted even though total
unity is not yet secured. The ecclesial/eucharistic connection is not obscured for either the communicant or observers.
Where the ecclesial constituents are either denied, lacking

or in doubt, the Secretariat considers that the essential relation between "eucharist and Church" is lacking or obscured;
consequently, the SPCU determined, with papal approval, that
communicants of such Churches and ecclesial assemblies should
only be given the eucharist in urgent necessity.[45]

The eucharist is believed to be the expression of full doctrinal and ecclesial communion, and thus, of the full visible
unity of Christ's Church. It preserves and deepens the very
ecclesial unity which produced it. The Secretariat does not
think it allowable to reduce this awesome Eucharistic sacrament to a *means* for seeking unity among Christians divided in
belief.[46]

The 1973 *Note* ends by casting a longing eye on the final ecumenical goal of creed, cult and code: one faith, one bread,
one body.

> We express the hope that the ecumenical move-
> ment will lead to a common profession of faith
> among Christians, and so allow us to celebrate
> the Eucharist in ecclesial unity...[47]

In a notable, mutual interchange of official delegations between Rome and Constantinople, Pope Paul VI indicated that a
common eucharist would be a final and crowning act signifying
full union between the Catholic Church and the Orthodox
Church. Paul VI declared that the Holy Spirit has shown us
more clearly that

> the Catholic Church and the Orthodox Church
> are united by such a deep communion that very
> little is lacking to reach the fullness au-
> thorizing a common celebration of the Lord's
> Eucharist.[48]

Demetrios I, Patriarch of Constantinople, had decided to set
up a special commission for dialogue with Rome; he had also
persuaded the Orthodox Churches to compose a pan-Orthodox
commission to prepare for an Orthodox theological dialogue.[49]
On the occasion Pope Paul affirmed that both churches lived
the life of sister communities having the

> same sacraments,...the same priesthood which
> celebrates the same Eucharist of the Lord...
> the same episcopate received in the same
> apostolic succession....[50]

Although the foregoing expressions and sentiments: "deep communion," "very little lacking" for celebration, "sister churches" suggest that the restoration of Orthodox-Roman Catholic

unity is not far off, and although the division is now appreciated as "intolerable, disproportionate,...ruinous...and un-
sustainable with regard to the divine plan bent on making the
scattered and multiform flock of Christ 'one flock and one
shepherd' (Jn. 10:16),"[51] nevertheless profound difficulties
still block the road to Orthodox/Catholic unity.

This historic division took place in a formal act at the top.
The steps and expressions leading toward reunion are taking
place at the top. But each community's massive body of
faithful has grown apart in mind and history. The enormity
of the task is sensed when Paul VI voices hope amid the "difficulties that seem to make insoluble the problem of the re-
unification of divided Christians in the one Catholic Church
...the communitarian body of Christ...."[52]

Beyond the difficulties of differing histories and psycholo-
gies Pope Paul notes pointedly the

> ... question of overcoming the formidable and
> atavistic anti-Roman objection, unjustified in
> our opinion, but still surviving particularly
> on the theological and canonical front. How is
> it possible to bring about the restoration of
> the unity of Christians, recognizing the in-
> trinsic necessities of real ecclesiastical
> unity, without overcoming obstacles which the
> genius of division has worked for centuries
> to make inseparable?[53]

The Pontiff concludes that the needed change of mind, deeper
insight in studies, and modification of inter-Christian attitudes cannot produce the desired end without special divine
help, which must ceaselessly be sought in prayer.[54]

Within the framework of his closing greeting to all Christians, Pope Paul first mentions "Catholics, who enjoy with us
the inestimable gift of the unity of the Church", and then,
"all our Christian brethren still separated from us, so that
they may know they are remembered, loved and awaited;...."[55]
Thus, Paul combines the council's doctrinal belief with his
own pastoral outlook. He reaffirms what he cannot change;
in changeable matters he has executed many far-reaching modifications within the Roman Catholic community. In seeking
the fullness of the gift of unity, he has declared his intention of continuing to remove every removable obstacle to that
fullness.[56] The persons, the assemblies of the separated
brothers are remembered, loved; their changes and overtures
are awaited.

Who belongs to the Church?

On another occasion, in a remarkable speech, Pope Paul indicated quite clearly that separated brothers are in the Church,
even though in a less visible and less full way.   In his letter to the Ephesians, the Apostle Paul did not hesitate to
speak of "members of the Church" (Eph. 1:15-19); Vatican II
chose to consider only remotely and in principle the question
of membership in the Church.   Pope Paul confronted it by asking directly, "Who belongs to the Church?"[57]

Having constructed the question, the Pope gave a simple first-
level answer, "through baptism...a person enters the Church."[58]
Bypassing the life-giving implications of Christian initiation into Christ's Church, his Mysterious Body, the Pope
formulated the more difficult question about his separated
brothers.

> Are all those who have been baptized, even
> those who are separated from Catholic Unity,
> in the Church? In the true Church? In the
> one Church? Yes.[59]

In rapid succession, the Pontiff cited Vatican II, the Creed,
Patristic, and Papal writing in support of this great and
far-reaching implication of baptism.   The sense of the grades
of union placed his primary affirmation in its modern perspective.   The doctrine of baptism pervades the ecumenical
question in Roman Catholic thought.

> This doctrine is the basis of our ecumenism,
> which makes us regard as brothers the Chris-
> tians who are separated from us, and all the
> more so if, with Baptism and faith in Christ
> and in the Mystery of the Blessed Trinity,
> they preserve many other treasures of our
> common Christian heritage.[60]

In noting the Christian elements which constitute bonds, the
opposite side of the picture is clearly implied. As one
thinks of other sacraments such as penance, anointing of the
sick, priesthood, etc., one notes that the absence of these
elements as common belief constitutes division. Thus, the
Pope develops his thought into the perception of full or
partial union.

> But is Baptism and a certain amount of faith
> enough to belong fully to the Church? We have
> to recall that this fullness, this perfect com-
> munion is a profound and inextinguishable re-
> quirement of the religious order established

> by Christ. If belonging to the Church in at
> least an initial or partial way is highly
> valuable, then it is just as desirable for
> this belonging to reach its full measure.
> The Church is one and unique. There are not
> several Churches standing by themselves and
> sufficient unto themselves. The sovereign
> law of unity intimately governs the religious
> society established by the Lord.[61]

This papal statement, starting with the unity of baptismal
life, then acknowledging the points of partial separation,
and closing with the hoped-for goal of fully healed or restored unity, suggests an analogy of the recuperation of a
badly wounded accident victim, or better perhaps, a soldier.
Severely wounded in battle, but not mortally, the soldier
would be recovering his wholeness, his fullness, as his torn
limbs knit together again. The analogy is not urbane, but
neither is the picture of the partially knit, partially severed assemblies of Christ's one Church.

The analogy safeguards the radical unity of life, the organic
unity of Christ's unique Church, while keeping visible its unhealed, its partially severed, state. Many have become so accustomed to the Church's unhealed, wounded condition, that
they seem satisfied with the divided state, as if one member
(or assembly) of the body could say to another, "I do not
need You." There is only one Church, but many different local
assemblies. "There are, indeed, many different members, but
one body. The eye cannot say to this hand, 'I do not need
you.'"[62]

The analogy seeks to preserve the visible Christ-given unity,
while acknowledging the manifest wounds of division. It affirms the one life in all the parts. The analogy likewise
implies the program of healing; it further envisions the goal
of the fullness of unity restored. It also tends to preclude a return to the idea of an invisible church, or the
notion that there are two churches, one visible and one invisible.

Seeing the struggle between the unity-seeking and autonomy-
seeking forces in the Christian world, Pope Paul insists on
the Roman Catholic commitment to the side of unity.

> Rome, certainly not faultless...stubbornly
> affirms and promotes this unity as her duty.
> ...It is the authentically ecumenical and
> unitarian force, which is seeking its prin-
> ciple and its center, the base which Christ
> ...chose and fixed in his stead, to signify

and perpetuate the foundations of his kingdom.

> The unity of the Church...is already a real-
> ity, in spite of the deficiencies of the men
> composing it. However it is not complete, it
> is not perfect in the statistical and social
> framework of the world, it is not universal.[63]

Thus, do the determinations and documentary expressions of
Vatican II continue to be presented and reworked in further
detail by the Council's acknowledged authoritative leader.
Pope Paul's weekly addresses are generously laced with the
concepts of Vatican II. From the Apostolic See, the believed
"center of unity,"[64] the Pontiff, personally and through the
Secretariat for Promoting Christian Unity, has, in the mid-
seventies, stressed the ecumenical duty of the local (diocesan) churches and their national conferences. The fullest
expression of this was the Vatican Secretariat's publication
in 1975 of the document entitled, *Ecumenical Collaboration
at the Regional, National and Local Levels,*[65] more conveniently referred to by the title *Ecumenical Collaboration.*

Ecumenical Collaboration

This document is a collaboration guide comparable to the previously issued *Dialogue Guide*. It was developed by the Secretariat as an aid to the Catholic bishops of the world. As
a whole, it does not enjoy the same juridicial status as the
Directory, nevertheless the contents of it, which derive from
the conciliar documents and the Vatican's official decisions,
do have the force of law.[66] John Cardinal Willebrands, President of the SPCU, was the responsible signer of the document; Pope Paul VI approved it as an aid to the bishops.

Ecumenical Collaboration considers the relation of the diocesan Church to the ecumenical movement; it lists the many
forms of local ecumenism open to the local church. Starting
from strictly religious acts such as sharing in prayer and
worship, the document enumerates cooperative activities of
slightly diminishing religious character extending out even
into the health field.[67] The point of view seems to be an
extension outward from the center of Christian belief. Somewhat as the Council considered primarily the core matters of
the Church, and afterwards considered the extension of Apostolic influence to the world's besetting problems in *The Pastoral Constitution on the Church in the Modern World (Gaudium
et Spes)*, so this collaborative document seems to follow a
similar centrifugal path.

Common Bible work, joint pastoral care, shared premises and
educational concerns can readily yield a workable Christian

common denominator, whereas health work, national emergencies and
social problems are frequently beyond the capacity of a local
ecumenical body to resolve, even though not beyond its Christian concern and possible influential activity. The modern
state is usually the primary agent in these latter areas of
human need. Collaborating churches can contribute a Christian motive and perspective.

From another point of view, the contents of this thirty-page
document appear to combine the concerns of Faith and Order
and those of Life and Work under the umbrella title of *Ecumenical Collaboration*. Bilateral doctrinal dialogue groups
and the more pervasive social development groups are both described as forms of local ecumenism. Thus, this 1975 collaboration document has many points of contact with the documents of the World Council of Churches.

Ecumenical Collaboration repeats the Papal and Conciliar acknowledgment that the "ecumenical movement is a movement of
the Spirit wider than any of the particular initiatives
through which it is manifested."[68] The Bishops of Vatican II
believe that the same Holy Spirit led them to the "accentua-
tion of the Christian positive" as contained in their *Decree
on Ecumenism*.

Among the separated brothers, the movement had *ascended* from
local agency form to the international level of the World
Council; in the Roman Catholic world, Vatican II had achieved
the critical turn-about and its insight and directive had *de-
scended* and been hesitantly and unevenly effected at the level of
the diocese.* In conciliar view, the union of Christians professing one faith and gathered in the one Church of Christ in
its one eucharist must take place at the diocesan (local)
level if ecumenism is fully to reach its term. Thus, the
diocesan or particular church is critically important.

In a diocesan church, its bishop (in union with the other
bishops and the pope) is the visible and basic principle of
unity.[69] The particular diocesan church is the universal
Church in a precise locality. *In* these local churches *and of
them*, but not merely of them as of a doctrinally-divided col-
lectivity, the one and unique Catholic Church exists.[70] The
point of view is that of the one living Church rooting itself
in local diversities, rather than of a collection of diversified organizational entities searching for a common base to

---

    *From the point of view of terminology, diocesan
church, particular church, Cathedral or Episcopal Church,—
all identify the same units within the Church Universal.

become a single ecclesiastical reality. *Ecumenical Collaboration* sees local diversity and the limits of that diversity
as an out-reach rooted in unity.

> ...the dynamic of Catholic life as the local
> church makes it present both in its particu-
> larity and in its concrete universality. With
> the awareness that in a given place it is the
> vehicle of the presence and action of the
> Catholic Church which is fundamentally one,
> the local church will be ready to take care
> that its free initiatives do not go beyond
> its competence and are always undertaken
> within the limits of the doctrine and disci-
> pline of the whole Catholic Church, particular-
> ly as this touches the sacraments.[71]

Where the faithful are thus united with and in the Universal
Church,and locally with their bishop in lived faith and a
love which contains any necessary obedience, they, as local
church, are a visible sign of the universal Church, and
hence of the invisible Christ's effectiveness. Some local
poverty in faith and love always clothes the visible sign
with shadows of inadequacy; yet, despite this, the local
flock gathered about its faithful shepherd is a sign.

By such local and universal bonds of communion in the particular church "an irreplaceable sacramental expression is given
to the living unity of the Catholic Church," according to
Ecumenical Collaboration."[72]

Added to this given unity,the document affirms another aspect
of unity which, based on baptism, has produced a real, but
yet deficient, communion between Christian churches and ecclesial assemblies; existent ecumenical activities and organizations give expression to this definite but incomplete unity,which is to be prudently fostered by the bishops.[73] The
ecumenical activities and organizations present a providential opportunity for growth toward the fullness of unity while
simultaneously presenting "problems and difficulties which
have to be solved in the light of Catholic principles of ecumenism."[74]

With the vantage point of input from all the dioceses of the
world the 1975 collaboration document notes that the observ-
ance of the Prayer-for-Unity Week, either in January or before Pentecost,"continues to be in most places the chief occasion on which Catholics and other Christians pray together."[75]
Further, common worship within the canonical limits prescribed
in previous documents is definitely promoted, as "normal Catholic ecumenical activity."[76]

Ecumenical Collaboration encourages common research, translation, production and distribution of the Bible and cooperation in pastoral care in such places as hospitals, armed
forces and prisons; however, the norm for the sharing of
premises is that "Catholic *Churches* are reserved for Catholic
worship" with exceptions permitted in response to needs and
emergencies.[77] Apparently, serious doctrinal differences can
lead to architectural barrenness, as well as new acrimony.

In almost every field of collaboration there are some areas
in which the cooperation can be full and wholehearted, while
at the same time there are other areas in which division in
belief precludes unity of action. Education is another example of this divided terrain in the collaboration document.
Sharing of most buildings, libraries, and even many common
classes can be achieved.

> But as long as Christians are not fully at one
> in faith, *catechesis,* which is formation for
> profession of faith, must remain necessarily
> the proper and inalienable task of the various
> churches and ecclesial communities.[78]

This same disjunction marks the Secretariat's presentation on
"councils of churches," whether on the local, national, or
regional (a group of nations) levels; the World Council is
considered as a different category.[79] *Ecumenical Collabora-*
tion notes that these councils throughout the world differ
in their activities and constitutions even though, in general,
they foster common service, some seeking of Christian unity
and some limited witness.[80] For the most part,the various
levels of councils are not structurally related to each other
as local organizations of national bodies or vice versa;
rather, despite nominal similarity, they are independent and
differently constituted bodies. Thus, each diocesan bishop
on the local level, and conferences of bishops on the national level, must make a theological and prudential judgment on
the question of joining the given council of churches.[81]

In English,the very concept of "council," which in Latin and
other languages[82] requires one word for consultation (*con-*
silium) and a different word for a union of persons (*concil-*
ium), gives rise to an ambiguity requiring some care in use.
The basis of the second Vatican Ecumenical Council or a national council (conference) of Catholic bishops is defined
as:

> ...a full and substantial communion of local
> Churches among themselves and with the Church
> of Rome which presides over the whole assembly
> of Charity.[83]

Creed, cult, ministry and tradition in common enable the local, national or world-wide assembly "to express the communion of the Catholic Church", according to the Secretariat. [84]
This concept of council expresses "Church." Such a council
or assembly is an act of the one communion or people. Thus,
the very expression "Council of Churches" suggests an ecclesial dimension which is open to misunderstanding. It is
necessary to distinguish a *Christian Council* from a *Council
of Churches;* both of these are different from a *Church Council.*

A *Christian Council,* composed of "Churches plus other agencies," is a distinct concept. The more the character of the
churches differ, the less such a council can have in common.
An inverse ratio governs this relationship.

Further, a council composed exclusively of churches which
agree in some Christian beliefs,while radically disagreeing
in others, is a different concept. This latter is called a
Council of Churches, as distinguished from the "churches plus
agencies" grouping above. Both are basically consultative.
Neither constitutes a full religious communion.

The mixed or Christian council (churches and other agencies)
has less of a base for seeking ecclesial unity and common
witness; on the other hand the council of churches, although
divided in belief, has a fuller base for seeking unity and
giving common witness in some degree proportionate to the dynamic force of its common belief. The World Council of
Churches is this latter type of consultative council on the
world level. The fellowship of doctrinally-divided churches
which it embodies "does not suppose at all the same degree of
communion expressed by ecumenical and provincial councils" [85]
previously noted in the *Ecumenical Collaboration* definition.

Common social work, common quest for more unity, and limited
common witness seem to characterize the consultative *consilium* (or fellowship) of churches, whereas one creed, one cult,
one ministry and common faith-life characterize a *concilium*
(or communion) of particular churches which is one universal
Church. Vatican II was a Church Council.

One may wonder whether the *consilium* (fellowship) is the be-
ginning of a new *concilium* (communion), whether the World
Council is the beginning of a new and great ecumenical
Church. [86] The Secretariat does not think so.

> ...councils of churches...do not in and of
> themselves contain in embryo the beginnings
> of a new Church which will replace the com-
> munion now existing within the Catholic Church.

They do not claim to be churches nor do they
claim authority to commission a ministry of
word and sacrament.[87]

Because *councils of churches* have a fuller ecclesial character than *Christian councils* (churches plus other agencies),
the Secretariat focused its attention on the former.

It observed that *councils of churches* although similar in nature were not uniform, nor were they subordinate parts of
each other,such that joining a local council meant joining a
national council, which in turn meant joining the World Council. Any given joining is a separate act with a differently
constituted organization.

In general these councils are not "church union" brokers,nor
are they the only organs through which churches can cooperate.
The authority of these councils is limited to that which the
member churches have granted them; each church governs its
own commitment to the council's acts.[88]

In view of the ecumenical *Decree's* directive of collaboration,
and in view of the foregoing practical principles among most
councils of churches, the Roman Catholic Bishops of nineteen
different countries have led their particular churches into
membership in their respective national councils of churches.
Thus, opening the 1980s

> ...the Catholic Church has [at least] full
> membership in 19 national councils of churches.
> In addition, there is considerable Catholic
> collaboration with councils and certain of
> their programmes at various levels.[89]

The World Council/Roman Catholic Joint Working Group (JWG) is
an example of collaboration at the international level, as
also is the joint agency for society, development and peace
known as Sodepax.[90]

The commended cooperation with councils of churches has thus
been initiated; however, the areas involved are in relatively
small countries,with fewer dioceses than the United States.
The collaboration has engaged particular or diocesan Roman
Catholic Churches as churches. The very document which promotes this collaboration does not hesitate to remind the
bishops that the local Church's entry into the ecumenical
arena is distinctly modified by the unity which their Church
enjoys and still has to bring to perfection.

> The documents of the Second Vatican Council
> expound clearly the conviction that the unity

which is the gift of Christ already exists
in the Catholic Church, although susceptible
of completion and perfection, and this qualifies significantly the Catholic participation
in the ecumenical movement.[91]

The dioceses contemplating collaboration are reminded again
by the forty Bishops of the Secretariat that rivalry is to
be shunned and the "appearance of indifference or of unwar-
ranted intermingling" is to be avoided.[92] Also, they are
cautioned that dealing with other churches (which are believed to lack the theological fullness of Christ's Church),
par cum pari is in no way to diminish the faith that the
unique Church of Christ "subsists in the Catholic Church."[93]

Interestingly, yet alarmingly for many, it is a declared diminution of faith in the uniqueness of the Church, and more
especially, in the supernatural transcendence of the Mass and
sacraments, that occasioned a schismatic movement led by
French Archbishop Marcel Lefebvre and some priests (he ordained) who came from different nations. The Archbishop,
now suspended from his priestly and episcopal rights and
duties, claims:

If we follow the Vatican now—this orientation which began in Vatican II—then we are
becoming Protestant, we are losing the Catholic faith.[94]

Ecumenical equality?

Holding the equal-partner (*par cum pari*) operational posture
in ecumenical collaboration, while preserving the faith conviction that Christ's Church subsists essentially in the Roman Catholic Church, with only elements of it elsewhere, is
rather difficult. It takes clear instruction to see and
maintain this equal/unequal collaboration, this matter of
being equal as representatives in a council of churches but
representing unequal ecclesial entities.

The equal use of the term 'Church' is against
it; the one-man/one-vote sense is against it;
the equality of persons militates against successful maintenance of this equal-representa-
tives/unequal-churches relationship.

Failure to maintain the equality side seems like a return to
triumphalism; failure to achieve the unequal side appears to
be the cessation of Catholicism and the acceptance of sectarian equality. Reverend Kenneth Baker, an editor of a 76-year
old Catholic Journal, far less extreme than Archbishop

Lefebvre, nevertheless expresses his alarm in similar terms.

> Millions of Catholics are confused-and that
> confusion has led to division. It seems to
> me that we are witnessing a wholesale Protes-
> tantization of the Catholic Church....[85]

On the other hand, many, who claimed the Roman Catholic Church
did not move far enough in the direction of other baptized
Christians, have left their Church.[96]

Other theologians, who have remained faithfully in the Church,
are also convinced that the Catholic Church has not moved
fast enough or far enough. Impatient with the pace of the
Vatican and the synodal meetings of bishops, these theologians
are calling for the start of the third ecumenical Vatican
Council.[97]

The spectrum of theological opinion within Roman Catholicism
has widened considerably since Vatican II. Archbishop Lefebvre is a type of a holding-back extreme; Father Hans Küng is
one on the other extreme who went beyond, and even *against*
Vatican II; he opposed defined Catholic doctrines.

Both have some difficult-to-measure influence on Church thinking; the end-point of one is apparently change-nothing, of
the other, it seems to be change nonchangeable doctrines. In
a day of avoiding censures, both men have been publicly rep-
rimanded by the Vatican; the Archbishop more, apparently because, as an archbishop, he is a church-maker, thus a schism-
maker. Father Küng has been deprived of his canonical mission
as a Catholic theologian; "...he can no longer be considered
a Catholic theologian nor function as such in a teaching
role."*

The Vatican documents maintain the position that not everything is changeable, yet much is changeable in mode but not
in faith content. Much has been changed, and continues to be
changed throughout the vast body of the Roman Catholic world.
The changes, which effect the whole body of Catholic believers,
continue to come about through the body of bishops in communion with Rome.[98] Thus, local bishops use the Vatican's *Ecumenical Collaboration* as an aid for the participation of the
local church in a local phase of the ecumenical movement.

---

*Sacred Congregation for the Doctrine of the Faith,
"Vatican Declaration on the theological Doctrine of the Reverend Hans Küng," *New York Times,* December 19, 1979. The
Times published the Vatican translation of the Latin text on
page A8.

When the local bishop leads his particular church in the local council of churches, he appears to acknowledge publicly
that the other churches are churches in some theological
sense of the term, even though he holds that they are not
fully the one Church of Christ. He also acknowledges that
the local council is a useful instrument for collaboration,
for working toward a fuller unity, and for some common witness.[99]

Again in each place, the difficult distinction of equal/un-
equal identity of member churches needs to be kept clear constitutionally and in the public view or else be lost in the
general sense of the people; vagueness here induces practical
indifferentism and false irenicism. Failure to join a local
council of churches makes the bishop appear 'above it all'
and indifferent to the acknowledged theological dimension of
the other Christian churches.[100] The document *Ecumenical
Collaboration* points out the Scylla and Charybdis between
which the local bishop must prudently navigate to avoid dis-
aster.

Although the local bishop may guide his particular or diocesan church into a local council of churches in a move which
is recognized as ecumenically positive, it is not at all
clear that this move is a way to the "church unity willed by
Christ" better than another way.

On the contrary, the division of beliefs represented in most
councils of churches tends to narrow their fields of operation to common actions in the practical fields of little or
no theological significance. As already suggested, the "immediate and bilateral"[101] interchange between Paul VI and
Dimitrios I appears closer to eucharistic concelebration than
does common action (in practical social matters). "Creed and
Moral Code" equivalence is more properly and proportionately
related to cultic or eucharistic unity (concelebration) than
common social, action which may nevertheless be an atmosphere
preparation for the higher goal.

Furthermore, some councils of churches make official *declarations*. Such declarations take positions which implicitly
teach. A particular church which disagrees with the declared
statement as to timing, propriety or content finds itself in
the untenable position of having its voice usurped, rendered
doubtful, and possibly contradicted before the church's own
members.

Consequently, more than ordinary foresight and leadership
integrity, added to constitutional safeguards, appear necessary to preserve the right of minority dissent and expression.[102] Acting on behalf of justice is truly a part of the

Gospel outreach, but the acceptable means to attain the ends
of justice can be difficult to formulate in some of society's
complex problems. Churches in councils need a guarantee
against being stampeded.[103]

Bishops and national episcopal conferences are reminded in
Ecumenical Collaboration that their decisions as to the ac-
ceptability and appropriateness of a given form of local ecumenical action or structure should be made "in cooperation
with the appropriate organ of the Holy See."[104] Also, as regards local conciliar *discussions,* it should be made clear to
all that "when Catholics take part in a council, they can
enter into such discussions only in conformity with the
teaching of their Church."[105] Moreover, delegates to a local
council need sharp awareness "of the limits beyond which they
cannot commit the Church without prior reference to higher
authority."[106]

Despite these limiting prescriptions, *Ecumenical Collaboration* positively encourages cooperation in prayer, dialogue
and action, especially when these are based on "common baptism
and a faith which in many essentials is also common."[107]
Bishops are urged to educate Catholics "concerning the implications of such participation."[108]

This document, *Ecumenical Collaboration,* ends a decade in
which the Roman Catholic Church had moved from a contemplation of her own unity, which almost excluded all others, to a
contemplation of that ecclesial unity which included, in at
least some way, all other baptized Christians. The emphasis
shifted from condemnation of theological errors to affirmation of true ecclesial elements; consequently, it proceeded
to theological dialogue and pastoral collaboration. The
change in priority from condemnation of error to affirmation
of the true continues to have incalculable effects.

In the process, this Church has reverbalized her entire sac-
ramentary; she then translated these reverbalizations into
the world's languages. She has shed some legitimate, prereformation, nonscriptural orders, such as subdiaconate and
minor orders, in order to highlight the continuity of the New
Testament's ministerial orders: bishop, presbyter, and deacon.
She is probing and reverbalizing her theological understandings and expressions in each country's catechetical guide.
Her entire code of canon law is fully rescructured and re-
stated.

But all the while she has focused her eyes on the one and
unique Church of Christ, which she believes continues to subsist in her, as the only final goal of authentic ecumenism.
She believes: that the one and only visible Church of Christ

never could, or can, be two churches; that in some way all
Christians must be gathered as Christ's one pilgrim people
in one ecclesial body around the petrine center Christ fixed
for it—one fold with one shepherd. She continues to modify
herself, and to re-express her creed, cult, code, and communion to enlarge her capacity for diversity within the unity
Christ intended: the Church realizes that her unity must
signify the mysterious, transcendent unity of Christ with His
Father.

Some similar reflections appear in the post-Amsterdam documents of the World Council of Churches. These later expressions, which must be examined, do not seem to be focused on the
same goal as the Vatican documents.

CHAPTER ELEVEN

FROM CONSULTATION TOWARD CHURCH

The World Council of Churches is essentially a consultation (as *conseil* in French, and *Rat* in German indicate) of doctrinally separated churches seeking the unity of the one Church of Christ. The divided communions consult and seek joint action where possible until it can be made visible that they have become the Scriptural one flock with one shepherd. The World Council is a consultation-instrument to achieve this end. When the end is achieved the instrument will have completed its usefulness. Like the scaffolding in a post-disaster reconstruction, it will be in the way when the work is done.

This appears to be the "emergency-stage" position expressed by Willem A. Visser't Hooft for the very assembly which, in 1948, voted the World Council into existence.

> We are a Council of Churches, not *the* Council
> of the one undivided Church. Our name indi-
> cates our weakness and our shame before God,
> for there can be and there *is* finally only one
> Church of Christ on earth. Our plurality is a
> deep anomaly. But our name indicates also that
> we are aware of that situation...that we would
> move forward towards the manifestation of the
> One Holy Church. Our Council represents there-
> fore an emergency solution—a stage on the road
> —a body living between the time of complete
> isolation of the churches from each other and
> the time—on earth or in heaven—when it will
> be visibly true that there is one Shepherd and
> one flock. [1]

Thus Visser't Hooft, one of the principal architects of the World Council as its first General Secretary, envisions the WCC as an "emergency solution" and a "stage on the road," a "body living between times," in a word a temporary instrument. He kept open the option that the temporary may last until the end-time and thus be permanent while life on earth lasts.

Despite Visser't Hooft's influence and stated position, the
World Council did not include in its constitution any explicit recognition that it was constructed as a temporary instrument or scaffolding for rebuilding Christ's one Church, or
any plan that it should decrease as Christ's one Church increased.[2]

On the contrary, the World Council set itself up with organizational mechanisms for an unending continuity in time. Also,
it seemed to take its major thrust from the "Life and Work"
(L&W) Movement rather than from the "Faith and Order" (F&O)
Movement. The confluence of these two ecumenical streams
principally constituted the World Council. Common work on
society (L&W) more easily engaged the energies of the great
new world organization than theological work (F&O) on the
churches themselves.

Visser't Hooft had said that the World Council "would move
forward towards the manifestation of the One Holy Church," but
even this guarded expression of the goal was not incorporated into the WCC constitution at Amsterdam. The objective
of the ecclesial unity willed by Christ was, at best, contained within the title of the "Faith and Order" movement's
new relationship under the larger umbrella of the World
Council structure.

If the Faith and Order Commission could steer the whole Council, then the port of Christian ecclesial unity might be
reached. If, on the other hand, F&O became merely one more
commission among other demanding committees which stressed
pressing social needs, then its call for unity, already muf-
fled because of its division of theological postures, would
be largely muted.

When the Council founders asked what the World Council was
for, instead of saying "*for* regaining the ecclesial unity
willed by Christ," they said, "It is constituted *for* discharge
of the functions set out below."[3] The first of the seven
functions was "to carry on the work of the two world movements for Faith and Order and for Life and Work."[4] The other
functions were to facilitate and promote (2) common action,
(3) cooperation in study, (4) ecumenical consciousness, (5)
interrelation with other ecumenical entities, (6) creation of
world conferences, and (7) the churches' evangelism.[5]

Despite the Faith and Order preeminence as the first function
in conjunction with Life and Work, it, in fact, became one of
four subordinate committees under the title, "Division of
Studies," which itself was one of four divisions.[6] It appears that the goal of the whole was buried by the structure.
The different parts of the whole Council structure were

aiding churches and people with communications, ideas, position papers and even (after World War II) with construction
materials and money. The Council as a whole was doing many
things for its member churches, and the question was raised
is the World Council itself the super-church?

Divided churches had begun to experience more of a universal
unity than they had known since prereformation days. Some of
the World Council's functions were similar to those which
the Vatican performed for particular churches. Would the
World Council through its large assembly legislate for its
member churches, and thus slowly control and forge them into
one great world church?

Landmark Toronto Statement

The "super-church" question had arisen before Amsterdam; that
Assembly had, by resolution, responded that the World Council
did not desire to take over the proper functions of its member churches, but sought rather to serve them as an instrument for dialogue, common witness, and collaboration.[7] But
the question persisted, in some quarters hopefully, in others
anxiously. Two years after its constitutional assembly, *the
Central Committee* of the WCC addressed this insistent question of the World Council's ecclesiological significance in
its 1950 Toronto meeting with a document entitled, *The Church,
The Churches and The World Council of Churches*.[8] This brief,
defining document is commonly called the *Toronto Statement*.

In its introduction, this statement reminded the churches
that the World Council at Amsterdam had determined, by constitution and resolution, that it did not desire to legislate
for or control its member churches; further, it disavowed

> any thought of becoming a single unified church
> structure independent of the churches which have
> joined...or a structure dominated by a centra-
> lized administrative authority.[9]

The greatness, in terms of actual world input and outreach,
of the new and unprecedented Council continued to evoke the
sense of the World Christian Church, despite its initial word
to the contrary. Even though it rejected the name "church"
for itself, the WCC in some way manifested something of unity
and universality which marks Christ's Church.

The *Toronto Statement* observed that its member churches
avoided precise definitions of the Church, consequently

> it is not to be expected that the World Council
> can easily achieve a definition which has to

take account of all the various ecclesiologies of its member Churches.[10]

The Central Committee, nevertheless, showed that it had at
least some definite convictions about the nature of Christ's
Church because it pointed out that the existing ecclesial
divisions "contradict the very nature of the Church."[11] The
Toronto Statement affirmed that the World Council does have
ecclesiological implications which it proceeded to delineate
by a series of negative and positive assertions.[12]

On the negative side, the *Toronto Statement* declared that the
World Council is not a super-church or the *Una Sancta* of the
Creed; it is not a union-negotiator for its divided member
churches, nor can it be based on any one particular conception of the church, since it does not wish to "prejudge the
ecclesiological problem."[13]

This last negation seems to be pragmatically inspired; it
withdraws from the Faith and Order goal of seeking church
unity. It can be argued that too clear an affirmation of
essential notes of Christ's Church would exclude certain member-churches from the World Council and thus defeat the purpose of calling Christian "churches" together for consultation.

On the other hand, too long a refusal to seek and affirm
which position (among contradictory ecclesiological positions) most conforms to the will of Christ, can reduce the
World Council to a frustrating *everybody-is-right* fellowship. In this latter event, mere social and secular projects will make the World Council irrelevant to the inspiration of Church unity which brought it into existence.

Different ecclesiologies seem to dominate the World Council
in different conferences or utterances.[14] This intended non-
determination of the ecclesiology willed by Christ enables
the World Council to remain open to the ecclesiology of every
church which accepts Christ as Savior and God; it stresses
the consultation nature of the WCC.[15]

However, the group pressure toward intercommunion implies a
free-church ecclesiology, which discards apostolic succession
and the sacrament of sacred orders as nonessential to the
Church of Christ. The very latitude which accepts any Christ-
professing Church as an equal partner seems to imply the reduction of all member churches to the status of incomplete
parts or sects of Christ's Church. Yet this implication is
simply denied by the *Toronto Statement*.

Membership in the World Council of Churches

does not imply that a Church treats its own
conception of the Church as merely relative.[16]

Although both friends and critics have interpreted the equal
partnership principle as inherently latitudinarian, the
statement insists that the equality does not apply to conceptions of the Christian Church, or the proper unity of Christ's
Church.[17]

The *Toronto Statement* declares that "The Council stands for
Church unity."[18] However, it neither declares what constitutes the unity it stands for, nor does it give a directional
signal among the different positions on unity which it perceives.[19]

The statement distinguishes as observable the unity-posi-
tions: of (1) creedal consensus only, (2) cultic and church-
order unity only, (3) creed, cult and church-order unity (4)
unity only in certain fundamentals of faith and order (5)
universal spiritual fellowship only, (6) invisible unity
only.[20]

Although the Council rejects for itself the image of a spiritual church which is not visible or tangible, it nevertheless
includes among its members churches which believe that the
true Church is essentially invisible. According to the document, membership in the WCC does not imply acceptance of the
invisible Church concept of the equal-partner churches which
hold this doctrine.[21]

Thus, the *Toronto Statement* declared that the WCC was *not* a
super-church, nor a union-broker, not based on a particular
church-concept, nor a relativiser of its members' ecclesial
concepts, not troubled by its members' contradictory doctrines on church unity or visibility. It exists to bring the
divided Christian Churches into dynamic consultation.

After disposing negatively of what is considered misunderstandings or inadequate conceptions of the World Council, the
Central Committee proceeded to "define the positive assumptions which underlie the World Council of Churches and the
ecclesiological implications of membership in it."[22]

In the negative part of the *Toronto Statement,* the Central
Committee had declared what the World Council is not; in the
positive part, the committee *shifted its focus* from the council as a whole to the assumed beliefs, recognitions and implied insights of its members. Constitutionally, its only
members are churches.[23]

The members believe that their consultation and collaboration

must be based on: (1) the recognition of, and submission to,
the Headship of Jesus Christ in His Church, (2) the belief
that the Church of Christ is and can only be one, (3) the
recognition that the membership of Christ's Church *includes
more* than the membership of their own Church body.[24]

The combination of these last two points (viz. 2 and 3) presents the difficulty that Christ's Church is one and is *in some
way different* from the member's own Church. Thus, it seems
that there are two different churches and that the member's
own church is not Christ's Church. This difficulty is a real
one; it plagues ecumenical dialogues, writings, and especially
media presentations. The pathway of solution is the recognition that the word "church" has at least two different senses:
one, a *theological* sense, implying all and only the essential
constituents which Christ willed for His Church, and the other,
a *sociological* sense, as a public institution which bears some
semblance to Christ's Church and which people label "church."

It is also noteworthy that the *Toronto Statement* shifted its
focus to membership. The document even has the non-member [of
the WCC] Roman Catholic Church in mind. It reads:

> All the Christian Churches, including the Church
> of Rome, hold that there is no complete identity
> between the membership of the Church Universal
> and the membership of their own Church. They
> recognize that there are Church members '*extra
> muros*,' that these belong '*aliquo modo*' to the
> Church, or even that there is an '*ecclesia extra
> ecclesiam*.' This recognition finds expression in
> the fact that with very few exceptions the Chris-
> tian Churches accept the baptism administered by
> other churches as valid.[25]

The Roman Catholic Church recognizes principally the *aliquo
modo* expression and the expression *extra muros* in the sense
of her members who have separated themselves from full communion, but the expression "a church outside the church"
moves into the use of the term church in at least two different senses: sociological versus theological; also "church
taken in some sense deficiently" versus "church taken in the
sense of Christ's own essential constituents." The Roman
Catholic Church believes that Christ's essential Church subsists in her continuously from the apostolic age.[26]

The different senses of the word "church" are noted in *Ecumenical Dialogue*, in which it is pointed out that:

> where councils or conferences of churches are
> dealt with, generally the term 'church' is to

be understood in a sociological sense and not
in a technical theological sense.[27]

The belief that validly baptized Christians belong to the
Catholic Church in some real but incomplete way was expressed
in the post Vatican II speech of Pope Paul, previously cited,[28]
and in a documentary way in the rite of receiving already-
baptized persons *fully* into the Roman Catholic Church. The
post Vatican II official Ritual of Church reception is entitled "Rite of Reception of Baptized Christians into Full
Communion with the Catholic Church."[29]

The official Roman Ritual carries the "full/not-full" distinction to the practical point that it calls for a new understanding of the term "convert." "Convert" is not to be
applied to any validly baptized person who moves from partial
communion into full communion with the Roman Catholic Church;
the term is to be reserved for those who come "from unbelief
to Christian belief."[30]

The term "convert" is viewed as inappropriate to describe one
who had already been united to Christ by baptism and thus
brought into Christ's mysterious body. Even though the baptism took place in a separated ecclesial community, the Roman Catholic Church believes that the baptized person is
thereby in a real but incomplete way united to her.[31] The
full process of initiation involves baptism, confirmation,
and eucharistic unity; in the future this initiation is to
take place in the context of the eucharistic liturgy as the
sign of full unity achieved. A separated Christian's prior
baptism has already started, but not completed, the process
of initiation.

Thus, the *Toronto Statement's* expression of "no complete
identity between the membership in the Church Universal and
one's own church" is seen by the Catholic Church not as an
absolute disjunction which can produce two distinct and valid
churches theologically, but rather as the radical union of
all the baptized, who are thereafter either fully or partially
in communion in Christ's one Church. The *Toronto Statement's*
expression *aliquo modo* (in some mode) describes this relationship in a way that the expression "a Church outside *the*
Church" fails to do so. The *Statement* proceeds by affirming
the mysterious bond which deeply unites the baptized, while
confining the dividing element to more of a surface level of
understanding.

This problematic "Christ's Church/own Church" relationship
is to be the subject for mutual consideration in the World
Council, while no member-church (despite equal partnership)
need regard "the other member churches as Churches in the

true and full sense of the word."[32]   Here again are different
senses for the word *church*, such that each member of the WCC
may consider itself truly and fully the one Church of Christ
while considering the other members to be inadmissibly usurping the title.   This proposition thus retains the conceptual
deadlock of the previous centuries.

The *Statement's* next positive proposition suggests the pathway through the impasse which had previously blocked dialogue.

> The member churches... recognize in other
> Churches *elements of the true Church*.   They
> consider that this mutual recognition obliges
> them to enter into a serious conversation with
> each other in the hope that these elements of
> truth will lead to recognition of the full
> truth and to unity based on the full truth.[33]

In the search to find theological realities which unite divided Christians, expressions such as *vestigia ecclesiae*
(vestiges or remnants of the Church), gold-bearing fragments,
relics, traces, and elements have been tried.   The term *elements* has thus far been found most helpful.

This term remains free of the pejorative connotations of others; it more easily bears the up-building sense of baptism
and the Word of God, which Christians believe to be *unity-
tending* realities.   However, this rather new term remains
open to the suggestion of numbering (how many elements?) and
measurement, both of which thrusts appear less than suitable
for the pursuit of the unity of Christians.

Baptism is believed by all Christians to be the entrance to
Christ's Church.   Some believe it to be merely symbolic; Roman Catholics and many other Christians believe that baptism
initiates the recipients into a unique sharing of the life-
giving gifts of God, making them mysteriously, but limitedly,
"sharers of the divine nature" (2 Peter 1:4).   Thus, this
element of baptism is thought to provide a divinely dynamic
gift, which tends toward the union of believers with each other and with God.   The *Toronto Statement* refers to such essentials "not...as mere elements...but powerful means by
which God works."[34]

The remaining positive propositions of the *Toronto Statement*
assert the member churches' willingness to consult for the
sake of witness;[35] recognition of solidarity for the sake of
mutual assistance and restraint of nonbrotherly actions;[36]
actual entering into spiritual relationships for the building
up of the Body of Christ and the renewal of the life of the
churches.[37]

The *Statement* perceives that despite their divisions, which
render total common witness impossible, the member churches
have enough in common so that "something of the unity"[38] may
be manifested as witness to the world. Thus, the Central
Committee has explicitly acknowledged positions which in various ways are suggested by the very existence and constitution of the World Council of Churches.

These positions are taken as signs pointing to further degrees of cooperation, both materially and psychologically.
The WCC's existence stands as testimony to "something of the
unity" both achieved and acknowledged among divided Churches.

However, the *Toronto Statement* was noticeably silent as regards the specifics of the final goal. Expressions like "fuller unity," "real unity," and elements that "will lead to
unity" surface in the document,[39] but the working, visible
constituents of Christ's one Church are not mentioned. The
matter-of-fact working constituents of ecumenism's final goal
seem ethereally vague; the reference to the one Lord "Who
knows only one flock"[40] seems more calculated to evoke the
risen Good Shepherd *in absentia* as the only source of practical unity, despite the fact that the tangible, visible WCC
claimed that it had already achieved "something of the unity"[41] and "a very real unity" "...the most precious element
of its life."[42]

The principle motive of the document seems to have been to
lay to rest the anxious fears of an emerging "super-church."
Perhaps the effort to define the final unity would have inflamed rather than allayed such fears.

Although the full title of the document is *The Church, The
Churches and The World Council of Churches,* very little content touches *The Church*, i.e., Christ's Church. The overall
concept of the World Council seems to be that it is an instrument designed to aid the many divided Churches to become the
one Church of Christ,[43] or perhaps to make visible the hidden
unity which their differences cover.

Concerning *The Church*, the document says only that the WCC is
not the Church of Christ, that on the basis of the New Testament His Church is one, that membership in His Church is
wider than membership in any other church, and finally, it
seems to distance itself from any one particular conception
of The Church.[44]

Although the New Testament contains more about Christ's Church
than merely its unity, the *Toronto Statement's* reticence concerning other essentials seems dictated by its overriding wish
not to offend any potential member. Speaking of its foregoing

positions, the *Statement* concludes:

> None of these...is in conflict with the teach-
> ings of the member churches. We believe there-
> fore that no Church need fear that by entering
> into the World Council it is in danger of deny-
> ing its heritage.[45]

The *Toronto Statement* could readily overcome the fear that
the World Council was, or was becoming, the super-church by
emphasizing its provisional nature as Visser't Hooft had done
two years before at Amsterdam. Visser't Hooft wrote and corrected drafts of the Toronto document.[46] The temporary nature of the World Council is left unsaid.

At least one member of the Central Committee strongly held
that "the World Council expresses the form which unity is
ultimately to take."[47] This position, if adopted, would certainly have driven out the Orthodox Church. The Committee
withdrew from this assertion and voted that its *Statement* not
express a position on the nature of the final unity.[48] Further, the Orthodox did not have to consider any other church
as truly and fully being the Church of Christ.[49]

The *Toronto Statement* was decisive in retaining the hesitant
membership, small as it was, of the Orthodox.[50] These inner
tensions regarding Church unity (viz. the WCC is the final
form versus the WCC has no doctrine of the final form) go far
in explaining the World Council's documentary vagueness regarding Christ's one Church. If the WCC is locked into the
lowest common denominator among its member churches, its
final achievement may be limited to talk, partial collaboration and partial witness.

By its series of negative statements and positive assumptions
in 1950 the *Toronto Statement* was influential in correcting
the trajectory of the new World Council projected into the
Christian world at Amsterdam. The *negatives,* that the WCC:
is not the super-church, is not a union-broker, does not have
one concept of church, does not have one concept of church-
unity, does not relativize any member's own concept of church,
quieted the fears of the anxious churches. The *positive* assumptions—that all the WCC's member churches believed and
recognized: the Divine Christ's headship of His Church, the
oneness of His Church, His Church's greater *inclusiveness*
than their own, their obligation to examine this inclusiveness, their awareness of Christian *elements* in other churches,
their obligation of mutual consultation, their growing sense
of *solidarity* and their entrance into renewed *spiritual relationships,* helped to align the expectations of the ecumenical
leaders.

Faith and Order at Lund

The World Council's "Faith and Order Commission" (now only a
WCC commission which still, however, retained its right to
run worldwide theological conferences) continued the modern
ecumenical inquiry at Lund, Sweden, in August 1952. The two-
week Lund Conference sharply focused its vision on *The Church*,
its continuity and unity, its worship and intercommunion.
Lund's 225 Church delegates, overwhelmingly Protestant (nine
were Orthodox), argued the merits of pre-examined position
papers on the foregoing topics.[51] The Churches represented
were: 35 Protestant, 4 Orthodox.

Willem A. Visser't Hooft, the general secretary of the WCC,
was also an officer of the Lund Conference on Faith and Order;
Oliver S. Tomkins, its secretary, edited the official conference report.[52] Tomkins himself, in speech and report, probed,
beyond the *Toronto Statement,* the implications of membership
in the World Council of Churches.

Tomkins (Church of England) sought to capture the meaning of
the World Council as a whole. The World Council was a new
kind of Christian institution which, although it lacked full
unity, had lessened the significance of separated denominations. He saw this as a paradox, namely that living in the
WCC's larger Christian unity reduced the significance of
daily life in the smaller denominations to which they all belonged. To Tomkins the World Council, as provisional, symbolized conflicting tensions.

> To put the ecumenical paradox more clearly
> and more brutally, the World Council of
> Churches is a Council of Denominations,
> whilst its very creation has destroyed the
> justification of denominations.[53]

The *Toronto Statement* had pointed out that member-churches
need not view other members as true churches. Tomkins observed that many official delegates had not yet grasped this.
The fact and, even more, failure to grasp it, embarrassed
their communications.

> It is equally embarrassing to have one's own
> Church treated as though it were not really a
> Church, and to have to treat bodies which one
> does not believe to be churches practically as
> though they were. But to wish it otherwise
> would...not be the Council into which we have
> in fact been led.[54]

Tomkins unfolded the implications of Amsterdam's determination

"to stay together," and the basis of growing cooperation,
namely, unity. He felt that mere comparison of denominations
(referred to as comparative ecclesiology), which tended to
justify divisions rather than get at the *Una Sancta*, was at an
end. [55]

As he proceeded, Tomkins struck harder; the implication of
entering the World Council is that "...we have already willed
the death of our denominations." [56]

Shifting his focus from the constitutive denominational units
of the World Council to the range of the Council itself,
Tomkins perceived:

> The peril of the World Council is that it might
> encourage the permanency of the units upon which
> it rests, and it is the peculiar vocation of
> Faith and Order to bear witness in every part of
> the Council's life that it has come into being
> only in order to die as a 'Council of Denomina-
> tions.' [57]

Tomkins disclaimed any wish to destroy a denominational
church in which a delegate had learned of Christ, but he did
insist that cherished denominational barriers incompatible
with the *Una Sancta* must be changed. His definition of the
WCC as a "Council of Denominations" implied that all member-
churches were denominations and consequently, needed changing.
From this point of view, it is clear that joining the World
Council is taken as an acknowledgment of denominational or
limited status. It seems to imply nonuniversality, noncatho-
licity. If this be true, then the very act of joining makes
an ecclesiological statement. The Church joining appears to
acknowledge that it is not the *Una Sancta*.

As a faithful son of the Church of England, Tomkins wished to
cast off anything of denominational loyalty so that his loyalty would be totally to the *Una Sancta*.

> My Church has no desire to be a 'denomination.'
> It desires simply to be the Church of God in
> England. We claim no peculiar doctrines or
> practices; we desire to take our stand...
> simply upon the Catholic faith, witnessed to
> in the Catholic creeds, ministering the Catho-
> lic sacraments, and maintaining the Catholic
> ministry. [58]

If there be a discrepancy between the desire and the fact,
then the denominational encrustations must go: "Faith and
Order exists to remind each other that as denominations, we

must die."[59]

Tomkins expressed his conviction that new forms of common
life must be found; activities, including worship, must be
done together, except where irreconcilable convictions forced
member churches to worship separately.[60]

Finally, Tomkins disclosed what he considered to be the core
problem of the Church's relationship in the World Council.

> We claim that we have a unity in Christ, we
> cannot show that we have unity in His body,
> the Church, that is the heart of our dilemma,...

> Nothing in the biblical conception of the
> Church, nor in the lives of the primitive
> Christians, will allow us to affirm for ever
> that we have unity in Christ and deny that we
> have unity in the Church. We must face this
> ...as a common problem, allowing each other no
> escape from the vigorous demands of accepting
> the Lordship of Christ.[61]

Acknowledging, in his closing paragraphs, that the Faith and
Order work was only a small part of the current Christian-
unity movement, Tomkins also indicated that his thoughts embraced the Roman Catholic Church:

> Although the Roman Catholic Church does not
> cooperate formally in our work, the manifest
> concern of Roman Catholics both clergy and
> laity, has never been absent from my thoughts
> in everything I have said.[62]

In his own more detached way, Visser't Hooft, of the Swiss
Reformed Church, also pointed to the same dilemma as Tomkins.

Visser't Hooft said that their unity in Christ, while remaining divided as churches, displayed apparently contradictory
tensions; yet the two tensions do exist and each is important.[63]

> It does not help to deny the existence of one
> of the two sides of the dialectical situation.
> To talk as some do of the 'World Church' as if
> it existed as a historical reality today is ut-
> terly misleading and is to minimize the serious-
> ness of our theological divisions, to our sepa-
> rateness in worship and sacrament, of our
> organizational self-centeredness. On the other
> hand to talk as if we live still in an era of

> complete denominational isolation, is to forget
> that...something of the reality of the Church
> Universal has become manifest as the churches
> have spoken, acted and lived together.[64]

Thus, "something of unity—yet divided churches" was dis-
tilled as the crucial problem in the thoughts of prominent
leaders at Lund. Preparatory to this distillation, Visser't
Hooft had interpreted Amsterdam as significantly creating "a
new fact,...a covenant, a fellowship of a permanent character."[65] What Amsterdam saw only dimly, the *Toronto Statement*
unfolded explicitly, namely that the World Council is

> a body which seeks to prepare the way for mani-
> fest, tangible unity, because that is clearly
> what the New Testament understands by unity.[66]

Since Toronto, it has become clear that all barriers to unity
must be dismantled. Separation, denominationalism are forces
of division. No longer are denominational divisions to be
regarded as normal.[67] Visser't Hooft perceives clearly that

> ...you cannot speak with conviction about the
> new and real unity which has grown up among
> the Churches and complacently accept the fact
> that our denominational forms of organization
> and action continue to give the impression
> that each denomination remains a law unto
> itself.[68]

In seeking to crystallize the central problem which Visser't
Hooft, as General Secretary of the WCC, wanted the Faith and
Order Commission to address at the next assembly of the World
Council (Evanston, Illinois, 1954), he suggested as a title
for the core problem: "The Unity which we have in Christ and
the Disunity of our Churches."[69]

The Conference at Lund condensed Visser't Hooft's suggested
subject to the title, "Our Oneness in Christ and our Disunity
as Churches,"[70] and accepted it as the Faith and Order theme
for the WCC Assembly to be held at Evanston.

The influential interpretations of Visser't Hooft and Tomkins
strongly influenced Lund's official *Report* and *Message* to the
churches. By definition, neither the WCC nor constituent
commissions, such as Faith and Order,[71] can legislate or make
obligatory resolutions for the member churches. They achieve
their influence by formulating and voting for conference documents which are sent to the member churches for study and
possible implementation. Lund's report and conclusions were
accepted by the Conference as a whole.

Lund's delegates had the impossible job of preventing the
Lund report from becoming a dead letter "back home." Lund
brought the nature of the *Una Sancta* into prominence and insisted that the church unity being sought was "full *visible*
unity."[72]

Lund confronted more theologically-controversial issues and
probed more sharply than previous assemblies and conferences
had done.[73] Thus, some of its agreed positions influenced
later World Council practices and postures. Delegates to
Lund came from over 110 different Protestant churches and
about four Eastern Rite churches. Consequently, efforts to
formulate common agreements concerning such theological realities as Church, worship and intercommunion were very difficult, and in many instances impossible.

One Eastern-Church delegate, speaking to the assembly near the
conference end, said "I have felt...that we have been trying
to find words and phrases to cover up our differences."[74]

Nevertheless, some common beliefs were newly expressed by the
Conference of the 39 Churches. These expressions lend themselves to presentation as paraphrased propositions related to
the six parts of the Lund *Report* which contain them.

Preface[75]

   oThe nature of the Church is the central theme.[76] The
      Christ/Church/Holy Spirit focus is termed *primary* and
      decisive for the advance of the ecumenical movement.

I. Word to the Churches

   oThere can be no real advance toward unity if we only com-
      pare our respective concepts of Church (comparative
      ecclesiology).[77]
   oCloser to Christ means closer to one another.[78]
   oA faith in Christ's one Church, not implemented by acts,
      is dead.[79]
   oChurches should act together in all except acts wherein
      theological conviction compels separation.[80]

II. Christ and His Church

   oChrist and His Church belong inseparably together.[81]
   oTo manifest Christ's one Church, we must change (implies
      denominational diminution).[82]
   oThe Church is not a human contrivance; it is God's gift
      for the Salvation of the World.[83]

III. Continuity and Unity

○*All* agree on some form of ecclesial continuity from
  Christ's time to the present; all emphasize continuity
  of Christian life; *most* think that the Gospel and sacraments are essential means of ecclesial continuity;
  the *majority* think that some form of commissioned ministry is essential.[84]
○*Some* think episcopal order is necessary; *others* presbyteral; *others*, congregational; *others*, no clear line of
  order is in the New Testament.[85]
○Some believe that the historic episcopate in apostolic
  succession is *essential* and the only sufficient safeguard of the historic continuity of the *Una Sancta*.[86]
○It is clear that here is an obstinate difference held with
  deep conviction and in a good conscience, which cannot
  readily be resolved.[87]
○The Ecumenical Movement is proof that a given unity exists
  among Christians. We *differ* in our understanding of
  the relation of our unity in Christ to the visible,
  holy Catholic and Apostolic Church. We are agreed that
  there are not two Churches, one visible and the other
  invisible, but one Church which must find visible expression on earth; we *differ* in our belief as to whether certain doctrinal, sacramental, and ministerial
  forms are of essence of the church itself.[88]
○We are striving toward a visible fellowship.[89]
○Some hold the unity of the Church must be organic; others,
  only a covenant.[90]

IV. Worship

○The conviction is strengthened that worship no less than
  Faith and Order, is *essential* to the being of the
  Church.[91]
○The conferees *agreed* that: they worship the Trinity; faith
  is a gift; worship involves the whole man; Gospel and
  sacraments are God's gifts; worship has an ecclesial
  character. The conferees *disagreed* as to: the use of
  material things in worship; what is liturgical; the
  character of ministry (sacred orders); sacrificial
  character of Lord's supper; veneration of saints,
  especially Mary. Ministry differences continue to be
  grave obstacles to unity; differences on Mary's place
  reveal deep divergence.[92]

V. Intercommunion

○The Orthodox see the liturgy as an act of the Church; differing churches cannot concelebrate; the very word
  'intercommunion' misrepresents the problem.[93]

°The rest of the conference   nevertheless regards intercommunion as a necessary part of any satisfactory
   church unity.[94]
°The majority believe that WCC membership requires joint
   sacramental communion; there will be no perfect solution of differences until there is *full visible unity*.[95]
°A conference may be regarded as an expression of *the
   Church,* even though only a temporary and local expression.[96]
°The recommendations urged intercommunion, yet without the
   violation of any member's conscience.[97]
°The divergences of the doctrine of the Church are still
   unreconciled.[98]

VI.   Where do we stand?

°We confess our faith in the One, Holy, Catholic and Apostolic Church which is God's gift for the salvation of
   the world.[99]
°We are convinced of an underlying unity of life in Christ;
   we differ about the authority of the Church.[100]
°We are now at a point at which our divergences stubbornly
   resist easy solution.[101]
°We are faced with the dilemma of combining proper denominational loyalty with obedience to the richer unity of
   Christ's one Church;[102] ('denominational autonomy/one
   church' dilemma).
°We meet a tension between the Roman and non-Roman expressions of Catholicity.[103]
°At Lund, in confronting the fundamental issues of Christian unity, we have been working at a level far more
   profound than previously; we have not resolved our
   crucial differences, nor designed a simple path toward
   unity.[104]

Interestingly, Lund modified Toronto's position that the WCC
had no definite stand on the nature of the Church's unity,
whether visible or invisible. Lund clearly characterized the
unity sought as *full visible* unity.[105] Furthermore, it was
an "already given" unity. The "one church" is God's gift,[106]
hence the characteristic oneness shares in the givenness of
the original gift. Thus, after Lund, the unity of the Church
is recognized by many Protestants as a "God-given, visible
unity."[107] These modifiers of unity, however, are generally
mentioned separately rather than together as one phrase.

The predominantly Protestant Conference, examining the nature
of Christ's Church, turned to the New Testament. "When we
think of the unity of the Church...we are all agreed that we
must relate to it the other qualifications of the Church in
the New Testament."[108] The *Lund Report* refers to Christ's

Church in both heading and text as "His Church."[109] Yet one
searches in vain for any reflection on the Petrine texts in
which Matthew's Gospel presents Christ's reference to the
Church as "My Church" (Matt. 16:18), and John's Gospel presents the Good Shepherd's reference to his people as "My
sheep" (John 21:17).

The conference admittedly faced a profoundly difficult task,
and perhaps texts such as these would have produced more heat
than light, but the conference report did claim:

> From the unity of Christ we seek to understand the
> unity of the Church on earth and from the unity of
> Christ and His Body we seek a means of realizing
> that unity in the actual state of our divisions on
> earth.[110]

The spectre of the ecclesial character, "church-likeness" or
"super-church," appearance of the World Council with its
structural parts was not laid to rest by the *Toronto Statement*. A Conference, such as that at Lund, is called an "expression of the church,"[111] even though only temporary and
local. Such a concept, namely "the people of God for common
work and thus common witness," implies a free church ecclesiology.[112] This concept, preserved by vote in an official
report, undoubtedly contributed to the hesitant posture
adopted by the Orthodox. One could not be sure that a later
assembly would refrain from changing the note of "local" to
universal, and the note of "temporary" to permanent.

If a passing conference such as *Lund* could be referred to as
a temporary and local expression of the Church, surely the
World Council headquarters was engaged in many more Christian
works than any of its subordinate conferences, and it clearly
was more universal and more permanent. A few years after the
Evanston Assembly, Visser't Hooft would again have to address
this question.[113]

CHAPTER TWELVE

WORLD COUNCIL'S SECOND
ASSEMBLY (EVANSTON)

After the Toronto Statement (1950) and Lund (1952) the World
Council of Churches continued its work in a Second World Assembly held at Evanston, Illinois, in the summer of 1954. As
at Amsterdam, the member churches had publicly proclaimed
their intention "to stay together," so at Evanston, in a manner somewhat less succinctly, they expressed a mind *to advance together*[1] toward a unity which was named but not defined.

The official *Message From the Assembly* noted Amsterdam's intention of "staying together" and continued:

> We enter now upon a second stage. To stay
> together is not enough. *We must go forward.*
> As we learn more of our unity in Christ, it
> becomes more intolerable that we should be
> divided. We therefore ask you: Is your
> church seriously considering...our Lord's
> prayer...that we may all be one? Is your
> congregation...doing all it can do to ensure
> that your neighbors shall hear the voice of
> the one Shepherd calling all men into the
> one flock?[2]

The World Council's agenda at Evanston was divided into six
sections, the first of which was run by the Faith and Order
Commission under the title, "Our oneness in Christ and our
disunity as Churches." The second section dealt with a topic
chiefly associated with the International Missionary Conference, namely: evangelism. The remaining four sections dealt
with topics formerly associated with "Life and Work," namely,
social problems, international affairs, racial tensions, and
the Christian Laity in the sphere of daily work.[3]

The theme of the assembly, "Christ—the Hope of the World,"
was somewhat loosely connected with the topics of each session.[4]

In an expression paralleled with Amsterdam's "we intend to
stay together," the Official F&O report stated, "we intend to
unite."[5] The affirmation was modified in the text by an introductory clause, "as the Holy Spirit may guide us," and at
the report's end, by the phrasing "we dedicate ourselves to
God anew, that He may enable us to grow together."[6]

Collaboration was one thing, union was quite another! The
delegates (with varying theological competence) who attended
the Faith and Order section had difficulty widening the theological base of their unity, while the great majority of
delegates understandably moved into the sections on social
problems, racism, and international problems.

The Evanston Assembly focused its attention primarily on social problems.[7] Pastor Marc Boegner, an officer of the Assembly, wrote, "we have been forced to be superficial in our
work."[8] The World Council was dealing with so many diverse
problems that the profound ecclesial problem at the core of
ecumenism faced increasing difficulty in claiming center-
stage. The attention and energy directed toward social problems make the attainment of ecumenism's goal more remote.

The F&O commission strengthened some of the expressions Lund
had formulated, but advance toward its target of visible unity is certainly not highlighted. The F&O theme was made more
commanding and abrupt by replacing the "and" of the title
with the verb "contradict," and thus the WCC acknowledges
"...our disunity as Churches contradicts our unity in
Christ."[9]

The *Report (Evanston Speaks)* tried to make clearer what the
delegates believe about this real, not merely sociological,
rhetorical or sentimental, unity.[10] A scale ranging from
"somewhat-realized unity" to "fully-shown unity" was affirmed.
Expressions such as "partially realized"[11] and "unity as fully manifested"[12] implied the sense of a unity gradient having
a beginning, a partial state, and a full and perfect state.

Within such a context, the Evanston *Report* spoke of a "growth
from unity to unity"[13] having the sense of "growth from initial unity to fully achieved unity."[14] At the same time, the
original unity given to the Church was termed "indestructible,"[15] but never fully realized by the Church.[16] That the
perfect unity said to characterize Christ's second coming has
never been fully realized, or that the church's members are
short of perfect in their achievement of unity, justifies the
sense of this assertion. But the implication that the *Una
Sancta* has never yet known a blossoming of the given gift of
visible unity seems somewhat short of the mark.

The Evanston *Report* was heavily documented with New Testament
texts addressing the question of the unity Christ gave His
Church. Again one searches in vain for the Petrine texts in
which Christ is presented by the texts as referring to "My
Church" and "My sheep"; such texts are widely known for their
implications concerning the kind of unity Christ intended.

As at Lund, so again at Evanston, the Orthodox delegation
separated itself from the Assembly report and presented a
special statement of its own regarding Faith and Order.[17]

A later World Council reflection on the significance of Evanston cites its F&O achievements as "the beginning of an attempt to spell out what we mean by 'oneness in Christ.'"[18]
This work of defining the meaning of church unity reached a
new and fuller expression at the World Council's third Assembly in New Delhi in 1961.

At Evanston, F&O ended its official report with suggestions
to the member churches: only *churches* can actually effect a
fuller unity; the World Council and its departments can promote it, but only the Christians, as assemblies, can produce
it. Evanston's suggestions, in paraphrases, are:

- Thank God for the given unity we now partially
       share; act together unless deep conviction
       compels otherwise.
- Together study Holy Scripture and also Christian
       Tradition.
- Consider frankly the non-theological (social and
       cultural) obstacles to unity.
- Speak and practice the truth in love; don't
       falsely agree or disagree.
- Explore again the Baptism/Eucharist connection
       for the possibility of intercommunion.
- Examine again the possibility of mutual recogni-
       tion of ministry.
- Divided witness is necessarily defective witness;
       it is a scandal; we must bear witness together.
- Pray together especially in the Week of Prayer
       for Christian Unity; the degree to which we
       pray for unity is a measure of our concern for
       unity.[19]

In a manner somewhat less forceful than the foregoing suggestions, Evanston indicated that unity in Christ may concretely
"require obedience unto the death" [of one's denominational
separateness].[20] Further, diversity which "disrupts the
manifest unity of the Body...becomes sinful division."[21]

Incidentally, Evanston was the final ecumenical gathering

attended by John R. Mott, whose enormous energy and talent
had started the modern ecumenical movement in 1910 at Edinburgh. Some weeks after Evanston, "God called back to himself this valiant servant...then nearly ninety years of
age"[22] writes Marc Boegner, an early, influential coworker in
the movement.

A proposal which started at Evanston '54 and came to flower
at New Delhi '61, requested a re-examination, and an extension, of the World Council's all-important basis along "biblical and trinitarian lines."[23]

Four Roman Catholic observers had been officially appointed
to attend the Faith and Order Conference at Lund in 1952,
whereas two years later at Evanston, Chicago's Cardinal
Stritch had forbidden the attendance of any Roman Catholics,
even in the role of observers, at the Second Assembly of the
World Council of Churches.

At Lund, the president of the Conference officially welcomed
the Roman Catholic observers, the first at any such gathering,
as an "important sign" while making reference to the "great
Church of Rome." The denominational parallelism to "Church
of Sweden," "Church of Ireland" was a bit jarring to minds
that never thought or wrote of themselves in such reformational
terms. The observer's presence signified to the conference
president that:

> ...the great Church of Rome is not indifferent
> to what is being done in order to further a
> better understanding between Christians of dif-
> ferent traditions, and that an amity of souls
> can exist in spite of ecclesiastical barriers
> that appear insurmountable.[24]

Unity of individual souls distinct from their ecclesial union
in Christ seemed a bit wide of the mark to persons present
primarily as representatives of *Churches*.

Also, the published writings from the Lund conference have
identified the "deepest difference" as that between the whole
Catholic corporate tradition and the whole corporate Protestant tradition; the wide challenge to such an analysis was
duly reported.[25] Evanston did not pick up this thread.

Lund's Theological Secretary in a probing speech had perceived that "the differences which divide us in practice are
rooted in different conceptions of the Church," and that
"underlying all particular questions is that of the nature of
the Church";[26] he went on, further, to say in the context of
organic unity:

> None of the Churches represented in this con-
> ference holds that for purposes of jurisdiction
> the Church should be organized like the Church
> of Rome, a pyramidal system in which all members
> are subject to an earthly head at its apex.[27]

Evanston chose to ignore this analysis, but perhaps Lund's
theological positions contributed to the Roman Catholic authorities' refusal to send observers to Evanston. If Christians are ever to be reintegrated, such deep convictions
need to be expressed, but bi-lateral dialogues between churches seem more aptly designed than open convention speeches
to get at mutual understandings. Private "Visser't Hooft/
Bea and Willebrands" conversations more effectively paved
the way for Roman Catholic observers to attend New Delhi.

World Council - Superchurch?

Between the assemblies at Evanston and New Delhi, Visser't
Hooft, the WCC's general secretary, again addressed the nag-
ging charge that the World Council of Churches was becoming
the new Christian superchurch. His article was published in
the WCC's journal, *The Ecumenical Review*[28] and also as a separate reprint.

From the article it appears that certain fundamentalist movements were painting the World Council with the same brush
that had been long used to paint the Vatican as the Babylon,
the "mother of harlots," of the Apocalypse.[29]

Visser't Hooft acknowledged "...the unhappy and even tragic
experiences which humanity has had with the Superchurch,"
but, he argued, the epithet was not applicable either theo-
retically or existentially to the World Council of Churches.[30]

In the article, Visser't Hooft constructed a Church definition of an almost totally political character without reference to Christ, faith, creed, or worship. His construction
of the Superchurch is "a centralized ecclesiastical institution of world-wide character which seeks to impose unity and
uniformity by means of outward pressure and political influence."[31] This institution is then monopolistic, integrative of
Church and state, centralistic, uniformity-demanding and con-
ceives unity as an end in itself.[32] His citation of the
struggles of John Hus, Martin Luther, and John Knox as free-
dom-fighters against the "domination of the Roman Super-
Church" leaves the reader no room for shades of gray in this
heavy black/white portrait.[33]

Perhaps Visser't Hooft wished to assure the World Council's
fundamentalist critics that he had not succumbed to any

institutionalizing or centralizing tendency, because he
noted that these latter dangers "threaten every church."[34]
In any event, he denied that any of his chosen "superchurch"
characteristics could be predicated of the WCC. The World
Council's characteristics were only biblically motivated,
oriented to spiritual unity, liberty-promoting, avoiding the
dangers of centralization and seeking unity as part of a
rather vague whole church.[35]

This surprising, reformation-type essay, hardly calculated
to win a Roman Catholic hearing for the World Council, was
published near the tenth anniversary of the WCC. More gener-
ally-applicable shades of gray would have appeared less inaccurate to the real world, from Apostolic times to the present,
than did the frightening-black and snow-white of the article.

The essay quoted the Amsterdam Assembly, Central Committee
reports, and the *Toronto Statement* to affirm that the World
Council rejected the idea of becoming the superchurch. In
its put-down of the Roman Catholic Church, the article blamed
its mixing of spiritual with political and social motives.
"In the long run the Church lost far more than it gained...
it lost its identity and integrity as the Church of Christ."[36]
Lund had said that Christ's Church was visible; it had added
that the Church had been given a unity which was indissoluble
and indestructible, as already noted, but the essay remained
silent about these previous acknowledgments.

In clearing the World Council of any worldly purposes, Visser't
Hooft, more clearly than in the *Toronto Statement,* verbalized
the goal of the ecumenical movement. He said:

> The ecumenical movement does not seek a return
> to the sociological unity of the Corpus Chris-
> tianum, but promotes the spiritual and manifest
> unity of churches which seek together to be the
> Church in the world.[37]

Thus, the ecumenical vision appears to be that the original
Church of visible continuity has "lost its identity," and the
presently divided churches are "seeking together to be the
Church." The bond of unity holding the separated churches
together is to be "spiritual and manifest." This is one of
the clearest expressions of the target toward which Visser't
Hooft tried to lead the WCC. It seems to make the World
Council a sort of an instrument which helps to dismantle the
denominational barriers so that the underlying spiritual unity of the *Una Sancta,* long hidden, might again become manifest.

The separated churches seek to be the Church, the *Una Sancta;*

by a sort of midwifery, the WCC promotes the process of spiritual unification until that unity is manifest. The essay
does not push ahead to the relationship between the Church
and the WCC at the point at which the process is achieved.
The article seems to have dismissed the Roman Catholic Church,
numbering about half of the world's Christians, from the process.

Visser't Hooft was not so sanguine as to think his article
would completely prevent the superchurch label from being attached to the World Council. He concluded,

> We cannot expect that the accusation that the
> World Council is on the way toward becoming a
> super-church will ever disappear completely.[38]

He felt that "the WCC would fail in its pastoral duty, if it
did not seek to explain itself patiently and persistently,"[39]
thus attributing to the WCC the duty of a church. He noted
that the World Council's *very existence,* the influence of its
statements and references to it as "the World Church" contributed to the superchurch image.[40]

On to New Delhi

Three years later, in 1961, the Central Committee, headed by
Franklin C. Fry, adopted a general report to present to the
Third Assembly of the World Council at New Delhi; this report
summarized the WCC work in the period from Evanston to New
Delhi.[41] The WCC's General Secretariat under Visser't Hooft
prepared the report which the Central Committee made its own.

Between assemblies the Central Committee,in its annual meetings,is in effect the World Council; its executive committee,
which meets twice a year, and the General Secretariat,in
daily operation, carry on and in effect are the World Council
in continuous reality.

In this official Central Committee (referred to simply by the
initials CC in World Council writings) document, Chairman
Fry repeated the "WCC/*Una Sancta*" relationship, previously
noted, when he wrote "...the story of a Council of Churches,
however great its achievements, can never be a success story
until the moment when it ceases to exist as a Council because
of the emergence in reality of the *Una Sancta.*"[42] It does
not seem to be a "John the Baptist" model of the WCC's de-
creasing while the *Una Sancta* emerges and increases,because
the World Council continues to increase even as the unity, at
least of dialogue and collaboration, continues to increase;
its structure and variegated services grew faster than any
"deliberate policy for enlarging the scope and activity of

the Council."[43]   In any event, the envisioned end will not
arrive until the WCC ceases to exist and the *Una Sancta*
emerges in reality.

In Chairman Fry's conception, which echoes ideas expressed at
different times by Visser't Hooft, it seems clear that the
WCC is not the *Una Sancta,* nor that it is to become the *Una
Sancta* in some "acorn to oak" fashion. Perhaps, however, the
concept admits the possibility that the WCC could be a federation which, on the elimination of denominational barriers,
would then evolve from the World Council of Churches into
the World Church. Fry's expression does not seem to contain
this idea, but neither does it fully exclude it. Fry implies
that ecumenism is a movement which must advance to its end.

In his epilogue to the same Central Committee report, *From
Evanston to New Delhi,* General Secretary Visser't Hooft unfolded a bit further the meaning of the World Council. He
first observed as factual that the World Council's growth
made it "more truly a *World* Council," that the Church's *missionary* dimension was more diffused throughout its structure,
that the Faith and Order commission had "renewed emphasis on
the calling of the Churches to concrete, visible unity" and
finally that the WCC had "become more deeply involved in the
struggle for just and peaceful human relations."[44]

From the foregoing data, Visser't Hooft concluded that the
thirteen-year-old World Council had become "an *indispensable
part* of the life of the member churches...a part of the ecclesiastical structure which the Churches need and desire to
have in our time."[45] He acknowledged that the Council's development

> ...has led to a certain 'institutionalization,'
> which is both necessary and natural in a body
> which the churches have created to serve them
> on the international plane...the relevant ques-
> tion is whether the institutional aspect of the
> World Council...is an adequate instrument.[46]

Visser't Hooft emphasized that the churches could not remain
satisfied in their present relationships. The ecumenical
movement must push on from the state of cooperation and some
life together "toward the full concrete manifestation of
their unity."[47]

> ...the World Council is an institution which
> seeks to transcend its own life and to point to
> a reality beyond itself, that is to the full
> unity of God's people.

> This has been so from the very beginning.
> 'Faith and Order' brought into the World
> Council its calling 'to promote the essen-
> tial oneness of the Church of Christ.' The
> World Council is an instrument created by
> the churches to fulfill...the purposes of
> the ecumenical movement...It must constantly
> hold the vision of the *Una Sancta* in its
> unity and purity before the Churches.[48]

Visser't Hooft here seems to throw out the notion of the
World Council as a federation. Expressions such as the *Una
Sancta* in its unity and purity," "full concrete manifestation of their unity," WCC pointing to "a reality beyond itself," "full unity of God's People," and "essential oneness,"
go beyond the relatively loose association of independent
and autonomous members which might be termed a federation.

At the same time, Visser't Hooft's conclusion that the World
Council was an "indispensable part of the ecclesiastical
structure" and yet intended to "transcend its own life," allow the impressions that the future, fully-visible, concrete
Una Sancta would dispense with the indispensable. An uncom-
fortable tension appears to lie between the facts and his
vision.

Visser't Hooft faced this tension in a provisory way. If the
WCC controlled the churches by legislation etc., the movement
would die; on the other hand, if the member churches kept the
Council as their council, as truly a Council of Churches, then
the WCC could continue to be an instrument for, a leaven for,
and a signpost to, the *Una Sancta*.[49] Such things as an instrument, leaven, and a signpost do not exist for themselves;
when the end is achieved they have fulfilled their purpose.
Thus, Visser't Hooft may be recognized as saying that the
presently indispensable WCC may be dispensed with when the
concrete, actual *Una Sancta* is fully manifest or visible.

Further, the WCC already represents "something more" than
merely its collection of member churches.[50] Even more than
a chord goes beyond the sum of the musical notes which produce it, the WCC represents a "something else," a "new dimension," a "plus,"

> ...which belongs to the mystery of the Church's
> unity and fellowship and through which the di-
> vine truth is seen in fuller proportion, and so
> the voice of the Council is at the same time a
> voice of the churches and a voice to the chur-
> ches. It is both institution and movement,
> instrument and leaven; its calling is both to
> serve and to challenge.[51]

In this passage, Visser't Hooft identifies the Council as
having a representative function for its member churches,
and also a prophetic, challenging function with reference to
their duty. The *quid extra* (extra something) which accrues
to the Council, as an assemblage of churches, partakes of
the mystery of the *Una Sancta* and has for its source the
[Holy] Spirit. Thus, the World Council is, in Visser't Hooft's
view, something more than any of its member churches, as a
representative voice and a prophetic conscience; this extra
dimension is from the [Holy] Spirit and belongs to the mystery of the *Una Sancta*.

Of great concern to the Central Committee and Visser't Hooft
was the fear that the member churches were giving a dispropor-
tionately small response to the insights, wisdom and exhorta-
tory resolutions of the World Council. Consequently, Visser't
Hooft closed the Central Committee's report with sharp emphasis on the influence the World Council must have in every local congregation. Too easily could the ecumenical movement be
a movemdnt of theologically sophisticated elite,talking to
themselves and their own committees. Such "think and decide"
bodies were necessary for ideas,trend-analysis, and task orientation

> But it is even more important that the World
> Council is rooted in the life of the congre-
> gations,....At this point our main task re-
> mains yet to be accomplished.[52]

Elsewhere in the CC's report, *From Evanston to New Delhi,*
were the long-worked-on determinations to integrate the International Missionary Council (IMC) with the World Council,
to receive the Russian Orthodox Church (the largest of the
Orthodox Churches) into World Council membership,[53] to extend
the constitutional basis of the World Council to include belief in the Trinity,[54] and to strengthen the Faith and Order
commission within the WCC.[55]

Each determination was in the form of a report which had already gone through the Committee of origin, the General Secretariat, the Executive Committee, and the Central Committee.
By the time of the Assembly, each report was carefully detailed and correlated with the WCC's other units and decisions. The assembly, for the most part, approves such reports; generally minor modifications, arising from the assembly floor, are incorporated into the text.

The WCC's concept of Church-unity, with a continuing awareness that any synthesis also touches the Roman Catholic
Church, comes into focus in the *Evanston to New Delhi* report
on Faith and Order. As a department in the Division of
Studies of the WCC, Faith and Order deepened its theological
probings after its Lund Conference. It sought to go beyond

mutual presentation of each denomination's current theological position, to search for the roots common to all the churches.[56] This penetration beneath the obvious differences
led to the question left unanswered by the *Toronto Statement*:
what kind of unity is to be sought—"what kind of unity does
God require of His Church?"[57]

After much consultation, the F&O Commission presented, and
the Central Committee accepted, a definition of the kind of
unity that must be sought. It has been called the *St. Andrew's Statement,* a name derived from the place of its first
presentation.

> ...the unity which is both God's will and His
> gift to His Church is one which brings *all in
> each place* who confess Christ Jesus as Lord
> into a fully committed fellowship with one
> another through one Baptism into Him, holding
> the one apostolic faith, preaching the one
> Gospel, breaking the one bread, and having a
> corporate life reaching out in witness and
> service to all, *and* which at the same time
> unites them with the whole Christian fellow-
> ship *in all places* and all ages in such wise
> that ministry and members are acknowledged by
> all and that all can act and speak together as
> occasion requires for the tasks to which God
> calls the Church.[58]

The formula's expression, "all in each place," captured
Visser't Hooft's intent that the movement not be confined to
an international elite, but rather, that it reach to the congregations in every town and village and lead them into one
local Christian fellowship. "All in each place," became a
catch-phrase that evoked the definition of unity which the
Central Committee approved for the New Delhi Assembly.

Some churches thought that this theological consensus on "the
nature of the unity sought" reflected what they largely already had, others, that it reflected the Lambeth Quadrilateral.[59] A Roman Catholic could rejoice in the formula's reference to "His Church" yet wonder about the lack of reference
to texts where the Gospels present Christ as saying "my
church," "my sheep."

The Church as a single organism with a framework of unitary
structure seems likewise to be rejected. The expression
"superchurch" has already been given a pejorative, political
content by Visser't Hooft. In speaking of the basis of unity
in a Faith and Order Conference he said:

> It is a dangerous misunderstanding to think
> that the only alternative to disunity is a
> monolithic, centralized and imperialistic
> super-church, a sort of ecclesiastical
> leviathan.[60]

The Central Committee in its report to the Assembly at New
Delhi, restrained those who thought that one church meant one
visible ecclesial structure.

> By its very nature such a unity is visible,
> but it does not imply a single centralized
> ecclesiastical institution—which is very gen-
> erally set aside as being undesirable. It is
> compatible with a large degree of institution-
> al and liturgical diversity, but it is neither
> 'federal' nor merely spiritual.'[61]

The St. Andrew's formula for the unity sought was judged by
the Central Committee to be a step beyond the *Toronto Statement;* it was further thought to confront the New Delhi Assembly with a radical choice: "yes" to the unity formula
would undoubtedly be a step forward (beyond denominational
autonomy); "no" to the unity formula meant refusal to go beyond the divided "status quo."[62]

> What seems clear is that this new definition
> presents both a new doctrinal question for
> consideration by the World Council of Churches,
> particularly in reference to the Toronto State-
> ment of 1950 and one of the most crucial eccle-
> siological issues which the ecumenical movement
> as a whole has yet faced.[63]

CHAPTER THIRTEEN

THIRD WORLD COUNCIL ASSEMBLY
(NEW DELHI, 1961)

The third assembly of the World Council of Churches faced the
crucial ecclesiological issue head on; it even intensified
the St. Andrew's formula for unity by voting to approve a re-
statement of it which proclaimed that the unity God wants is
in fact being made visible. This present active sense nevertheless keeps the formula substantially the same as that presented to the assembly by the Central Committee.

Unity Formula: "all in each place"

> We believe that the unity which is both God's
> will and his gift to his Church is being made
> visible as all in each place, who are baptized
> into Jesus Christ and confess him as Lord and
> Saviour are brought by the Holy Spirit into one
> fully committed fellowship, holding the one
> apostolic faith, preaching the one Gospel,
> breaking the one bread, joining in common
> prayer, and having a corporate life reaching
> out in witness and service to all and who at
> the same time are united with the whole Chris-
> tian fellowship in all places and all ages in
> such wise that ministry and members are accepted
> by all, and that all can act and speak together
> as occasion requires for the tasks to which God
> calls his people.
>
> It is for such unity that we believe we must
> pray and work.[1]

The Lambeth Quadrilateral (Scripture/Creeds/Sacraments/His-
toric Episcopacy), harmonizes with only three equivalents
(Gospel/Apostolic Faith/Baptism and one bread) in the New
Delhi unity-formula. The fourth New Delhi term, ministry,
may include the historic episcopacy, but certainly does not
require it. Thus, the new unity formula, a step forward perhaps for some WCC members, falls significantly short of the
Anglican Quadrilateral.

253

The Orthodox saw the formula as defective in mentioning only
two sacraments and seeming to restrict the sense of full liturgical worship to "one bread" with the unacceptable opening
toward deficient ecclesiology and intercommunion.[2]

Added to the foregoing, Roman Catholics note the expression
"his Church" in the formula,while it omits the thrust of the
Scriptural texts in which Christ refers to "my church," "my
sheep." By such criteria, the formula seems to be characterized by a Protestant "free-church" perspective; the overwhelming Protestant majority in the World Council appears to
be synthesizing a consensus. The World Council, itself,
seems more structured than its formula for the *Una Sancta*.

The World Council had grown to such an extent that the Central Committee divided the New Delhi Assembly into three different kinds of sessions: (1) *General* Sessions for Addresses,
common prayer and ceremonies, etc.; (2) *Deliberative* Sessions
for reports of the Assembly sections which considered the
three chosen and prepared papers on Worship, Service and
Unity; (3) *Business* Sessions,which considered nominations,
changes in constitution, new member churches, etc.[3]

There was no voting in the General Sessions; voting flourished in the Business Sessions. However, the Deliberative
Sessions,in which the "unity formula" was presented, were
regarded as

> of such a theological or general policy nature
> that they ought not to be amended in so large
> a body...the only recommendation in order...
> was that the Assembly approve the substance of
> the document, and commend it to the Churches.[4]

If enough floor strength could be mustered the report could
be sent back to the section which presented it. Despite this
restraining rule,the formulating committee modified the text
somewhat in response to limited reactions from the Assembly.[5]
An Orthodox-Anglican majority would presumably have rejected
the unity formula.

Thus, although some delegates dissented,and the Orthodox made
a separate statement, the Assembly voted to approve the unity
report. Its key paragraph is the unity formula previously
quoted; the remainder of the report comments on the formula
and suggests possible consequences on levels identified as
local, denominational, and world.[6]

The "Unity Report" identifies the unity formula as "our common goal."[7] The report acknowledges that the World Council
is "not yet of a common mind on the interpretation or means

of achieving the goal we have described."[8] However, this
picture of unity is termed a "stage beyond" the *Toronto
Statement* which itself was "a landmark in the World Council's thinking about itself and its relation to work for
unity."[9]

The incorporation of Faith and Order into the World Council
had brought the "F&O" primary focus on unity to the wider
assembly, so that "the vision of the one Church has become
the inspiration of our ecumenical endeavour. We reaffirm
that we must go forward to seek the full implications of this
vision."[10] When the anxious thought of the "one Church/de-
nominational autonomy" *conflict* arose, the approved report in
general terms insisted:

> The achievement of unity will involve nothing
> less than the death and rebirth of many forms
> of church life as we have known them. We be-
> lieve that nothing less costly can finally
> suffice.[11]

Although the Assembly, and its elected Central Committee, have
legislative authority over the subordinate divisions of the
WCC organization itself,[12] nevertheless its voted reports do
not bind the member churches. The Assembly can only vote to
recommend the reports for the reflection and possible action
of the member churches. Thus, the report's wished-for unity
of worship of "all in each place" continues as a dead letter
in any given town or village in which different WCC members
continue as separated congregations.

The practical difficulties readily become magnified when one
contemplates a town in which Orthodox, Episcopalian, Presbyterian, Lutheran and Congregationalist WCC members have local
churches. Perhaps "eucharistic division," held intolerable
by some, while its contrary is held intolerable by others,
most sharply points up the problem at the local level.[13] Although the report judges that a general solution cannot be
found at this local level yet, it discretely approves those
who *risk* intercommunicating, while it gently *pushes* the question of the possibility of "intercommunion before full
union."[14]

Thus, the World Council pragmatically favors a non-episcopal
free church ecclesiology as against the position of those who
believe that there is no true eucharist without valid episcopal continuity from Apostolic times. This WCC ecclesiology
is utterly unacceptable to the Orthodox and High Church Episcopalians.

This matter is so phrased in terms of taking "responsible

risks" and exerting "pressure on the limits of our inherited
traditions," that the force of the document is mainly against
those who hold the necessity of continuous episcopacy.[15]   The
risk is rather one-sided!

So while the *Toronto Statement* (1950) declared that the WCC
can hold no particular conception of the Church, and the *New
Delhi Report* (1961) declares that "the Toronto Statement
still best expresses our understanding of the Council's nature,"[16] the WCC, in fact, clearly favors a free-church ecclesiology.

To put the matter another way, a non-episcopal ecclesiology
will more easily enable the World Council to achieve its
formula of unity. *Diakonoi, Presbyteroi,* and *Episcopoi* (deacons, priests, and bishops respectively) are much more common to the New Testament picture of unity than they are to
the "unity formula" which the *New Delhi Report* identifies as
"a commonly accepted picture of our goal."[17]   In a separate
F&O study, springing from Lund's questions but not published
as an interim report until shortly *after* the New Delhi Assembly, the necessity of episcopal and presbyteral elements
in a reunited church was recognized.[18]   This post-script to
New Delhi added the quadrilateral fourth element (Gospel/
Creeds/Sacraments/*Episcopacy*) missing from the new unity
formula.

Concept Problems

The New Delhi document next considers the *denominational
level* and its approach to union in doctrine, sacraments and
service at that level.   The Orthodox do not accept the status of a denomination as a church in any relation to their
own self-concept of Church because "the Church itself is essentially undivided";[19] others, however, conceive of the
overall relationship of denominations as "divisions *within*
the church."[20]   To bypass this ecclesiological difficulty,
the Unity Report *limits* its attention to the "same Christ"
and "certain crucial elements" (Gospel, baptism, eucharist,
service) which WCC members recognize as contained in "a
variety of corporate traditions."[21]   Thus the term "denomination" is kept and, for the Orthodox, need only mean that
they recognize the same Christ in a definite corporate tradition which contains certain crucial Christian elements.

Following this, *The New Delhi Report* briefly examined the
areas of doctrine, sacraments and service in which it showed
its member churches "a next step towards unity",[22] that is,
its own formulated concept of unity.

Under the title of doctrine, the report noted that "formulas

of faith are not identically the same as the actual faith itself" and that "community (*koinonia*) in Christ is more nearly
the precondition of sound doctrine (*orthodoxia*) than vice
versa."[23] These insights, without further precisioning, were
used to urge each denomination to re-examine its doctrinal
bases "in the light of the primacy of Scripture."[24]

Under the titles of baptism and the eucharist, the *New Delhi
Report* affirms that baptism is the "essential basis" of the
ecumenical fellowship, as Paul points out, "we were all baptized into one body."[25] Mutual recognition of baptism has
aided the motion toward unity; but further gains require the
realization that baptism is a *dynamic* starting point leading
to Christian growth and full union in Christ.[26]

"Eucharistic separation" reveals the contradiction of doctrinal position and the practical failure "to live and act as
one visible and united body."[27] The document holds that the
impasse can be broken through "wherever existing convictions
allow" by celebrating "intercommunion between churches...
without waiting for consensus...in the ecumenical movement
as a whole." Thus, "ecclesial intercommunion without waiting"
can become a slogan bypassing the need for continuous, apostolic episcopacy. This is free-church ecclesiology.

This section closes with the "Life and Work" recognition that
common witness and service unite; their extension to ethics
and discipline, common Christian education, even perhaps for
ordinands, is the suggested path ahead.[28]

Finally, *The New Delhi Report* examines the World Council
level itself for the implications consequent upon its new extended picture of the ecclesial unity to be sought. The document proposes "faithful prayer for the unity of Christ's
Church as and when he wills it" as "our deepest responsibility."[29] It then notes that while the WCC should not impose
any one concept of unity, it should, nevertheless, proclaim
the unity of Christ's Church and help its member churches to
comprehend it and achieve it more fully.[30]

Pushing out further than prior position statements, this document indicates that the WCC considered that "education for
unity," "consultative help" for uniting churches, "consultations on church union," and "directly requesting churches to
react" to unions already achieved are within its constitutional competence.[31] Moreover, the report decided to make
inquiry into the institutional or church structures which im-
pede unity, and the actual processes of the early Conciliar
period.[32]

In looking at the World Council itself, the Assembly left the
door ajar for future super-church reflections by saying with
a flourish of solemnity, "We are learning what the Council is
by *living* together within it; and so it shall be."[33]   Persons
come together for a consultation, but they live within a community, a communion or a church; the translated "amen" adds a
surprising note of determination or "accomplished fact" to
the expressed insight.   Continuing the thought, the Assembly
desires to know "the theological meaning of our new life in
the Council", which "is not something wholly other than the
member churches.   It is the churches in continuing council."[34]

Churches within a constant communion (this is *koinonia's*[35]
primary sense) and sharing a new life which vitalizes both
local church and conciliar communion, "should speak of the
Council as 'we' rather than 'it' or 'they.'"[36]   The Assembly
affirms divine approval for itself by adopting the proposition that

> many Christians are now aware that the Council
> is in some new and unprecedented sense an in-
> strument of the Holy Spirit for the effecting
> of God's will for the whole Church, and through
> the Church for the world.[37]

That the Council can instrumentally effect God's will for the
whole *Una Sancta* and the world is a rather sweeping assertion
of totality and divine support.   This statement certainly involves and implies an overarching posture with reference to
denominational churches; it encourages the concern that the
World Council cultivates the superchurch idea, or at least
that concept of a divinely-initiated, super-instrument over-
seeing the member denominations.

With the WCC as a continuing *koinonia* fostering a new life
for member bodies living within it and effecting God's will,[38]
it becomes difficult to visualize the necessity of world denominational bodies such as the Lutheran World Federation
(LWF), or the World Alliance of Reformed Churches (WARC), once
the Lutheran and Reformed Churches join the WCC.   It appears
that the increasingly-magnified WCC and the world denominational bodies are on a collision course, unless perhaps the
WCC incorporates them under its own world structure.

The *New Delhi Report* briefly addressed the problem of these
other world bodies: "opinion today is divided over the effects of their existence."[39]   Some think they are a present
barrier to full unity until they deepen their domination's
sense of the *Una Sancta;* others see the WCC as interfering
with a denominational unity which may lead to a wider unity;
the report favors the notion that a denomination "will not

consider the union of one of their churches (with the WCC)
as a loss, but as a gain for the whole church."[40]

The unity section of the report closes with a return to the
anguish of separate communions at the WCC level, and the urgency of hopes "for the adjustment of Church policies on
intercommunion."[41] The final paragraph reminds the member
churches that the unity sought is neither "for its own sake,
or even for our sake. It is for the Lord's sake and for that
of the world."[42]

High Points at New Delhi

The excitement of the New Delhi Assembly, and its memorable
high points, appear to rest in actions other than the unity
section.[43] Chief among the exciting events was the integration of the International Missionary Council (IMC) and the
WCC. Other highlights were the changing of *The Basis,* the
admission of the Russian Orthodox and the presence of Roman
Catholic observers.

The Missionary Council under John Mott at Edinburgh in 1910
had been the acknowledged starting point of the modern ecumenical movement. It had remained apart but "associated
with" the WCC, on the ground that the World Council would as-
similate the missionary body, diminish it, and lessen its
missionary thrust.

However, in the half century from Edinburgh to New Delhi,
"the activities of the two councils had become increasingly
interdependent,"[44] many of the same people "were involved
in the life of both bodies,"[45] and the conviction had grown
that mission and Christ's Church are so intimately connected
that neither is complete without the other;[46] consequently,
the WCC would injure itself if it neglected to encourage the
missionary work of its member churches. Thus, on the opening day, with all details previously worked out, the IMC was
integrated with the WCC under the name of the World Council
"without a dissenting vote."[47]

On the other hand, some voices dissented when the Constitutional *Basis* of the WCC was changed; it was extended to include the Trinity and the expression, "according to the
scriptures." The Orthodox churches wanted the first; the
Norwegian Lutherans wanted the second.[48] The opponents of
change feared that the "Basis" was being slowly converted
into a fuller dogmatic church formula which would be the
touchstone of membership in the council; fears were expressed
in words like a "new universal church," "creedal extension
retards religious cooperation," "a step toward confessionalism," "creed belongs to church, not the World Council," "the

Basis is becoming doctrinally burdensome."[49]   Finally the vote
was taken; there were "383 in favor, 36 against, 7 absten-
tions"[50] for the *new Basis* which reads:

> The World Council of Churches is a fellowship
> of churches which confess the Lord Jesus Christ
> as God and Saviour according to the Scriptures
> and therefore seek to fulfill together their
> common calling to the glory of the one God,
> Father, Son and Holy Spirit.[51]

This expected inclusion of the Trinity in the basis of the
World Council "played a very important role in the decision...
made to join the WCC" on the part of the Russian Orthodox
Church.[52]   The much smaller Orthodox churches of Bulgaria,
Rumania and Poland, undoubtedly influenced by the Russian
Orthodox decision, were among the twenty-two other smaller
churches which joined the WCC at New Delhi. At the same Assembly, it was voted no longer to receive into membership
a "church with an inclusive membership of less than ten thousand."[53]

As the number of member-churches swelled at New Delhi, so also
did the number of official observers; among the latter were
included five Roman Catholics,[54] all priests, from the newly-
formed Secretariat for Promoting Christian Unity (SPCU). Visser't Hooft and Bea had prepared the way for these observers
a year before the New Delhi Assembly, as well as reciprocally
inviting World Council observers to the Second Vatican Council.[55]   In his address at New Delhi's opening session, Visser't Hooft welcomed the five observers and hoped that it
would be clear that New Delhi and Vatican II were not opponents seeking self-gain but rather both servants of Christ.[56]

At Evanston in 1954, WCC leaders wondered whether the Council
could, with integrity, hold together; at New Delhi in 1961;
they wondered whether the WCC was "able to become a World
Council in the full sense of the word."[57]   Its integration
with the IMC, its significant inclusion of more Orthodox
churches, as well as African and Asian churches, its widening
of the "Basis," and its welcoming of Roman Catholic observers, certainly brought the Council closer to world dimensions
than it had been.

At the same time collaborative world-type activities vis-a-
vis hunger, racism, international tensions, etc., (all extra-
ordinarily good works), seemed to gain more attention and support than the newly precisioned Faith and Order formula for
unity. Moreover, at New Delhi, the Faith and Order Committee
recorded its complaint that the F&O position in the WCC is
"neither satisfactory...nor appropriate to the specific nature

of its purpose or task," and it requested the Central Committee soon to consider elevating its position to "the status of
a Division."[58] Yet, Visser't Hooft seemed to have his gaze
fixed on Life and Work activity when he ended his reflections
about New Delhi with a paraphrase on S. M. Cavert's report of
the Assembly:

> 'They [the Churches] were not only determined
> to stay together [as at Amsterdam] and to grow
> together [as at Evanston] but to move out to-
> gether into the World struggle for social jus-
> tice and international peace.' I hoped that
> he was right.[59]

CHAPTER FOURTEEN

FOURTH WORLD COUNCIL
ASSEMBLY (UPPSALA, 1968)

Before, during, and after the New Delhi Assembly, the inter-
communications of the Roman Catholic Church were winding into
high gear in preparation for the second ecumenical council at
the Vatican. Pope John XXIII (1958-1963) had interpreted the
Council in 1959 as an *aggiornamento* for the Church and as an
"inducement of the faithful of the separated communities to
follow Us amicably in this quest for unity and for grace."[1]

In 1960, Pope John had set up the Secretariat for Promoting
Christian Unity (SPCU) and approved the plan of its president,
Cardinal Bea, to send five observers to the New Delhi Assembly, as well as to invite observers from all Christian communities to Vatican II;[2] about 150 came.

After the New Delhi Assembly the significant event which attracted Christian attention was Vatican II. In reporting on
the interim period from New Delhi 1961 to Uppsala 1968,
Frankin C. Fry, Chairman of the WCC's powerful Central Committee, could write in 1968:

> In historical perspective there is no question
> what the towering event—or rather series of
> events—of this period of this Central Committee
> has been. It is the change in, indeed the
> transformation of, the relations of the World
> Council to the Roman Catholic Church...dele-
> gated observers...were welcomed...at the Second
> Vatican Council. Following the Decree *de
> oecumenismo*...conversations began...which is-
> sued in the decision to approve the formation
> of a joint working group on a continuing basis.[3]

The dialogue of Cardinal Bea and Secretary Visser't Hooft had
thus issued in a continuing linkage between the World Council
and the Roman Catholic Church. The linkage was informal and
exploratory, but it was official, and it reinforced the conviction that there was really only one ecumenical movement as

263

far as the World Council and the Roman Catholic Church were
concerned. Both bodies professed the Trinitarian Basis, both
acknowledged the inspiration of the Holy Spirit in the modern
ecumenical movement, but deep differences were recognized by
both as to the nature of the Church, the World Council, and
the goal of the movement.

However, a shift of focus was occurring. As Visser't Hooft
had hoped, the churches of the World Council "moved out together into the world struggle for justice and peace."[4] This
motion toward the world tended to do two things: it increased
the number of contact points at which the nonmember Roman
Catholic Church could cooperate with the deployed agencies of
the WCC, but at the same time this contrifugal force diminished the focus of the World Council's attention on the ecclesial problem at the heart of the ecumenical movement.
Multiform secular-type activity diverted from the theologic-
ally-oriented thrust toward the *Una Sancta*.

It appeared that the old Soederblom principle of "cooperating
in service, while relegating doctrine to an indefinitely later consideration" was commanding the WCC direction. Doctrine
was indeed rather cursorily examined, but the motion toward
worldly involvement dominated and excited attention as the
World Council held its fourth Assembly in Uppsala, the birth-
place of Soederblom's Life and Work movement.

A year and a half before Uppsala, Willem Visser't Hooft, General Secretary from 1938 to 1966, retired. The Central Committee, acknowledging the difficulty of replacing this extraordinary leader, finally appointed Rev. Dr. Eugene Carson
Blake of the United Presbyterian Church in the USA to this
most influential post in the WCC.[5] Rev. Dr. Visser't Hooft
continued his valuable service to the World Council as a permanent honorary president with an office in the General Secretariat at Geneva.[6]

Focus on "the World"

At Uppsala, E. C. Blake, the new General Secretary, strongly
endorsed the World Council's engagement in "new activities
and emphases in the service of the world."[7] Citing Archbishop Soederblom's inspiration in the Life and Work movement,
Blake rejoiced in the Assembly's location in Uppsala

> ...to make it entirely clear that its interest
> and involvement in justice and peace, in devel-
> opment and aid, are...a renewed emphasis on an
> early and essential part of what we are.[8]

Blake took issue with those who think that the World Council

is only for union of the churches, or that its bureaucracy,
supported by divided and sovereign churches, is a hindrance
to the unity sought.[9] Yet he did not show how the "church
toward the world" emphasis, which may be termed "secular ecumenism," would finally bring about the *Una Sancta*.[10] Rather,
he repeated and insisted that the world's problems, such as
poverty and racism, were pressing upon the churches and the
World Council,and must be met.[11]

Shortly after the meeting at Uppsala, Blake wrote a reflective
essay on the assembly and the World Council's future. He
noted approvingly that the world's Agenda had more deeply influenced the proceedings at Uppsala than had the divisions
among the churches.

> Every report received, document approved, and
> programme envisaged was affected by the state
> of the world even more than by the state of the
> church.[12]

Further, after mentioning the 235 member churches represented,
the expanded presence of the National Orthodox Churches, and
the new relationship of the Joint Working Group (JWG) with
the Roman Catholic Church, Blake approvingly identified what
he considered would be the most remembered characteristic of
Uppsala: "The emphasis on Christian service to humanity."[13]
The church-toward-the world movement appeared to be canonized
as primary. The Conciliarity of the WCC aided services;would
service reciprocally further conciliarity rather than the recovery of the *Una Sancta*? Did Life and Work eclipse Faith
and Order at Uppsala?

European Visser't Hooft, nurtured in continental theological
debates, had been able to hold the theological and activity
elements of the World Council in closer conjunction than
Blake whose American activist enthusiasm encouraged and even
led the way into the consumingly interesting maelstrom of the
world. Rather than unitive motions toward the manifestation
of the *Una Sancta*, Blake felt that "effective programmes...
are the essence of the World Council."[14] He apparently did
not want the Life and Work activity to obscure the Faith and
Order tradition,[15] and the record indicates that the eclipse
was not total, but many participants could hardly see the
barely visible moon in the brightness of the activist sun.

The packing of Uppsala's two-week agenda, the quantity of reports and committee meetings, the large number of delegates,
observers (including 150 students) and visitors[at the assembly, and even in the deliberative section devoted to the Faith
and Order question (Section I)] prompted the officially registered complaint:

...that a section of an assembly should *never
again* again be asked to produce a theological
document similar to that at Uppsala under the
conditions prevailing in the first four Assemblies. If a theological document is needed,
entirely different procedures must be devised
for its preparation, discussion, revision and
adoption.[16]

As at the three previous assemblies, so at Uppsala, the body
of approved participants was divided into sections to consider prepared materials which could be accepted, modified, or
entirely reworked in producing the official WCC report; this
would then be commended to the member churches for their free
response.

The Central Committee divided the Uppsala Assembly into the
following six sections:

        Section I   The Holy Spirit and the Catholicity
                            of the Church (F&O)
        Section II   Renewal of Mission (IMC)
        Section III   World Economic and Social Develop-
                            ment (L&W)
        Section IV   Toward Justice and Peace in Inter-
                            national Affairs (L&W)
        Section V   Worship (a new topic germain to F&O)
        Section VI   Towards new Styles of Living (L&W)[17]

Only Sections I and V dealt with theological concerns pertinent to the ecumenical goal of manifesting the unity of
Christ's Church; the WCC had committed itself to this goal in
its landmark *Toronto Statement*.[18]

Section V on Worship (a subject not yet directly considered
by a WCC Assembly), produced a document which represents a
hesitant start on the topic.[19] An Anglican clergyman and
Dean of King's College, Cambridge, was asked to give his reaction to the Worship Section's debate and final document.
He observed candidly:

        ...this document represents a beginning. By
        taking worship as one of its themes, the Fourth
        Assembly showed that the problem is not to be
        left in the respectable obscurity of Faith and
        Order. Nor is it to be submerged in enthusiasm
        for the social Gospel....Perhaps for the sake
        of the world; the next Assembly should be more
        theological.[20]

The Faith and Order Commission gave its own major attention

to the *Una Sancta* in Section I which considered the topic of
"the Holy Spirit and the Catholicity of the Church."[21] Despite the title, the Section's final document confined its
thoughts on the Holy Spirit mainly to paragraph 8, but ranged
expansively over the Church's attributes, classically called
her identifying marks. As named in the Apostle's Creed, they
characterize the Church of Christ as: one, holy, catholic and
apostolic.

The debate and document suffered from an ambiguous use of the
term "church" from the struggle between the Orthodox definite-
ness of "unbroken *visible* eucharistic unity" versus the free
church tendency to reserve visibility to an indefinite future
manifestation, and from an ambivalent application of the quality, catholicity, either theologically or phenomenologically.
Despite these weaknesses the finally-approved document broke
new ground for a WCC Assembly.[22] First, the document made
general comments, then it briefly considered diversity, continuity, and unity with reference to Christ's Church, and
finally, considered the unity of mankind. Thus, in a sharply
condensed and reworked form, some significant ground, at least
newly confronted, follows. The condensed form shows the con-
textual setting from which the ultimate WCC goal of *a new conciliarity* emerges.

General[23]

　°World's criticism: the struggle for church unity is irrel-
　　evant to the world's crises; forget it.
　°F&O reply: the same God who gives us light on the world's
　　crises, is bringing us together in His one Church.
　°God shows us fresh meaning in the oneness, holiness,
　　catholicity and apostolicity which in close interde-
　　pendence have always characterized the authentic life
　　of the Church. Each basic gift is God's gift and our
　　task.
　°Christ's purpose is to bring people of all times, all
　　races, all places, all conditions into an organic and
　　living unity in Christ.
　°Catholicity is opposed to particularism; (the context op-
　　poses universality to denominational particularity).

a) Diversity[24]

　°Distinguish a diversity which frustrates unity (bad) from
　　a diversity which encourages unity (good).
　°There is a variety of gifts (1 Cor. 12-14); there are di-
　　verse ways of presenting doctrine, of celebrating
　　liturgy and organizing the Church.

b) Continuity[25]
   (Apostolicity)

   °The Church, discernible through the centuries, is revealed
     as the one Body of Christ; its continuity is actualized
     in - faith, worship, and sacraments, continuous succes-
     sion of apostolic ministry, preparation for diakonia,
     and witness.
   °All that makes the Church to be the Church is from Christ
     through the Apostles; fidelity to the mission of the
     Apostles also makes the Church apostolic.

c) Unity[26]

   °New Delhi said "all in each place"; continue to seek this
     unity in common: profession of faith, observance of bap-
     tism and eucharist, and one accepted ministry for the
     whole Church.
   °To "all in each place," now add "all in *all* places."
   °Regional Councils, world denominational fellowships give a
     unity which is inevitably *partial*. Regional Councils
     and the World Council "may be regarded as a transition-
     al opportunity for eventually actualizing a true uni-
     versal, ecumenical, *conciliar* form of common life and
     witness. The members of the World Council of Churches,
     committed to each other, should work for a time when a
     genuinely *universal council* may once more speak for all
     Christians, and lead the way into the future," (para-
     graph 19).[27]

d) Unity of Mankind[28]

   °The Church claims to be a sign of the unity of mankind;
     the world is skeptical; the outsider thinks the Church
     irrelevant; the Church needs new openness.
   °Technology is forming a single secular culture; this shows
     the unifiability of man. The Christian believes man-
     kind's unity is from: one God, one creation, one
     Christ's salvation, one Church, and one end: God.
   °By this divine truth we must reject the humanly divisive
     elements in racism, classism, nationalism, rich/poor
     disparity, etc.
   °Catholicity, God's gift, is the sacramental experience of
     incorporation into Christ of which the Church is the
     form.

The inclusion of the secular charge of "irrelevance" near the
beginning and end of the eight-page document on "the Holy
Spirit and the Church's Catholicity" manifests the influence
which the shift toward secular ecumenism had on the assembly's
most clearly focused *Una Sancta* section.

The solicited reaction of a qualified participant affirms
that, "the need and challenge of the secular world were continually present and pressing in the work of this section, as
throughout the Assembly."[29] This same participant mentions
the lack of time, basic theological unpreparedness, the unacceptable kind of "theology-by-show-of-hands," and the obstacles posed by language barriers, unfamiliarity of concepts
and procedural confusions.[30]

The *irrelevance charge* is an ax aimed at the very root of the
ecumenical movement. Christ's "that they may be one as we
are" (John 17:11) is the principal driving power of the movement; if that root is severed by secular disbelief then the
WCC's drive to manifest the *Una Sancta* is a dead issue.

Further, the WCC needs belief in its own basis to justify its
involvement as Christian, even in the world's problems. A
withering of its belief must surely deflate its moral authority before both the world and its own member churches. A
mid-point between arrival at the one Church and isolated
Christian activity in the world appears to be conciliar
Christian activity in the world, but even this activity needs
its belief basis to maintain its Christian character. The
irrelevance charge may be a danger signal warning that the
WCC's motion toward secular ecumenism is reducing its contact with its own basis.

Despite the foregoing danger, Section I managed to produce a
theological compromise statement; in it the Protestant majority manifested openness to the Orthodox and Anglican insistence on *ministry* (more special than the priesthood of all
the faithful), each time the constituents of Christ's Church
were mentioned. Thus, the ecclesial elements of creed, cult
and ministry appear three times in the brief document: once
under the heading of diversity, once as manifesting continuity, and once as constitutive of unity.[31] At the same time,
under the concept of cult, *only the two* sacraments of baptism
and the eucharist, generally acknowledged in Protestant Churches, are explicitly named.

Luther's and Calvin's definitions of the Church are surely
preserved in the constant insistence on evangelical faith and
the naming of baptism and the eucharist. On the other hand,
expressions such as "celebrating liturgical events," "continuous succession of the apostolic ministry," "one ministry
recognized by the whole church," "a ministry for the whole
church," added to "an organic and living unity in Christ"
suggest the Anglican and Orthodox influence.[32]

The ability to evaluate diversity in the Church, and its dis-
cernibility through the ages from the Apostolic era, imply a

visibility to the Church (and its characteristic qualities of
unity and catholicity) which stems largely from Orthodox and
Anglican input.[33]   At Uppsala, the visibility of the Church,
acknowledged at Lund (1952), is almost taken for granted;
the Church is more than the assembly of the invisibly predestined.

The invisible divine and humanly external components of the
Church are affirmed in the different expressions of *Catholic-*
ity, as "the sacramental experience of...incorporation into
Christ...of which the Church is the form"[34] and Christ's purpose of bringing people "of all times, of all races, of all
places, of all conditions into an organic and living unity in
Christ."[35]

This latter formulation echoes Christ's great Gospel command,
"make disciples of all nations...teach them all I have commanded you...I am with you always" (Matt. 28:19f). The authority mentioned in the Matthean passage accrues to the
Apostles; the World Council of autonomous churches has yet to
grapple with the meaning of this authority for the unity of
the *Una Sancta*. Nevertheless, Uppsala added the new emphasis
of *Catholicity* to its formula for unity.

New Delhi had explored the pragmatic possibility of Christian
unity for "all in each place." The stress had been on the
joining of local Christian congregations of varying beliefs
to form one church in each town. Uppsala chose to emphasize
additionally that the churches in the different towns were to
keep themselves open to the next stage of being one assembly
with the church in the next town also. This additional perception was encased in the formula "all...in *all* places,"
thus:

> to the emphasis on 'all in each place' we would
> now add a fresh understanding of the unity of
> *all Christians in all places*. This calls the
> churches in all places to realize that they be-
> long together and are called to act together...
> it is imperative to make visible the bonds which
> unite Christians in universal fellowship.[36]

The Assembly manifested little, if any, evidence that the
"all in each place" had had much effect, in its seven year
tenure,[37] so the newly-stressed "all in all places" can be
viewed mainly as a conceptual understanding of the road ahead,
if, by chance, the enormously difficult first stages should
be somewhat achieved in a given region.

Assemblies Cumulatively Defining "Church"

In adding Uppsala to New Delhi, a definition begins to emerge
that the Church is a single, visible, universal, apostolical-
ly connected organic unity in Christ of all Christians in all
places, individually and collectively. "All in each place"
stresses the local church; "all in all places" collects the
local churches into larger *national* or regional groupings;
thereafter, the report of Section I opens out to a consideration of the form of the Church's life at the international
level.

Denominational fellowships, federations, or alliances, although providing a sense of universality, are at the world
level "inevitably partial"[38] consequently, Section I envisions a World Council form of ecclesial life and activity,
thus making the experience of universality co-terminous with
the world. The development goes from "all in each place" to
"all in the world" but *only* in a *conciliar form.*

> The ecumenical movement helps to enlarge this
> experience of universality, and its regional
> councils and its World Council may be regarded
> as a transitional opportunity for eventually
> actualizing a truly universal, ecumenical,
> conciliar form of common life and witness. The
> members of the World Council of Churches, com-
> mitted to each other, should work for a time
> when a genuinely universal council may once
> more speak for all Christians and lead the
> way into the future.[39]

Is this a case of the segmented caterpillar being transformed
into the butterfly or rather of the caterpillar diminishing
its segment markings and adding wings? Is this the WCC becoming the *Una Sancta* or the WCC remaining the World Council
and calling itself the Church? The question is asked, not
capriciously, but rather searchingly, to find an analogical
model of the goal which the World Council seriously sets for
itself.

If the butterfly model is accurate, then it seems that the
World Council is aiming at becoming another approximately
500-million-member Catholic Church, which will be an alterna-
tive to the already existing approximately 500-million-member
Roman Catholic Church. Or is the aim to become the billion-
member Catholic Church with the Roman Catholic Church coming
under its umbrella as a denominational or confessional family,
despite its being one Church? The Faith and Order Committee
of the Assembly juggled terms and concepts thus to classify
the Roman Catholic Church.

> There is so wide a variety of world confes-
> sional families...that it is very difficult
> to find a general name for them. The term
> is now used as a convenient designation to
> include not only the world wide organizations
> of churches stemming from the Reformation,
> but also the Roman Catholic Church and the
> families of Orthodox and Oriental Churches.[40]

Eugene Carson Blake, the WCC's new general secretary, chose
to highlight the Uppsala "Conciliar form" concept in his
analysis of Uppsala's meeting. He characterized the Uppsala
Report's lines about a universal council as "perhaps the most
startling sentences of this report."[41]

> Here the next stage, 'a genuinely universal
> council,' is for the first time seriously ar-
> ticulated by the official representatives of
> the Churches in an Assembly. Note the points:
> (i) no final structure...is envisioned. (ii)
> But the World Council is seen as an instrument
> of transition to the next stage of world unity
> —a central and crucial instrument for that
> transition. (iii) The next stage is flatly
> stated to be a truly universal council able to
> speak for all Christians with the kind of au-
> thority of the seven ancient ecumenical Coun-
> cils of the Church.
>
> If this vision finds approval in the Churches,
> it will become the most important guiding ac-
> tion for the future of the ecumenical movement.
> ...It does definitely project the guide-lines
> for ecumenical work in the next period....
>
> A position has been taken which cannot be ig-
> nored in the future; it must be adopted or
> amended.[42]

Visser't Hooft, an honorary president of the WCC, delivered
a key address at Uppsala. His modest assessment that the
then-twenty-year-old World Council still "is only a small
beginning"[43] provides a counterbalancing note of realism to
the overall picture.

At the same time, Visser't Hooft frequently mentioned that
the 1925 Life and Work Question of "the relation between the
Church and the world" is a "perennial issue," "again the basic
issue," "the center of the stage."[44] He mentions the difficulty in closing the gap between the vertically minded members of the World Council and the horizontally-minded

participants. He sees the two aspects related in mankind's
unity: "The vertical dimension of its unity determines the
horizontal dimension."[45]

Visser't Hooft did not mention any ultimate 'conciliar form'
of Church unity, but he did use the occasion to affirm that
there "may be very many different forms of church order."
"My point," he says, "is simply that there seems to be no
really urgent reason to identify unity with acceptance of one
and the same church order."[46] He seems to rest on cultural
pluralism rather than on the scriptural 'episcopal, presby-
terial, diaconal' structure of the Pauline and pastoral epistles as normative; it is not clear that his closing question
on church unity: "Must we not draw the conclusions that there
can be real fellowship in faith and in sacrament even when
structures differ"?[47] allows other than a Reformation definition of the Church.

Yet he had previously written that "the best cooperation and
the most intensive dialogue are no substitutes for full fellowship in Christ."[48] He wishes "one reconciled, united family with no internal walls of separation"[49] without acknowledging that he is proposing a free church ecclesiology,
radically unacceptable to the Orthodox and others who believe
that the structure of apostolic episcopal succession is constitutive of Christ's Church.

Kindred to Visser't Hooft's concepts are the questions placed
in the Uppsala report by the Assembly Committee of Faith and
Order, namely, "whether a diversity of ecclesiologies is
found in the New Testament and whether this justifies a multiplicity of denominations."[50] This same committee agreed to
the study of the Unity of Christ's Church in a wider context
of the unity of mankind; it posed the further question of
whether unity could be regained simply by an increase in the
manifestation of unity, or whether some internal constituent
needs to be recovered.[51]

Thus, by a sort of cross-pollination of interrelated affirmations and a search for some consensus, which seems more like
a compromise[52] than a synthesis of Christ's intentions and
teachings, the World Council sets its course. This consensus-
course can hardly fail to influence its member-churches in
ways which may allow consensus to replace Christ's own plan
of salvation.

Roman Catholic Membership

In joining the World Council, Faith and Order had retained
its right to accept, as full-fledged members, qualified *persons* who belonged to nonmember churches. Thus it was that

nine Roman Catholic priests, qualified theological scholars,
were added to the list of the Faith and Order Commission as
full members.[53]

Membership of individual Roman Catholics in the Faith and
Order Commission unavoidably reintroduced the larger question
of the membership of their church in the World Council of
Churches. The formation and continuation of the Joint Work-
ing Group (JWG) in 1965 had first crystallized the inquiry.
The World Council, on the basis of its wish to include all
Christian churches among its members, affirmed its readiness
to receive any qualified Christian Church.

At Uppsala, this readiness was repeated in a statement,
adopted by the Assembly, concerning the World Council's relation with the Roman Catholic Church.[54] This adopted statement remarked that:

> ...the ecumenical movement has expanded to in-
> clude the Roman Catholic Church. The Second
> Vatican Council explained *in a new way* the Ro-
> man Catholic Church's understanding of and
> attitude to other churches. By the adoption
> of such texts as the Decree on Ecumenism...it
> laid the basis for dialogue and cooperation.
> This change has had a deep effect on the ecu-
> menical movement.
>
> The Roman Catholic Church has also shown a new
> interest in the World Council of Churches. It
> has agreed...to the establishment of a Joint
> Working Group....The World Council of Churches
> reaffirms its *eagerness to extend its membership
> to include all* those Christian churches at pres-
> ent outside its fellowship.[55]

The Uppsala statement approved the JWG's report on its bilateral exploratory work. The Assembly particularly liked the
JWG's speaking of "one ecumenical movement" and expressed

> ...its conviction that the guiding principle of
> future effort should be to bring this *one* move-
> ment towards complete manifestation.
>
> In the World Council of Churches, separate
> churches have been drawn into a koinonia by
> common acceptance of its Basis and by a cove-
> nant to fulfill their common calling together.
> The Assembly affirms its belief that this
> koinonia is essential to the one ecumenical
> movement and that it must be more fully manifested.[56]

Despite this clear World Council eagerness to extend its membership rolls, General Secretary Blake felt that the theological and practical problems implicit in Roman Catholic Church
membership rendered this practical step "at this time...pre-
mature."[57]

Dr. G. Fisher, former Archbishop of Canterbury, aware of the
ecclesiological ambiguity in Roman Catholic Church membership
in the World Council proposed:

> ...that the Council should be transformed into
> an organization for inter-Church aid, an organ-
> ization loose enough to present the Roman Cath-
> olic Church with no difficulties in joining its
> membership.[58]

If the WCC had chosen the English name "World *Consultation* of
Churches" to correspond more closely with the French,
"*Conseil*" *Oecuménique des Eglises,* or the German, *Ökuemischer*
"*Rat*" *der Kirchen,* the ambiguity in the WCC rhetoric and ex-
pression might have been eliminated. However, Blake's ex-
plicit call for a truly universal council, implying "the kind
of *authority* of the seven ancient ecumenical Councils of the
Church,"[59] seems to pack more ecclesiology into the World
Council's English title than its sense in the other official
WCC languages allows.

In any event, the question of Roman Catholic Church membership in the World Council presents at least a double-barreled
problem. If Rome does not join, how is the World Council
truly *world* representative with the Roman Catholic half of
the Christian world out of it? On the other hand, if the
Catholic Church does join, isn't it admitting that it is not
"Catholic" (universal, world), and that its Councils from
Fourth Constantinople (870) to Vatican II (including Trent),
were not *ecumenical,* as they have been named from the beginning, as well as for the intervening eleven centuries?

A member of the Vatican's Secretariat for Unity, Reverend
Roberto Tucci, was invited as an Assembly guest to address
Uppsala's plenary session.

In the context of praise for the World Council's privileged
place in the Ecumenical Movement, Tucci faced the problem of
Roman Catholic Church membership in the World Council.[60]
Speaking "merely in a personal capacity,"[61] Tucci opined, on
the one hand, that *nonmembership* may increase "catholic/non-
catholic" tensions in the ecumenical movement, and would
serve to constitute the WCC as a non-Roman institution *de
facto,* and even *de jure* if exclusion were established on
theological principles; further, such exclusion would

restrict the consultative scope of the WCC, "which is essentially a place of dialogue."[62]

On the other hand, membership of the Roman Catholic Church in
the World Council would have to face the ecclesiology of Vatican II which need "not constitute an insuperable obstacle."[63]
Tucci felt that the psychological and practical problems of
Roman Catholic Church membership presented the greater obstacles. To give the largest church one vote appears absurd;
whereas to give each independent local church, that is, each
diocese, one vote would have a swamping effect on the organization, activities and style of the presently constituted
World Council.[64]

Prior to Tucci's address, the Joint Working Group had judged
that the Roman Catholic Church's membership in the World
Council at the time of Uppsala would not be an aid in seeking
the unity of Christians. Marc Boegner, Patriarch of French
ecumenism, thought this decision "eminently reasonable."[65]
It appeared to Boegner, even more strongly than to Roberto
Tucci,

> ...quite unrealistic to believe that in the
> present state of theology the entry of the
> Roman Church into the 'family' of 223 member-
> Churches of the Council can be envisaged for
> a single moment; there is...an immensity of
> problems that must be studied in common.[66]

Aside from the membership question, Tucci's carefully prepared address at Uppsala contained reassuring insights for
the assembled delegates. He pointed out from authoritative
quotes that ecumenism after Vatican II was an inherent part
of the papal apostolate and an essential ingredient of the
Church's pastoral work.[67] He identified the WCC's place in
the ecumenical movement as "special and privileged,"[68] as a
"providential institution and instrument,"[69] as being "essentially a place for dialogue."[70] Tucci accepted the interpretation of "equality in encounter" for the phrase *par cum
pari,* as long as it precluded the notion that each WCC member-
church is the equal of Christ's Church.[71]

Further, Tucci pointed out that Vatican II had focused its
attention on the mystery of Christ's Church and the *differing
degrees* of participating in that mystery. In this light, the
Council Fathers saw other churches and ecclesial communities
as having genuine ecclesial status, as being efficacious regarding salvation, and as sharing already existing (although
varying) *degrees of communion* with each other and with the
Catholic Church.

In the same line of thought, Tucci indicated that church's
belief in her uniqueness and in the insoluble gift of unity
Christ had given her. He did not hesitate to acknowledge her
need for purification and constant renewal; these processes
prepared for a restoration of unity (Unitatis Reditegratio)
among Christians rather than the "return" of the pre-Vatican
II church.

Tucci acknowledged that we cannot today foresee the possible
form of the future's one visible organic union of which
Christ is the center.[72] Veteran ecumenist, Norman Goodall,
the editor of Uppsala 68, characterized this speech as "the
remarkable utterance of Father Tucci."[73]

Uppsala was already well set in its pursuit of the world's
agenda,[74] rather than pursuit of Church unity via the "increasing degrees" pathway implicit in Tucci's speech. Increasing collaboration in secular ecumenism, with its possible
Christian witness, was more and more displacing the goal of
Church unity in the WCC activity. From the mountain peak of
Uppsala 68 to the next mountain peak of Nairobi 75, the same
trend appears to characterize the World Council's activities.

To those who complain that the WCC has suffered a focus shift,
from what critics disparagingly call "official or churchy ecumenism"[75] to secular ecumenism, the response is given that
"the Church-to-the-world" orientation was there from the beginning, in Soederblom's "Life and Work" movement.

Soederblom's conviction that "doctrine divides; service
unites" surfaces in the modified form "service unites; doctrinal divisions will heal along the way," as if the rigidity
of cold contradiction will evanesce beneath the beams of
friendly cooperation. Warm feelings and active cooperation
surely help in the mutual analysis of radically differing
convictions, but such feelings cannot forever cover profoundly differing beliefs about the nature of the Una Sancta.

Visser't Hooft's "we believed that unity has to grow out of
the actual living and working together of the churches"[76]
seems to elevate the "Life and Work" dimension to the detri-
ment of "Faith and Order." Soederblom is lavishly and widely praised; Brent is hardly mentioned, outside of the subordi-
nated Faith and Order Commission. The Central Committee is
occupied mainly with church-to-the-world programs; the Faith
and Order commission, as one of many, reports to the Central
Committee.

Further, student observers (tomorrow's delegates) at Uppsala
preferred the worldly agenda to the theological. At earlier
meetings students had called for action in the world now;

less church, less mission, more welcome to the world was
their insistent emphasis "...at the Assembly in Uppsala it
became clear that this new orientation had come to stay."[77]

Development, racism, trouble in Africa, Ireland, and the Near
East are all totally legitimate matters of concern to people,
to nations, to the United Nations. If this also continues as
the primary agenda of the WCC, shall not the World Council
become merely a Christian United Nations?

Visser't Hooft insists that the WCC must preserve both its
vertical and horizontal interests in dynamic tension, and he
even assigns an ultimate priority to the vertical,[78] but Visser't Hooft's more mature conviction, too little incorporated
into the WCC structure, seems unable to deflect the World
Council from its headlong horizontal course.

At the World Council's fifth Assembly in Nairobi, Kenya, there
is scarcely any evidence that the 75 year-old Visser't Hooft
influenced the Assembly. Methodist Rev. Dr. Philip Potter
had replaced Presbyterian Rev. Dr. Eugene Blake as general
secretary in 1972. Canadian Anglican Bishop, Edward Scott,
was elected Moderator (the former title had been chairman)
of the powerful Central Committee. The influential leadership emphasized the world's agenda.[79]

From Uppsala 1968 to Nairobi 1975

After Uppsala, the unity-target shifted from the *Una Sancta*
to a "genuinely universal council," the trend toward the
domination of secular ecumenism continued, and the Geneva/
Rome collaboration increased, while the Roman Catholic membership question continued unresolved.

(1) Universal Council. The manner in which the World Council's influence spread was manifested in the tenth decennial
meeting of Anglican bishops at Lambeth (known as Lambeth X),
immediately following the close of the Uppsala Assembly.
Resolution No. 44 asked each Anglican bishop to give priority
to local-level ecumenism, and to take seriously Lund's principle that separated Christians should do all together save
where conscience keeps them apart; further, the resolution in
a routine manner

> endorsed Uppsala's hope that the Church would
> 'work for the time when a *genuinely universal
> council* may once more speak for all Christians.'[80]

The following year at its annual meeting, the World Council's
Central Committee approvingly received notice of this Anglican resolution in the report of Rev. Dr. Lukas Vischer,

Director of the Secretariat of the Faith and Order Commission.
Vischer's report praised the trend that work for such a general council would also be used by Lambeth as a directional
indicator of ecumenical progress. Moreover, Vischer hoped
that other confessional families, at their world-level meetings, would follow the Anglican example.[81]

Vischer's report concerning "a genuinely universal council"
was received as a personal assessment which invited further
inquiry.[82] Vischer noted that the term "Council" had clearly
been shifted at Uppsala from its consultation sense (its
original sense as noted by Tucci) to the sense corresponding
to the one Church's early ecumenical councils; it is a distinct change in meaning from *conseil* to *concile* in French and
from *Rat* to *Konzil* in German.[83]

The change is much more than merely a word change. The modern phenomenon of the WCC started, and until Uppsala had continued, with the principle that each denominational member
church could accept or reject any or all WCC recommendations
on its own denominational authority. The theological implication of "ancient Council", such as Nicea, is that its authority manifests the will of God and, as a universal or ecumenical council, binds the whole Church in conscience. The ancient council spoke with the same authoritative assertion
that the Apostles used at their meeting in Jerusalem (Acts
15:28) "It is the decision of the Holy Spirit and ours
too,...."

At Uppsala, Roman Catholic speaker, Tucci, had advisedly said
that the World Council "is essentially a place for dialogue."[84]
Reformed theologian Vischer, a year later, says to the Central
Committee: the entity which the WCC is becoming is a "place for
binding decision." The WCC was primarily a dialogue, a consultation leading to collaboration; Nicea was a special event
of the *koinonia*, the full communion of Christians; Nicea's
decision defined the faith of the whole Church to the present
day. Vischer strongly affirmed that dialogue is not enough;
full genuine fellowship, i.e. *koinonia*, is the goal of the WCC.
Vischer declared:

> ...it is surely most misleading to equate dia-
> logue and koinonia, the real goal of the ecu-
> menical movement is full fellowship, and the
> dialogue which will characterize that fellow-
> ship is different in quality from the dialogues
> which we now have.[85]

Theologian Vischer had been Visser't Hooft's, and the Central
Committee's, choice to attend, as observer, all four sessions
of Vatican II. The dialogue there, of bishops and theologians

who shared creed, cult and acknowledgment of authority, probably for Vischer, contrasted sharply with the theologically-
divergent dialogue of the divided churches at Uppsala. In
any event, Vischer perceived a real difference between the
dialogue of a *koinonia* and the dialogue of the consultative
WCC. The goal must be a full fellowship, but he seems to
transpose this into a "council" (which is an event) instead
of into the *Una Sancta*, the full communion of faith, worship
and authority, which is the presupposition of an authoritative
defining council. Vischer moves from consultative Council
to conscience-binding (truly Ecumenical) Council thus:

> ...dialogue...must aim resolutely at the es-
> tablishment of fellowship; and the time may
> have arrived for the Churches to envisage
> together this goal more explicitly and con-
> cretely than before.

> In what goal might they ultimately meet? The
> Fourth Assembly made a suggestion. It said
> that the ecumenical movement had to work for
> the time when a *genuinely universal council*
> might speak for all Christians.[86]

Vischer used the idea of the council as a norm or a test to
measure the ecumenical progress of the WCC member churches.[87]
He felt that the conditions prerequisite for such a "genuinely universal council" were: the obliteration of historic ex-
communications, common eucharist, a sense of universal solidarity, and breaking through denominational barriers.[88]

From the Swiss reformed ecclesiological position, which Vischer shares with Visser't Hooft, Vischer appears to classify
Orthodox and Roman Catholics as denominations which can do as
many others do who freely practice intercommunion. He sees
the eucharist, the Body of Christ, as a means, instead of as
the end. Interestingly, his design of getting all these big
and little churches together into one "genuinely universal
council" seems more pragmatic than theological and scriptural.
Christ is not absent from his report, but Christ's mind does
not seem to be the basis of the unity to be achieved. Vischer
takes a strong position for changing church structures.

> The church has undergone changes even when it
> believed it stood as a rock amid the swift cur-
> rent of the ages. Indeed, if it is to pass on
> its message it must change its structures.
> Structures of unchangeable permanence falsify
> its real nature.[89]

The Central Committee received, but did not adopt as its own,

Director Vischer's report. Three Orthodox members (one Greek,
one Russian, the third from Syrian Orthodoxy) objected that:
Vischer was describing a new council different from the World
Council, that the "unity of the Church," not a council, is
the objective of the ecumenical movement, that the eucharist
is the conclusion of unity achieved, that change does not
mean revolution.[90]

A Roman Catholic delegated-observer concurred by remarking
that eucharistic unity was "against the discipline of the Roman Catholic Church," while indicating that Vischer had courageously raised serious questions which needed consideration.[91]

Vischer's focus on the "genuinely universal council", with its
implication of doctrinal definition and binding legislation,
evokes Visser't Hooft's spectral image of the "superchurch."
In an article published under the aegis of Faith and Order
that same year, Vischer considerably deflates the ghostly
image of referring to "thoughtless and obstructive...anxious
talk of a 'superchurch' (that spook which like all spooks is
spoken of again and again but never really described)", while
acknowledging that there is perhaps a limited correctness in
the delineation.[92]

In the same article Vischer pointed out that Uppsala had newly included the *universality* of the Church's fellowship in
the ecumenical discussion, and expressed the desirability of a
"really universal council."[93] He thought it worthwhile to
"unfold the essence of the church under the viewpoint of 'conciliarity'" and to conceive "the total life of the Church in
conciliar fashion."[94]

In pursuit of this "the Church is *essentially* conciliar" objective, Vischer declared "conciliar consultations are of the
nature of the people of God,"[95] "conciliarity is among the
marks of the Church,"[96] "conciliar consultation is the truest
possible face of the Church,"[97] "the ecumenical movement can
actually be understood as the preparation of a future universal council."[98]

Vischer's position as Director of the WCC's Faith and Order
Secretariat indicates the prevailing direction of Church-
unity thinking as the WCC approached Nairobi. The goal appears to be a visibly universal Council which can speak with
one binding voice for presently autonomous churches.

In his lengthy article, Vischer insisted on the necessity of
common service-structures for the Church's *visible universality*; he even endorsed the need for a *center* but felt that the
center might better be the "universal council" moving from

place to place (the practice of the young WCC), than a static
geographical fixture which "inhibits," "burdens," and "nar-
rows the variety" of the church, and even takes on a nonscriptural, legally defined place and weight of its own.[99]
The mobile center position was in contrast to *the claim*, paraphrased by Vischer, that

> primacy and jurisdiction over the whole Church
> is due to the bishop of Rome as the successor
> of Peter. This claim makes Rome the geographic
> *centre* of the Church. The universal unity of
> the Church can become clear only if it is 'Ro-
> man Catholic.'[100]

The Vatican documents emphasize the *Petrine* centrality more
than the geographic location; where Peter is, there is the
visible center.

Vischer acknowledged that the Papal See has achieved some remarkable accomplishments,

> even today it contributes to holding churches
> together and strengthening them in their uni-
> versal mission. The consciousness of uni-
> versal fellowship is, in no church as strongly
> developed as in the Roman Catholic Church.[101]

However, according to Vischer "the claim" has caused schisms;
the Latinity has constricted the Church's rightful variety;
moreover, he thinks that the world's present technical, se-
cularized, global-village situation calls for a new central
structure "subject to the judgment of the church as a
whole."[102]   Thus, within the WCC, the conciliarity goal was
strongly advocated.

Two years after Vischer's 1969 presentation to the Central
Committee and his extensive article pointing to the Uppsala-
inspired goal of a "genuine universal council," English Congregationalist, Rev. Dr. Norman Goodall, the editor of *Uppsala
68* (Uppsala's Official Report), reinforced the "universal
council" theme and Vischer's insistence that this goal cannot
be reached unless the denominations undergo radical changes.[10]

Goodall perceives that the conciliar goal will evoke a "long
and involved process of debate" and that intercommunion or
eucharistic fellowship is implied as a *prerequisite* for its
attainment.[104]   He estimates that Uppsala's proposal of a
"genuinely universal council" is

> as yet a very tentative one—its importance lies
> in a widespread awareness that the ecumenical

movement must either move or peter out,....

Goodall observes that in the decade of which he writes (1961-1971), there has been a "petering out" or overall "loss of momentum" in the drive toward organic union; this slowdown occurred among the very Protestant churches which have entertained merger efforts toward a stage of limited unity. After noting that "organic union" proceeds much more readily in cases of like with like (Lutheran with Lutheran, Reformed with Presbyterian, etc.) than across the episcopal boundary, Goodall, from his survey of church union negotiations, concludes that

> The decade under review, and especially the
> latter part of it, has undoubtedly been marked
> by a loss of momentum in the pursuit of or-
> ganic union.[105]

(2) Secularity Trend. Goodall judged that the prevailing operative mood, especially popular among the young, is that church union is irrelevant in the face of the world's pressing problems of hunger, racism, development and war and peace.[106]

Goodall thinks that the reasons for the loss of momentum toward the final goal in Faith and Order circles, and consequently in the WCC, are reappraisal of the problems concerning the nature of the Church and the nature of the unity that the *Una Sancta* demands.[107] Lund's study of the nontheological factors, and Uppsala's trend toward primary concern with the world's problems diffused the movement's driving power. *Secular* "catholicity" and "apostolicity" look toward the "going out of the Church to the world"; these approaches diverted the thrust away from organic union.[108] Confusion of goals seems to be leading to diffusion of energies, time and resources.

Goodall perceives that in response to urgent human problems the World Council has become

> more and more involved in questions concerning
> the right ordering of society. These questions,
> social and economic with inescapable political
> implications, have never been absent from the
> life of the World Council.[109]

At Uppsala, the fascinating question of the development of peoples "found expression at fever heat."[110] With racism, rich/poor, human rights, and rigid institution sub-themes filling the air, one may wonder whether a World Council Assembly is capable of the *Una Sancta* question. As a matter of

fact, the development theme "spilled over into almost all the
sections and featured largely in the great plenary sessions
of the Assembly."[111]

(3) Membership Question. The question of Roman Catholic membership in the World Council continued to be regarded as a
complex question whose implications were deliberately being
given time to ripen; Goodall qualified as "memorable and very
significant" the step taken by Pope Paul VI when,on invitation,he entered the Ecumenical Center in Geneva.[112] On that
occasion in June 1969, Pope Paul appreciatively affirmed the
utility of dialogue and increased collaboration between the
World Council and the Catholic Church,but considered that the
membership question needed more theological and pastoral
cultivation for its maturation.[113]

As Pope John had identified himself to his Jewish visitors,
"I am your brother, Joseph," somewhat similarly Pope Paul
identified himself to the Christian gathering at Geneva, "Our
name is Peter."[114] He merely recalled that Christ had given
the meaning to the name and briefly indicated the functions
of fisher of men and shepherd with which Christ had charged
Peter.

The Pope asked,"Is not the World Council a marvelous movement
of Christians, of 'children of God who are scattered abroad'
(John 11, 52), who are now searching for a recomposition of
unity?"[115] He recognized the union which already binds, although incompletely, all baptized Christians. Pope Paul
publicly professed his belief that God is guiding "all Christians in the search for the *fullness* of that unity which
Christ wills for His one and only Church."[116]

After noting the manifold fruitful points of contact already
established through the Joint Working Group, the Roman Pontiff responded to the question: Should the Catholic Church
become a member of the World Council?

> In fraternal frankness we do not consider that
> the question of the membership of the Catholic
> Church in the World Council is so mature that
> a positive answer could or should be given.
> The question still remains a hypothesis. It
> contains serious theological and pastoral im-
> plications. It thus requires profound study
> and commits us to a way that honesty recognizes
> could be long and difficult. But this does not
> prevent us from assuring you of our great re-
> spect and deep affection. The determination
> which animates us and the principles which
> guide us will always be the search, filled

with hope and pastoral realism, for the unity
willed by Christ.[117]

Pope Paul concluded with the Johannine excerpt of Christ's
prayer for unity (John 17).

Visser't Hooft, who was part of the capacity audience addressed by Pope Paul, commented on the divided reaction of the
papal visit, and especially his self-identification, "My name
is Peter." The negative side felt that the historic Papal
visit to the World Council center was not the occasion to imply the claim of universal jurisdiction which they felt to be
ecumenism's greatest obstacle. Some, with Visser't Hooft, on
the other hand, held it better to express deep convictions
openly. The occasion's significance lay in the prayer which
the man, who called himself Peter, said in common with those
who did not so regard him.[118]

During this period between Uppsala '68 and Nairobi '75, the
Faith and Order Commission continued to emphasize the theme
of conciliarity for the future,[119] and Visser't Hooft, as
the WCC's elder statesman, concurred, almost on the eve of
Nairobi, in that theme, while promoting the World Council's
preoccupation with the world's agenda.[120] "High worldmanship
rather than high churchmanship" appeared to be the note of
the future; a horizontally-oriented view focused theology on
the world rather than on the denominational differences which
continue to flourish, or on the picture of the one Christian
Church of the future.[121]

Visser't Hooft, acknowledging that member-Church adoptions
of WCC decisions have had very meager results, nevertheless
insisted that the World Council ideas were making successful
headway in such areas as proselytism, admission to communion,
theology's ecumenical spirit, East-West Christian relations,
and some reunions actually effected.[122]

Idea-persuasion, rather than universal jurisdiction, appears
to be Visser't Hooft's convinced way of arriving at common
witness, unity for a church, the world council, and finally
the genuinely universal council.

It is in this way that the World Council must
and can be the school in which we rediscover
the genuine conciliarity which was a feature
of the ancient Church.[123]

This makes it appear that the WCC is to be the consultative
path of a true ecumenical council (*Concile*, *Konzil*) which,
in turn, will become the stepping stone to, or be, the recovered *Una Sancta*. Visser't Hooft's disinclination to

manifest his final concept of the future Church to be recovered led Oliver Bristol, the invited writer of his "Foreword,"
to lament

> I could wish that he had paid more attention
> to the question of the form which the Church
> must take if its unity is to be evident with-
> out its freedom being impaired.[124]

At Uppsala, Visser't Hooft had strongly stressed the horizontal "Church to the world," orientation ("denying responsibility for any of the world's needy is as heretical as denying
an article of faith"); this "secular ecumenism" thrust was so
popularized that, five years later, Visser't Hooft could say
that if he had known of this popularity he would have added
to it the necessity of its vertical component: namely, that
the denial of God's reconciliation through Christ is as
heretical as refusal to help in the struggle for justice and
freedom.[125]

The year before the Nairobi Assembly, Visser't Hooft again
tried to right the movement's tilt toward secular ecumenism
by explaining that the construction of a choice between ecclesial and secular ecumenism yielded false alternatives; he
declared the two are interdependent and inseparable.[126]

> An ecumenical movement which is *only* interested
> in doctrine remains in the air. An ecumenical
> movement which is *only* concerned about action
> loses its identity as a Christ centered movement
> and so becomes a tool of the forces which are
> drawn up against each other in the social and
> political field.[127]

Visser't Hooft's rhetoric not infrequently bypasses the ecclesial reality of the *Una Sancta* as he expresses his man-to-
man or man-to-Christ (or God) relationship. The Church of
Christ continues to have vague lines in much of his writing;
it does not appear to have been as incarnated (or enfleshed)
as Christ himself was. In any event, the WCC's next Assembly
continues, and even increases, the tilt toward secular ecumenism, whose upstaging of ecclesial ecumenism progressively
diminishes the thrust toward the *Una Sancta*. For its fifth
assembly (1975), the World Council chose a new continental
meeting place: Africa.

CHAPTER FIFTEEN

FIFTH WORLD COUNCIL
ASSEMBLY (NAIROBI 1975)

At its fifth Assembly in Nairobi, Kenya, the WCC gave added impetus to the "general universal council" direction and the church-toward-the-World trend. Intercommunion pressure was still an unsolved tension and the Roman Catholic Church, through the JWG, increased contacts with the World Council but refrained from seeking membership.

Under the Assembly theme: "Jesus Christ frees and unites," the World Council divided its assembly program into the following sections which still carry on the character of the separate initiating movements of mission, Faith and Order (F&O), Life and Work (L&W). The six sections were:

I.   Confessing Christ Today (Evangelism, Mission).

II. What Unity Requires (F&O: "Christ and Trinity" basis).

III. Seeking Community (from various faiths, cultures) (L&W).

IV. Education for Liberation and Community (L&W).

V.   Structures of Injustice and Struggles for Liberation (L&W).

VI. Human Development[1] (L&W).

Of primary interest to the search for the common goal of ecumenism in WCC and RCC documents, is Section II which carries forward the Faith and Order drive for "full" ecclesial unity. If one puts the Section II title in the form of a question, "What does unity require?", the Nairobi document proposes the specific answer: a "genuine universal council" which had been set as a target at Uppsala.[2] This conciliarity necessarily implies some concept of *Church*. Is it Christ's Church still remains the crucial question.

(1) Conciliarity. Surrounding the specific answer stand the
prior and more pressing questions of the movement's accepted
goal, "visible unity," hopeful compassion in the struggle
for justice, and a fuller understanding of the context of
unity in terms that embrace the handicapped, women, structured organizations, and political realities.[3] These con-
textual surroundings distract attention from, but do not
mute, the dominant conciliar note of the document.

A target of conciliar fellowship seems to correspond as a
necessary centerpiece to the many-faceted concerns of the
multichurch council. A strong kind of organizational center,
or hub, is needed to preserve even a pragmatic unity among
such disparate activities.

Nairobi reaffirms the goal of visible unity sought by the
previous Assemblies. *New Delhi '61* had called for the visible unity of "all in each place" and even, but less sharply,
"all in all places." *Uppsala '68* sharpened the "all places"
emphasis and identified itself with the ecclesial note of
visible unified Catholicity. Thereupon, *Nairobi '75* sought
to equate specific visible unity with a "conciliar unity or
fellowship."[4] On the anvil of intramural debate the F&O
Commission hammered out the concept which Nairobi approved.

> The one Church is to be envisioned as a *con-
> ciliar fellowship* of local churches which are
> themselves truly united. In this *conciliar
> fellowship,* each local church possesses, in
> communion with the others, the fullness of
> catholicity, witnesses to the same apostolic
> faith, and therefore recognizes the others as
> belonging to the same Church of Christ and
> guided by the same Spirit. As the New Delhi
> Assembly pointed out, they are bound together
> because they have received the same baptism
> and share in the same Eucharist; they recognize
> each other's members and ministries. They are
> one in their common commitment to confess the
> gospel of Christ by proclamation and service
> to the world. To this end, each church aims at
> maintaining sustained and sustaining relation-
> ships with her sister churches, expressed in
> *conciliar gatherings* whenever required for the
> fulfillment of their common calling.[5]

This is an ideal envisioning of the WCC's goal; it seems to
equate Christ's one Church with "a conciliar fellowship of
local churches." But, as stated, the local churches are *already* previously *one* ("truly united") in faith, worship (baptism and eucharist) and mutuality of membership, ministry

and evangelical service to the world.

The real denominational churches of the WCC are divided, and
are, in fact, not fully one faith, worship and ministry. If,
indeed, they enjoyed Christ's fullness of the "creed, cult
and ministry" elements, they would be much closer to the *Una
Sancta,* whether they were meeting in the special event of a
genuinely universal council, or not. A council is an event;
it is not the Church. A conciliar meeting is something the
church may have occasionally, but the church is the essentially continuing reality for the decades, and even centuries,
between such special events.

All ecumenists appear to acknowledge that the Church was the
Church for the centuries before Nicea met in 325. Thus, it
seems confusing, if not misleading, to say that the one
Church, the *Una Sancta* is, or is to be envisioned as, a conciliar fellowship. Is Nairobi trying to say the Church is a
conciliar unity, or fellowship, in each place, a conciliar
unity in all places and a conciliar world unity? If so, it
is making conciliarity the primary element of the Church's
definition. It is making the "series of events" be the
Church instead of merely the Church's occasional act.

The Nairobi document complains that the term "conciliar fellowship" is often taken erroneously and that the concept is
merely an elaboration of the New Delhi unity statement ("all
in each place, and in all places").[6] The document seems neg-
lectful of the *concilium/consilium, Konsil/Rat* ambiguity, and
the deeper difference between the early authoritative ecumenical councils and the modern ecumenical consultations.

Such radical differences may be commonplace to the World
Council's leadership, but those who rhetorically paint the
visions need to distinguish between reality and rhetoric. The
Secretariat for Promoting Christian Unity (SPCU), on the eve
of Nairobi, judged that consultative and collaborative councils of churches (such as the WCC)

> do not in and of themselves contain in embryo
> the beginnings of a new Church which will re-
> place the communion now existing within the
> Catholic Church. They do not claim to be
> churches nor do they claim authority to com-
> mission a ministry of word and sacrament.[7]

Nairobi declared that the term "conciliar fellowship" is "intended to describe *an aspect* of the life of the one undivided
Church at all levels."[8] The aspect (different from the Nairobi definition) is that of publicly manifested unity, and a
display of the charismatic quality of Christian life which

the assembled local churches cultivate.[9]

If stating that the *Una Sancta* is a "conciliar fellowship of
local Churches" represents a congregationalist ecclesiology,
then the Orthodox input brought the Nairobi document to a
more mystery-laden declaration of conciliarity and sharing of
divine nature (theosis);[10] the Orthodox did this in the long
passage in which they pointed out that true councils require
a pre-existing unified Church. "True Conciliar fellowship
presupposes the unity of the Church."[11]

Nairobi juxtaposes radically different "theologies of Church",
which the document-drafters cannot merge; yet, the overwhelmingly Protestant unity section and full Assembly approved the
position that all member churches share in the Orthodox view
on conciliarity.

> True conciliarity is the reflection in the life
> of the Church of the triune being of God. It is
> that unity for which Christ prayed....The source
> of the Church's unity...is the meeting...with
> [Christ's] living presence in the midst of the
> eucharistic fellowship....Thereby [Christians]
> share a common participation in the divine nature
> and become living members in the one living Body
> of the risen Christ. Though...different local
> communities do and should manifest a rich di-
> versity...nevertheless no...difference can alter
> the integrity of the one apostolic faith....The
> One...Son of God is incarnate in the One Church.
> ...[Christians] commune with him who said: 'I
> am the truth.' This Living Truth is the goal
> towards which all churches who seek for unity
> tend together. Conciliarity expresses this
> interior unity of the churches separated by
> space, culture, or time,...[local churches]
> seek from time to time by councils...to express
> their unity visibly in a common meeting.[12]

This intimate interweaving of theology and eucharistic liturgy,[13] the sharing in the divine nature (theosis), emphasis on
the Trinity, and action of the Holy Spirit, mark, especially
in combination, the Orthodox contributions to the ongoing
theological dialogue. Immediately following this paragraph,
Nairobi acknowledged that the present

> interconfessional assemblies are *not councils*
> in the full sense *because* they are not yet
> united by a common understanding of the apostol-
> ic faith, by a common ministry and a common
> Eucharist.[14]

This acknowledgment is a lucid perception that Christian community of faith, worship and ministry is needed for true conciliarity.

However, the Nairobi Assembly looks toward the day when one
of its assemblies will be listed as the next in the line of
the ancient ecumenical assemblies. Orthodox delegate Pere
Cyrille Argenti, in addressing a plenary session, prayed that

> through the participation in the World Council
> by all the Christian Churches (and in particu-
> lar the very ancient and venerable Church of
> Rome, our elder sister,...)—if not the Fifth
> or Sixth Assembly of the Council of Churches
> then at least the 7th Assembly will be recog-
> nized by the whole Christian people as the 8th
> Ecumenical Council of the One, Holy, Catholic
> and Apostolic Church of Christ.[15]

Nairobi identified itself as a motion toward, and a foretaste
of, such full conciliar fellowship.[16]

Philip Potter, the third General Secretary, spent much of his
official report pointing out that global problems need global
perspectives, in line with which he aimed at the target: "The
one Church is to be envisioned as a *conciliar fellowship of
local churches* which are themselves truly united."[17] Potter
defined the post-Nairobi work of the WCC as the furthering of
the goal: full conciliar fellowship.

> The World Council exists to assist the churches
> to move forward into the fullness of conciliar
> fellowship—that unity of a fully committed,
> charismatic fellowship of all churches in each
> place and in all places. Our task at this as-
> sembly will be to see how the World Council can
> be the privileged instrument of God to further
> this goal in the coming years.[18]

Since, according to Nairobi, true conciliar fellowship presupposes true ecclesial unity, it could be argued backwards
that the production of an authoritative council will thereby
prove that all the local churches throughout the world are
already one. This argument was nowhere found explicitly, but
seems implied in the insistent thrust for a genuine world
conciliar fellowship. It seems that the leaders want the appearance of the real thing without requiring its member churches to become one in faith, worship and apostolic authority.
It appears that the outer appearance is sought more than the
acknowledged inner essentials.

Denominational barriers are proving very obstinate;[19] also,
there is fear that the WCC must achieve some significant advance in ecclesial unity or lose credibility and remain simply as a dialogue and collaboration agency of some Christian
churches.

Nairobi constructed the thrust toward a truly universal council into its ongoing activities by means of an Assembly
guideline which is to govern the Central Committee, the Executive Committee and the General Secretariat of the World
Council:

> ...all programmes of the WCC should be con-
> ceived and implemented in a way which enables
> the member churches to grow towards a truly
> ecumenical, conciliar fellowship. In this
> respect, the programmes...should...foster
> growth toward fuller unity.[20]

In an admirable thrust to deepen the World Council's program,
the Nairobi Assembly changed the WCC constitution to select
visible unity, rather than the specific "general council", as
the *first* of the World Council's new ordering of functions
and purposes: "to call the churches to *the goal of visible
unity* in one faith and in one eucharistic fellowship expressed in worship and in common life in Christ, and to advance towards that unity in order that the world may believe."[21]

Some proposals for global programs, designed to engage the
local congregations themselves, were so forceful that the Assembly simply bypassed the denominational authorities, as if
the WCC were itself the "superchurch" telling or leading the
rest of the member churches. Orthodox churches objected to
such activity on ecclesiological grounds; "In the Orthodox
structure," they said, "only the bishop has jurisdiction of
the congregations and the WCC cannot bypass him."[22]

(2) Seculiarity Trend. Anglican Canon David Paton, the editor of Nairobi's official Report, tentatively accepted the
evaluation of the Fifth Assembly as a "consolidating assembly
in which there was nothing remarkably new in the order of
ideas."[23] Paton, in his post-Assembly assessment, pointed up
the problem of the evangelical groups who see the World Council's commitment to social action as a diversion from its
professed evangelical objectives.[24]

Also, Paton perceived that this division between objectives
and interests emerged throughout the Assembly. He condensed
its emergence to a

number of contentious issues. A major one
was susceptible of many descriptions: Evangelicals versus Ecumenicals, and 'vertical'
versus the 'horizontal' dimensions in Christian discipleship; Evangelism or Social Action; Prayer or Politics;...it cropped up
all over the place.

Another was about Human Rights...unoffici-
ally it ramified everywhere.[25]

The 676 voting delegates, representing 286 member churches,
were the core of the Assembly which totalled almost three
times that number, counting delegated observers, advisers,
stewards, guests and press. For most of the official delegates (about 80%), Nairobi was their first World Council Assembly.[26] Thus Paton conceded:

It is difficult...to see how a large hetero-
geneous body would be able to do anything
much more than exchange experiences...if it
was not presented with a sizeable block of
common material to digest and react to.[27]

In the first of its two and a half weeks this group, so het-
erogeneous in language, nationality, and theological education, engaged in exchanges on "dialogue with other religions
on the uniqueness of Christ; on racism; on oppression, rebel-
lion, violence; on the relation of the WCC to the member
churches."[28] How can an assembly of this kind arrive at the
mind of Christ regarding the reuniting of entrenched auton-
mous denominations in his *Una Sancta*?

Editor Paton had been to three assemblies; after Nairobi he
pointed out the great differences among the delegates, the
diversity of the matters considered, the "frantic drafting"[29]
of reports as the less than three-week period of speeches,
celebrations, discussions, and meetings rushed inexorably to
its end. Lack of clarity frequently characterized section
reports. Sections had a compulsion to say something in their
official reports on which they would stand or fall.[30] Thus,
Paton questions whether *the churches*, through their assembled
delegates, do in fact control the WCC.

It has, I think, to be said that the problem of
how an Assembly can control the actual work of
the World Council of Churches has not yet been
solved; and it may in fact be insoluble.[31]

Paton recognizes that the Central Committee, the Executive
Committee and the General Secretary, chosen for these posts

by others than their churches, in fact, run or control this
new, modern mostly Protestant giant: the WCC.

There is a widespread recognition that a difficult-to-bridge
gap exists between the top of the World Council and the actual churches which legally and financially constitute it as
a Council of Churches.[32] Overextension of programs, coupled
with inflation, has confronted the WCC with the financial
necessity of critically weighing its priorities in the post-
Nairobi period.[33] Paton argues, however, that the WCC must
continue, thus:

>   Since the World exists, and the Christian
>   family exists around the world, the WCC is a
>   necessity; and if it did not exist, it or
>   something very like it would have to be in-
>   vented. Since it is necessary, it has to be
>   worked at and paid for....[34]

One may wonder whether the secular dimension of WCC work has
blurred, or crowded out, the goal of regaining Christian unity. The denominationally divided members of the WCC are
still sending divided signals into the mission fields.

Those interested in the mission work of the Church have not
infrequently charged that the WCC is too engrossed in secular
and social ecumenism to give adequate attention to the more
primary ecclesial work of missions. General Secretary Potter
estimates that the criticism of overinvolvement with social
issues is not justified because the Christian message is at
the heart of the Council and Christian duty demands response
to people's needs.[35] Potter appears convinced that the unre-
lenting demands of the social gospel must be attended to by
the World Council which cannot turn back but must be involved
in the various ways of witnessing to Christ in the world.[36]

The complaint of secular overextension continues to harass
the WCC; Potter acknowledged the complaint and suggested his
exasperation when he rebuffed "those who perversely and almost parrot-fashion say that the World Council is giving far
too much attention to social and political issues and not
enough to work for the unity and evangelistic task of the
Church."[37]

Later, when mentioning the F&O, L&W, and Missionary branches
of the World Council, Potter admits "the fact is that we have
all found it very difficult to keep together these three essential callings of the church...."[38] Nairobi recognized the
continued presence of this problem and "it emphasized the
need for the work of the Council to be seen as a comprehen-
sive whole."[39]

Potter thinks the problem goes deeper; he judges that the
member churches themselves have failed to integrate the function of prophetic witness on secular activities into their
own ecclesial lives and thus the crisis is in the churches,
and thence in the World Council.[40] His solution remains the
global, or all-movements-together, view. He does not suggest
that Christians should first be one, so that they may preclude
contradictory gospel witness; rather he seems to highlight
the L&W tradition of service to the World.[41] Without question, the solution to problems of racism, development, mili-
tarism, transnational corporations and political ethics are
important, but such attention-getting concerns practically
side track interest in the quest for the *Una Sancta*.

As the person is prior to the person's own actions, so in
some analogous way the one Church is prior to the Church's
own actions. Thus, the exhaustive efforts to construct the
Una Sancta's common prophetic voice to the world, from a
grouping of partly united and partly seriously-divided autonomous churches, appears to contain the nucleus of permanent
frustration. Global (everything together) solutions seem to
hide and compound the problem rather than solve it.

If the WCC misguides its members in the quest for the *Una
Sancta,* it will become, not an instrument in the solution,
but a part of the problem. The primacy of the ecclesiological nucleus problem needs priority of attention; and this is
a problem of recovery, not of construction or remaking. Yves
Congar, perhaps the foremost pioneer of Roman Catholic participation in the Modern Ecumenical movement, made his own
the conviction of Orthodox ecumenists:

> Man cannot remake the Church of the Apostles;
> he can only reunite himself to it. 'If the
> Church has not always existed, if she does
> not trace her origin from Christ Himself,
> then she never will exist. Congresses, con-
> ferences, interconfessional reunions may be
> the sign of a new ecumenical spirit in
> Christendom but they cannot claim to create
> a Church which is for the first time in his-
> tory truly ecumenical.'[42]

The *Una Sancta* problem will not go away. It is deeply im-
planted in every member church of the WCC; as a result, it
emerges in every World Council Assembly. Moreover, the relationship of Christ to his Church is a question of faith; consequently, those who seek a covenant conciliarity based only,
or even mainly, on Life and Work collaboration in external
affairs are merely submerging the Christ/Church inseparability as if *it* were the obstacle to unity; "such a pact harbors

within itself the seed of new divisions."[43]

(3) RCC Membership. At Nairobi, the Assembly again took up
the question of the relationship between the World Council
and the Roman Catholic Church. It noted with approval that
collaboration in common studies, in Bible translation, in
social development work had increased, and that "mutual engagement had become irreversible."[44] At the same time, it
was posed as a problem that the Roman Catholic Church had not
become a member of the World Council of Churches. What are
the obstacles to its membership? In its official document,
Nairobi said:

> The principal difficulty has been to find ways
> to witness together as a fellowship of churches.
> The Roman Catholic Church is constituted as a
> universal community. Its belief that the one
> Church of Jesus Christ subsists in it does not
> exclude dialogue and cooperation with other
> churches, but the emphasis it places on its
> *identity* and proper initiative makes it diffi-
> cult to act with other churches. The interna-
> tional juridical recognition given to the Holy
> See makes cooperation between it and the World
> Council of Churches especially difficult in
> areas like International Affairs (especially
> representation at the United Nations), and in
> Relief and Aid, etc. Similarly, the emphasis
> on *identity* of member churches of the World
> Council can create obstacles to further coopera-
> tion.[45]

This statement manifests the World Council's difficulty in
recognizing the RCC's self image as radically unique, while
simultaneously attempting to see it as not essentially different from its other member-churches. Is it simply the same
as any church which broke from it, or is it in some way different? The question has serious theological and pastoral
difficulties.

Despite a caution to move carefully in such difficult questions, Nairobi voted to push the question of RCC membership
by saying:

> This Assembly looks forward eagerly to the
> day when it will be possible for the Roman
> Catholic Church to become a member of the
> World Council of Churches.[46]

This nudge toward membership was contained in the Nairobi
statement which unanimously adopted the Joint Working Group's

report on the WCC/RCC relationship. This JWG report cited
the progressive development of dialogue and collaboration between its parent bodies (namely the WCC and the RCC). Such
development naturally led to the question of membership.
After studying this question the JWG reported:

> an application by the Roman Catholic Church
> for World Council membership would not be
> made in the near future.[47]

To the question: Why not?", the JWG replied that there are
factors which militate against such a visible relationship
between the World Council of Churches and the Roman Catholic
Church. The factors are:

> To a much greater degree than other churches,
> the Roman Catholic Church sees its constitu-
> tion as a universal fellowship with a universal
> mission and structure as an essential element
> of its identity. Membership could present real
> pastoral problems to many Roman Catholics be-
> cause the decision to belong to a world-wide
> fellowship of churches could easily be misun-
> derstood. Then there is the way in which au-
> thority is considered in the Roman Catholic
> Church and the processes through which it is
> exercised. There are also practical differ-
> ences in the mode of operation, including the
> style and impact of public statements.[48]

Thus, the JWG, half of whose membership is from the World
Council, recognizes that the Roman Catholic Church's: (1)
constitution as a universal community; (2) authority concept;
(3) public statement posture; and (4) pastoral responsibility
—prevent membership in the rather new World Council as it is
presently constituted.

But the World Council is a changing organization. It changed
its constitution at Nairobi to identify the goal of "visible
unity in faith, eucharistic worship and common life" as its
first purpose.[49] Thus, the future is open.

Nairobi itself, in its documentary report, recognized the
Roman Catholic Church's constitution as a universal ecclesial
community. It further recorded that Church's belief that
"the one Church of Christ subsists in it" and its consequent
sense of special identity and proper initiative. These very
elements present the World Council with factors which do not
square with the Tomkins' definition that the WCC is a *council
of non-universal denominations* which have to die so the *Una
Sancta* can emerge.[50]

John Cardinal Willebrands, "as representative of the Catholic
partner" in the JWG, addressed to the World Council's General
Secretary a commentary on the JWG's *Fourth Official Report*.[51]
The Cardinal assured Secretary Potter that the Catholic reaction to the report was positive and approving; the document
was useful as a springboard to the way ahead. The "multi-
faceted" ecumenical movement was an enabling Christian instrument in the contemporary world. "Yet it loses its meaning unless it has as both its initial impulse and its ultimate goal *the unity* which is the gift of Christ to his faithful people."[52]

Willebrands continued with thoughts taken from the Vatican
Council's *Decree on Ecumenism* (articles 1 and 2):

> In our understanding therefore, the essential
> characteristic of the ecumenical movement is
> a longing 'for the *one visible Church* of God,
> a Church truly universal and sent forth to the
> whole world so that the world may be converted
> to the Gospel and so be saved, to the glory of
> God.'
>
> There is a sense in which the unity of the
> Church is an end in itself since it is meant
> to be the living illustration of that mystery
> of unity which is the life of the Trinity.[53]

Willebrands appears to be widening the notion, flourishing
in the World Council, that the only reason for the Church is
evangelism. He praised some insights of conciliarity, but indicated that conciliarity, a feature of Church life, is not
the same as organic union.[54] Willebrands frankly specified
the Secretariat's understanding of the report with a view to
the JWG's post-Nairobi work. He said he wished "to manifest
as fully and authentically as possible the real, if imperfect, communion that already exists."[55]

In a post-Nairobi speech Visser't Hooft observed that this
awareness of a "real but incomplete unity" had been sensed
at Lausanne in 1927.[56] Much nineteenth century Protestant
theology had taught that "invisible unity" was enough; the
Protestant majority at Lausanne, led by the Anglo-Catholic
conviction of Bishop Brent, felt that the already present
unity must be manifested.[57] It is that "real, but partial,
unity" which is the bed-rock of the modern ecumenical movement. As Visser't Hooft points out, "We...learned to distinguish between a unity already realized and the complete
unity which we have to seek."[58]

Following the Nairobi Assembly *visible unity* was relocated to

a very prominent place in the constitution. But is this visibility of the unity applied to the "conciliar fellowship" or
to the "one Church"?

CHAPTER SIXTEEN

TOWARD VANCOUVER

As The World Council of Churches (WCC) moved on after its
Assembly in Nairobi (1975), its Faith and Order (F&O) Commission had been granted a new position of strength among the
WCC's numerous sub-units. By no means had F&O achieved the
magnitude of influence of Life & Work, its founding co-
partner, but it had gained a primacy of position in the revised constitutional listing of the "Functions and Purposes"
of the WCC. Further, its first-place listing engages the
WCC in the work of ecclesial unity in the same words as those
which direct the F&O commission to its goal.

This inquiry is interested in the WCC's striving to regain
the *Una Sancta*. This ancient expression is found in the
Nicene Creed, which refers to the Church Christ founded as
the *Una Sancta Apostolica Ecclesia* (the one holy apostolic
church). The WCC's serious efforts to make visible, or recover (or be?), the one Church of Christ for its divided member churches is a striving for a unity which can be appreciated as it progresses. Some ideas unite, others divide,
still others, despite noteworthy efforts to activate them,
merely stand in place. It appears that Faith and Order has
been the WCC's primary cutting edge (sometimes frustrated)
in producing manageable ideas which attempt to define the
constituents of the *Una Sancta* goal, and to ascertain the
steps necessary to achieve it.

Thus, Faith & Order's place within the ever-ready-to-expand
complex of the WCC can facilitate or diminish F&O's progress.

The WCC constitution's "Title III" lists seven "Functions
and Purposes" in the following order: (i) unity; (ii) common
witness; (iii) mission work; (iv) justice & peace; (v) religious renewal; (vi) ecumenical contacts; and now in last
place the catch-all function of (vii) advancing the work of:
Faith and Order (F&O), Life and Work (L&W), the International
Missionary Council (IMC), and finally the World Council on
Christian Education (WCCE).[1]

The first article of the constitution's "Title III" reads as
follows: "The World Council of Churches is constituted for
the following functions and purposes:

> (i) to call the churches to the goal of visible unity
> in one faith and in one eucharistic fellowship expressed
> in worship and in common life in Christ, *and to advance*
> *towards that unity* in order that the world may believe.

It is worthy of note that the WCC identifies this purpose
with the expressions: "to call...and to advance"(italicized
above); whereas F&O (below) specifies its more restrained
aim with the words: "to proclaim...and to call..."

The comparable passage in the By-Laws of the Faith and Order
commission (Title 2. AIM AND FUNCTION), is quoted here that
the reader may see the forthrightness of the present F&O influence. It reads:

> *The Aim* of the Commission is to proclaim the one-
> ness of the Church of Jesus Christ and to call the
> churches to the goal of visible unity in one faith
> and one eucharistic fellowship, expressed in wor-
> ship and in common life in Christ, in order that
> the world may believe.[2]

Such straightforward documentary statements greatly hearten
those who are convinced that ecclesial unity in faith, worship and common life should precede the members further de-
ploying their churches' still divided and dividing voices to
all the peoples of the globe. However, constitutional language is one thing; achievement of its aim in the multi-
diversified WCC is another. Further, at the time that the
Nairobi Assembly revised Title III of its constitution, two
members raised cautions implying serious future division.

First, Bishop Nikolainen of the Lutheran Church of Finland
required that the minutes contain the understanding that "the
goal of visible unity does not necessarily mean unity of
jurisdiction or church government."[3]

Secondly, the Salvation Army's Commissioner Williams objected
to the imbedding of the phrase "eucharistic fellowship" as
standing against the beliefs of the Salvation Army and the
Society of Friends.[4]

General Secretary Potter responded that the World Council's
"functions are not binding upon the member churches but are
what the WCC is expected to promote."[5] Potter is the WCC's
principal leader; as such, he is expected to promote the
whole WCC program, which, itself, is supposedly designed to

achieve the final goal of the visible unity of the Church of
Christ. However, the diffusion and interlacing of the whole
WCC program appears to be so complex as to swamp or dislo-
cate the final goal.

1.   WCC COMPLEXITY

The ever-growing complexity of the WCC's structure and
operations strongly militates against its efficient pursuit
of the *Una Sancta* Ecclesia (One Holy Church) goal.   In 1971,
the young WCC sought to simplify and restructure its already
complex operating program.   It reduced its way of working to
what it now terms three programme units: Unit Programme I,
Unit Programme II and Unit Programme III.

Unit Programme I seems to contain the common inner core
of *theological speculation* (Faith and Order type matter);[6]
Unit Programme II appears to be focused on *practical
work* (Life and Work type matter);[7]
Unit Programme III is centered around teaching, under
the title "Education and Renewal."[8]

Unit Programme I has four sub-units working under its
supervision:

SUB-UNIT 1[9]is titled Faith and Order (F&O); this is
the continuation of the original Faith and Order Commission,
which now has about 120 members, of whom twelve are Catholic
theologians.   F&O has preserved its right to invite persons
of nonmember churches to become full members of its theo-
logically-focused Commission.

SUB-UNIT 2 is called the Conference on World Mission
and Evangelism (CWME); it also is a large commission whose
overall task is mission and evangelism (the work of the former
International Missionary Council, which joined the WCC at
New Delhi '61).

SUB-UNIT 3 is known by the name "Dialogue with People of
Other Faiths and Ideologies" (DFI).   Its name identifies its
work.

And finally SUB-UNIT 4, titled "Church and Society"
(C&S), whose attention may be glued to any ethical issues
which arise either in government, business or science, etc.,
encompasses a very wide spectrum, indeed.

Unit Programme II starts with a management unit which
guides five sub-units and at least four other active programs,
all of which require personnel and secretariat desks which

keep the information traffic going up and down as well as
sideways to the desks of the other sub-units related to a
programme in any way. All of these sub-units appear to be
engaged in Life and Work type activities. These five sub-
units, under the Unit Executive Group (UEG), are:[10]

SUB-UNIT 1 is the Commission of the Churches on international Affairs (CCIA).

SUB-UNIT 2 is the Commission on Interchurch Aid, Refu-
gee and World Service (CICARWS).

SUB-UNIT 3 is known as the "Programme to Combat Racism"
(PCR). This is the sub-unit involved in very controversial
acts of giving funds to the forces fighting aparteid in
South Africa.

SUB-UNIT 4 is the Commission on the Churches' Participation in Development (CCPD). It concerns itself with an ongoing analysis of global activities and structures, and their
effects on people, especially the world's poor people.

SUB-UNIT 5 is named "Christian Medical Commission" (CMC).
Its work as an enabling organization is to promote health
and healing as a Christian service.

Unit Programme III[11]. This unit, which seems presently
to have five sub-units, is entitled "Education and Renewal".
The structure of the unit has been changing up into the 1980s,
and has been characterized by a constant readiness to try new
concepts and plans.[12] Its present sub-units are:

SUB-UNIT 1 seeks to shape Christian education into an
ecumenical design.

SUB-UNIT 2 is entitled Programme on Theological Education (PTE).

SUB-UNIT 3 deals with Renewal and Congregational Life
(RCL).

SUB-UNIT 4 explores the concerns of Women in Church and
Society (WCS).

SUB-UNIT 5 is simply named Youth.

As some of the sub-unit names indicate--especially the names
of these last sub-units--their interests cut across practically all of the other sub-units, and even the major units.
The admittedly difficult effort to define functions in any
organization is somewhat like trying to cut a pie into clean

slices. When another knife cuts at cross purposes to the intent of the original cutter, the cross-action inevitably pro-
duces overlapping, and intrusions into the responsibility of
others, with a consequent loss of time, energy and enthusiasm,
not to mention the unecumenical loss of sub-unit prestige.

Intra- and Inter-unit communications add to the complexity of
the WCC operations. For example, Unit Programme I has four
subunits: F&O, Missions, Other-religions dialogue, and Church
and Society. All are of different size, goal, structure and
style; yet all in some hard-to-measure degree overlap.[13]
F&O and Mission, in common, claim belief in the apostolic
Christian faith; yet, F&O seeks to formulate one common statement of that faith, while Mission assists divided voices to
carry their divided "good news" to non-believers!

The official report also notes that the subunits named are
"working largely as separate entities."[14] In the same place,
the report frankly notes that differences of mandate, short-
age of personnel and lack of money contribute to the lack of
collaboration between the three big programme units.[15] As
complexity increases, can the drive toward the *Una Sancta* be
accelerated?

Churches *alone,* as churches, constitute the membership of the
WCC. This was a critical requirement of the WCC's foundation.
However, useful relationships were maintained with other
"*ecumenical agencies.*" Further, since Nairobi, many councils
of churches have joined the World Council under the title of
associate membership. Their interests are as multiform as the
countries and regions they come from; this added complexity,
with its necessary scattering of attention, time and energy of
the World Council's personnel, simply reduces, that much more,
the concentration of effort needed for the reconstitution of
unity among its member churches.

These "councils," frequently formed by both churches and
agencies, are generally staffed by full-time personnel engaged in communication, organizational, and promotional activities, similar to much of the WCC's L&W-type work on the
world level. They are apt and ready contacts for the World
Council. The development of a network of such centers can
readily lead the WCC toward becoming an *active fellowship of
non-voting ecumenical agencies!* This fellowship of agencies
is precisely what Visser't Hooft sought to avoid before the
WCC was founded. One can visualize the churches' diminished
influence and meaning as members, in proportion as the WCC
agency-nerve-center takes on a professional non-ecclesial
character.

This increased interaction with "national agencies" tends to
give the World Council's center in Geneva a life of its own,
separated from the churches which give the WCC its *primary*
meaning. This "life-of-its-own," reality, already emerging
in official reports, is simply exacerbated by an increase of
non-ecclesial attachments. The *Nairobi To Vancouver* report
already indicates that the leadership complex of units and
subunits, with networks of programs and action groups around
the world, tends

> to create an atmosphere of isolation from each
> other and from the official church bodies. As
> a result, the work of the Council is not always
> seen and experienced as a comprehensive whole,
> which in turn sometimes strains the relationship
> between the churches and the Council.[16]

In proceedings aimed at visible ecclesial unity, churches
must deal with churches, not with agencies. Agencies may assist if they are not too cumbersome, and get out of the way
in time. And in this matter, the WCC appears to be acting
more like an agency. Thus, in church unity matters, the
Catholic Church can talk with an Orthodox Church, or an Anglican Church, or a Lutheran Church, but it really cannot deal
with an agency about these churches. It can dialogue with an
agency; it can collaborate in a limited way with some agencies; but the work of reintegrating visible unity is the work
of churches, not agencies.

2.   SECULARITY DISPLACING UNITY FOCUS?

But, more pointedly, how can this multiform dispersion
of energies contribute to the reintegration of Christian
Churches into Christ's intended *Una Sancta* ecclesia? One can
well imagine that persons engaged in the foregoing increasing-
ly-diversifying pursuits for decades may conclude that the
unity Christ intended is eschatological, that is, it will
only be achieved in the end-time, after life on earth (as we
know it) is finished!

This structural picture, with its required large number of
diversely directed people, makes it difficult to see how
such scattered activity will effectively aid in reconstitut-
ing the unity of divided, differently structured churches.
It appears that the WCC is making (has made?) it practically impossible for itself to let go of its own institutional being in the process of assisting its member churches to
unify themselves on the basis of the Scriptural truth to become *even something like* the organism of Christ's *Una Sancta
Apostolica Ecclesia* (one holy apostolic Church).

This apparent difficulty, of course, in no way releases either
the World Council or the Roman Catholic Church from the obligation of striving to reach this goal of Christ's intention.
Both bodies are committed to the Scriptural belief that God
"...whose power [is] now at work in us can do immeasureably
more than we ask or imagine..."[17]

Readily, and with praise, one can acknowledge that the WCC
work itself is valuable; also that the Christian motivation
for all of this is of a high order, but it appears that the
basic drive for the *Una Sancta* Ecclesia is so submerged in
the midst of the multitudinous other activities that it cannot be attained as an imminent goal. It seems likely that
some WCC officials and staff, from many denominations, engaged in this constantly demanding complex of institutional
activities, will tend to think of their UNITY IN THIS WORK
as beginning somehow to constitute the ecclesial unity which
is the goal of the Ecumenical movement.

Despite rhetoric that sounds identical when it speaks of "ecclesial unity", the phrase connotes two very different realities. The text of the Nicene Creed means "one church"; the
post-Nairobi expression persistently means, not "one church",
but a "truly ecumenical *conciliar fellowship*". General Secretary Rev. Dr. Philip Potter authored an "Introduction" (18
pages) to the "official report" of the WCC covering the period between Nairobi and Vancouver, which identifies the WCC's
goal as "conciliar fellowship".

In this important seven-year summary by the WCC's acknowledged
leader, Dr. Potter identifies the WCC as an "expression of
faith," estimates that the world situation has deteriorated
sharply, and then focuses his attention on the World Council's
mandate from Nairobi. The mandate consisted of three exten-
sively worded "guidelines", from which the Central Committee
focused the Secretariat's attention on what it termed "areas
of concentration."[18]

Very briefly, the three guidelines respectively require that
all the WCC programmes are to help the member churches:
(1) to grow towards a truly ecumenical, conciliar fellowship...; (2) to reach a common understanding of Gospel and
tradition for a fuller common witness...; and (3) to participate in the struggle for human dignity and social justice...[19]

The effects of the third guideline seem to have overwhelmed
the others. However, the question here is concerned with the
precise goal, or center-target, on which the WCC continues to
set its sights. That goal is precisely "a conciliar fellowship," not the one Church of Christ, not the *Una Sancta* of
Peter and Paul.

The World Council of Churches is by definition a "fellowship of churches". The elements which constitute this council are "churches". Hence, it appears that the most fundamental principle which should guide the WCC is the Christ-given nature of "His Church." To get at the nature of anything, one must know what it is for. Thus, to gain insight into what the WCC, composed of churches, is for, one should ask what is Christ's *Church* for.

On this question, the World Council and the Roman Catholic Church do not seem to be in agreement. The World Council of Churches appears, by the sheer magnitude of its agenda, dedicated to United Nations-type problems, to define itself as a secular-agenda organization; and by persuading its member churches to vote for, support, and even to adopt, this ecclesially-clothed activist agenda, it seems to be making the churches into images of itself--instead of the other way around.

Whereas, the Roman Catholic Church, which also works through a complex bureaucracy, known as the Vatican Curia, nevertheless clearly believes, as it states in its newly revised *Code of Canon Law,* that "the salvation of souls...is always the supreme law of the Church."[20] Thus, there is a constantly applicable norm against which the existence and function of each Vatican Curial office may be measured. Always allowing for human weakness and inefficiency, the norm, today at least, is definite and clear, and tends *a priori* to question excursions into what is primarily the secular domain.

In his Introduction to the official report to the Vancouver assembly, Dr. Potter noted that the WCC had published a prayer guide, *For All God's People;* such an act among Roman Catholics is an act of the Church requiring an *imprimatur.* It also published a hymnal, *Cantate Domino.* Such acts are guiding functions for the authorities who lead the church in its Christian belief. At this point in his report and in the light of the landmark 1950 *Toronto Statement,* Dr. Potter cites the need "...to examine afresh the ecclesial nature of the World Council."[21]

3.   CHANGING GOALS?

       The effort to analyze the most basic focus of the WCC and the RCC in no way seeks to denigrate the value of the excellent work that the WCC has done. It is rather to ask the questions: "has the WCC moved away from its primary business?" "Has the WCC become a Christian 'UN', rather than continue as a spearhead of the movement for ecclesial unity?" Is not the WCC making itself less able (or possibly unable?)

to reconstitute unity among its doctrinally-divided member
churches?

In the report which its most influential leader, Rev. Philip
Potter, general secretary of the WCC, gave to the WCC's Central Committee, he seemed to affirm that the World Council
has, indeed, changed its organizational sights from the primary ecclesial business of church unity to the business of
economics, politics and society of the world.

Again, these are very important arenas of good Christian activity, but is it the primary business of a church, or consequently of the World Council as a "fellowship of Churches"?

In his report, given at Kingston, Jamaica, three and a half
years after the 1975 Nairobi Assembly, Potter said:

> In the first twenty years of the life of the
> Council [1948 to 1968] we had a clear mandate
> to promote the unity of the Church through re-
> newal of the Churches in mission and service
> to the world. In more recent years [1968 to
> 1979], two aspects of ecumenism have come to
> the fore. *Oikoumene* has acquired its original
> meaning of the *whole inhabited earth* which be-
> longs to the Lord (Psalm 24:1). The whole
> life of humankind comes under God's rule and
> *therefore the concern of the churches*. We are
> bound to work for the unity of humankind and
> this means being engaged in the struggle for a
> just society in which barriers of class, race
> and sex are broken down....[22]

Some six or seven years after this Kingston speech, Potter is
still firmly minded that the WCC's emphasis should be keyed
toward the agenda of "secular ecumenism." In 1983 he wrote:
the "brokenness of our human situation in the world context
has necessarily been a major preoccupation for the Council."[23]
As he neared the end of this same essay, after enumerating
such emphases as human rights, unjust power structures, foundations of a just and sustainable society and action for
social change, he wrote: "This indeed is the crux of the very
nature and calling of the Council...."[24] The UN and other
secular world societies are working on these gigantic problems, but how, then, will the WCC focus its major attention
on the Unity of Christians willed by Christ?

It appears that no one would argue that injustice done by man
is the business of Christ's Church. But Christ's way was to
convert the sinning man or woman, to proclaim God's truth to
the leading Scribes and Pharisees. He converted Simon the

the Zealot to become his disciple; he did not give him money
to overthrow Pilate. His words can be directed against the
evils done by persons, whether Jewish followers or pagans,
whether anawim or tax-collector, but He does not work to
overturn either the Sanhedrin or the Roman Empire. In fact,
to the one who cut off the ear of the high priest's servant,
Matthew (25:51f.) quotes Christ as sharply correcting the
swordsman: "Put back your sword where it belongs. Those who
use the sword are sooner or later destroyed by it."

In his report, Potter notes that the giving of money to combat racism (Unit II's subunit 3: Programme to Combat Racism)
in South Africa caused "much fury in some quarters."[25] Further, "several churches and groups have raised the question
of supporting violence which cannot be the action of the
Church."[26]

The first General Secretary, Willem Visser't Hooft, in a 1980
reflection paper, now thinks of ecumenical work chiefly as a
process of serious conversation, profession of faith and worship. Visser't Hooft says:

> ...in the process of dialogue, in common con-
> fession before the world, in common worship,
> it is possible for the churches in the plural
> to become more and more the Church in the
> singular.[27]

The present WCC leader, Philip Potter, seems to be steering
the ship further away from the port now clearly envisioned
by its founding patriarch and first general secretary,
Willem Visser't Hooft.

The Rev. Edward Scott, moderator of the powerful Central Committee, in his foreword to the 1983 official report, asks the
question: "Does the report indicate that the Council [WCC]
has been true to the vision of those who brought it into
being?"[28]

Despite the magnitude of the "secular-ecumenism" agenda,
some of the many worthwhile publications produced through
the WCC were centered on the substantive ecclesial problems
which have divided Christians.

One document, entitled *Common Witness,* done under the aegis
of the JWG (the "Joint Working Group," composed of WCC
sponsored theologians and Vatican-appointed theologians), was
produced by the Commission for World Mission and Evangelism.

Another, done through the services of Unit Programme I (Faith
and Witness), examines the path *Toward a Confession of the
Common Faith.*

A Third, which has generated the most wide-spread interest of all, is identified as a convergence statement on *Baptism, Eucharist and Ministry,* already commonly referred to as the BEM document, from the first letters of the three principal words in the document's title.

4. THE BEM DOCUMENT

From the time of Episcopal Bishop Charles Brent's founding of the Faith and Order organization in 1927, questions on the nature of the Church, and the constituents which form it, such as baptism, eucharist and ministry, have been present on its agenda. It can, in truth, even be said that pioneer John Mott's refusal to allow these very questions in the famous 1910 Mission meeting in Edinburgh, sparked Brent's drive to design the Faith and Order movement which has nurtured a convergence among its member theologians who produced the theological statement on *Baptism, Eucharist and Ministry* known as the *BEM document.*

This so-called "convergence"[29] was unanimously agreed to in 1982 at the Faith and Order Commission meeting of over a hundred theologians of different traditions at Lima, Peru. Hence the document is also known as the *Lima document,* and the liturgy written in its light as the *Lima Liturgy.* The BEM text, or BEM, as it is conveniently named, is one of the most forthright, concentrated, Christian theological documents ever published under the auspices of the WCC. It may be Faith and Order's and thus the WCC's, most significant church-unity document since the Toronto Statement in 1950.

The official report evaluates its significance thus:

> The period since Nairobi may well be remembered as a time of genuine breakthrough in search for visible church unity. Faith and Order's text of *Baptism, Eucharist and Ministry* (1982) has now been sent to the churches with a request for official response by the end of 1984...[30]

This BEM text is indeed a breakthrough, and unprecedented! Moreover, the aggressive action of the F&O commission (with the Central Committee's authorization), respectfully inviting "*all churches* to prepare an official response to this text at the highest appropriate level of authority,"[31] was a further unprecedented move into unchartered waters. F&O had previously invited responses to a prior BEM statement from the WCC's member churches; over a hundred of the three hundred had responded. But this invitation, *to all churches,*

includes all nonmember Protestant and Orthodox churches, and
also the Catholic Church. It was a bold move! Apparently,
F&O's Catholic members felt free to participate in the agreement decision without any qualifying hesitations. Another
move which is going to evoke official pause and some rejection is a sort of test or challenge, thus:

> As concrete evidence of their ecumenical
> commitment, the churches are being asked to
> enable the widest possible involvement of
> the whole people of God at all levels of
> church life in the spiritual process of re-
> ceiving this text.[32]

The text is not an easy document; some theologians find unacceptable statements in it. The preface acknowledges that
the BEM text is incomplete. However, it omits some critically important matter, especially on the topic of ministry.
Yet the text contains many sound points of age-old Christian
doctrine. Thus, it seems more prudent that it be examined
by competent, ecumenically-minded people in those churches
belonging to the WCC. This unanimously-agreed text was completed under the chairmanship of British Methodist Geoffrey
Wainwright,[33] long-time F&O commission member.[34]

In many places, the text shows, so-to-speak, some of the
voiceprints of its origin. Surely "epiklesis" and "anamnesis"
emphases manifest the traditional Orthodox presence; the
avoidance of the "Christ to Apostles to successors" sequence
suggests the non-episcopal Protestant presence; the language
of reality-under-sacramental signs and "real presence" language appears to reveal Catholic interventions.

In some places the text seems verbose, as it leads somewhat
tentatively toward a critical assertion. It seems, at times,
as though it might be adding interventions to please an in-
tervener, or might, perhaps be helping to instruct those who
have lost the critical-ecclesiological sense of Baptism,
Eucharist and Ministry.

This BEM document (English edition) is a 33-page attractive
booklet consisting of a preface, three sections (one each on:
Baptism, Eucharist and Ministry) and a final appendix page
suggesting reference readings and uses.

Baptism is treated in 23 numbered and popularly worded paragraphs; six of the paragraphs have commentary attached to
them. The *Eucharist* text has 33 paragraphs with commentary
attached to six. The *Ministry* text consists of 55 numbered
paragraphs with 14 attachments.

From the churches, the Faith and Order Commission would like
to know with all possible precision: "the extent which your
church can *recognize* in this text the *faith of the Church
through the ages*"; it also wishes to know: the "consequences"
your church can take for ecclesial interrelations, the "guidance" for itself and "suggestions" that may aid the ongoing
unity-seeking study of the F&O Commission.

The text, in general, is orderly; for example, the baptism
text proceeds from institution, through meaning, relation to
faith, and practice, and ends with the celebration of baptism. This section (as well as eucharist and ministry) opens
with the traditional New Testament citations which thin out
as the paragraphs proceed. Moreover, the document does explicitly acknowledge some support coming from *tradition* as
expressed in the writings of the Fathers:

> The universal practice of baptism by the
> apostolic Church from its earliest days is
> attested in letters of the New Testament,
> the Acts of the Apostles, *and the writings
> of the Fathers.*[35]

This reference to the "writings of the Fathers" certainly
invites greater confidence from those Christian communities
for whom the teaching of the Fathers gives the traditional
sense of the Church and its understanding of Scripture in
that period of time. The preface also manifests F&O's intention to reflect "the common *Christian tradition* on essential elements of Christian communion.[36] "The faith of
the Church through the ages" will certainly be manifested in
the Fathers' development of the apostolic tradition.

This F&O document's *preface* importantly identifies the goal
sought as "visible Church unity,"[37] thus distinguishing itself from the more specific, and non-center-target expression, "conciliar fellowship," which the *Nairobi to Vancouver*
report had frequently used, but which seems somewhat at odds
with the test of: "the faith of the Church through the ages."
The faith of the Fathers can in places throw a penetrating
light on passages in the Lima text.

Baptism

The *preface* observes (apologetically ?) that "the language
of the document is still largely classical in reconciling
controversies" (p. ix), yet it seems reluctant to name baptism as a sacrament in the section on baptism; however, a
comment, in the later section on the eucharist, says:
"Since the earliest days, baptism has been understood as

a the *sacrament* by which believers are incorporated into the
body of Christ...." Augustine was already using *sacramentum*
in place of the Greek word, *musterion,* in the fifth century.
His thought contributed to the classical sense of baptism as
a *signum efficax gratiae* (an efficacious sign of grace).[38]
The BEM text freely uses the word *sign,* and also occasionally "grace", but seems hesitant to use the term "efficacious". At the same time, it implies the *efficacious* result
of baptism as it freely speaks of what baptism does. One
notable instance occurs when the document declares of the
baptized, that God

> marks them with a *seal* and implants in their
> hearts the first installment of their in-
> heritance as sons and daughters.[39]

In paragraph 13, the BEM text implies the efficacious result
of baptism in terse and forcefully prescriptive terms. The
document reads: "Baptism is an unrepeatable act. Any practice which might be interpreted as 're-baptism' must be
avoided."[40]

Many of the document's statements are directly theological
and critical for defining a goal of unity which can command
the attention of believing Orthodox, Catholics and others;
for example, baptism: "is a gift of God, and is administered
in the name of the Father, the Son, and the Holy Spirit";
"it unites the one baptized with Christ and with his people";
it raises persons "now to a new life in the power of the
resurrection of Jesus Christ"; "it is incorporation into
Christ"; "it is a sign and seal of our common discipleship";
"it is a basic bond of unity"; "it has a dynamic which embraces the whole of life, and extends to all nations"; "it
looks to growth."[41] These expressions, and others like them,
inform believing Christians that the Faith and Order Commission of the WCC is seriously dealing with Christian beliefs
about which there must be agreement before any radical
Christian unity can take place. "The faith of the Church
through the ages," is surely recognizable here.

The text treads softly on the "infant baptism vs. believer's
baptism" debate, which arose, in emotional times, after
fifteen centuries of not being a problem. The Orthodox have
to wonder how this could, after so long, have arisen as a
problem.[42] The text highlights ground common to both positions as it points out that "both forms of baptism embody
God's own initiative in Christ and express a response of
faith made within the believing community."[43]

In pursuit of the ecumenical goal, the BEM text calls for a
mutual recognition of baptism among the Christian churches.

"Wherever possible, mutual recognition should be expressed
explicitly by the churches."[44]

Eucharist

As the *BEM* text had treated baptism, so it dealt with the
eucharist; it considered the institution, the meaning and
the celebration of this summit doctrine of Christian worship. The document bases its starting points on the New
Testament texts found in the synoptic Gospels (Matthew,
Mark, Luke) and the *earliest written formulation* of Christian belief in the eucharist as found in Paul's first letter
to the Corinthians (chapter 11). Paul's sentences are
quoted fully in the document.

The "meal" aspect of Jesus' Last Supper with his apostles is
highlighted. It is identified as a "sign of the kingdom,"
an "anamnesis of his death and resurrection" and a "*sacramental* meal"; its sacrificial character appears to be studiously avoided in this initial "institution" presentation.
So studious is the omission, that the expression entirely
familiar to Catholics, "the sacrifice of the mass," is
omitted in the listing of the many names by which the "Lord's
Supper" is known. The commission chose to use only the more
common name, "mass". This "institution" treatment ends with
the factual observation that the celebration of the Lord's
Supper "continues as the central act of the Church's worship."[45]

Under the heading, "The Meaning of the Eucharist", the BEM
text identifies the eucharist as a sacrament, and in paragraph 4 as a "sacrifice of praise". Paragraph 5 comes out
quite directly and affirms

> The eucharist is...the *living and effective
> sign of the sacrifice* accomplished once and
> for all on the cross and still operative on
> behalf of all humankind.[46]

Paragraph 8 expresses the belief even more simply with the
sentence: "The eucharist is the sacrament of the unique
sacrifice of Christ, who ever lives to make intercession
for us."[47] Orthodox scholar George Bebis presents a reflection from Irenaeus on the eucharist as a "pure sacrifice,"[48]
which might help to highlight the "faith of the Church
through the ages."

Also very strongly, paragraph 13 quotes Christ's words of
institution, "this is my body; this is my blood", and declares:

> What Christ declared is true, and this truth
> is fulfilled *every time* the eucharist is
> celebrated. The Church confesses Christ's
> real, living and active presence in the
> eucharist.[49]

The text appears to indicate that Christ's *real presence* is
objectively independent of a given communicant's faith.
This seems to imply an objectivity independent of even the
celebrant's faith. Further, the commentary on this paragraph specifies the power to effect this utterly transcendent reality as the power of the Holy Spirit, without indicating anything about the competency or the valid power of
orders of the human agent through whom the Holy Spirit is
acting.[50]   The commentary on paragraph 19 speaks only of the
acknowledgement of the "*right* to participate in or preside
over eucharistic celebration."[51]   Deeper than the question
of a personal *right,* however, is the Orthodox, Anglican and
Roman Catholic question of *capability,* especially with regard to one presiding over the eucharistic celebration.
This BEM deficiency, critical for many Christians, comes
more to the fore in the document's section on "ministry."

While these questions are vitally important, it must be remembered that the BEM document is admittedly incomplete, and
it is not a text book. With these and other cautions in
mind, it can be said that the BEM text strives to affirm a
high eucharistic theology and an implied high Christology.[52]
It is an evocative document, which engenders a reexamination
of "the faith of the Church through the ages," and facili-
tates ecumenical dialogue.[53]

The essential invocation of the Holy Spirit (epiklesis) and
the special nature of the eucharist as a living memorial
(anamnesis) are addressed, whereas the motion toward "intercommunion" (happily, this uncomprehending, non-liturgical
term is not used) so common in WCC reports and activity, is
broached very delicately in paragraph 33.   The Lima text
simply suggests that the broadening theological convergence
"may allow some churches to attain a greater measure of
eucharistic communion among themselves...."[54]

Finally, the terms consecration and transsubstantiation are
avoided, as well as any raising of the question of the precise moment at which Christ is actually present in this
unique, sacramental mode. However, the BEM text does
specify that Christ's instituting words and acts "stand at
the heart of the celebration."[55]

Germane to the whole topic of the eucharistic celebration,
of course, is the question of how and to whom Christ intended

to transmit the function of presiding at the living eucharistic memorial of his once and for all sacrifice. This is
the most complex question of all, namely the question which
some identify as the sacrament of sacred orders, while
others tend to speak generically of ministry, under which
title they subsume, and sometimes bypass, the question of
the power Christ gave to his Church.

Ministry

On the topic of "ministry", the F&O Commission addressed six
large headings, namely: I. The Calling of the whole people
of God; II. The Church and the Ordained Ministry; III. Forms
of the Ordained Ministry; IV. Functions of Bishop, Priest
and Deacon; V. Ordination; and finally, VI. Towards the
Mutual Recognition of the Ordained Ministries.

Very interestingly, the Commission's BEM document devotes
its first three numbered paragraphs to God (the Father), the
Son and the Holy Spirit, respectively, in establishing *the
Church*. The Constitution on the Church (*Lumen Gentium*) of
Vatican II had devoted its articles 2, 3 and 4 to the acts
of the Father, Son and Holy Spirit in establishing and continuing *the Church*. Both documents are pleased to recognize
that the described sacred realities originated from the Tri-
une God as divinely granted gifts, designed for the salvation of all who will respond to his gracious invitation.
This belief in the Trinity is the profound, enabling, common ground which gives hope for continued progress in F&O's
search for steps leading toward ecclesial unity.

BEM's paragraphs 4, 5, and 6 deal with (*Christ's) Church*,
the gifts given for the upbuilding of the Church, and the
declared need to work "from the perspective of the calling
of the whole people of God,"[56] if the effort to overcome
the differences among the churches is to be serious.

At the key point on *the nature of the Church* (paragraph 4),
the F&O commission declined to address this always-present
question; instead, it deflected the text to the messianic
signs of the Nazareth Manifesto (Luke 4:18), and then led
the reader to consider the "varying political, social and
cultural contexts" in which the Church is carrying out its
mission of salvation.[57]

This section strongly conveys the impression that it is trying to persuade the non-episcopal churches of the utility,
traditional basis, and even the necessity, of regaining the
traditional ministerial three-fold structure of "*bishop,
presbyter and deacon*", especially episcopacy, if ecclesial

unity is ever to be achieved. Imbeded in this position, of
course, is the question of authority, and also the question
of the persons to whom Christ gave that authority. The
modern debilitating atmosphere against even proper religious
authority appears to nag BEM's ministry section, and makes
it the weakest section of the Lima document.

On the one hand, the stronger statements made by the BEM
document are texts such as the following: "to fulfill its
mission, the church needs persons [ordained ministers] who
are publicly and continually responsible for pointing to its
fundamental dependence on Jesus Christ, and thereby provide...a focus of unity....The ministry of such persons...is
constitutive for the life and witness of the Church.[58]; "a
ministry of *episkope* [= supervision in Greek; = episcopacy
in English] is necessary to express and safeguard the unity
of the body."[59] A forceful line is given in the paragraph
(9) in which the text declares that there were different
roles in the Church from its very beginning; in fact, "The
Church has *never* been without persons holding specific authority and responsibility."[60]

On the other hand, weakness undercuts the presentation when
the text speaks of: Christ choosing the apostles, and Christ
still choosing his ministers as if he bypassed the very
apostles to whom he had given the original commission. This
weakness is manifest in, at least, paragraphs 11 and 15.
The Scriptural evidence indicates that, as Christ chose his
apostles, so his apostles chose their successors. Thus, to
the present, most Christians hold that continuous apostolic
succession is an essential characteristic of Christ's Church.

Also, the document can find *no real distinction* between the
priesthood of the laity and the ordained priesthood (including episcopacy). The implication is that there is no
sacrament of Holy Orders. Consequently, episcopacy and
priesthood may be considered as useful and historical (and
perhaps even necessary for unity because of the nineteen
centuries of Church tradition), but not essential for the
constitution of Christ's Church. Is not this an old, but
critical, stumbling block? Geoffrey Wainwright, addressing
the question, says:

> The notion of the ordained ministry as a
> focalizing and enabling 'representation' is
> good, and helps to break through the *badly-
> formulated alternative* of a difference in
> kind or degree between the ordained and the
> rest.

This contrasts sharply with the Vatican II position of the

more than 2000 bishops (plus their expert theologians) who
expressed their belief in the *Dogmatic Constitution on the
Church*, thus:

> Though they differ *essentially* and not only
> in degree, the common priesthood of the
> faithful and the ministerial or hierarchical
> priesthood are nonetheless ordered one to
> another; each in its own proper way shares
> in the one priesthood of Christ.

A bit further on, Vatican II affirms that:

> ...the bishops have by divine institution
> [ex divina institutione] taken the place of
> the apostles, in such wise that whoever
> listens to them is listening to Christ and
> whoever despises them despises Christ and
> him who sent Christ.[61]

The conflict of beliefs thickens a bit more when the BEM
text declares in paragraph 38 that the non-episcopal communities cannot accept any suggestion of their own ministerial invalidity until "it enters into an existing line of
episcopal succession."[62]

A group of eight slowly uniting Protestant Churches, whose
prior writings appear to have echoes in the BEM text, responded to the episcopal succession question by saying,
"...the uniting church will not require any theory or doctrine of episcopacy or episcopal succession which goes beyond the consensus stated in this document," after having
already agreed that:

> The uniting church intends that its bishops
> should stand in continuity with the historic
> ministry of bishops as that ministry has been
> maintained through the ages and will ordain
> its bishops in such a way that recognition of
> this ministry is invited from all parts of the
> Universal Church.[63]

The eight Churches have identified their 20-year process
of unity meetings as the *Consultation on Church Union* or,
more briefly, as *COCU*. The COCU formulation of the episcopal succession question appears to be paving the road ahead
more smoothly than the seemingly intransigent language of
the BEM text.

The BEM text appears counter-indicative in its suggesting
(the apostles differ from their successors) that the

unrepeatability of the apostles' experience somehow rendered
them impotent in conferring, on chosen followers, the *same
power and responsibility* to carry on what Christ gave them
to do, for all nations and until the end-time. This weakness in Bem's ministry section hardly reflects "the [experi-
enced] faith of the Church through the ages."

The orderly transmission of Christian faith and life under
successive apostolic episcopal authority has been and continues to be a majority characteristic of the Christian
world. As Paul checked for fifteen days with Peter, and
again years later with the Jerusalem leaders, lest his
preaching be in vain (Galatians 1 and 2), so ecumenists need
reminding that Christian faith is not merely a personal possession that can be manipulated. Roman Catholics are explicitly reminded, by the newly-revised *Code of Canon Law,*
that their public Christian-unity positions involve the competence of those burdened with the continuous safeguarding
of the apostolic faith and unity, thus:

> 1. It is within the special competence of
> the entire college of bishops and of the
> Apostolic See to promote and direct the par-
> ticipation of Catholics in the ecumenical
> movement, whose purpose is the restoration
> of unity among all Christians, which the
> Church is bound by the will of Christ to
> promote.
>
> 2. It is likewise within the competence of
> bishops and, in accord with the norm of law,
> of conferences of bishops to promote the same
> unity and to issue practical norms for the
> needs and opportunities presented by diverse
> circumstances in light of the prescriptions
> of the supreme church authority.[64]

Although the origin of the Christian priesthood from the
presbyterate does not share the same post-New-Testament
support as the episcopacy, nevertheless its ancient place
as subordinate to and authorized by the bishop is attested
to.[65] Thus, one suspects that the document's least-common-
denominator treatment of the traditional priesthood will
tend, in the lay communities in which the document is diffused, to diminish the priesthood's attractiveness, and
consequently undercut budding vocations. Bishops, suffering long-range shortages in the ranks of the diocesan
priesthood, will hardly be advised to spread the BEM text
among their people.

Why the document veils the emergence of *the three-fold*

pattern (bishop, presbyter, deacon) until the second and
third centuries remains a bit of a mystery. These authoritative offices (admittedly with changing functions) are already in evidence in the Pastoral epistles (80's). Further,
they are identified a number of times (and not as anything
new!) in the authentic letters (Philadelphians, Magnesians,
Trallians, Smyrnaeans) of Ignatius of Antioch, who was
martyred by 110 A.D.[66] BEM's commentary 19 refers to the
Ignatian letters. However, their content naturally ante-
dated their writing; consequently, one might expect the BEM
authors to acknowledge the first century origins of the
three-fold pattern (bishop, presbyter, deacon).

In his letter to the Trallians, Ignatius, speaking of the
significance of the bishop, presbyters and deacons in the
Christian community, says: "without these, it cannot be
called a Church."[67]

Ignatius' letter to the Smyrnaeans manifests the values
(prior to the year 110) with which the ecclesial ministers
should be held:

> You must all follow the bishop as Jesus Christ
> follows the Father, and the presbytery as you
> would the Apostles. Reverence the deacons as
> you would the command of God. Let no one do
> anything of concern to the Church without the
> bishop. Let that be considered a valid
> Eucharist which is celebrated by the bishop,
> or by one whom he appoints. Wherever the bishop
> appears, let the people be there; just as wherever
> Jesus Christ is, there is the Catholic Church.[68]

These quotations from Ignatius are not intended to claim
that the three-fold structure (bishop-presbyter-deacon) was
equally in place throughout all the Christian communities
by 110 A.D., the time of Ignatius' death. But it appears
to show that these authoritative, structural Christian offices, already mentioned in the pastoral epistles (80's)
and Luke's *Acts of the Apostles* (about 90 A.D.), were already rather widespread along the Antioch-to-Rome trail of
the Gospel's western flow. A recent searching study positively affirms Antioch's established church structure, thus:
"...within two decades of Matthew [i.e., Matthew's Gospel],
...a firm authoritative structure of single-bishop, presbyters, and deacons had made its appearance at Antioch."[69]

Robert Stephanopoulos, commenting on the Orthodox sense of
the essential ecclesial need of the *continuing* office of
bishop, incisively remarks:

> Not by episcopal succession alone, but cer-
> tainly not without episcopal succession, can
> there be any discussion of the recovery of
> the true unity in the one Church.[70]

Further, when a document, interested in the authentic unity
of Christ's Church, and treating, *ex professo*, of ministry
in that Church, fails to acknowledge Christ's relationship
to Peter in that presentation, then it raises the question
about the requisite unity of the topics treated! The F&O
Commission owes it to its readers to say why it chose not to
include in its treatment the reality expressed in the scriptural texts. The BEM text admirably avoided "fundamentalism"
in its frequent but selective use of the New Testament. It
appeared also to have avoided the opposite extreme of a liberal skepticism. The document's use of Scripture seemed to
reflect the scholarly realism reflected in Martin Hengel's
Acts and the History of Earliest Christianity:

> It is probable that by far the majority of
> narratives and sayings in the gospels will
> have had a *historical basis* in the activity
> of Jesus, though perhaps in a different
> form.[71]

Rejecting the outmoded practice of a sweeping attribution of
texts to the inventiveness of anonymous and amorphous communities, Hengel notes Peter's significance when he observes:

> The transmission and formation of the oral
> tradition about Jesus certainly did not just
> by-pass the leading figures of the first com-
> munity. Simon Peter, who is so often given
> pride of place, must have had a particularly
> prominent position in it.[72]

In the study *Peter in the New Testament,* done by a group of
Protestant and Catholic scholars, Peter's role was noted as
very significant. After extensive study, the group concluded cautiously to the minimum that it could forthrightly
affirm. "*Peter was the most important of the twelve* in
Jerusalem and its environs...Peter served as spokesman of
the twelve...Peter [was perceived as] the confessor of the
true Christian faith...it becomes clear to the [post-Easter]
Christian community that with this faith Peter is the rock
on whom Jesus has founded his church..."[73]

In the study's final chapter, the scholarly group again cautioned the reader that their study had merely affirmed an
inescapable minimum about Peter.

> Although we have listed the minimal facts about
> Simon Peter of which we have some historical
> certitude, this does not do justice to the
> whole New Testament picture.[74]

One may guess the F&O Commission's fear that facing certain
New Testament texts now might, perhaps, be counterproductive.
On the other hand, written texts, once released, take on a
history of their own, and this glaring omission suggests the
question: Is the Reformation still more present on the Faith
and Order Commission than the desire to discover the unity
Christ wants for his Church? It is hard to repress the
sense that the unity Christ willed, and wills, for his
earthly community's reflection of the Trinity will never
come until Christians face those texts, the reality that
flows from them, and the Church's need for a flesh and blood
unifying center.

How does one explain that the WCC and the Faith and Order
Commission claim to be seeking, on the basis of Sacred Scripture and now Christian Tradition, Christ's *Una Sancta Ecclesia* and yet studiously avoid texts which must in some way
be connected with that quest?

Matthew (Mt. 16:18f.) presents Christ as saying: "you are
Peter [kepha], and on this rock [kepha] I will build my
Church"; and "I will give you the keys of the Kingdom of
heaven"; and [in Luke's Gospel (Lk. 22:32), to Peter alone]
"you, in turn must strengthen your brothers"; and "feed my
lambs,...tend my sheep,...feed my sheep" [in John's Gospel
(21:15ff.), again to Peter alone]. Paul also enters this
picture (Gal. 1 and 2) when he goes to see Peter (Cephas)
for fifteen days; years later, Paul again goes to Jerusalem
"to make sure the course I was pursuing, or had pursued, was
not useless." The *Acts of the Apostles* (1 to 15, passim)
fleshes out the origins of the primeval Jerusalem Church
with its focus on the Apostles and especially Peter.

The various criticisms (literary, form, redaction, and historical) each serve to throw some light on the scriptural
texts. These services are valuable, but limited. They do
not deny, nor exhaust, the multiple foundational attesta-
tions and ecclesial implications of the texts. These valuable but limited criticisms (mostly cerebral, and dryly academic) are largely unable to assess (perhaps even to discern)
the lived Christian faith and love which produced the canonical Scripture texts. The Ephesian husbands are exhorted to
love their wives "as Christ loved the Church" (Eph. 5:25).
He is head of the Church, his body. "Christ cares for the
Church...we are members of his body" (Eph. 5:29). "The love
of Christ drives us on" (II Cor. 5:14).[75] Some degree of

this love unifies the members of his one body, and assists
the inspired authors to discern the historical and post-
resurrectional ligaments which bind the body to its Sacred
Head. The Matthean, Lukan, Johannine and Pauline texts all
involve Peter.

These texts are not going to go away. Sooner or later, they,
and other pertinent texts, may be calmly faced in Faith and
Order's dialogue on *ministry in Christ's Church*. "The
faith of the Church through the ages" must be surprised at
the void in a treatment on Christian ministry which omits
the centuries-old, foundational and unifying petrine leadership of more than half of the world's Christians.

These last few pages have sought to note a few strengths and
weaknesses in the *breakthrough* BEM document. Theologically,
the section on baptism appears to be the strongest, and the
section on ministry the weakest. Nevertheless, the enterprise as a whole is worthwhile. The Faith and Order Commission has facilitated the modern ecumenical dialogue in a
theological and far-reaching way. But the euphoria of the
breakthrough is realistically moderated by the profound
problems still ahead.

But worse still is the dead-end sensed by BEM leader Geoffrey Wainwright when he suggests that the BEM document

>   comes as close as we are historically likely
>   to come to substantial and practical agree-
>   ment on the stated themes.[76]

One hesitates to think that the theologians have drawn a
paper plan while neglecting the personal and ecclesial
metanoia needed to correspond to the Divine design. Pious
substitution of human heritage in place of elements needed
to fulfill the divine will for unity appears to be a terminal pit. Some parts of a so-called ecclesial heritage need
pruning. Is, perhaps, the opinion in the air that only one
ecclesial community must do all the changing?

One consequence of the theological work was the production
of a eucharistic liturgical text formulated by Max Thurian.
The text has become known as the *Lima Liturgy*.[77]

The Lima Liturgy

In brief, this liturgy, prepared for the Faith and Order
Commission, was first used at the Lima meeting on January
15, 1982. It consists of three parts: (1) the introductory
section (6 brief parts); (2) the liturgy of the Word (10

parts); and (3) the liturgy of the Eucharist (19 parts).[78]

Observant Roman Catholics will readily recognize the overall framework of the Mass, with its details, for the most part, in relatively the same order. Orthodox will recognize their liturgy in the Lima formulation, but may be surprised at an invocation of the Holy Spirit (Epiclesis I) before the prayer of Institution as well as after the memorial prayer (Anamnesis). Protestants who have retained or regained the ancient liturgy will recognize the familiar elements of their communal prayer life.

Max Thurian, a liturgical scholar, rather successfully knit together liturgical elements from the major Christian traditions to fashion the 35 parts of a coherent and attractive liturgical form. The text appears to be doctrinally sound. Perhaps Thurian's efforts to accommodate each community's prayer life made the text overly inclusive; its multiple acclaims suggest a litany; the split epiclesis, perhaps, yields a sense of *deja vu*.

Thurian clearly marked the parts to be said or done by the presiding celebrant, concelebrants, other officiants and the congregation. He rested on the BEM document to observe that Christian liturgy should be observed every Lord's day as well as feast days.[79] In his preparatory observations, Thurian noted the places where the Lima formulation can readily be contracted or expanded. Gently, he reminded the readers that on special occasions the participants would be "those authorized by their own church to concelebrate."[80]

Thurian indicated that the Lima Liturgy would be used in August 1983 at the sixth Assembly of the World Council of Churches to be held in Vancouver. Although this liturgical formulation of the so-called *Lima Liturgy* seems to have the essentials needed for either an Orthodox Liturgy or a Roman Catholic Mass, critical belief questions remain. For Orthodox and Catholics, concelebration is a sign of *unity achieved;* this most sacred act is not a mere means for something greater. Furthermore, only those with valid orders may concelebrate. The continuous ancient tradition allowed only ordained men to preside at the sacred liturgy. Would the WCC Assembly at Vancouver honor such beliefs?

CHAPTER SEVENTEEN

SIXTH WORLD COUNCIL ASSEMBLY
(VANCOUVER 1983)

Founded in 1948, the World Council of Churches has lived through *five prior assemblies:* Amsterdam (1948), Evanston (1954), New Delhi (1961), Uppsala (1968), and Nairobi (1975). The intention to recover the unity of Christ's One Holy Church (*Una Sancta Ecclesia*) is still one of its driving motives. The question of "what that Church is" emerges explicitly or implicitly in every assembly. As one among the many questions and purposes of the Council, it waxes and wanes in importance from assembly to assembly.

The question of *the nature of Christ's Church* and the *progress* in the WCC's effort to define and recover it have aroused considerable and serious theological interest, not only among Protestant churches (the WCC's majority), but also among Orthodox churches and the nonmember Roman Catholic Church as well. Attendant *questions* about "conciliar fellowship" and/or "church", about "Life and Work" activity overshadowing the "Faith and Order" unity drive, and about the Roman Catholic Church's relationship with the World Council, - are part of the overall church-unity interest. Through its Faith and Order (F&O) Commission, the World Council gave a significant worship and doctrinal *impulse* to the modern ecumenical movement at its sixth Assembly.

1.   THE ASSEMBLY ITSELF

The World Council of Churches held this sixth Assembly in Vancouver, Canada, from July 24 to August 10, 1983, on the campus of the University of British Columbia. Some thirty retiring officials and 847 voting delegates, claiming to represent 400,000,000 people in 300 member churches, were the primary participants. Some 3500 others also attended; these consisted of delegated representatives, delegated observers, advisors, staff, guests and members of the press, who participated in various roles in this sixth Assembly. All told, about 4500 people were in daily attendance.[1]

Although the following churches are united as members of the
World Council, and thus publicly and explicitly united in
the belief positions (on the Trinity and the Divinity of
Christ) required for WCC membership, they, and presumably
their delegates, are, nevertheless, theologically, and thus
denominationally, divided on such remaining Christian doctrines as: the nature of Christ's Church, sacraments, authority, divorce, etc. Despite the seriousness of the doctrinal
divisions, the public unity, based on the transcendent com-
monly-believed doctrines, is a singularly significant phenomenon in this century.

Integrity in the search for Christian *Church unity*, which
the WCC identifies constitutionally as *its first purpose and
function*,[2] will hopefully preserve this phenomenon. At
present, however, the ecclesial divisions are still in place.
The relative distribution and the consequent relative voting
strengths of the divided churches' delegates follow:[3]

Reformed	(176)	Oriental		Pentecostal	(11)
Lutheran	(122)	Orthodox	(44)	Kimbanguist	(6)
Eastern		Baptist	(38)	Mar Thoma	(3)
Orthodox	(125)	Moravian	(11)	Menonnite	(2)
Anglican	(89)	Disciples	(13)	Brethren	(2)
Methodist	(95)	Old Catholic	(8)	Other	
United	(82)	Independent	(6)	Churches	(14)

As with previous WCC assemblies, there was a great effort to
do more than the mostly new, multi-lingual delegates (a first
assembly for 80% of them!) could accomplish in a brief "eighteen frenzied days and nights."[4] There was no assurance that
such novice delegates were effective, either to the assembly
or, on their return home, to the churches which sent them.
The Assembly report merely expresses *a hope* that they would
come as representatives.[5] Not counting the three basically
free Sundays, twenty-three plenary sessions, daily worship
services, and a multitude of small and middle sized meetings
crammed the remaining fifteen days[6] of the WCC's sixth Assembly.

Pope John Paul II sent "Greetings" to the Vancouver Assembly
as had Pope Paul VI to the WCC Assemblies in Uppsala '68 and
Nairobi '75. Such greetings had not been sent to Amsterdam
'48, Evanston '54, nor New Delhi '61. However, *Delegated
Observers* have been sent from the Vatican to all the Assemblies since 1961: 5 to New Delhi, 12 to Uppsala, 12 to Nairobi and 20 to Vancouver. The Pope praised the Assembly's
theme: "Jesus Christ-the Life of the World"; he also praised
what had been done to further the cause of Christian unity,
expressed hope for increased progress under the Holy Spirit's
guidance, and closed with St. Paul's farewell to the

Corinthians, "my love be with you all in Christ Jesus."[7]

On July 25, the first working day of the Assembly the Secretary of the Vatican's Christian Unity Secretariat, Fr. Duprey, addressed the ecumenical gathering with Pope John Paul's message. In a preface to the greetings, Duprey indicated the assessment of the World Council which the Pope had given to the Roman Curia three years prior to the Vancouver Assembly. After affirming that the Catholic Church is irreversibly committed to the ecumenical movement, Pope John Paul said:

> ...it is convinced of the importance of the
> multilateral dialogue and of its collaboration
> with the World Council of Churches. The Coun-
> cil is *a privileged instrument* of the ecumeni-
> cal movement.[8]

Whereas in former assemblies the Faith and Order group, Mission-interest group, Life and Work group, etc., were identified by the term "Sections", new terms "*Issues*" and "*Issue Groups*" were chosen for use at Vancouver. The WCC preparation-committee divided the delegates into eight *Groups* to discuss and determine action on the following eight *Issues,* thus deriving the name *Issue Groups*. The eight issues were:

1. Witnessing in a Divided World
2. Taking Steps toward Unity
3. Moving toward Participation
4. Healing and Sharing Life in Community
5. Confronting Threats to Peace and Survival
6. Struggling for Justice and Human Dignity
7. Learning in Community
8. Communicating Credibly.[9]

The reports and recommendations of the eight *Issue Groups* occupied the *third* major section of the 355-page Assembly report. Section *one* was David Gill's "story of the Assembly," and section *two* synopsized speeches on the theme and subthemes presented in the plenary sessions. Following the Issue Groups' reports came the work of Policy Reference Committee I (section *four*) and Policy Reference Committee II (section *five*). The report ends with 12 appendices (reproducing the highest officials' reports, selected theme speeches, reports of the Guidelines and financial committees, lists of officers, delegates, other participants and the presently operative constitution).

Mindful that the primary reason for founding the WCC was the recovery of Christ's *Una Sancta Ecclesia,* one may easily identify Issue 2 as closest in content to the goal sought.

At the same time, it seems apparent that the excitement generated by some of the secular-agenda topics would practically sidetrack theologically-unprepared delegates from the
pursuit of the less-tangible topic of ecclesial unity. So
short a meeting for so many and such diverse topics mili-
tated against the preparation of profound Assembly documents.
The official Assembly report, entitled *Gathered for Life*,
and edited by David Gill, indicates that:

> Each Issue Group comprised over 120 people.
> They met eight times, in smaller groups and
> in plenary, and then submitted their reports
> to the whole Assembly. Some of these reports,
> it must be said, will win no prizes for the
> quality of their theological or social
> analysis, not to mention their prose. With
> the exception of the document *Taking Steps
> Towards Unity,* all show signs of the time
> pressure under which Issue Groups worked.
> The pressure was even greater when the dele-
> gates in plenary session, already behind with
> their agenda, had to deal with the reports in
> rapid fire succession.[10]

2.   ISSUE GROUP 2: CHURCH UNITY

Nevertheless, *Issue Group 2* (Taking Steps Toward Unity)
produced a developed and orderly report. Its numbered paragraphs start with the constitutional goal of *Church unity,*
briefly survey the chief unity elements of previous Assemblies, identify Nairobi's "conciliar fellowship", and indicate that "it is the implication of such Church unity for
the destiny of the human community...which has impressed this
Vancouver Assembly."[11]

The *organic unity* which Issue Group 2 contemplates will be
a credible witness to Christ before the world. It will be
recognizable by: (1) a common understanding of the apostolic
faith; (2) a common possession of the BEM realities (baptism,
eucharist, ministry); and (3) common ways of decision-making
and of teaching authoritatively. The way forward consists
of the promotion in the churches of the three items just
mentioned (taking BEM first however), and another step of exploring and verbalizing the interrelationship of eucharist
and church and the influence this relationship can have in
bettering the human community (the world).[12]

The Issue Group 2 report appears to be strongly influenced
by both the BEM document and the Lima Liturgy. The "church/
eucharist/world" connection seeks to convince the WCC's

doctrine-only enthusiasts and their opposing world-agenda
devotees that each represents opposite sides of the same one
coin. "As Christians we want to affirm there can be no such
division between unity and human renewal, either in the
Church or in the agenda of the WCC."[13] The question of getting the Christian act together first before fixing the
world was not posed in this analysis. Doctrine-first would
prevent the missioning of divided and dividing missionaries
to an already divided world.

Issue Group 2 strongly endorses the holding of a Fifth World
Conference on Faith and Order in 1987 or 1988. At that time
the response to, and the reception of, the BEM document and
the experimental Lima Liturgy should be well documented. The
doctrinal and pastoral problems which it will undoubtedly
reveal will need to be addressed to clear the way forward
toward the goal.[14]

In closing its report, which the Assembly accepted as its
own, *Issue Group 2,* without citing any external source, declared "The World Council of Churches is a *privileged instrument* of the ecumenical movement." In terms which
scarcely suggest modest understatement, it went on to de-
clare further of itself:

> The fellowship of churches which constitutes
> the World Council of Churches is a *preliminary
> expression of that unity* which is God's will
> and gift for which Christians pray and work.[15]

After indicating the WCC's nature as an encounter-forum and
a framework for Christian cooperation, witness and service,
the report went on to identify the critical operatives in
any motion toward ecclesial unity, thus:

> While the World Council of Churches is an
> expression of the ecumenical movement, *the
> real agents* of that movement are the Chris-
> tian churches themselves.[16]

3.   WORSHIP AT VANCOUVER

    Worship, indeed daily public worship, appears to have
been the most significant and memorable *characteristic* of
the Sixth Assembly of the World Council of Churches. Not
worship in the sense of the official liturgical prayer of
one member Church, but rather worship in the sense of public,
group praying of large numbers of Christian delegates; there
was, besides, ample evidence of the non-liturgical worship
of private prayer. Also, on some occasions, the delegates

were invited to participate in the official liturgy of their
own separated churches.

Gill, who edited the English edition of the Vancouver report,
quoted the reflections of both an active participant and an
observer on their overall impressions of worship at Vancouver:

> Ms. Jean Skuse...of the retiring Central Com-
> mittee...named one thing she would never for-
> get about the Sixth Assembly: 'I have never
> sung so many alleluias or kyries before in my
> life!' Msgr. Basil Meeking of the Vatican's
> Secretariat for Promoting Christian Unity
> called Vancouver 'the praying Assembly.'[17]

Beside his editing, David Gill also authored parts of the
Vancouver account which the WCC adopted as its official Assembly report. Gill perceived that the flame which enthused
and inspired Vancouver's activity was:

> ...the Assembly's worship, centered on a huge
> gold and white tent set up on the lawns at
> the University of British Columbia. That
> canvas cathedral became the abiding symbol
> of the Sixth Assembly.

Further on, Gill wrote that in the light of his fifteen
years of WCC experience, including Uppsala '68 and Nairobi
'75,

> Vancouver towers above them all for the
> quality of its liturgical life.[18]

4.   THE LIMA LITURGY

On one special occasion, the delegates were invited to
participate in the recently formulated experimental liturgy
known as the *Lima Liturgy*. Gill observes that for many this
event marked "the high point of the Sixth Assembly."[19] The
WCC's official report, *Gathered for Life,* contains a picture
of Anglican Archbishop Runcie centering a group of non-
Anglican women and men ministers celebrating the Lima Liturgy which highlights the eucharistic texts.

Unfortunately, neither the picture's caption nor the text's
description of the liturgy noted the Archbishop's *significant introductory remark* regarding the basic ecclesial division in this very event. Orthodox and Roman Catholic
priests shared acceptable prayers and readings, but did not
participate in the experimental liturgy's principal

section.[20] Pertinent here are the radically serious questions of who at the Vancouver altar has complete and valid
Holy Orders, and whether, in Christ's intention, women can
validly receive Holy Orders. Centuries of Christian tradition from the foundation of the Church have answered the
latter question in the negative. The revised *Code of Canon
Law* encourages women's participation in many ministries, but
not in Holy Orders.

Orthodox and Roman Catholic priests could not concelebrate
or communicate in this experimental liturgy, as Anglican
Archbishop Runcie, the principal celebrant, publicly noted
in his introductory remarks, which did not appear to be in
the official Assembly report.[21]

> Not all of those present at the Vancouver
> celebration could participate by receiving
> communion but even the sadness of this un-
> avoidable separation was put in a positive
> context by the sensitive words of Archbishop
> Runcie as the liturgy began.[22]

The Orthodox churches, which are member-churches of the
World Council, do not acknowledge the validity of the
eucharistic celebration of the WCC's non-orthodox churches.
Thus, on principle, the Orthodox cannot concelebrate any
eucharistic liturgy with such churches, let alone an experimental liturgy, recently composed for the mixed-religious
Faith and Order Commission at Lima. Some years ago, the
American Orthodox bishops adopted ecumenical *Guidelines*
which, on faith and validity principles, restrict access
to the Eucharistic mysteries. The Orthodox Church admits
to Holy Communion

> ...only her baptized and chrismated children
> who confess the full Orthodox faith, pure and
> entire, and by it she shows forth their one-
> ness with her and with her Divine Spouse....
> Further the Church teaches that the Eucharist
> *cannot be found,* and must not be sought, *out-
> side of her convenanted mysteries....*the
> Eucharistic Mystery is the end of unity, not
> a means to that end, and....therefore, decis-
> ions regarding Holy Communion reached by Chris-
> tian bodies outside of the Orthodox Church have
> *no significance of validity* for the Orthodox
> Church or her members.[23]

However, although they cannot concelebrate, or communicate
at the heart of the liturgy, Orthodox clergy and laity may
participate in ecumenical services involving prayers and

scriptural readings.[24]   Roman Catholic *delegated observers*
are in a similar position.   Gill indicates that both Orthodox and Catholics participated in the prayers and readings
prior to the start of the canon (anaphora) of the liturgy.[25]

Roman Catholics make the distinction, previously seen, between a common participation in acceptable prayers and participation or communication in sacred liturgical acts.   The
first is identified with the expression, *communicatio in
spiritualibus* and the second, which is used to designate
the Church's official liturgical acts, is identified with
the expression, *communicatio in sacris* (communication in
sacred [implying official or liturgical] *acts*).

An example of the communication or participation in commonly
acceptable prayer (in spiritualibus) is the "Week of Prayer
for Christian Unity," annually shared by Catholics, Orthodox and Protestants at the parish level.   Pope John Paul's
prayer service in a Lutheran Church in Rome was another
outstanding and symbolic example of this communication in
prayer.

On the other hand, the sharing of the *sacred acts (in sacris)*
of the Sacraments is *ordinarily* recognized as theologically
unacceptable, or in the case of *baptized* non-catholics, as
extraordinary.

Sacraments, in Catholic belief, have an *ecclesial dimension*.
They are acts of Christ's Church, not merely acts of the
individual person who happens to perform them.   Thus, the
newly revised *Code of Canon Law* reads:

>   Liturgical actions are not private actions
>   but celebrations of the Church itself, which
>   is the 'sacrament of unity,' namely, a holy
>   people assembled and ordered under the bishops;
>   therefore liturgical actions pertain to the whole
>   body of the Church and manifest it and affect
>   it,....[26]

The next canon identifies for Catholics the *authority* responsible for preserving the unity and integrity of the
Church's liturgy.

>   #1.   The supervision of the sacred liturgy de-
>   pends solely on the authority of the Church
>   which resides in the Apostolic See and, in
>   accord with the law, the diocesan bishop.
>   #2.   It is for the Apostolic See to order the
>   sacred liturgy of the universal Church, to
>   publish the liturgical books, to review their

> translations into the vernacular languages
> and to see that liturgical ordinances are
> faithfully observed everywhere.[27]

In the light of the belief that apostolic authority has been
transmitted through the succession of validly ordained
bishops, the concern for safeguarding the integrity of the
eucharistic liturgy is manifested in a later canon. A concelebration with those not believed to be validly ordained,
as at Vancouver's experimental liturgy, falsifies the ecumenism it proposes to advance by its illusion of unity.
Thus, the Catholic Church restricts concelebration; full
communion with the Catholic Church is the test. Concelebration's sacred act is a sign of unity achieved, involving the
Glorified Person of Christ (as is believed); concelebration
may not be used as a means to an end.

> It is forbidden for Catholic priests to con-
> celebrate the Eucharist with priests or
> ministers of churches or ecclesial communi-
> ties which are not in full communion with the
> Catholic Church.[28]

Under *extraordinary* conditions, previously identified, persons, whose faith position on the given sacrament is essentially and truthfully one with Catholic faith, may share
some sacramental acts.

Pope John Paul, in a 1978 address to the Secretariat for
Promoting Christian Unity, noted that, "It would be a very
unenlightened charity that expressed itself at the expense
of truth."[29]

These clear teachings and cautions of the highest Catholic
authority are not well known by Catholics generally, especially by the post-Vatican II generation. Further, they
are neither known, nor readily understood when known, by
the majority of Protestants, who may easily interpret the
failure of sacramental reciprocity on the part of Catholics
as a withdrawal from the claimed desire for Christian unity.
Thus, in his article, "An Ecumenical Eucharist for a World
Assembly" in *America*, Rev. Thomas Rausch, S.J., can write
that despite Runcie's cautioning words to the effect that
Orthodox and Catholic doctrine precludes eucharistic
sharing,

> ...nevertheless, it was very widely noted
> that a number of Roman Catholics felt that
> their consciences allowed them to partici-
> pate beyond what the official norms of their
> church permitted.[30]

What Rausch describes appears to be a growing "snowball" effect. Undoubtedly, the Lima Liturgy, now also referred to
as the liturgy at Vancouver (WCC's Liturgy?), will be par-
ticiapted in by growing numbers of Protestants at ecumenical
meetings and, even perhaps, at the end of the annual week for
Christian unity. The enthusiasm at Vancouver was apparently
very great. As already observed, the Lima Liturgy could
easily be viewed as if it were a Catholic Mass. If Catholics do not realize that *validity* pertains to the very reality of the eucharistic celebration, they may well be
"snowballed" into false ecumenical and counterproductive
practices.

While the Protestant ministry, in general, is considered by
Catholics to be beneficial, its eucharistic practice is
thought to lack a required fullness on the part of the celebrant. This deficiency is believed to flow from the deficiency of Sacramental Orders. In article 23 of the *Decree
on Ecumenism,* the assembly of all the Catholic Bishops at
Vatican II, speaking of the Reformation churches, said:

> ...we believe they have not preserved the
> proper reality of the eucharistic mystery in
> its fullness, especially because of the ab-
> sence of the sacrament of Orders, neverthe-
> less when they commemorate the Lord's death
> and resurrection in the Holy Supper, they
> profess that it signifies life in communion
> with Christ....Furthermore, their worship
> sometimes displays notable features of a
> liturgy once shared in common.[31]

This middle ground between *partial value* in ministry and
liturgy, *but not the fullness* of Holy Orders and eucharistic
liturgy, is ground difficult for the laity to hold in the
face of increasing pressure toward "intercommunion" during
ecumenical meetings. This is particularly true in the light
of the mass-like *Lima Liturgy.* To participate is to acknowledge what is not fully there; to refrain is confusing,
if not insulting, to highly motivated, well-intentioned
Protestants. Although he neither approved nor disapproved
what the communicating Catholics did at Vancouver, Rausch
thinks that facing the issue cannot be avoided:

> ...the inability of the Roman Catholic Church
> to welcome even occasional intercommunion will
> become even more difficult for Catholics to
> explain and for Protestants to understand.[32]

The public confusion is evident; in some mixed marriages the
pain is palpable. Yet it appears that neglecting present

restraint will later compound public confusion as to the
reality of both the eucharist and holy orders.

Despite these difficulties, which scarcely gave pause to the
Assembly, it appears, in an overview, that the *worship at
Vancouver* was successful and influential for the WCC.

   a)   It seems that the worship was done for the sake of
worship, i.e., for the glory of God (ad gloriam Dei) and not
merely as a means to break down barriers or win hesitant ad-
herents.[33]   It increased the WCC's credibility.

   b)   The WCC magnified and supported its Faith and
Order Commission's BEM work and the Lima Liturgy.   In the
prior twenty years, the World Council seemed to let its
LLife and Work" (L&W) activity overwhelm its F&O initiatives,
in line with the early unhappy slogan, "doctrine divides;
service unites."

   c)   On the principle that prayer influences and supports the ground of belief (lex orandi est lex credendi), the
WCC's worship emphasis advanced the sense of ecclesial unity
among its participating delegates.   The ripples, from the
pebble thrown in the lake at Vancouver, will touch all the
lake's shores.   However, nonsacramental and nonliturgy-
minded churches will probably experience some future tension
from the *BEM* document as well as the *Lima Liturgy*.

   d)   Liturgical differences between member churches,
especially between Orthodox and Protestant churches, should
lead to a deeper understanding of the relationship between
Church and liturgy.   If Christ's offering to the Father is
seen as the highest and necessary expression of Christ's
Church, then a profound ecumenical breakthrough will have
occurred.

5.   CONCILIAR FELLOWSHIP AND/OR CHURCH UNITY?

   While the common public worship at Vancouver to some
degree heightened the participants' sense of what *ecclesial
community* means and requires, the rhetoric at the assembly
focused on the target of *conciliar fellowship*.

The Church *in se* is neither its worship nor one of its conciliar meetings, although these are some of its acts.   However, General Secretary Philip Potter, as General Secretary
Eugene Carson Blake before him, continued to steer the ship
toward this conciliar-fellowship goal.

In his final major report to the Assembly, Potter, citing

the image of the "*house of living stones*" from the first
Epistle of Peter (1 Pet. 2:4-5), envisioned the divided
Christian churches as the scattered stones of the totally-
broken Church.[34]   Potter's imagery seems to picture the
World Council's (and its General Secretary's) overall job
as rebuilding the house whose stones have fallen apart.
Yet the living stones of the petrine image all enjoyed
koinonia (faith and worship community-life), which the
living stones of Potter's vision do not.

Thus, the petrine image admits of an alternate development;
such as the continuation of the original "*house of living
stones*" into the present, with most if its stones fitted
under the capstone which is Christ, while some stones have
fallen off the house.   In the first case, a human architect
must make a new design into which to place the stones; in
the second, the original design with its capstone remains,
and the loosened stones need only be reclaimed for their
rightful places.

Throughout his report, Potter refers to Peter, but he apparently confines his remarks to the contents of the *First
Epistle of Peter*.   Peter's words and actions flourish
throughout the Gospels and Acts.   In fact, his name occurs
more than the names of all the other original Apostles put
together.   More significantly still, Peter's name is the
principal name attached to the texts which treat of *Christ's
Church* about which Potter and, indeed, the Assembly, were
supposed to be treating, but nowhere within Potter's report
or the Assembly Report can the most significant texts be
found.[35]

The *Gospel According to Matthew* (ch. 16) quotes Christ as
saying, "you are kepha (rock = Peter) and on this kepha *I
will build my Church*"; in *Luke's Gospel* (ch. 22) Christ
prays for Peter's faith so he can strengthen the others;
in the *Gospel According to John* (ch. 21) Peter is the one
commissioned to "feed my sheep"; the *Acts of the Apostles*
lucidly highlights Peter's carrying out of his commission.
Even a detached but knowledgeable observer cannot help
wondering why the WCC, which claims "the scriptures as our
criterion,"[36] continues, Assembly after Assembly, to shun
these texts.

Further, many of the Assembly's speakers make claims for
themselves "*as Church*" which are applicable only to the
Orthodox or Roman Catholic Churches; they seem to be un-
aware of the enormity of the debt their more recently designed foundations owe to the communities continuously in
existence since before the First Letter of Peter was
written.

Toward the end of his report, Potter did affirm that "all
that has been said before is about the confession of the one,
holy, catholic and apostolic Church."[37] At this point he
briefly reviewed the achievements of prior assemblies and
reasserted the unity definition of New Delhi:

> unity in each place and in all places and
> all ages is one eucharistic fellowship ex-
> pressed in worship and in common life in
> Christ that the world may believe.

After mentioning the gains of bilateral and multilateral dialogues, he concluded:

> We see the way forward in working for *con-
> ciliar fellowship* expressed in various ways,
> however feebly, not least in the World
> Council.[38]

The New Delhi unity definition is implicitly antidenominational; Potter's rhetoric was gently antidenominational;
whereas the *conciliar fellowship* model allows and even encourages the continued autonomy of the denominations. In
this final report, Potter's conciliar fellowship goal may
be seen as a final goal having the "all in each place" unity
characteristics previously described.

In such a picture, then, Christians in each town would be
called on to form a town *conciliar fellowship,* and so on for
states, nations and the world. If this be the ultimate grand
design, then *council* has supplanted *Christ's Church* in the
WCC's thinking, since the apostolic Church far exceeded the
dimensions of a council. In this exploratory picture, autonomous denominations would continue to flourish.

On the other hand, if *conciliar fellowship* is only a step
along the way, then the steps in the grand design have not
yet been blueprinted for the public examination. But it
would seem that, at the end-point of the design, the dis-
mantling of the conciliar scaffolding would yield the reunion of Christians in the *una sancta ecclesia*. In this
latter picture, denominations would have yielded their autonomy to the *universal Church*.

Despite a few mergings of smaller denominations into larger
ones, tenacious denominational independence is showing no
signs of diminishing or going away. The Assembly's important
"Programme Guidelines Committee" (PGC) observed with concern
the "...tension between growing confessionalism and conciliar
unity."[39] Yet, one wonders how a denomination can give up
its confessional life and identity in favor of "conciliar

unity"? The expression is used rhetorically by WCC spokes-
persons as if they wanted some vague movement like this to
take place.

The goal or target of *Conciliar Fellowship* seems to be somewhat off-center of the WCC's early aim. The original center
had many times been identified as the *una sancta Ecclesia*
(the one holy Church of the Nicene and other ancient creeds).
The "one holy Church" goal and a "conciliar fellowship" goal
are not identical things. They may appear on the same target,
but only the *una sancta Ecclesia* can possess the *faith, worship and life in Christ* of the target's center.

The "una sancta Ecclesia" may occasionally initiate a council
for itself, as at Nicea, Ephesus, Chalcedon, but that is a
free event in the life of the ecclesia. It is an act of the
ecclesia; it is not the ecclesia itself, as the Council of
Jerusalem (Acts 15) was an act of the Apostolic Church, but
only something the Church did in passing. The Apostolic
Church lived before, through and after the event.

On the matter of *denominationalism,* a very serious constitutional flaw still plagues the WCC. It has become more con-
specuous since the elevation of F&O's unity function to the
prime position in Article III of the constitution.

Article II gives each member church one vote; while article
III calls the member churches to visible unity.[40] This combination concludes to: more church division = more voting power;
and conversely, more unity = less voting influence in the WCC.

Thus, if ten 35,000 member churches become one church, the
new church has a WCC influence of only one vote in place of
the former ten votes controlled while separated. Reversing
the process, a 350,000 member church would gain more control
over the WCC if it broke up into ten independent denominations! The WCC's prestigious "Policy Reference Committee I"
(PRC I), without examining the question, merely reported:

>   Concern was expressed that uniting churches
>   can *sometimes* be penalized for uniting by
>   losing seats on committees, etc. The matter
>   should be studied.[41]

Sometimes? Such a constitutional discrepancy insures the
continuation of denominationalism and the emasculation of the
forces of ecclesial unity. If this anomaly continues, nothing other than *conciliar fellowship* is possible to the WCC.

Perhaps *Issue Group 2* (on unity) expressed the need for attention to the underlying doctrine on the *Church* when it saw

that a *common apostolic creed,* with a common explanation of
it and a common profession of it, was a prerequisite step
for achieving the unity of the apostolic Church. Issue Group
2 declared about this step of a common creed:

> It will be impossible to take this common step
> if in this study of the apostolic faith we do
> not give special attention to the nature and
> mystery of the Church of God, since the confes-
> sion of the one, holy, catholic and apostolic
> Church belongs to the apostolic faith.[42]

6.   RCC MEMBERSHIP?

The powerful Policy Reference Committee I (PRC I), consisting of 33 members, of whom seven were Orthodox, reviewed
the *reports* of

la)   The Most Rev. Edward Scott, Moderator of the Central Committee (CC) (which committee is, in effect, the WCC
between Assemblies); lb) General Secretary, Rev. Philip
Potter; and lc) the report of Dr. McCloud (Finance Committee
of the WCC); McCloud indicated that financially speaking,
"the Council would not be able to sustain its existing structure much beyond 1985."[43]

2)   It next examined the relationship of the World
Council to its member churches (301 after Vancouver).

3)   It considered also the WCC's *relationship with the
Roman Catholic Church,* and with

4)   Christian World Communions (formerly identified as
World Confessional Families).

5)   After this it attended to nominations and elections.

6)   Finally, it considered Programme Guidelines,[44] and
the cost of the Vancouver Assembly itself.

A number of points of this Committee's [PRC I] report are of
interest, but the one which most focuses on the WCC/RCC question is report number 3. The PRC examined and commented on
the report of the *Joint Working Group,* or *JWG*, which had been
formed in 1965, the last year of the Second Vatican Council.
This small (15 to 20 theologians) JWG had been a sort of
interface consultative group focused on the overlapping interest areas of its two parent institutions. In its two
decade life, the JWG has composed four reports prior th the
Fifth Report (1983) which it presented to Secretary General
Potter at Vancouver.

The earlier reports highlighted studies which explored areas

of common ground. This last report reviewed the prior twenty
years, identified the present status of the WCC/RCC relationship and pointed ahead to the work of formulating a common
profession of the apostolic faith.

A member of the Church of Scotland felt that there had been
"a lack of progress and a hesitancy about the [WCC/RCC] relationship on the Roman Catholic side." Msgr Basil Meeking, a
delegated observer of the RCC, responded by speaking of the
gradually advancing WCC/RCC relationship in terms of

> '...substance and maturity.' It had, he said,
> gone beyond the stage of polite friendship.
> Recently Pope John Paul II asked that *collab-*
> *oration* with the WCC be intensified in all
> fields *where it is possible*--a commitment that
> is seen, for example, in the fact that every
> episcopal conference has been asked to study
> the BEM document.[45]

Meeking's declaration that the Catholic episcopal conferences
of the world have been asked to study the BEM text indicates
that dialogue on this F&O Commission breakthrough document is
the cutting edge of ecumenical dialogue.

The Policy Reference Committee's discussion on the JWG's report clarified an *overall norm* governing the Catholic Church's
ecumenical relations.

> Overarching all considerations of continual
> relationships between the RCC and the *member*
> *churches*,...should always be the awareness of
> the common ground and the vision of the com-
> mon goal of the ecumenical movement.[46]

The common ground and the common goal are the parameters of
the continuing relationship; also, it is primarily a church
to church relationship rather than a church to agency relationship. The *common ground* refers to the ground common to
baptized believers in Christ (Christ, baptism, Sacred Scripture, etc.), which supports a real but incomplete unity
among separated Christians; the *common goal* is the organic
unity of Christ's *una sancta Ecclesia,* which Article III of
the WCC's constitution expresses more cautiously in terms of
some critical ecclesial elements, namely "visible unity of
faith, eucharist and common life in Christ." (As previously
noted, the doctrine on the eucharist in the BEM document is
too much for some member churches and too little for others.)

These parameters of common ground and common goal enable "the
RCC and the WCC and its member churches [to] have *general*

criteria to evaluate various forms of *collaboration* in ecumenical solidarity."[47] These general criteria enable the
ecumenical partners to answer only some of the questions concerning the RCC/WCC relationship. For example, RCC membership in the WCC is a separate matter. Thus questions can be
answered:

1) Dialogue? Yes, until all Christians are one church.
2) Collaboration? Yes, within the parameters.
3) *Membership?* No, 1972's 'not in the immediate future'
   still remains the answer to this inquiry.[48]

The *Information Service* *(IS)* of the Vatican Secretariat for
Promoting Christian Unity (SPCU) contains the fifteen-page
report of the WCC/RCC Joint Working Group, which the Policy
Reference Committee was considering. The Joint Working
Group's report, after researching common ground, turned its
attention to the acknowledgment of continuing differences
between its WCC and RCC parent bodies. Differences remain

> ...particularly on the international level,
> which still justify the answer given when the
> possibility of Roman Catholic membership in
> the Council was raised in the 1970s--'not in
> the immediate future.' Nor is it a question
> which is yet ready to be taken up again.[49]

The reasons cited in the JWG's report were differences in
authority, structure and operation. The JWG consists of a
small number of theologians, about seven of whom are Catholic, and about nine of whom come from different member churches of the World Council. Their analytic explorations
sometimes find new ways of expressing ongoing relationships.
Thus, in speaking of the RCC's self-image, the JWG report,
using WCC-type language, says of the Catholic Church:

> It believes itself to be constituted as a
> 'universal fellowship with a universal mis-
> sion and structure as an essential element
> of its identity'....Thus it gives importance
> to the differences of structure between it-
> self and the WCC member churches, and the
> differences of operation on the world level.
> [Acknowledging the unity of the ecumenical
> movement, the Catholic Church] accepts the
> challenge of undertaking increased collabora-
> tion with the World Council of Churches and
> its member churches, despite its own nonmember
> status.[50]

In view of the RCC's distinctive and identifying structure,
it cannot become a singly organized structure with the WCC.
Hence, disparities must inevitably flow from the differences
in structure and types of authority identified with these
differences. Yet increasing collaboration is workable, and
the JWG sees a role for itself in exploring this ground as
"servant to the two partners."[51]

7.   RCC'S WILLEBRANDS TO WCC'S POTTER

Cardinal Willebrands, President of the Secretariat for Promoting Christian Unity (SPCU), wrote to the WCC's General
Secretary Potter that the JWG's "Fifth Report" had been given
general approval from the Catholic side. The Cardinal
thought that some observations would aid in understanding the
report. Very briefly, some of the remarks made by SPCU's
president follow:[52]

1) The WCC is an *important instrument* of the ecumenical movement, thus the Catholic Church is pleased to collaborate with different of its activities, particularly its
Faith and Order work. The wide ecumenical movement embraces
not only the WCC's multilateral dialogue, but also the many
complementary bilateral dialogues in which the RCC freely
engages.

2) The RCC/WCC relationship seems to be what Pope Paul
VI called *a Fraternal Solidarity*, rather than a mere "collaboration". The relationship involves not only collaboration, but also common theological and practical reflection,
prayer and a common calling to respond to the intention of
Christ for the unity of all his followers. Commitment to
the ecumenical movement and to a "fraternal solidarity" does
not require membership in ecumenical agencies, nor does it
require uniform relationships with existing agencies and
instruments of the movement. In expressing a caution, the
Cardinal wrote:

> The Roman Catholic Church puts strong emphasis
> on the *unity given by Christ* through the Holy
> Spirit and sees it as central to its own ex-
> istence. It finds its own reality as Church
> both in the variety of the local churches and
> in the communion among them, building up the
> unity of the Body of Christ in the one Holy
> Spirit. This reality finds also expression in
> its constitution 'as a universal fellowship with
> a universal mission and structure.' Likewise it
> understands the being of the Church, as mystery
> of Christ and sacramental sign of his salvation,

to be inseparably spiritual reality and
visible structure. Hence it cannot admit
in its ecumenical relations any project or
action which may seem to sit lightly to or
reject these ecclesiological realities.[53]

The Cardinal went further to indicate that the WCC's increasing involvement with non-churches will condition future
relationship and collaboration. The very basic problem at
issue is the division among Christians. Willebrands continued:

Inevitably the very different nature of the
two bodies affects the relationship. Yet
surely for a true perspective we must be
aware that *the basic anomaly is the division
among christians* and the attitudes of mind
and heart which perpetuate it. Provided the
reality of the difference in nature between
the two partners is respected in practice,
experience shows the relationship is one
which has a healing effect on that underlying anomaly of division.[54]

3) The letter noted the *considerable encouragement*
felt when the WCC at Nairobi identified "visible unity of
the churches" as its first aim. Yet ecumenists must realize
that any advance toward such unity can only result from
patient persistence, as experience has shown. It took fifty
years for Faith and Order to bring its reflections on baptism, eucharist and ministry (BEM) to its present stage of
understanding. Such growth and maturation (though incomplete) are not begotten in an environment of impatience and
of the press of schedules and deadlines. The new factor of
Catholic beliefs and traditions in BEM can bring disquieting
problems to the World Council.

Of course the way in which this reality and
others of a similar kind are dealt with will
condition the Roman Catholic Church/World
Council of Churches relations.[55]

4) In closing, the letter pointed to the considerable
amount of work already invested in F&O studies which are
still relatively unknown. Willebrands was pleased that the
post-Vancouver period would give *priority to ecumenical formation,* especially its theological content. He also noted
that caution must accompany social collaboration whose underlying theological presuppositions require careful examination.[56]

Some of the Cardinal's remarks found responsive chords within the Assembly, others did not. How widely its contents
were known is not manifest in the record. However, the letter to General Secretary Potter is cited in the Policy Reference Committee I (PRC I) Report approved by the Assembly.
The PRC record reads that while accepting the Joint Working
Group's report, "the Assembly also gratefully acknowledges
the response of 'general approval' [of the JWG's report] from
the Roman Catholic Church, in the official letter to the WCC
General Secretary...."[57]

8.   SECULARITY UPSTAGING UNITY?

The Cardinal's letter and the RCC Observer's post-Assembly reflections both warmly emphasized the Faith and
Order influence at Vancouver. On the other hand, some concern was manifested at the widening and more diffusive *non-
church-unity* interests to which the Council *of Churches* was
giving its energies.

The theme, "Jesus Christ--The Life of the World", was tailor-
made for emphasis on Christology and the ecclesiology flowing from it. Yet these theological emphases were scarcely
observable in the record or the discussions of the eight Issue Groups. The Orthodox insight into *Theosis,* the Father's
reflection on the Divine gift of the new life in Christ, the
union of persons with God and each other communally in
Christ--these are not the well-springs of the Issue Groups'
recommendations. Rather the Issue Groups, after an opening
modest bow to the theme, turned full attention to the world.

> Life was considered in many of its secular
> implications and *in terms of* economics,
> politics and situations of injustice.[58]

The Programme Guidelines Committee (PGC) had the task of
sorting out the proposals from the Assemblies' official
reports and from Issue Groups. Over 120 proposals came from
the Issue Groups alone! The PGC report declares:

> The Programme Guidelines Committee has received
> a vast number of specific proposals for particu-
> lar programme areas....Recognizing that the As-
> sembly cannot act responsibly on all of these
> proposals, the [PGC] has limited itself to
> identifying a number of broader priority areas.[59]

The most secular and least ecclesial agenda in the overall
Assembly report seems to be the agenda of Policy Reference
Committee II (PRC II). Its report, which is entitled "World

Affairs in Ecumenical Perspective", starts off with a self-
justification (as ecumenical?).

> The making and breaking of human life anywhere
> and for whatever reason is the legitimate and
> necessary concern of Christ's Church: on that
> score the churches as they work together through
> their World Council have never had any doubts....
> But where to start? Where to stop? And how
> select? The Sixth Assembly, like its predeces-
> sors, was in that quandary.[60]

One does not argue that human problems are the concern of
Christ's Church. Nor does one argue with the profound sense
of Christian compassion which motivates that concern. At
the same time, the Church's *primary business* is the present
and eternal union of persons with God in Christ; salvation
of souls is the supreme law of its activity.

Removing obstacles to unity among the denominations of
Christians present at Vancouver is far closer to their *primary and possible* church-activity than spreading anxieties
to all delegates about problems which most did not know existed and which they can scarcely solve (by scattershot
statements) even when they learn about them. Every country
in the world has multiple human problems! As PRC II recognized: where do you start? Once started, what principle
allows the PRC II or the WCC to stop? What principle gov-
erned PRC II in handling the human rights of the child in
the womb?

On this one problem, which is *decisively moral* and much
closer to the action of delegates and their local churches,
the Orthodox effort of theme-speaker Rev. Dr. Theodore
Stylianopoulus to extend WCC concern "to embrace the human
rights of the unborn"[61] seems to have been shelved (or rejected?). Thus in a serious moral matter *important for ecclesial unity* there appears to be a sizable gap. The continuous traditional Christian belief identifies a deliberately procured abortion as a very serious evil; the belief of
the world's Catholic bishops (at Vatican II) that abortion
is an "*abominable crime*"[62] met no recorded correspondence of
belief at Vancouver.

PRC II had to pick and choose among 50 requests to have the
WCC at Vancouver speak out on various of the world's social
problems which have real (but more difficult to define) moral
dimensions, such as: Caste in India, Religion in Albania,
Claims of the Aboriginal Canadians, nuclear deterrence, mi-
grant workers, USA in Central America, Russia in Afghanistan
(what about Poland, Hungary, Iran, etc., etc., etc.).[63]

Criteria were developed to help the Council choose which issues to make statements about. The criteria had nothing explicitly ecclesial about them; the immediacy of the Christ-
life was, at best, a very remotely applicable norm.

When one adds to the foregoing the pace of the Assembly, the
realization that 80% of the voting delegates are first-timers,
the questions of theological competence on moral questions
and adequate knowledge on the U.N.-type secular questions,
one may justifiably wonder about the priority and percentage
of limited time given to such a scattershot of concerns by a
Council of Churches. Is not this thrust overshadowing and
forestalling progress in the WCC's pursuit of its primary
goal: the visible unity of Christians in faith, worship and
life in Christ? Are Christians finding it easier to criticize someone else's house than to fix their own house?

In an overview of this Assembly, *"secular ecumenism"* did not
overshadow the Faith and Order ecumenical (reunion of Christians) thrust as much as at Uppsala '68 and Nairobi '75. Some
reasons for this appear to be: (1) the dominant sense of
worship around which the WCC designed the Vancouver Assembly,
(2) the enthusiasm generated by the experimental Lima Liturgy, and (3) the emergence of F&O's BEM document as a truly
ecumenical response to the theme, "Jesus Christ--The Life of
the World". Time and the future decisions of the Executive
and Central committees will tell. Before the year elapsed,
another significant event took place. Pope John Paul II
visited the World Council headquarters in Geneva!

9.   THE POPE VISITS THE WCC

        On June 12, 1984, Pope John Paul II, on the occasion
of his visit to the Catholic Church in Switzerland, responded
to an *invitation to visit* the headquarters of the World Council of Churches in Geneva. These visits had been planned
prior to this date, but an almost successful assassination
attempt on May 13, 1981, had hospitalized the Pontiff and
forced a major readjustment of his schedule.

Pope Paul VI (1963-1978) had visited Geneva fifteen years
before, nearly to the day, of this 1984 visit. It may be
recalled that in John XXIII's period of service to the Church
(1958-1963), one has difficulty in locating even the name of
the World Council of Churches in his public addresses or
documents.

On the occasion of his almost three-hour visit, Pope John
Paul II and those with him joined Rev. Dr. Philip Potter,
General Secretary of the WCC, the staff and invited guests

in a 90-minute worship service consisting of prayer, an act
of penitence, readings from the Old and New Testaments, addresses by Potter and the Pope, and concluding with a "Song
of Mary".[64]

General Secretary Potter spoke about: (1) priority given to
visible unity, (2) the need for common Christian witness,
(3) the collaboration program known as SODEPAX (Society, Development and Peace), which had lasted from 1967 until its
mutual termination in 1980, and (4) the effort to mobilize
the whole people of God. In making his fourth point, Potter
suggested that the present WCC/RCC cooperative efforts should
be extended to something more, in these words:

> Your Holiness, your presence among us at the
> feast of Pentecost is a clear indication of
> our united determination to proclaim and live
> the Gospel in word and deed and also to seek
> to follow the prayer of our Lord that we may
> be one that the world may believe that he
> whose name we bear was sent for its salvation.
> But this determination must be expressed in
> our active involvement together, *beyond* formal
> collaboration....[65]

Pope John Paul II, following Potter, spoke for 37 minutes
in French. The Vatican's English translation of the papal
address consists of 15 numbered paragraphs. In his speech,
the Pope, after thanking his host for the invitation and
noting the fittingness of the Pentecost occasion, indicated
that his presence, at the World Council headquarters, as the
bishop of Rome, was *a sign* of his will for unity. Pope John
Paul continued:

> From the beginning of my ministry as bishop of
> Rome, I have insisted that the engagement of
> the Catholic Church in the ecumenical movement
> is *irreversible* and that the search for unity
> was *one of its pastoral priorities.*[66]

The Holy Father chose to speak about the elements which the
Vatican II *Decree on Ecumenism* highlights as present and
unitive for Western Christians. In separate paragraphs, he
enlarged upon the commonly believed realities of baptism,
the Word of God, the whole role of the Holy Spirit, prayer
and collaboration. A thread running through his text was a
focus on truth and the work of the Holy Spirit from the
fourth Gospel: "he will guide you into all truth" (Jn. 16:13).
The Pontiff used Paul VI's expression, "fraternal solidarity",
to identify the RCC/WCC relationship. He mentioned the older
Assemblies, Uppsala and Nairobi, and also the last one at

Vancouver which, in praise, he characterized as dominated by
the reality of common prayer.

The special point which gave the address its title, *Ecumenism
and the Role of the Bishop of Rome,* was developed in the second paragraph. It is most significant for the future of the
ecumenical movement and an understanding of the relations of
the Catholic Church with its partners in the multilateral and
bilateral dialogues. Pope John Paul calmly emphasized the
point that the belief which Catholics brought to dialogues
and collaboration was a *conviction* that the role of the Bishop of Rome is an integral part of the patrimony with which
Christ endowed his Church. The Pope's words were:

> To be sure, the Catholic Church entered on the
> hard ecumenical task bringing with it a *convic-
> tion.* Despite the moral afflictions which have
> marked the life of its members and even of its
> leaders in the course of history, it is convinced
> that in the ministry of the bishop of Rome it has
> preserved the visible pole and *guarantee of unity
> in full fidelity to the apostolic tradition* and
> to the faith of the fathers. St. Ignatius of
> Antioch in his time greeted the church 'which
> presides in the region of the Romans' as that
> 'which presides in charity' over the communion.
> The Catholic Church believes that the bishop who
> presides over the life of that local church,
> which is made fruitful by the blood of Peter and
> Paul, received from the Lord the mission of re-
> maining as witness to the faith which was con-
> fessed by these two leaders of the apostolic
> community and which, by the grace of the Holy
> Spirit, brings about the unity of believers.
>
> To be in communion with the bishop of Rome is
> to give visible evidence that one is in communion
> with all who confess that same faith, with those
> who have confessed it since Pentecost and with
> those who will confess it until the day of the
> Lord shall come. That is *our Catholic convic-
> tion and our fidelity to Christ forbids us to
> give it up.* We also know that it is a difficulty
> for most of you, whose memories are perhaps
> marked by certain sorrowful recollections for
> which my predecessor Pope Paul VI asked your
> forgiveness. But we have to discuss this in
> all frankness and friendship, with the serious-
> ness full of promise shown in the work done to
> prepare the Faith and Order study on baptism,

eucharist and ministry. If the ecumenical
movement is really led by the Holy Spirit,
the time for that will come.[67]

After touching on dangers in the world today, on evangelical
works and on evangelism, the Pope, in paragraph 13, turned
his attention to the bishops in the Catholic Church who, in
union with the bishop of Rome, have the responsibility of
safeguarding the faith, evangelization and ecumenical work
of their dioceses. The Pope continued:

The harmonious development of a collaboration
with the Catholic Church demands that this
conviction about the mission of the bishop,
which is also shared by several of the member
churches of the World Council, should be taken
into account.[68]

After concluding with the Lord's Prayer, an hour of private
discussion, a snack, an exchange of gifts, and a farewell
exchange of peace, Pope John Paul departed.[69]

Two days later, the Pope met with the Swiss Protestant Evangelical Association. In his remarks to them, he noted their
celebrations honoring Huldrych Zwingli and John Calvin. He
took the occasion of their invitation to respond to the
president's suggested opening that "communion at separate
tables means disobedience toward Christ's call." Pope John
Paul, referring to Zwingli and Calvin, said:

On the one hand, we cannot forget that the work
of their reform remains a permanent challenge
between us and makes our ecclesial divisions
actual even today. But on the other hand, no
one can deny that the elements of the theology
and spirituality of each of them retain profound links among us....The memory of the
events of the past ought not to limit the freedom of our present efforts, with a view to re-
pairing the damage those events caused.[70]

The Pope suggested that a Reformation history written jointly
by Catholics and Reformed would help to clarify those troubled
memories.   He mentioned the baptism which unites all believers, although some serious differences in faith still
divide us. Then he said of the eucharist:

The eucharistic celebration is indeed a profession of faith in action for the church, and
complete accord in the faith is the presupposition for a common eucharistic celebration which

is really faithful and true. We cannot give a
deceptive sign. All our dialogue tends toward
such a common celebration. It would be useless
to do away with the suffering of the separation
unless we remedy the cause of this suffering.[71]

The Holy Father suggested trying to do together everything
that is possible to do together in truth. Doing the truth
brings one to the light (Jn. 3:21).

10.   NEW SECRETARY GENERAL ELECTED

     About a month after the Pope's visit to the World Coun-
cil, the governing Central Committee, which is effectively
the WCC between Assemblies, met to elect a successor to the
62-year-old Dr. Potter. As the third General Secretary,
Potter had led the Council for twelve years. During his
leadership, the WCC's interests seemed directed more toward
the Life and Work agenda than the agenda of Faith and Order.
Time could write:

     To the growing dismay of conservative church-
     goers in the U.S. and Europe, the World Council
     of Churches seems to have been moving increas-
     ingly away from its avowed purpose of fostering
     Christian Unity.[72]

The WCC's Central Committee, by a very wide margin, chose as
their fourth General Secretary 57-year-old Emilio Castro who,
born of Roman Catholic parents, had been baptized in that
faith.[73]

As a youth he had moved from playing with Methodist young-
sters near their church to becoming a Methodist himself. He
studied under Karl Barth, worked as a pastor and had served
at the WCC headquarters as the director of the Commission on
World Mission and Evangelism. His five-year term will begin
next year.[74]

11.   TOMORROW?

     Yesterday, the partial unity was acknowledged; *today,*
the serious effort is afoot to diminish the partial disunity
stubbornly remaining; *tomorrow,* the partial unity will be
increased, but the goal of the visible organic unity of all
Christians in Christ's *UNA SANCTA ECCLESIA* seems well beyond
the present horizon.

Christ called it "my church" in Matthew's account, which, in

view of the RCC's acceptance of the stages in the formation
of the Gospels,[75] may be considered to have been written in
the light of the Risen Christ's final intentions.[76]

Renewal in faith encourages optimism that today's noble vision, although still not entirely clear to most, will become
tomorrow's Christian unity in full profession of faith, worship and apostolic ministry. Nothing less can be a full
Christian unity for hundreds of millions of Christians!

From a secular point of view, this vision appears discour-
agingly impossible, but faith believes in the Person who
converted the cross of infamy into the crucifix of salvation.
It is "HIS CHURCH".

APPENDIX I

ADDRESS TO WORLD
COUNCIL OF CHURCHES
BY
POPE JOHN PAUL II

At the headquarters of the World Council of Churches in Geneva, Switzerland, Pope John Paul II delivered this address on "Ecumenism and the Role of the Bishop of Rome" on June 12, 1984.

Grace to you and peace from God our Father and the Lord Jesus Christ (Eph. 1:2).

1.   Thank you for having invited me to visit you here in the Ecumenical Center during my visit to the Catholics of Switzerland.   How fitting it is that we should meet to pray together and to talk as brothers and sisters at this season of the year when Christians throughout the world celebrate the event of Pentecost.   For in the words of St. Irenaeus:

> 'At Pentecost...the Spirit came down upon the disciples with power to grant all nations entry into life and to open the New Testament.   And so in every language they sang a hymn to God in unison.   For the Spirit brought the scattered race together into unity and offered to the Father the first fruits of all the nations' (St. Irenaeus, *Ad Hear*. III, 17, 2).

Pentecost, the gift of the Spirit, is for the church the ever-living source of its unity and the beginning of its mission.   Our meeting coincides with the spirit of these days.

The simple fact of my presence here among you, as bishop of Rome paying a fraternal visit to the World Council of Churches, is a sign of this will for unity.   From the beginning of my ministry as bishop of Rome, I have insisted that

355

the engagement of the Catholic Church in the ecumenical movement is irreversible and that the search for unity was one
of its pastoral priorities (cf. Invitation to Prayer for the
Sixth Assembly of the WCC, July 24, 1983, L'Osservatore
Romano, July 25, 1983). The new Code of Canon Law as well
expresses very clearly the obligation of the Catholic bishops to promote the ecumenical movement in conformity with
Christ's will (Canon 755, 1).

2. To be sure, the Catholic Church entered on the hard
ecumenical task bringing with it a conviction. Despite the
moral afflictions which have marked the life of its members
and even of its leaders in the course of history, it is convinced that in the ministry of the bishop of Rome it has
preserved the visible pole and guarantee of unity in full
fidelity to the apostolic tradition and to the faith of the
fathers. St. Ignatius of Antioch in his time greeted the
church "which presides in the region of the Romans" as that
"which presides in charity" over the communion. The Catholic Church believes that the bishop who presides over the
life of that local church, which is made fruitful by the
blood of Peter and Paul, received from the Lord the mission
of remaining as witness to the faith which was confessed by
these two leaders of the apostolic community and which, by
the grace of the Holy Spirit, brings about the unity of believers.

To be in communion with the bishop of Rome is to give
visible evidence that one is in communion with all who confess that same faith, with those who have confessed it
since Pentecost and with those who will confess it until the
day of the Lord shall come. That is our Catholic conviction,
and our fidelity to Christ forbids us to give it up. We
also know that it is a difficulty for most of you, whose
memories are perhaps marked by certain sorrowful recollec-
tions for which my predecessor Pope Paul VI asked your for-
giveness. But we have to discuss this in all frankness and
friendship, with the seriousness full of promise shown in
the work done to prepare the Faith and Order study on baptism, eucharist and ministry. If the ecumenical movement
is really led by the Holy Spirit, the time for that will
come.

3. The Catholic Church and the member churches of the
World Council of Churches have a long history in common. We
share painful memories of dramatic separations and reciprocal polemics which profoundly wounded unity. It is a history in which we never ceased to have in common many of the
elements and endowments which together build up and give
life to the church (cf. Decree on Ecumenism, 3). Now this
history is becoming the discovery of the incomplete but real

communion which exists between us. All the elements which
go to make it up, or ought to do so, are progressively put
in their true perspective with all the consequences that
this new perception signifies for collaboration between us
and for common witness.

4. To begin with, we have become aware of our common
baptism and its significance. Here the affirmations of the
New Delhi or Evanston assemblies express the same conviction as the Second Vatican Council's Decree on Ecumenism.

"By the sacrament of baptism, whenever it is properly
conferred in the way the Lord determined, and received with
proper dispositions of soul, man becomes truly incorporated
into the crucified and glorified Christ....Baptism therefore constitutes the sacramental bond of unity existing
among all who are reborn through it" (no. 22).

Sure enough, "baptism, of itself, is only a beginning,
a point of departure, for it is wholly directed toward the
acquiring of fullness of life in Christ" (*idem.*). But baptized with a true baptism, we are all enveloped in the same
indivisible love of the Father, given life by the same indivisible Spirit of God, incorporated into the only Son.
If we are divided among ourselves, we are all held in the
same clasp by what St. Irenaeus called "the two hands of
the Father" (the Son and the Spirit). That is what impels
us to knit again the communion between us. It is a matter
of accepting what we are for God in virtue of "one baptism"
because of "one God and Father of us all who is above all
and through all and in all" (Eph. 4:6). Although we are
still divided, we are nevertheless all in the mystery of
Pentecost, which is reversing Babel. In this way our divisions stand out against the existing unity and because
of it are only more scandalous.

5. Together we have learned to be in communion in our
respect for the word of God. Thanks to the renewal of
biblical studies, in which the exegetes of all Christian
confessions have worked side by side, some of the old
polemics which have set us against each other for centuries
are shown to be futile. Here we cannot but mention Cardinal (Augustin) Bea, who consecrated to the service of unity
the last 10 years of a long life dedicated to the study and
teaching of scripture. When the Second Vatican Council
affirmed, "It follows that all the preaching of the church,
as indeed the entire Christian religion, should be nour-
ished and ruled by sacred scripture" (Dogmatic Constitution
on Divine Revelation, 21), it was only expressing a common
certitude. More and more the word of God is understood in
reference to the life and witness of the ecclesial community,

which is animated by that Spirit of whom Jesus said: "He
will teach you all things," "he will guide you into all
truth" (Jn. 14:26; 16:13). Even if we are not yet fully
in accord on the interpretation of certain important points
of this word of God, must we not stress the positive significance of this growing unanimity?

6. There is another aspect of the Christian mystery
which brings us together more than in the past. Together
we have learned to understand better the whole role of the
Holy Spirit. Now this rediscovery, which marks the renewal
of the Catholic liturgy, has made us sensitive to new dimensions of our ecclesial life. The Spirit is the source
of a liberty which allows renewal in the fidelity which we
receive from the generations which have gone before. He
knows how to find new ways as soon as there is question of
moving together toward a unity at once founded on truth and
respectful of the rich diversity of really Christian values
which have their source in a common patrimony (cf. Decree
on Ecumenism).

7. This new attention to the presence of the Spirit
gives a particular accent to our prayer. To begin with, it
is open to the thanksgiving in which we detach ourselves
from our own cares to fix our gaze on the work of God and
the marvel of his grace. This attention to God gives us a
more lively awareness of God's design for his people, animated by a certitude of the primacy of the divine initiative. We can no longer be content simply to pray and to
intercede together. We are now anxious to bless God for
the work of his grace.

Prayer holds pride of place in our concerns. Although
it is not yet possible for us to celebrate the eucharist
together and communicate at the same table, more and more
we set our hearts on making common prayer the center of our
meetings, even when they are austere working sessions. From
this point of view, it is significant that last summer the
assembly at Vancouver was dominated by this reality of common prayer, which took place every day with dignity and
fervor, and the tent where the prayer was held became the
symbol of this very important ecumenical event. Today we
also meet in prayer. This common growth in fidelity to the
apostolic order, "Pray constantly. Give thanks in all circumstances" (1 Thes. 5:17-18), is the undoubted sign of the
Lord's spirit in the midst of our pursuit. It shows we are
on the right way.

8. Going forward together in the experience of prayer
and thus drawing closer to each other, it has become possible for us to develop what Pope Paul VI called real

"fraternal solidarity" (Message to the Fifth Assembly at Nairobi, 1975) with the World Council and its member churches. So a wide range of collaboration has developed. In the first place this is found in the serious and persevering research of the Faith and Order Commission. This is a fundamental theological work, for unity in the profession of the faith conditions the outcome of all the efforts made in common, while these efforts in their turn are an important means of progressing toward this unity in the faith.

9. In fact a common service of humanity in the name of the Gospel is a necessary way of doing the truth and of going toward the light (cf. Jn. 3:21). It is not by accident that the declarations of the assembly at Uppsala on the service of creation and those of the Second Vatican Council's Pastoral Constitution on the Church in the Modern World intersect at several points. The quest of the World Council of Churches for justice and peace, its commitment to the service of the poor and the unfortunate, its incessant work for the defense of liberty and human rights meet the constant care of the Catholic communities.

The defense of human beings and their dignity, their liberty, their rights, the fuller meaning of their existence are a major concern of the Catholic Church. Wherever it can, it strives to make its contribution to promoting the conditions required for human development in the full truth of human existence created and redeemed by God, convinced that "man is the primary route that the church must travel in fulfilling her mission" (*Redemptor Hominis,* 14).

By intervening in favor of human beings, whatever the political regime of the country, it insists on making the distinction and relative autonomy of church from state. It is respectful of the noble and difficult function of those who have charge of the common good. It undertakes a dialogue with them and enters into the stable relation of a common agreement to enable peace and justice to progress. At the same time, it judges that it is not its role to intervene in the forms of government which people choose for their temporal affairs or to preach violence in order to change them. But it invites its lay members to take an active part in their administration and orientation according to evangelical principles, and it keeps its freedom in order to judge from an ethical point of view the conditions which favor the progress of people and of communities or which, on the contrary, are gravely harmful to the rights of people or to civil and religious liberty (cf. Pastoral Constitution on the Church in the Modern World, 42, 75).

On the latter point the Catholic Church desires that
other Christian churches and communities raise their
voices along with hers so that the citizens' authentic
freedom of conscience and of worship is guaranteed as well
as the liberty of the churches to train their ministers
and to provide them with the means they need to develop
the faith of their peoples. Many persons of good will and
from international organizations understand today the importance of this fundamental right. But faced with the
gravity of the facts, it seems to me necessary that, together, all Christians and Christian communities—when
they have the possibility of expressing themselves—should
give their common witness on what is vital to them.

10. Further we should meet together more and more in
all fields where human beings, because of the burden of
their environment, experience great difficulties on the
social, ethical or religious levels in living according to
the dignity of their vocation. So many human values—
equity in relationships, authenticity of love, fraternal
and generous openness to others—are obscured in the lives
of individuals and of families. Despite our separations
and the frequent differences in methods of operation, we
often meet on the level of social thought and action, and
we witness to one and the same vision, based on the same
reading of the Gospel. Certainly it happens that we differ about the means. Our positions on ethical questions
are not always the same. But what unites us already allows us to hope that a day will come when we shall arrive
at a convergence on this fundamental ground.

Yes, the will "to follow Christ" in his love for those
who are in need leads us to common action. And temporary
though it be, this communion in evangelical service lets
us glimpse what our whole and perfect communion in faith,
charity and the eucharist could be, will be. It is not
then a purely chance encounter inspired only by pity in
the face of misery or a reaction in the face of injustice.
It belongs to our march together toward unity.

11. We also find ourselves together in apprehension
about the future of humanity. Our faith in Christ lets us
share in the same hope for facing the forces of destruc-
tion which assail the human family, erode its spiritual
foundations and lead it to the brink of the abyss. The
creative and redemptive work of God cannot be engulfed by
all that sin kindles in the human heart nor be definitive-
ly stopped. But that leads us to a keen perception of our
own responsibility as Christians facing the future of humanity and also to an awareness of the gravity of our divisions. To the extent that they obscure our witness in a

world tempted by suicide they are an obstacle to the proclamation of the good news of salvation in Jesus Christ.

12. Our communion in action is based, in fact, on our
sharing in a common concern for evangelization. It is not
simply a coincidence that you, Dr. Potter, were invited to
speak to the bishops who met in Rome for the 1974 synod
and whose profound reflection on evangelization in the modern world is contained in the apostolic exhortation *Evangelii Nuntiandi*. You outlined before the synod the way in
which the World Council of Churches understands the missionary task. Already on that occasion it was apparent
that the great questions for the urgency of evangelization
and of its methods, of dialogue with other religions, of
the relation of Gospel and culture, face all Christians
and invite them to new faithfulness in mission.

Our meetings and our exchanges on this topic have shown
that we are in agreement that "there is no true evangelization if the name, the teaching, the life, the promises,
the kingdom and the mystery of Jesus of Nazareth, the Son
of God are not proclaimed" (*Evangelii Nuntiandi,* 22). But
we also recognize "that it is impossible to accept that in
evangelization one could or should ignore the importance
of problems so much discussed today concerning justice,
liberation development and peace in the world. That would
be to forget the lesson which comes to us from the Gospel
concerning love of our neighbor who is suffering and in
need" (*idem,* 31).

13. For the Catholic Church it is the bishops who have
the responsibility of orienting and coordinating all aspects of the effort of evangelization, of helping them
keep their authentic inspiration, of respecting the essential freedom of the commitment of faith and of keeping
them from being degraded in proselytism or enslaved to the
ideologies of the moment. The harmonious development of a
collaboration with the Catholic Church demands that this
conviction about the mission of the bishop, which is also
shared by several of the member churches of the World
Council, should be taken into account.

14. It is just 15 years since my predecessor Pope Paul
VI came here to visit you and expressed his joy at the
development of the relations between the World Council of
Churches and the Catholic Church. I want to express my
wish, as I have done several times, that this collaboration between us should increase and intensify wherever
possible. The joint working group between the Catholic
Church and the World Council of Churches has an important
task to accomplish. It must be imaginative in finding the

ways which here and now allow us "to join in the great
mission of revealing Christ to the world" (*Redemptor
Hominis*, 11). In doing this truth together we shall manifest this effort toward a common witness which is one of
the priorities assigned to the joint working group. It
will call for a new effort of ecumenical formation and a
deepening of doctrinal understanding. Our witness cannot
be truly and completely common until we reach unity in
the confession of the apostolic faith.

15. Today, before God and Jesus Christ, in the
strength of the Holy Spirit, we can give thanks for the
steps forward which we have taken together on the way of
unity. This progress forbids us to go back. As I thank
you for all that this council has done since it began to
help us to grow together, I can only remind you of the
firm determination of the Catholic Church to do everything
to ensure that one day the restored *koinonia* may shine
forth. And how shall we do this except in making every
effort to grow in mutual respect and reciprocal confidence
and in the common search for the one truth? The way is
long. The necessary steps have to be respected. But we
have faith in the Spirit.

Dear brothers and sisters in Christ, like my venerated
predecessor Paul VI at the beginning of the second session of the Second Vatican Council (Sept. 29, 1963), precisely at the moment when it broached the grave question
of unity, I want to be among you as a humble adorer and
servant of Christ, of the Christ in majesty as he is represented in our splendid churches of East and West. It
is he who, in the glory he shared with his Father, stands
above our assembly of believers and blesses it. We to
whom are confided so many responsibilities for the church
turn toward him and toward the Father, imploring the light
and strength of the Holy Spirit so that we may give better
witness and serve the salvation of men and women. Are we
not a little like the apostles gathered in the first cena-
cle with Mary the mother of Jesus? Christ the Redeemer
is our principle, our way, our guide, our hope, our end.
May he grant his church on earth to be more, in his mystery
and in his visible unity, an epiphany of the love which
unites the Father, the Son and the Holy Spirit.

CHAPTER EIGHTEEN

CONCLUDING REFLECTIONS

Since the modern ecumenical movement is still going on, an overall definitive conclusion is not possible. The novelty is gone, but the movement has grown deeper and wider than ever. It started with Protestants; the Orthodox Churches cautiously increased their interest in it; now the Pope, in his speech at Geneva, and all the Roman Catholic bishops, in examining the BEM (Baptism, Eucharist, Ministry) document, are involved in it. The *BEM* document of the World Council's Faith and Order Commission has focused attention on some of the theological essentials of Christ's Church. This document has been sent for reaction to the heads of all Christian churches in the world. The mixed reactions expressed have kept the modern ecumenical movement in a state of active ferment. A final assessment is beyond the horizon.

Despite the ferment in the movement, one can see clearly that the World Council's concept of ecumenism is *not exactly the same* as the concept actively espoused by the Roman Catholic Church. *Yet* the two concepts are *not totally different*. The conceptual areas overlap enough that the ecumenical movement can be identified as one movement. Yet, enough difference remains so that the movement toward its goal is impeded. Briefly, the conceptual overlap is impressive; the remaining differences are also significant.

Because of the separating differences, the modern ecumenical moving together (a unifying process in Christian faith and life) has been described as a *convergence*. But this term seems to reflect an *extrinsic* view of what is happening. It seems to this observer-participant that the ecumenical process needs rather to be an *intrinsic* one. It is a healing process—a *healing* in apostolic faith and Christian life. It is a recovery of integrity. A reintegration of all the elements required to be fully Christian is needed. St. Paul warned the Corinthians: "Christ cannot be divided."

Something of *shared* faith and generative-life already flourishes beneath the visible divisions. Participation

in the Christ-life which comes from Christian baptism gener-
ates a healing motion toward the unity which Christ wants.
Renewal in Christian faith and life has healed some parts, so
to speak, of the divisions among Christians; other parts remain painfully divided, but not as inflamed, as heretofore.

A constructive assessment of ecumenism' modern meaning requires recognition of *sameness and difference* in the concepts
of the partners having the dialogue. Today, unlike the previous four and a half centuries, consideration of *sameness*
precedes the discussion of *difference*. But the differences
must not be ignored as they were intentionally in the origins
of the Protestant International Missionary Conference (IMC/
1910) and the movement known as the International Christian
Conference on Life and Work (L&W/1925).

1. SAMENESS

     Deep *sameness* in the WCC/RCC concept of ecumenism is
grounded in totally common origins, some critically important
belief positions, and some general presentations of the ecumenical goal.

The partners (WCC and RCC) in the movement look back to unity
in *origin* from Christ and his Apostles, through the formation
period of the New Testament, the witness of the martyrs, and
the writings of the Fathers. Christ's Church was in the post-
apostolic period, as Luke (*Acts* 2) described it—a community
—a *koinonia*. Differences occurred within it but the differences did not destroy the overall koinonia. Groups departed
from it; a few of them remained in existence, but many disappeared. However, the original koinonia continued growing,
and for a thousand years Christian faith and life was *sub-*
stantially one in a way universally understood.

Western Christians share another five centuries of substantial common life, even identity. *Koinonia* (ecclesial community) was experienced and enjoyed across geographical, linguistic and cultural boundaries. Differences existed within
the Christian communion; but the differences did not radically separate the communicants, nor destroy koinonia. Much of
this *extensive Christian tradition,* deeply ingrained in terms,
expressions, self-image, and reactions, remains *common* to
Christians despite their present divisions.

In the matter of *present belief,* the Roman Catholic Church
and the World Council member-churches publicly are one in
confessing Jesus Christ as God and Savior and in seeking to
honor the one God who has revealed his trinitarian identity
as Father, Son and Holy Spirit (WCC basis). Both partners in
the movement (i.e., RCC and most of the WCC) believe that

Christ's sacrament of baptism *incorporates* persons into his
one holy Church (*Una Sancta Ecclesia*), not merely into its
divided Christian communities.

As a consequence of this baptismal belief, they hold that the
visible Church, which assimilated them to itself, nourishes,
strengthens and unites them to God and to each other. They
further hold, but now at various levels, that their believing
participation in their Church's re-enactment of Christ's Last
Supper makes them better human and Christian persons and more
pleasing to God. In a word, they *believe* that Christ's
Church and its actions are salvific, visible entities with
invisible divine effects.

Moreover, both partners believe the Bible to be Sacred Scripture which, when properly understood, expresses the plan and
intent of God for them. Furthermore, both believe that the
Holy Spirit, who can influence souls both within and outside
of the sacramental order, is, in fact, influencing persons
both, individually and communally in the ecumenical movement.
A desire, even a yearning, for unity among Christians has
been very widely experienced among the world's separated
Christians. Very many feel actively encouraged to recover
the ecclesial unity given by Christ who intended and prayed
that his followers should be one as he and his Father are one
(John 17:11f.).

Finally, in a general way, variously expressed, both partners
believe that the *goal* of the ecumenical movement is the unity
of Christians in the *Una Sancta Ecclesia,* as professed in the
year 325 by the Ecumenical Council of Nicea in its (Nicene)
Creed.

Thus the ecumenical partners, in their beginnings, present
activities and end, have a great deal which is common in
their vision.

2.   DIFFERENCES

Despite this *considerable sameness* in the theological
vision of origin, present belief, and goal, it is noticeable
that these common points could be expressed only in a *limited*
way. *To this limited extent,* the Roman Catholic Church and
the World Council of Churches can say that they have the *same
concept* of ecumenism.

Looking only at these generally phrased points of unity, many,
especially the impatient, are inclined to overlook all differences and insistently demand both that the Roman Catholic
Church join the World Council of Churches and that the World
Council quickly dissolve all denominational differences.

Misled by ecumenical rhetoric which stresses only WCC/RCC
sameness, the unwary wish the WCC to rbing about the
establishment of all Christians in the *Una Sancta*. Such
impatience with real differences is a present difficulty!

However, the very same areas of origin, present life and goal,
examined above, on closer scrutiny, yield *elements of difference* so deep as to indicate that many decades still separate
Christians from the union which is much desired.

The differences in interpretation of *origins* appear to be
soluble, in the light of the historico-critical method which
produced the common bible and is presently being applied,
more in the West than in the East, to the sub-apostolic and
patristic writings.

However, when some Western Christian ecumenists assume the
posture of returning to the Second Ecumenical Council of
Nicea (787), as if the councils since then produced *by their
own Catholic forefathers* were nonexistent, the consequent
dialogue assumes an unreal character. The serious conciliar
insights since Nicea and the consequent official faith-deci-
sions, which channeled the faith to modern Christians, perhaps need re-examination, but not repudiation. A further
difficulty arises when ecumenists selectively neglect books
or passages within the believed and accepted canon of Sacred
Scripture.

Differences in *presently-lived* faith-convictions constitute a
more difficult area of division. As an ecumenist examines
such disparities as "Protestants have 2 sacraments/Orthodox
and Catholics have 7 sacraments," "Protestants have only the
general priesthood of the faithful/Orthodox and Catholics
have also a special sacramental priesthood," "Protestants
acknowledge an authority of persuasion/Orthodox and Catholics
claim possession of jurisdictional apostolic authority (and
Catholics believe in the petrine authority as divinely intended)," he recognizes that all such questions are rooted
in the nature of Christ's Church. The *nature of the Christ's
Church,* thus, is central to the ecumenical problem. The
Church's founding was, for centuries, seen as coming from
the person, works and intent of Christ;[1] *what Christ intended*
is not negotiable in any reunion efforts.

The Roman Catholic Church believes that the Church of Jesus
Christ, in all its essentials, *subsists in her;* The World
Council in its *Toronto Statement* (1950) professes that it has
no position on what constitutes the essentials of Christ's
one church. Nevertheless, the World Council, in its rhetoric,
repeatedly manifests a *leaning toward a Protestant free-
church ecclesiology* (the assembly of those here and now

gathered by the Word) with an occasional expression of
Luther's definition as the community in which the Word is
rightly preached and the two sacraments (baptism and eucharist) rightly done. Absent from this definition are the
other five sacraments, especially holy orders, and also
absent is the authority which Christ conferred on Peter and
the apostles in His Church, and not on everybody or anybody
who gratuitously assumes it.

The Roman Catholic belief that the College of Apostles became the *college of Bishops* with Peter and the Pope as center respectively, is repeatedly affirmed in *Lumen Gentium*
(ch. 3) and the other Vatican Council documents. The Orthodox and some Anglican churches also profess the need of
successive Apostolic episcopacy as a constituent of Christ's
Church. This difference still massively blocks the road to
the unified concept of Christ's Church and to the full unity
of Christians in faith, worship and common life; consequently, it blocks the path to identity in the WCC/RCC definitions of ecumenism.

Whereas the World Council member churches largely view the
position and authority of the *papacy as an obstacle* to the
goal of Christian Unity, the Roman Catholic belief is that
the continuous petrine papacy is the Church's

> ...lasting and visible source and foundation
> of unity both of faith and of communion[2]

as it also believes that each bishop, in union with him, is
the principle and foundation of unity in his local or particular church.

Finally, as to the *goal* of the modern ecumenical movement,
the World Council has sharpened the sense of the goal *from*
a general, somewhat indefinite (invisible) sense of the one
church, *to* a new, definite *constitutional goal* of *"visible
unity in faith, eucharist and common life.* Its present rhetoric, witnessed at Vancouver in 1983 and after, is focused
on a *conciliar model* (like the WCC itself?) of the one
church; beside being off the center-target of the Apostolic
Church, this model evokes the unsettling spectre of the conciliarity period in the prereformation life of the Church.

The Roman Catholic goal is visible organic unity which implies some sort of a living organizational unity with the
episcopal heads of all particular churches in collegial
union with the one visible center, whose incumbent will be
the successor of Peter. The WCC's Conciliarity can be modified to be a feature of this *collegiate petrine model,* but
conciliarity simply cannot replace it or subsume it. Some

communities of separated Christians may die out and disappear, but the Apostolic Church, in which the Church of Christ fully subsists, is not going to disappear. Belief in Christ requires belief that he is with *his Church* continuously from its origin until the end-time.

Thus, in the goal of the modern ecumenical movement, even in the concepts which overlap, there remain significant differences. The "ONE CHURCH" seems presently to mean different things to the partners in the one movement. Yet, ecumenical rhetoric, at times, is so ambivalent that it appears to embrace both models!

From the Roman Catholic point of view, the concept of "return" (i.e., from Protestant division and incompleteness to Catholic unity and fullness) is seldom witnessed in spoken or written word.[3]

The word "return" appears to suggest that the Roman Catholic Church and other churches remained static, as at the point of the original departure. However, nothing could be further from the truth. The Catholic Church has changed dramatically, but not essentially, in the decades since Vatican II.

Some within and outside her membership have been dismayed by the diversity and subsidiarity which are *slowly* changing the Church's image from that of a pyramidal (pope to bishops to priests to laity only) picture to something like a circle with the hub and particular rim-centers linked by vital dual-flow spoke-lines. Those who "return", or "are reconciled" now are regaining their rightful place in a structured, but more flexible, Christian community.

Meanwhile, the Orthodox Churches are struggling to affirm a pan-Orthodox unity which seems to exist more in ideal than in actual reality because of the serious differences of perception, geography, language and culture (but not doctrine) which exist among the autocephalous Orthodox churches. The outcome of a pan-Orthodox synod, if achievable, cannot be foreseen.

Some Western Christian communities (Protestant) are regenerating a fuller liturgical, sacramental and ministerial life, including even celibate monastic groups. A healing, a reconciliation, a regeneration (flowing from the divinely-given gifts), not seen in nearly five centuries, is almost globally influencing this era. Thus the term "return" has frequently been replaced by the term "convergence" to give a more forward-looking sense to the phenomenon; this word suffers not merely because of its mechanistic and extrinsic

connotations, but perhaps more because it suggests secular
diplomacy and fails to reveal the transcendent realities
involved. Neither "return" nor "convergence" suggests the
bottom line reality. *"Doing the divinely-intended <u>truth</u>* at
any cost needs an image to give it popular, motivating
currency.[4]

The World Council of Churches has been extraordinary in the
great number of isolated Christian communities which it has,
in fact, brought together with strong commitment for dialogue, collaboration and selective common worship. Any
positive relationship to 400,000,000 people must be deemed
impressive and significant!

The WCC's call to union seems, at the same time, to have
strengthened the divisive, defensive, identifying, denominational bonds of some of its member churches. The Lutherans,
Anglicans, Reformed and others are strengthening their respective denominational ties. The outcome of these *opposing
motions* appears to be setting the denominations on a collision course with the overall call for the unity of Christ's
one Church. It looks like a resettling-in to an agreed
division.

From the point of view of the goal, there is a long distance
yet to go; but from the point of view of the starting point,
a greater distance may have been travelled in a relatively
short time. The separating has been going on for four and a
half centuries; the coming together, thus far, about three-
quarters of a century. Moreover, a great amount of reconciliation has been effected through the dedicated leadership
and services of the World Council. Still-flourishing pioneer, Rev. Dr. Willem Visser't Hooft, although unable to
attend the WCC's Sixth Assembly (Vancouver '83), continues
his moral and consultative support as the revered Honorary
President of the World Council. Deceased *World Council
pioneers* such as Mott, Brent, Soederblom, Germanos, and many
others, were heroic in their inspiration and self-sacri-
ficing efforts in pursuit of unity.

Despite those efforts, which continue through the work of
others, the *date of reaching the goal* is not in sight! It
would appear to be an effort to schedule God's deployment
of his gifts and Christians' response to them. Yet the intent of Christ, that his followers be one as He and the
Father are one, is clear and remains forceful. It permits
no cessation of effort. The RCC says it will not cease its
efforts; the WCC says the same. Will the WCC/RCC relationship be the same beyond the year 2000?

3.   WHERE TO, NEXT?

     The overall ecumenical movement is headed toward
Christian unity, but answers to: "What kind of unity", and
"When", etc. lie ahead.

Methodist theologian, Dr. Geoffrey Wainwright, who chaired
the Faith and Order Commission which produced the BEM (Baptism, Eucharist and Ministry) document (Lima '82) seems to
think that the BEM text is the upper limit of the ecumenical
movement's reach.   Speaking of the BEM text, he says that
this document

          ...comes as close as we are likely to come
          to substantial and practical agreement on
          the stated themes.[5]

If this be so, then those who rest content with this sentiment and stop before the movement reaches its goal will be
implying: thus far and no further to Christ's intent.   A
great void here appears to be the inability of some Protestant communions to acknowledge their historic departure from
the Catholic Church and the loss of essential ecclesial
elements at and after the time of their departure.   Acknowledging the fault of dividing appears to be a prerequisite
to reunion.   The RCC both in its head and all the bishops
for the whole Roman Catholic Community, in a formal and
public document said regarding the Community's sins against
unity:

          ...in humble prayer we beg pardon of God and
          of our separated brethren, just as we forgive
          them that offend us.[6]

The famous Catholic ecumenist Rev. Yves Congar O.P., considering the WCC/RCC relationship, fears that the WCC and
the RCC will run along parallel lines with certain limited
collaboration links between them.

In an essay entitled *Trials and promises of ecumenism,*
Conger viewed the future of union among Christians somewhat
pessimistically:

          Will organic unity ever be attained in History?
          Or is it rather eschatological?   I am more and
          more inclined to the latter view.[7]

However, Congar in no way considers giving up.   The reaching
out toward organic unity must continue in response to
Christ's prayer that all his followers be one.

The WCC and the RCC will continue in the SAME one ecumenical movement, yet Congar thinks that the special worldwide
character and strength of the Catholic Church "may raise
the spectre of a *parallel ecumenism*."[8]

This expression "parallel ecumenism" for the WCC/RCC relationship suggests the image of a *ladder* lying on the ground
with one side being the WCC, and the other the RCC, with a
number of contact rungs between the.   Perhaps a railroad
would provide a better *parallel tracks model* into which
Congar suspects that the modern movement is tending.   The
railroad track gives the impression of convergence, but
experience warns that the convergence will not take place
further down the line.

Would it not be a mistake for the RCC to become a member of
the WCC?   It would seem tantamount to a rejection of the
petrine function as foundation and preserver of unity.   It
would appear to be a denial of the Catholic Church's universality (catholicity), identity, and of its self-image of
being a sacrament of Christ as Christ is the Sacrament of
the Father.   It would seem to many Catholics like the
"protestantizing" of the Catholic Church—with a consequent
disorientation of all, including Protestants.   One may
wonder how long it would take the RCC to recover its
credibility?

It appears that *dialogue and collaboration* are the paths to
be sought until the truths of the revealed and lived Christianity clarify the theological and practical path of unity
in the one holy Church of Christ.   Meanwhile, doctrinal bilateral dialogues between ecclesial communities, more than
nondoctrinal associations with agencies (such as National
Councils of Churches) which are not themselves churches,
will likely be awarded priority.

> On the Catholic side bilateral dialogues
> are much appreciated, for they permit
> clearer delimitation of terms and con-
> clusions....[bilateral dialogues] achieve
> indisputable depth and precision;...[9]

Despite the obstacles which make the road ahead difficult
for the ecumenical movement, the goal, even some progress
toward it, makes the effort worth while.   Both the WCC and
the RCC believe the *Una Sancta Ecclesia* to be the *sign* of
Christ *for the unity of all mankind*.

Present partial unity yields encouragement, differences and
new questions[10] give pause; but that which unites Christians

is acknowledged as divinely given and consequently is greater than the human myopia and resistance which still divide Christian communities.

Finally, the dialoguing and collaborating partners in the ecumenical movement agree in principle that the movement's end is nothing less than the *Una Sancta Ecclesia;* that is what Christ in Matthew's Gospel (16:18) called "*My Church.*"

NOTES

CHAPTER ONE

[1]John Macquarrie, *Christian Unity and Christian Diversity* (Philadelphia: Westminister Press, 1975), p. 26.

[2]Ruth Rouse and Stephen C. Neill, ed., *A History of the Ecumenical Movement, 1517-1948* (Philadelphia: The Westminster Press, 1968). (Hereafter cited as *H.E.M.*).

[3]George H. Tavard, *Two Centuries of Ecumenism*, trans. by R. W. Hughes, Mentor-Omega Books (New York: The New American Library, 1962), p. 75.

[4]Samuel McCrea Cavert, *The American Churches in the Ecumenical Movement 1900-1968* (New York: Association Press, 1968), p. 7.

[5]Hugh T. Kerr, "Protestantism," *The Encyclopedia Americana, 1968*, XXII, pp. 684-689.

[6]Transliteration from the Greek and the omission of the accent and breathing marks appears to be acceptable practice in other than technical journals.

[7]George R. Berry, *The Classic Greek Dictionary* (New York: Follett Publishing Company, 1958), p. 477f.

[8]Charleton T. Lewis and Charles Short, *A Latin Dictionary* (Oxford: At the Clarendon Press, 1st ed. 1879, impression of 1962), p. 1257.
     In their Latin dictionary, lexicographers Lewis and Short classify the word as "postclassical" and spell among its English equivalents "oecumenical," a spelling which still is found in occasional use. For the most part, the Greek *oikoumene* or the English *ecumenical* is used.

[9]William A. Jurgens, *The Faith of the Early Fathers* (Minnesota: The Liturgical Press, 1970), p. 398. The recognition of Constantinople (381) "as an Ecumenical Council came about gradually: in the West, its Ecumenical character seems to have been recognized at the time of Ephesus (431) in the East.

[10]William J. Schmidt, "The Reformed Stance," *The Review of Books and Religion*, Vol. 4, Number 4, p. 12. (Article is the review of a book entitled, *Ecumenical Testimony*).

[11]Willem Adolf Visser't Hooft, "Appendix I," in *A History of the Ecumenical Movement*, ed. by R. Rouse and S.C. Neill (Philadelphia: Westminster Press, 1968), p. 736.

[12]*Ibid.*, p. 736.

[13]H.J. Schroeder, *Disciplinary Decrees of the General Councils* (London: B. Herder, 1937), passim.

[14]Cavert, *op.cit.*, p. 7.

[15]Visser't Hooft, *op.cit.*, p. 737 (emphasis added).

[16]Translation Department of W.C.C. *Ecumenical Glossary* (Geneva: World Council of Churches, 1967), p. 20.

[17]William J. Schmidt, "The Morphology of Ecumenism," *New York Theological Seminary Bulletin*, XXXVII (New York: Fall 1969), p. 9f.

[18]William A. Jurgens, *The Faith of the Early Fathers* (Collegeville: The Liturgical Press, 1970), p. 25.

[19]Bernard Lambert, *Ecumenism* (West Germany: Herder and Herder, 1967), p. 37.

[20]H.J. Schroeder, *Disciplinary Decrees of the General Council* (London: B. Herder Book Co., 1937), p. 16.

[21]*Ibid.*, p. 64.

[22]Lambert, *op.cit.*, p. 38.

[23]Lukas Vischer, ed., *A Documentary History of the Faith and Order Movement* (St. Louis: Bethany Press, 1963), p. 178.

[24]Lukas Vischer, *op.cit.*, pp. 7 to 23.

[25]One Holy (Church).

[26]Visser't Hooft, *op.cit.*, p. 740.

[27]Lambert, *op.cit.*, p. 31 (emphasis added).

[28]George H. Tavard, *Two Centuries of Ecumenism* (New York: New American Library of World Literature, 1962), p. xi.

[29] Schmidt, *op.cit.*, p. 9.

[30] John Macquarrie, *Christian Unity and Christian Diversity* (Philadelphia: The Westminster Press, 1975), p. 34.

[31] Yves M.J. Congar, *A History of Theology* (New York: Doubleday, 1968), p. 65ff and p. 202.

[32] William B. Murphy, et. al., *God and His Creation* (Dubuque: The Priory Press, 1958), p. 52.

[33] John Macquarrie, *Principles of Christian Theology* (New York: Charles Scribner's Sons, 1966), p. 1.

[34] Karl Rahner, *On the Theology of Death*, 2nd English ed. (New York: Herder and Herder, 1965), p. 7.

[35] Karl Rahner, Herbert Vorgrimler, *Theological Dictionary*, ed. by Cornelius Ernest, trans. by R. Strachan (New York: Herder and Herder, 1968), p. 456.

[36] Van A. Harvey, *A Handbook of Theological Terms* (New York: The Macmillan Company, 1968), p. 239.

[37] Ephesians, *The New Testament of the New American Bible* (New York: Catholic Book Publishing Co., 1970), p. 229.

[38] Xavier Leon-Dufour, *The Gospels and the Jesus of History*, ed. & trans. by J. McHugh (New York: Desclee, 1968), p. 271.

[39] James M. Robinson, Helmut Koester, *Trajectories through Early Christianity* (Philadelphia: Fortress Press, 1971), p. 277 (emphasis added).

[40] Edward Schillebeeckx, "Introduction" *A Survey of Catholic Theology 1800-1970*, T.M. Schoof ed. (New York: Paulist-Neuman Press, 1970), p. 1.

[41] *Ibid.*, p. 2.

[42] *Ibid.*, p. 1.

[43] N.Y. Times, Dec. 16, 1979.

[44] Robert C. Johnson "Who is Heinrich Ott"? in *New Theology No. 1*, ed. M. Marty & D. Peerman (New York: Macmillan Company, (1964), p. 37.

[45] *Ibid.*, p. 40.

[46]Gordon D. Kaufmann, "On the Meaning of 'God':
Transcendence Without Mythology," *New Theology No. 4*, eds. M.
Marty & D. Peerman (New York: Macmillan Company, 1967), p.
69 ff.

[47]The Epistles of John and Peter.

[48]Rudolf Schnackenburg, *The Church in the New Testament*,
trans. by W.J. O'Hara (New York: Herder and Herder, 1977), p.
130.

[49]Abbe Amann, *The Church of the Early Centuries*, trans.
by E. Raybould (London: Sands & Co., 1930), passim.

[50]Philip Hughes, *The Church in Crisis* (New York: Hanover
House, 1960), p. 32ff.

[51]H.J. Schroeder, *Disciplinary Decrees of the General
Councils* (St. Louis: B. Herder Book Co., 1937), p. 59ff.

[52]Augustin Bea, *The Unity of Christians* (New York:
Herder and Herder, 1963), p. 40.

[53]*Ibid.*, p. 40f.

[54]Georges Florovsky "The Orthodox Churches and the
Ecumenical Movement Prior to 1910," *A History of the
Ecumenical Movement, 1517-1948*, eds. R. Rouse & S.C. Neill
(Philadelphia: Westminster Press, 1968), p. 171.(Hereafter, H.E.

[55]Bea, *op.cit.*, p. 41.

[56]*Ibid.*, p. 41f.

[57]S.C. Neill, "Division and Search for Unity Prior to the
Reformation," *H.E.M.*,   p. 23.

[58]*Ibid.*, p. 23.

[59]Christopher Dawson, *The Dividing of Christendom* (New
York: Doubleday, 1967), p. 13f.

[60]H.J. Schroeder, *op.cit.*, p. 486.

[61]Martin E. Marty, *Protestantism* (New York: Doubleday,
1974), p. 42.

[62]John T. McNeill, "The Ecumenical Idea and Efforts to
Realize It," *H.E.M.*, p. 50.

[63] Literally, *Whose region, his religion.* This formula succinctly conveys the concept: whichever religious body controls tne region politically, to that same body belongs control of the religion.

[64] McNeill, *op.cit.*, p. 28.

[65] S.C. Neill, *op.cit.*, p. 24.

[66] George Tavard, *Understanding Protestantism*, trans. by R. Attwater (Glen Rock, New Jersey: Paulist Press, 1964), p. 9.

[67] *Ibid.*, p. 11.

[68] Martin Schmidt, "Ecumenical Activity on the Continent of Europe in the Seventeenth and Eighteenth Centuries," *H.E.M.*, p. 73.

[69] Roland H. Bainton, *The Age of the Reformation* (New York: Van Nostrand Co., 1956), p. 43.

[70] Crane Brinton, *The Shaping of Modern Thought* (New Jersey: Prentice-Hall, 1965), p. 68ff.

[71] *Ibid.*, p. 62.

[72] *Ibid.*, p. 62.

[73] *Ibid.*, p. 68.

[74] Dawson, *op.cit.*, p. 18.

[75] Schmidt, *op.cit.*, p. 77f.

[76] *Ibid.*, p. 77.

[77] *Ibid.*, p. 96.

[78] George Tavard, *Understanding Protestantism*, trans. by R. Attwater (New Jersey: Deus Books, 1964), p. 49f

[79] *Ibid.*

[80] Schmidt, *op.cit.*, p. 83.

[81] *Ibid.*, p. 84.

[82] *Ibid.*, p. 83.

[83] Henry Brandreth, "Approaches of the Churches Towards Each Other in the Nineteenth Century," *H.E.M.*, p. 294.

[84] Schmidt, *op.cit.*, p. 103.

[85] Dawson, *op.cit.*, p. 17.

[86] A. Simon, "Liberalism," *New Catholic Encyclopedia*, VIII, p. 701.

[87] Brinton, *op.cit.*, p. 119.

[88] *Ibid.*, p. 120.

[89] Dawson, *op.cit.* p. 212.

[90] George H. Tavard, *Two Centuries of Ecumenism* (New York: New American Library, 1962), p. 21.

[91] *Ibid.*, p. 21.

[92] Tavard, *Two Centuries of Ecumenism*, p. 20.

[93] *Ibid.*, p. 20.

[94] Rouse, "Volunatry Movements and the Changing Ecumenical Climate," *H.E.M.*, p. 331.

CHAPTER TWO

[1] Samuel McCrea Cavert, *The American Churches in the Ecumenical Movement* (New York: Association Press, 1968), p. 18.

[2] Rouse, "Other Aspects of the Ecumenical Movement," *H.E.M.*, p. 599ff.

[3] C.H. Jaquet, ed. *Yearbook of American Churches 1970* (New York: Council Press, 1970), pp 10-92.

[4] Samuel McCrea Cavert, *The American Churches in the Ecumenical Movement 1900-1968* (New York: Association Press, 1968), p. 15. (Hereafter   cited as *American Churches*).

[5] Cavert, *American Churches*, p. 15.

[6] *Ibid.*, p. 17.

[7] *Ibid.*, p. 18.

[8] Cavert, *American Churches*, p. 19.

[9] *Ibid.*, p. 19.

[10] Samuel McCrea Cavert, *Church Cooperation and Unity in America* (New York: Association Press, 1970), p. 13. (Hereafter cited as *Church Cooperation*).

[11] Cavert, *Church Cooperation*, p. 13.

[12] Corinthians 1:10-13 (New American Bible).

[13] Cavert, *Church Cooperation*, pp. 301-321.

[14] Cavert, *Church Cooperation*, p. 301.

[15] Martin E. Marty, *Protestantism* (New York: Doubleday, 1972), p. 11.

[16] Marty, *Protestantism*, passim.

[17] *Ibid.*, p. 77.

[18] Marty, *Protestantism*, p. 78.

[19] Marty, *Protestantism*, p. 78.

[20] Marty, *Protestantism*, p. 84.

[21] *Ibid.*, p. 174.

[22] Marty, *Protestantism*, Chapters 8 through 12 respectively.

[23] John Macquarrie, *Christian Unity and Christian Diversity* (Philadelphia: Westminster Press, 1975), p. 4.

[24] Cavert, *American Churches*, p. 10 (emphasis added).

[25] Cavert, *American Churches*, p. 258.

[26] Cavert, *Church Cooperation*, passim.

[27] Rouse, "Voluntary Movements and the Changing Ecumenical Climate," *H.E.M.*, p. 330.

[28] Cavert, *American Churches*, p. 52ff.

[29] *Ibid.*, p. 52.

[30] *Ibid.*, p. 484.

[31] Cavert, *American Churches*, p. 53.

[32] Harold E. Fey, "Confessional Families and the Ecumenical Movement," *History of the Ecumenical Movement*, II, ed. H. Fey (Philadelphia: Westminster Press, 1970), p. 118. (Hereafter this book will be abbreviated to *H.E.M.*, II).

[33] Cavert, *American Churches*, p. 71.

[34] Cavert, *American Churches*, p. 209 and passim.

[35] John R. Fry, *The Trivialization of the United Presbyterian Church* (New York: Harper & Row, 1975), passim.

[36] *New York Times*, Saturday, June 10, 1972, Article by G. Dugan, p. 35.

[37] Ian Henderson, *Power Without Glory*, p. 12 and passim.

[38] Cavert, *American Churches*, p. 259 (emphasis added).

[39] Cavert, *American Churches*, p. 213.

[40] Ian Henderson, *Power Without Glory* (Richmond, Virginia: John Knox Press, 1969), p. v.

[41] Cavert, *American Churches*, p. 72ff.

[42] Nils Karlstrom, "Movements for International Friendship and Life and Work," *H.E.M.*, p. 515f.

[43] Tissington Tatlow, "The World Conference on Faith and Order," *H.E.M.*, p. 414.

[44] Tatlow, "The World Conference on Faith and Order," *H.E.M.*, p. 428.

[45] Cavert, *American Churches*, p. 201.

CHAPTER THREE

[1] Rouse, "Voluntary Movement...," *H.E.M.*, 1, p. 331.

[2] Kenneth Latourette, "Ecumenical Bearings of the Missionary Movement and the International Missionary Council," *H.E.M.*, 1, p. 354f.

[3]Latourette, "Ecumenical Bearings...," *H.E.M.*, passim.

[4]Latourette, "Ecumenical Bearings...," *H.E.M.*, p. 362.

[5]Latourette, "Ecumenical Bearings...," *H.E.M.*, p. 364.

[6]*Ibid.*, p. 364.

[7]Latourette, "Ecumenical Bearings...," *H.E.M.*, passim.

[8]Stephen C. Neill, *Brothers of the Faith* (Nashville: Abingdon Press, 1960), p. 18 and passim.

[9]Latourette, "Ecumenical Bearings...," *H.E.M.*, p. 360.

[10]Neill, *Brothers of the Faith*, p. 44.

[11]*Ibid.*, p. 44. 'Professing Jesus Christ as God and Savior' became the membership basis for "Faith and Order" and later for the World Council of Churches.

[12]Neill, *Brothers of the Faith*, p. 45f.

[13]Neill, *Brothers of the Faith*, p. 29.

[14]Nils Karlstrom, "Movements for International Friendship and Life and Work," *A History of the Ecumenical Movement*, p. 520.

[15]Karlstrom, "Movements...Life and Work," *H.E.M.*, p. 527.

[16]Karlstrom, "Movements...Life and Work," *H.E.M.*, p. 529.

[17]*Ibid.*, p. 533.

[18]Karlstrom, "Movements...Life and Work," *H.E.M.*, p. 534.

[19]Karlstrom, "Movements...Life and Work," *H.E.M.*, p. 535f.

[20]Karlstrom, "Movements...Life and Work," *H.E.M.*, p. 538.

[21]Karlstrom, "Movements...Life and Work," *H.E.M.*, p. 538f.

[22]Nils Ehrenstrom, "Movements for International Friendship and Life and Work, 1925-1948," *H.E.M.*, p. 547ff.

[23]Ehrenstrom, "...Life and Work, 1925-1948," *H.E.M.*, p. 547.

[24]*Ibid.*, p. 553.

[25]Ehrenstrom, "...Life and Work, 1925-1948," *H.E.M.*, p. 551.

[26]Ehrenstrom, "...Life and Work, 1925-1948," *H.E.M.*, p. 573.

[27]Ehrenstrom, "...Life and Work, 1925-1948," *H.E.M.*, p. 574.

[28]Ehrenstrom, "...Life and Work, 1925-1948," *H.E.M.*, p. 574 (emphasis added).

[29]Ehrenstrom, "...Life and Work, 1925-1948," *H.E.M.*, p. 584.

[30]*Ibid.*, p. 591.

[31]Ehrenstrom, "...Life and Work, 1925-1948," *H.E.M.*, p. 592.

[32]Tatlow, "The World Conference on Faith and Order," *H.E.M.*, p. 408.

[33]Tatlow, "World Conference on Faith and Order," *H.E.M.*, p. 411.

[34]*Ibid.*, p. 413.

[35]Henderson, *Power Without Glory*, p. 8.

[36]Tatlow, "World Conference on Faith and Order," *H.E.M.*, p. 416.

[37]Tatlow, "World Conference on Faith and Order," *H.E.M.*, p. 416.

[38]Tavard, *Two Centuries of Ecumenism*, 1962 Mentor, N.Y., p. 94.

[39]Tatlow, "World Conference on Faith and Order," *H.E.M.*, p. 417.

[40]Tatlow, "The World Conference on Faith and Order," *H.E.M.*, p. 417. (emphasis added).

[41]*Ibid.*, p. 419f.

[42]"The World Conference on Faith and Order," *H.E.M.*, p. 420.

[43]Don Herbert Yoder, "Christian Unity in Nineteenth Century America," *H.E.M.*, p. 250.

[44]Henry R. Brandreth, "Approaches of the Churches Towards Each Other in the Nineteenth Century," *H.E.M.*, p. 265.

[45]*Ibid.*, p. 265.

[46]Brandreth, "Approaches...Century," *H.E.M.*, p. 265.

[47]Tatlow, "The World Conference on Faith and Order," *H.E.M.*, p. 424.

[48]"Lausanne," *A Documentary History of the Faith and Order Movement*, ed. L. Vischer (St. Louis: Bethany Press, 1963), p. 37.

[49]George Tavard, *Two Centuries of Ecumenism*, p. 79.

[50]Tatlow, "The World Conference on Faith and Order," *H.E.M.*, p. 426.

[51]*Ibid.*, p. 427.

[52]Tatlow, "The World Conference on Faith and Order," *H.E.M.*, p. 430.

[53]Willem Visser't Hooft, *Memoirs* (Philadelphia: Westminster Press), p. 76.

[54]*Loc. Cit.*

[55]Visser't Hooft, *Memoirs*, p. 77.

[56]Samuel McCrea Cavert, *The American Churches in the Ecumenical Movement* (New York: Association Press, 1968), p. 162.

[57]Cavert, *The American Churches in the Ecumenical Movement*, p. 162.

[58]*Ibid.*, p. 163.

[59]Visser't Hooft, *Memoirs*, p. 79.

[60]Ehrenstrom, "Movements for International Friendship and Life Work," *H.E.M.*, p. 592.

[61]*Ibid.*, p. 596.

[62]Visser't Hooft, *Memoirs*, p. 80.

[63]Visser't Hooft, *The Ten Formative Years 1938-1948*, pp. 25-27.

[64]Visser't Hooft, *Memoirs*, p. 81.

[65]*Ibid.*, p. 81.

[66]Visser't Hooft, *Memoirs*, p. 81f.

[67]W. A. Visser't Hooft, *The Ten Formative Years 1938-1948*, p. 7f. (Hereafter cited as *Formative Years*).

[68]Visser't Hooft, *Formative Years*, p. 18.

[69]Visser't Hooft, *Formative Years*, p. 12.

[70]*Ibid.*, p. 19.

[71]Visser't Hooft, *Formative Years*, p. 35.

[72]Ehrenstrom, "Movements for International Friendship and Life and Work," *H.E.M.*, p. 590.

[73]Tatlow, "The World Conference on Faith and Order," *H.E.M.*, p. 432.

[74] *Ibid.*, p. 432.

[75] Visser't Hooft, *Formative Years*, p. 21. (emphasis added).

[76] *Ibid.*, p. 23.

[77] *Ibid.*, p. 23.

[78] Visser't Hooft, *Formative Years*, p. 23. (emphasis added).

[79] *Ibid.*, p. 23.

[80] Visser't Hooft, *Formative Years*, p. 23.

[81] *Ibid.*, p. 24.

[82] Visser't Hooft, *Formative Years*, p. 12.

[83] Visser't Hooft, "The Genesis of the World Council of Churches," *H.E.M.*, p. 702.

[84] *Ibid.*

CHAPTER FOUR

[1] Visser't Hooft, *Memoirs*, p. 255 and passim.

[2] Norman Goodall, *The Ecumenical Movement* (London: Oxford University Press, 1961), p. 233.

[3] Visser't Hooft, *Memoirs*, p. 255.

[4] *Ibid.*, p. 260.

[5] Timothy Ware, *The Orthodox Church* (Maryland: Penguin Books, 1972), p. 139.

[6] Ware, *The Orthodox Church*, p. 332.

[7]*Ibid.*, p. 330.

[8]*Ibid.*, p. 330.

[9]Ware, *The Orthodox Church*, pp. 14, 51.

[10]Demetrios Constantelos, *The Greek Orthodox Church* (New York: The Seabury Press, 1967), pp. 24, 118.

[11]Constantelos, *The Greek Orthodox Church*, p. 47.

[12]Archbishop Iakovos, "Foreword" to *The Greek Orthodox Church*, p. 3.

[13]Constantelos, *The Greek Orthodox Church*, p. 29f.

[14]Ware, *The Orthodox Church*, p. 81. (emphasis added).

[15]*Ibid.*, p. 97.

[16]Carnegie S. Calian, *Icon and Pulpit* (Philadelphia: The Westminster Press, 1968), p. 26.

[17]Georges Florovsky, "The Orthodox Churches and the Ecumenical Movement Prior to 1910," *H.E.M.*, p. 203.

[18]Ware, *The Orthodox Church*, p. 332.

[19]Calian, *op.cit.*, p. 31.

[20]Ernst Benz, *The Eastern Orthodox Church*, (New York: Doubleday, 1957), p. 205.

[21]Visser't Hooft, *Memoirs*, p. 276.

[22]Stephen C. Neill, *Brothers of the Faith* (New York: Abingdon Press, 1960), p. 72.

[23]*Ibid.*, p. 72ff.

[24]*Ibid.*, p. 79.

[25]*Ibid.*, p. 72.

[26]Ware, *The Orthodox Church*, pp. 15, 317.

[27] *Ibid.*, p. 250.

[28] *Ibid.*, p. 319, footnote 3.

[29] Nicholas Zernov, "The Eastern Churches and the Ecumenical Movement in the Twentieth Century," *H.E.M.*, p. 672.

[30] Zernov, *op.cit.*, p. 673.

[31] Neill, *Brothers of the Faith*, p. 72f.

[32] Ware, *The Orthodox Church*, p. 328.

[33] Neill, *op.cit.*, p. 73.

[34] Nicholas Zernov, "The Eastern Churches...Twentieth Century," *H.E.M.*, p. 666.

[35] *Ibid.*, p. 667.

[36] Willem Visser't Hooft, "The Genesis of the World Council of Churches," *H.E.M.*, p. 717.

[37] A Christian Assembly at worship fits a reformed definition of the Church.

[38] *The First Assembly of the World Council of Churches*, ed. W. Visser't Hooft (New York: Harper and Brothers, 1949), p. 28.

[39] Samuel McCrea Cavert, *American Churches in the Ecumenical Movement* (New York: Association Press, 1968), p. 202.

[40] Marc Boegner, *The Long Road to Unity*, trans. by R. Hague (London: Collins, 1970), p. 224.

[41] Boegner, *op.cit.*, p. 224.

[42] *The First Assembly of the World Council of Churches* (the official report), ed. W. Visser't Hooft. (New York: Harper and Brothers, 1948), pp. 197-201. (Hereafter cited as *Amsterdam* and page number).

[43]*Amsterdam*, p. 197. The Apostolic Church might be
termed a fellowship (*koinonia*) of local churches which accepted Jesus Christ as God and Savior; but such a definition needs
further specification; cf Acts 2:42-47.

[44] Boegner, *The Long Road to Unity*, p. 58.

[45] Boegner, *The Long Road to Unity*, p. 58.

[46] David P. Gaines, *The World Council of Churches* (New
Hampshire: Noone House, 1966), p. 166.

[47] Gaines, *The World Council of Churches*, p. 164.

[48]*Amsterdam*, pp. 203-213.

[49] Gaines, *World Council of Churches*, p. 397.

[50]*Amsterdam*, p. 202. (emphasis added).

[51] Gaines, *op.cit.*, p. 164.

[52] Matt. 28:18-20, et al.

[53]*Amsterdam*, p. 203f.

[54] Richard P. McBrien, *Do We Need the Church?* (New York:
Harper and Row, 1969), p. 98f.

[55]*Amsterdam*, p. 202.

[56]*Ibid.*, p. 203.

[57]*Amsterdam*, p. 198. (emphasis added).

[58]*Amsterdam*, p. 198f.

[59] Gaines, *The World Council of Churches*, p. 396.

[60]*Ibid.*, p. 408f.

[61] Visser't Hooft, *Memoirs*, p. 296f. (At the time of the
Cyprus Crisis, Visser't Hooft issued a statement by himself).

⁶²Douglas Horton, *Toward an Undivided Church* (New York: Association Press, 1967), p. 57.

⁶³An alternate form of the General Secretary's last name.

⁶⁴Stephen Neill, *Brothers of the Faith*, p. 144.

⁶⁵Visser't Hooft, *Memoirs*, p. 348.

⁶⁶*Ibid.*, p. 37.

⁶⁷Visser't Hooft, *Memoirs*, p. 95. (emphasis added).

⁶⁸Daniel Jenkins, "Karl Barth," *Barth*, ed. James F. Andrews (St. Louis: B. Herder, 1969), p. 12.

⁶⁹J.C. Hoekendijk, *The Church Inside Out*, trans. by I.C. Rottenberg (Philadelphia: Westminster Press, 1966), pp. 24, 39ff.

⁷⁰Daniel Jenkins, "Karl Barth," *Barth*, ed. James F. Andrews (St. Louis: B. Herder, 1969), p. 12.

⁷¹*Ibid.*, p. 7.

⁷²Jenkins, *op.cit.*, p. 74.

⁷³Karl Barth, *Church Dogmatics: A Selection*, ed. H. Gollwitzer, trans. by G. Bromley (New York: Harper Torchbooks, 1961), p. 74.

⁷⁴*Ibid.*, p. 74.

⁷⁵*Ibid.*, p. 66. (emphasis added).

⁷⁶*Ibid.*, p. 68. (emphasis added).

⁷⁷*Ibid.*, p. 72. (emphasis added).

⁷⁸Barth, *op.cit.*, passim.

⁷⁹Karl Barth, "Recapitulation Number Three," *Barth*, ed. J.F. Andrews (St. Louis: B. Herder, 1969), p. 111.

[80]Avery Dulles, *Models of the Church* (New York: Doubleday, 1974), p. 80.

[81]Visser't Hooft, *Memoirs*, p. 134.

[82]David L. Mueller, *Karl Barth* (Waco, Texas: Word Books,
1972), p. 33.

[83]J.L. Witte, S.J. "A Talk with a Giant-Karl Barth,"
America, LXXIX, September 25, 1948, p. 568.

[84]Witte, *op.cit.*, p. 568.

[85]*Ibid.*, p. 568.

[86]Mueller, *Karl Barth*, p. 53.

[87]*Amsterdam*, p. 32.

[88]*Ibid.*, p. 9.

CHAPTER FIVE

[1]John Powell, *The Mystery of the Church* (Milwaukee:
Bruce Publishing Company, 1967), p. 4.

[2]Powell, *The Mystery of the Church*, p. 4.

[3]*Ibid.*, p. 4.

[4]H. Denzinger, ed., *The Sources of Catholic Dogma*, 30th
edition, trans. R.J. Deferrari (London: R. Herder Book Co.,
1953), p. 429. (Hereafter referred to as *Denz*, with a page
citation).

[5]*Denz*, p. 433 (from a letter sent by the Vatican to the
Catholic Bishops of the World).

[6]Roberti Bellarmini, Cardinalis, *Solida Christianae Fidei
Demonstratio*, Antverpii, 1611, p. 183. (De qua nostra
sententia est Ecclesiam unam tantum esse, non duas: & illam
unam & veram) caetum hominum euisdem Christianae fidei
professione, et eorundem Sacramentorum communione colligatum,
sub regimine legitimorum pastorum, as praecipue unius Christi

in terris Vicarii, Rom. Pontificis. (Translation is writer's).

[7]Bellarmini, *Solida Christinae Fidei Demonstratio*, p. 183.

[8]*Ibid.*, p. 183.

[9]*Ibid.*, index.

[10]"Bellarmine" *A Catholic Dictionary of Theology* (London: T. Nelson and Sons Ltd., 1962), p. 253.

[11]Ad. Tanquerey, *Synopsis Theologiae Dogmaticae Fundamentalis*, 24 ed., ed. J. Bord (Paris: Desclee et Socii, 1937), p. 412. Societas, a Christo instituta, hominum viatorum, qui eiusdem fidei professione et eorumdem sacramentorum participatione, sub R. Pontificis auctoritate, coadunantur, ad gratiam et salutem obtinendum. (Translation is writer's).

[12]"The Augsburg Confession," *The Book of Concord*, trans. and edited by T. Tappert (Philadelphia: Fortress Press, 1959), p. 32.

[13]*Ibid.*, p. 32.

[14]*Book of Concord*, pp. 338, 339, 344, 352, 363, 411.

[15]John Calvin, *A Compend of the Institutes of the Christian Religion*, ed. H.T. Kerr (Philadelphia: The Westminster Press, 1964), p. 155 (IV, i, 9).

[16]Calvin, *A Compend of the Institutes*, p. 152 (IV, i, 2).

[17]*Ibid.*, p. 152 (IV, i, 2).

[18]Calvin, *A Compend of the Institutes*, pp. 163-165.

[19]George Tavard, *Two Centuries of Ecumenism* (New York: American Library, 1962), p. 68.

[20]Roger Aubert, "Stages of Catholic Ecumenism from Leo XIII to Vatican II" *Renewal of Religious Structures* (New York: Herder & Herder, 1968), p. 184.

[21]Aubert, "...from Leo XIII to Vatican II," p. 184.

[22]Tavard, *op.cit.*, p. 71.

[23]Pope Leo XIII, "Praeclara Gratulationis," *The American Catholic Quarterly Review*, trans. James Gibbons, XIX, No. 76, Oct. 1894, p. 779.

[24]*Ibid.*, p. 780.

[25]*Ibid.*, p. 781.

[26]Pope Leo XIII, "*Praeclara Gratulationis*," p. 781.

[27]*Ibid.*, p. 782.

[28]*Ibid.*, p. 782.

[29]*Ibid.*, p. 783.

[30]Pope Leo XIII, *op.cit.*, p. 783.

[31]*Ibid.*, p. 789.

[32]Leo XIII, "*Satis Cognitum*," *The Irish Ecclesiastical Record*, Vol. XVII, Dublin, 1896, p. 748.

[33]*Ibid.*, p. 749.

[34]Leo XIII, "*Satis Cognitum*," p. 750 and passim.

[35]*Ibid.*, p. 751.

[36]*Ibid.*, p. 752.

[37]Leo XIII, "*Satis Cognitum*," p. 754 (I Cor. 12:12).

[38]*Ibid.*, p. 755.

[39]*Ibid.*, p. 755.

[40]Leo XIII, "*Satis Cognitum*," p. 755.

[41]Leo XIII, "*Satis Cognitum*," p. 834ff. The parallel phrases in the New Oxford Bible yield the same substantial

meaning: "Full authority has been committed to me...Make all nations my disciples...teach them to observe all that I have commanded you."

[42]Leo XIII, *op.cit.*, p. 836f.

[43]William A. Jurgens, *The Faith of the Early Fathers* (Collegeville: Liturgical Press, 1970), pp. 6-12.

[44]Raymond E. Brown, *Priest and Bishop* (New York: Paulist Press, 1970), passim.

[45]Leo XIII, "*Satis Cognitum*," p. 843.

[46]Leo XIII, "*Satis Cognitum*," p. 843.

[47]*Ibid.*, p. 844f.   The inserted kepha-kepha manifests the textual play on words.

[48]Howard Clark Kee, "The Gospel According to Matthew," *The Interpreter's One-Volume Commentary on the Bible* (Nashville: Abingdon Press, 1971), p. 629.

[49]*Ibid.*, p. 630.

[50]Oscar Cullmann, *Peter: Disciple, Apostle, Martyr* (London: SCM Press Ltd., 1962), p. 213.

[51]*Ibid..*, p. 213ff.

[52]L. Hertling and E. Kirschbaum, *The Roman Catacombs and Their Martyrs*, tr. M. Costelloe (Milwaukee: Bruce Publishing Co., 1956), p. 36.

[53]Leo XIII, "*Satis Cognitum*," p. 845.

[54]Leo XIII, "*Satis Cognitum*," p. 848.

[55]*Ibid.*, p. 849ff.

[56]Leo XIII, "*Satis Cognitum*," p. 851f.   (Leo quotes Chrysostom as using the word *college* in this context).

[57]*Ibid.*, p. 847.

[58] Leo XIII, *Divinum Illud*, trans. J. Bluett: (New York: The America Press, 1897), p. 4.

[59] Leo XIII, *Divinum Illud*, p. 9.

[60] *Ibid.*, p. 9.

[61] Leo XIII, *Divinum Illud*, p. 10.

[62] *Ibid.*, pp. 13, 16.

[63] Leo XIII, *Divinum Illud*, p. 14. (Pius XII later devoted an entire encyclical to this Pauline concept of the Church).

[64] *Ibid.*, p. 18.

[65] *Ibid.*, p. 18.

[66] Leo XIII, "Apostolicae Curae," *Denz,* p. 497.

[67] Leo XIII, *Apostolicae Curae*, trans. by G. Treacy (New York: Paulist Press, 1949), p. 17.

[68] Philip Hughes, *A Popular History of the Catholic Church* (New York: Macmillan Co., 1957), p. 245.

[69] Leo XIII, "Annum Ingressi," *The Great Encyclical Letters of Pope Leo XIII*, ed. J. Wynne (New York: Benziger Bros., 1903), p. 559.

[70] *Ibid.*, p. 559f. (emphasis added).

[71] Leo XIII, "Annum Ingressi," p. 560ff.

[72] *Ibid.*, p. 566.

[73] *Ibid.*, p. 567.

[74] *Ibid.*, p. 575f.

[75] *Ibid.*, p. 578, and passim.

[76] E.E.Y. Hales, *The Catholic Church in the Modern World* (New York: Doubleday, 1960), p. 228ff.

[77] *Ibid.*, p. 178ff. Also *Denz*, p. 508ff.

[78] Benedict XV, "Union of Minds," *The Church: Papal Teachings*, selected by Benedictines of Solesmes, trans. E. O'Gorman (Boston: St. Paul Editions, 1962), pp. 406, 412, 424.

[79] Benedict XV, "The Faith of Peter," *Ibid.*, p. 418.

[80] Aubert, *op.cit.*, p. 185.

[81] Benedict XV, "Romanorum Pontificium," *The Church: Papal Teachings*, p. 407. (emphasis added).

[82] Benedict XV, "Dante and the Church," *op.cit.*, p. 421f.

[83] James Simpson and Edward Storey, *The Long Shadows of Lambeth X* (New York: McGraw-Hill, 1967), p. 313f.

CHAPTER SIX

[1] Roger Aubert, "Stages of Catholic Ecumenism from Leo XIII to Vatican II," *op.cit.*, p. 186.

[2] Aubert, *op.cit.*, p. 187, passim.

[3] George H. Tavard, *Two Centuries of Ecumenism* (New York: New American Library, 1962), p. 102ff and passim.

[4] Tavard, *Two Centuries of Ecumenism*, p. 105.

[5] *Ibid.*, p. 106.

[6] Aubert, *op.cit.*, p. 187.

[7] *Ibid.*, p. 187f and passim.

[8] John McDonnell, *Catholic Action, Its Nature and Beginnings on the College Level*, Unpublished dissertation, Niagara University, New York 1951.

[9] Pius XI, *Mortalium Animos*, tr. R. McGowan, Washington, D.C., National Catholic Welfare Conference, 1928. (*Mortalium*

Animos has been a common reference to this eighteen page
encyclical devoted to the concept of Church Unity).

[10] Pius XI, *Mortalium Animos*, p. 16, passim.

[11] *Ibid.*, p. 3.

[12] *Ibid.*, p. 4.

[13] Pius XI, *Mortalium Animos*, p. 11.

[14] *Ibid.*, p. 12.

[15] *Ibid.*, p. 5f.

[16] Pius XI, *Mortalium Animos*, pp. 4, 7.

[17] *Ibid.*, p. 7.

[18] Pius XI, *Mortalium Animos*, p. 8.

[19] *Ibid.*, p. 8.

[20] Pius XI, *Mortalium Animos*, p. 8.

[21] *Ibid.*, p. 8.

[22] *Ibid.*, p. 8.

[23] Pius XI, *Mortalium Animos*, p. 9.

[24] *Ibid.*, p. 16.

[25] *Ibid.*, p. 14.

[26] Pius XI, *Mortalium Animos*, p. 17.

[27] *Ibid.*, p. 12f.

[28] Boegner, *The Long Road to Unity*, p. 68.

[29] *Ibid.*, p. 388. (The scriptural expression is from
1 Tim 3:15).

[30] Visser't Hooft, *Memoirs*, p. 319.

[31] Visser't Hooft, *Memoirs*, p. 65.

[32] *Ibid.*, p. 65f. (emphasis added).

[33] Pius XI, "Allocutio: Jan. 11, 1927" *Irenikon*, Vol. 3, 1927, p. 20.

[34] Aubert, *op.cit.*, p. 190.

[35] *Ibid.*, p. 191.

[36] Pius XII, "In the Service of Truth," *The Church*, p. 497.

[37] Pius XII, *The Unity of Human Society* (New York: America Press, 1939), p. 12f.

[38] Pius XII, *Mystici Corporis*, Vatican translation, National Catholic Welfare Conference, Washington, D.C., 1943, p. 35.

[39] *Ibid.*, p. 10.

[40] Pius XII, *Mystici Corporis*, p. 3.

[41] *Ibid.*, p. 39. (emphasis added).

[42] Visser't Hooft, *Memoirs*, p. 195.

[43] *Ibid.*, p. 206.

[44] *Ibid.*, p. 206f.

[45] Congregatio S. Officii, "Monitum," *Acta Apostolicae Sedis*, Vol. XL, No. 6, 15 Junii, 1948, p. 257 (canon 1325 was cited).

[46] *Ibid.*, p. 257.

[47] *Ibid.*, p. 257.

[48] Stanislaus Woywod (Revised by C. Smith), *A Practical Commentary on the Code of Canon Law* (New York: J.F. Wagner,

Inc., 1957), p. 109.

[49]Congregation S. Officii, "Instruction: De Motione
Oecumenica," *The Jurist*, Vol. X, Washington, D.C., Jan. 1950,
pp. 201-213.   (The official English Translation is appended).
This is commonly called *Ecclesia Catholica*, hereafter cited
as *Ecclesia Catholica*.

[50]Congregatio S. Officii, "*Ecclesia Catholica*," *op.cit.*,
pp. 201-213.

[51]Congregatio S. Officii, "*Ecclesia Catholica*," *op.cit.*,
p. 212.

[52]*Ibid.*, p. 208.

[53]*Ibid.*, p. 211f.

[54]Congregatio S. Officii, "*Ecclesia Catholica*," p. 207.

[55]*Ibid.*, p. 207.

[56]*Ibid.*, p. 207.

[57]Congregatio S. Officii, "*Ecclesia Catholica*," p. 210
and passim.

[58]George Tavard, *Two Centuries of Ecumenism* (New York:
Mentor-Omega Books, 1962), p. 185.   Also, Bernard Leeming,
The Churches and the Church (Maryland: Newman Press, 1961),
pp. 264-275.

[59]Visser't Hooft, *Memoirs*, p. 322.   (emphasis added).

[60]Visser't Hooft, *Memoirs*, p. 322.

[61]Pius XII, *Humani Generis*, tr. J.C. Fenton (Washington,
D.C.:   N.C.W.C., 1950), p. 3.

[62]Pius XII, *Humani Generis*, p. 3f.

[63]*Ibid.*, p. 4f and passim.

[64]Eirenism from the Greek root *eirene* (meaning peace) has
an alternate form, irenicism, in English to convey the same

notion in the papal texts.

[65] Pius XII, *Humani Generis*, pp. 4, 19.

[66] *Ibid.*, p. 4.

[67] Pius XII, *Humani Generis*, p. 9.

[68] *Ibid.*, p. 19.

[69] Visser't Hooft, *Memoirs*, p. 322.

[70] Lucas Vischer, "The Ecumenical Movement and the Roman Catholic Church," *A History of the Ecumenical Movement*, Vol. 2, Ed. H.E. Fay (Philadelphia: Westminster Press, 1970), p. 316f.

[71] Pius XII, "Allocutio: Fidelity and Adaptation," *The Church*, p. 738f.

[72] Pius XII, "Meminisse Juvat," *The Church*, p. 781f.

[73] *Ibid.*, p. 783.

CHAPTER SEVEN

[1] Vischer, *op.cit.*, p. 322.

[2] John XXIII, "Coronation Homily," *The Church*, p. 791f.

[3] John XXIII, "Consistory Allocution," *The Church*, p. 793f.

[4] John XXIII, "First Christmas Message," *The Church,* p. 795.

[5] John XXIII, "First Christmas Message," p. 796.

[6] John XXIII, "Speeches of January 25, 1959," *The Church*, pp. 797-800.

[7] John XXIII, "Allocutio: Venice, 1959," *The Church*, p. 802f.

[8] Vischer, *op.cit.*, p. 322f.

[9] *Ibid.*, p. 324.

[10]Visser't Hooft, *Memoirs*, p. 328.

[11]*Ibid.*, p. 328.

[12]*Ibid.*, p. 328.

[13]Visser't Hooft, *Memoirs*, p. 329.

[14]Visser't Hooft, *Memoirs*, p. 329.

[15]Augustin Bea, *The Unity of Christians*, Introduction by
G. O'Hara, ed. B. Leeming (New York: Herder and Herder, 1963),
p. xiv.

[16]*Ibid.*, p. xii.

[17]Bea, *The Unity of Christians*, p. 65.

[18]*Ibid.*, p. 66.

[19]*Ibid.*, p. 66.

[20]Bea, *The Unity of Christians*, p. 66.

[21]*Ibid.*, p. 67.

[22]*Ibid.*, p. 68.

[23]*Ibid.*, p. 69.

[24]Bea, *The Unity of Christians*, p. 69f and passim.

[25]*Ibid.*, p. 71.

[26]Bea, *The Unity of Christians*, p. 34.

[27]Xavier Rynne, *Letters from Vatican City* (New York:
Farrar, Strauss & Co., 1963), p. 94. The Conciliar
Commissions: 1. Theological (Faith and Morals), 2. Bishops
and dioceses, 3. Discipline (clergy and faithful), 4.
Religious, 5. Sacraments, 6. Studies and Seminaries, 7.
Missions, 8. Liturgy, 9. Oriental Churches, 10. Apostolate of
Laity, 11. Secretariate for promoting unity. (p. 90).

[28]John XXIII, *"Toward Christian Unity,"* *Letters from
Vatican City*, pp. 262-272.

[29]*Ibid.*, p. 265.

[30]*Ibid.*, p. 266.

[31] John XXIII, "*Toward Christian Unity*," p. 267.

[32] *Ibid.*, p. 268.

[33] John XXIII, "*Toward Christian Unity*," p. 269.

[34] *Ibid.*, p. 270.

[35] John XXIII, "*Toward Christian Unity*," p. 271.

[36] Xavier Rynne, *Letters from Vatican City*, p. 85 and passim.

[37] *The Documents of Vatican II*, ed. Walter M. Abbott (New York: Guild Press, 1966), p. 140. Hereafter cited as Vatican II: *Documents*. (emphasis added).

[38] John Powell, *The Mystery of the Church* (Milwaukee: Bruce Publishing Co., 1967), p. 62 and passim.

[39] Avery Dulles, *Models of the Church* (New York: Doubleday, 1974), pp. 186, 58ff.

[40] Vatican II, *Documents*, p. 141.

[41] Vatican II, *Documents*, p. 142.

[42] Rynne, *op.cit.*, p. 130 (day by day summary) and passim. (Liturgy: Oct. 22 to Nov. 13; Sources of Revelation: Nov. 14-21; Communication media: Nov. 23, 24; Unity with Orthodox: Nov. 26-30; Church: Dec. 1-7).

[43] Rynne, *op.cit.*, pp. 188-211.

[44] Henri Fesquet, *The Drama of Vatican II*, tr. B. Murchland (New York: Random House, 1967), p. 88.

[45] McBrien, *Church: The Continuing Quest* (New York: Newman Press, 1970), pp. 31-41. (The chapter headings are abbreviated for ease of comparison).

[46] Vatican II, *Documents*, p. 22.

[47] Vatican II, *Documents*, p. 23 (Art. 8). (emphasis added).

CHAPTER EIGHT

[1] Augustin Bea, "The Academic Pursuits and Christian

Unity," *Ecumenical Dialogue at Harvard*, eds. S. Miller and G. Wright (Cambridge: Belknap Press, 1964), p. 30.

[2] Rynne, *Letters from Vatican City*, p. 248.

[3] Paul VI, *Ecclesiam Suam*, tr. N.C.W.C. (Boston: St. Paul editions, 1964).

[4] Paul VI, *Ecclesiam Suam*, p. 18f.

[5] *Ibid.*, p. 17ff.

[6] *Ibid.*, p. 40ff.

[7] Paul VI, *Ecclesiam Suam*, p. 45.

[8] *Ibid.*, p. 46.

[9] *Ibid.*, p. 46.

[10] Paul VI, *Ecclesiam Suam*, p. 46.

[11] *Ibid.*, p. 46.

[12] *Ibid.*, p. 46.

[13] *Ibid.*, p. 47.

[14] Paul VI, *Ecclesiam Suam*, p. 48.

[15] *Ibid.*, p. 15.   (emphasis added).

[16] *Ibid.*, pp. 23-25, and passim.

[17] Fesquet, *op.cit.*, p. 301f.

[18] Visser't Hooft, *Memoirs*, p. 333.

[19] Fesquet, *The Drama of Vatican II*, pp. 298ff and passim.

[20] Bonaventure Kloppenburg, *Ecclesiology of Vatican II*, tr. M. O'Connell (Chicago: Franciscan Herald Press, 1974), p. 367.

[21] McBrien, *Church: The Continuing Quest*, p. 23ff.

[22] Dulles, *Models of the Church*, p. 26.

[23] *Ibid.*, p. 27.

[24] Yves Congar, *This Church That I Love*, tr. L. Delafuente

(New Jersey: Dimension Books, 1969), p. 9.

[25] *Ibid.*, p. 27ff.

[26] Congar, *This Church That I Love*, p. 11.   Theologian
McBrien in his *Church-Continuing Quest* estimates that Congar
is the greatest Catholic ecclesiologist of this century, p.
46.

[27] Vatican II, "Lumen Gentium," *Vatican Council II*, ed. A.
Flannery (Collegeville: Liturgical Press, 1975) Art. 18, p.
370.

[28] Vatican II, "Lumen Gentium," *Vatican Council II*, ed. A.
Flannery, Art. 22, p. 374.

[29] Vatican II, "Lumen Gentium," *Vatican Council II*, ed. A.
Flannery, Art. 19, p. 370. (emphasis added).

[30] Vatican II, "Lumen Gentium," *Vatican Council II*, ed. A.
Flannery, Art. 22, p. 375.

[31] *Ibid.*, Art. 22, p. 375.

[32] *Ibid.*, Art. 22, p. 375.

[33] Dulles, *Models of the Church*, p. 26.

[34] Vatican II, "Lumen Gentium," *Vatican Council II*, ed. A.
Flannery, Art. 20, p. 371.

[35] Vatican II, "Lumen Gentium," *Vatican Council II*, ed. A.
Flannery, Art. 23, p. 376. (emphasis added).

[36] *Ibid.*, Art. 23, p. 376.

[37] *Ibid.*, Art. 23, p. 377.

[38] William A. Jurgens, *The Faith of the Early Fathers*
(Collegeville Minnesota: Liturgical Press, 1970), pp. 17-25.

[39] Vatican II, "Lumen Gentium," *Vatican Council II*, ed. A.
Flannery, Art. 23, p. 378.

[40] *Ibid.*, Art. 26, p. 381.

[41] Vatican II, "Decree on the Pastoral Office of Bishops
in the Church," *Vatican Council II*, ed. A. Flannery, Ch. III,
pp. 586-588; also Paul VI, "Ecclesiae Sanctae," *Vatican Council
II*, ed. A. Flannery, p. 609. (This latter is the post
conciliar implementation of Episcopal Conferences).

⁴²B. Kloppenburg, *Ecclesiology of Vatican II*, tr. M. O'Connell (Chicago: Franciscan Herald Press, 1974), p. 229.

⁴³Vatican II, "Lumen Gentium," *Vatican Council II*, ed. A. Flannery, Art. 22, p. 375.

⁴⁴Paul VI, *Opening Address: Third Session of Vatican II*, tr. N.C.W.S. Service (Washington, D.C., NCWC, 1964), p. 8.

⁴⁵*Ibid.*, p. 8.

⁴⁶Paul VI, *Opening Address: Third Session of Vatican II*, p. 9. (emphasis added).

⁴⁷*Ibid.*, p. 11.

⁴⁸Fesquet, *The Drama of Vatican II*, p. 301.

⁴⁹Paul VI, *Ecclesiam Suam*, p. 46. (emphasis added).

⁵⁰Fesquet, *op.cit.*, p. 301.

⁵¹*Ibid.*, p. 302.

⁵²Visser't Hooft, *Memoirs*, p. 330.

⁵³Visser't Hooft, *Memoirs*, p. 331.

⁵⁴*Ibid.*, p. 331.

⁵⁵Vatican II, "Lumen Gentium," *Vatican Council II*, ed. A. Flannery, Art. 3, p. 351.

⁵⁶Paul VI, *Opening Address: Vatican II*, p. 5.

⁵⁷Vatican II, "Lumen Gentium," *Vatican Council II*, ed. A. Flannery, p. 351.

⁵⁸Vatican II, "Lumen Gentium," *Vatican Council II*, ed. A. Flannery, Art. 19, p. 321.

⁵⁹Vatican II, "Christus Dominus," *Vatican Council II*, ed. A. Flannery, pp. 564-591.

⁶⁰Vatican II, "Lumen Gentium," *Vatican Council II*, ed. A. Flannery, Articles 18, 19, 20, pp. 369-372.

⁶¹Vatican II, "Lumen Gentium," *Vatican Council II*, ed. A. Flannery, Art. 21, p. 373f. (*in eius persona* = in his person)

⁶²Paul VI, *Seven Addresses on the Church*, tr. USCC News

Service (Washington, D.C.: United States Catholic Conference, 1967), p. 3. (Hereafter cited as *Seven Addresses*).

[63] Paul VI, *Seven Addresses*, p. 24.

[64] Lawrence Cardinal Shehan, "Introduction," *The Documents of Vatican II*, ed. W. Abbott (New York: Guild Press, 1966), p. xv.

[65] Paul VI, *Seven Addresses*, p. 22.

[66] Paul VI, *Seven Addresses*, p. 23.

[67] Vatican II, "Lumen Gentium," *Vatican Council II*, ed. A. Flannery, Articles 2, 3, 4, pp. 350-352.

[68] Paul VI, *Seven Addresses*, p. 8f.

[69] Vatican II, "Lumen Gentium," *Vatican Council II*, ed. A. Flannery, Art. 8, p. 357.

CHAPTER NINE

[1] Thomas Stransky, "Commentary," *The Decree of Ecumenism*, tr. J. Long and T. Stransky (New Jersey: Paulist Press, 1965), p. 9. This small work is especially valuable because Stransky was a staff member of Bea's Secretariat.

[2] Stransky, "Commentary," *The Decree on Ecumenism*, pp. 7-11.

[3] *Ibid.*, p. 12.

[4] *Ibid.*, p. 13.

[5] Vatican II, "Decree on Ecumenism" (*Unitatis Redintegratio*) *Vatican Council II*, ed. A. Flannery, pp. 452-470.

[6] Vatican II, "Decree on Ecumenism" (*Unitatis Redintegratio*) *Vatican Council II*, ed. A. Flannery, p. 452.

[7] *Ibid.*, p. 452.

[8] *Ibid.*, p. 452.

[9] Vatican II, *The Decree on Ecumenism*, tr. J. Long and T. Stransky, Article 2, p. 47.

[10]Vatican II, *The Decree on Ecumenism*, tr. J. Long and T. Stransky, Article 2, p. 48.

[11]*Ibid.*, p. 49.

[12]*Ibid.*, p. 49, and [12a]p. 49.

[13]Vatican II, *The Decree on Ecumenism*, tr. J. Long and T. Stransky, Article 3, p. 49f. (Emphasis added).

[14]Vatican II, *The Decree on Ecumenism*, tr. J. Long and T. Stransky, Article 3, p. 50.

[15]*Ibid.*, p. 50.

[16]*Ibid.*, p. 50.

[17]*Ibid.*, p. 51.

[18]Bernard Leeming, *The Churches and The Church* (London: Darton, Longman and Todd, 1963), p. 280.

[19]Vatican II, *The Decree on Ecumenism*, tr. J. Long and T. Stransky, Article 3, p. 51.

[20]*Ibid.*, Article 3, p. 50.

[21]Vatican II, *The Decree on Ecumenism*, tr. J. Long and T. Stransky, Article 3, p. 51.

[22]*Ibid.*, Article 3, p. 51.

[23]*Ibid.*, Article 4, pp. 52-53.

[24]Vatican II, *The Decree on Ecumenism*, tr. J. Long and T. Stransky, Article 4, p. 53.

[25]*Ibid.*, Article 4, p. 54.

[26]Vatican II, *The Decree on Ecumenism*, tr. J. Long and T. Stransky, Article 4, p. 55.

[27]*Ibid.*, Article 7, p. 60.

[28]Vatican II, *The Decree on Ecumenism*, tr. J. Long and T. Stransky, Article 6, p. 59f.

[29]John XXIII, "Toward Christian Unity" (Opening Address of Vatican II) *Letters from Vatican City*, p. 268.

[30]Henri Fesquet, *The Drama of Vatican II*, pp. 107-109.

[31] Vatican II, *The Decree on Ecumenism*, tr. J. Long and T. Stransky, Article 7, p. 61.

[32] *Ibid.*, Article 8, p. 61.

[33] Vatican II, *The Decree on Ecumenism*, tr. J. Long and T. Stransky, Article 8, p. 62.

[34] *Ibid.*, Article 8, p. 62ff, passim.

[35] Vatican II, *The Decree on Ecumenism*, tr. J. Long and T. Stransky, Article II, p. 64.

[36] Vatican II, *The Decree on Ecumenism*, tr. J. Long and T. Stransky, Articles 13-24, pp. 68-83.

[37] Bonaventure Kloppenburg, *Ecclesiology of Vatican II*, tr. M. O'Connell (Chicago: Franciscan Herald Press, 1974), p. 128f, passim.

[38] T. Stransky, "Commentary," *The Decree of Ecumenism*, p. 26f.

[39] Vatican II, *The Decree on Ecumenism*, tr. J. Long and T. Stransky, Articles 13, 14, p. 68f.

[40] T. Stransky, "Commentary," *The Decree on Ecumenism*, p. 29.

[41] Vatican II, *The Decree on Ecumenism*, tr. J. Long and T. Stransky, Article 18, p. 76.

[42] Vatican II, *The Decree on Ecumenism*, tr. J. Long and T. Stransky, Article 14, p. 70f.

[43] *Ibid.*, p. 70f.

[44] *Ibid.*, Article 15, p. 73.

[45] Vatican II, *The Decree on Ecumenism*, tr. J. Long and T. Stransky, Article 16, p. 74. This is a rare expression in the pastoral documents.

[46] *Ibid.*, p. 74.

[47] *Ibid.*, Article 17, p. 75.

[48] *Ibid.*, p. 75.

[49] Vatican II, *The Decree on Ecumenism*, tr. J. Long and T. Stransky, Article 17, p. 75.

[50]*Ibid.*, Article 19, p. 77.

[51]Vatican II, *The Decree on Ecumenism*, tr. J. Long and T. Stransky, Article 15, p. 73.

[52]*Ibid.*, Article 19, p. 78.

[53]Vatican II, *The Decree on Ecumenism*, tr. J. Long and T. Stransky, Article 20, p. 78.

[54]Vatican II, *The Decree on Ecumenism*, tr. J. Long and T. Stransky, Article 21, p. 80.

[55]*Ibid.*, Article 22, p. 80.

[56]*Ibid.*, p. 80.

[57]Vatican II, *The Decree on Ecumenism*, tr. J. Long and T. Stransky, Article 22, p. 80.

[58]Vatican II, *The Decree on Ecumenism*, tr. J. Long and T. Stransky, Article 24, p. 82.

[59]*Ibid.*, p. 83.

[60]Vatican II, *The Decree on Ecumenism*, tr. J. Long and T. Stransky, Article 13, p. 69.

[61]Edmund Schlink, *After the Council*, tr. H. Bouman (Philadelphia: Fortress Press, 1968), p. 118.

[62]*Ibid.*, p. 118.

[63]Schlink, *After the Council*, p. 119.

[64]*Ibid.*, p. 124.

[65]Visser't Hooft, *Memoirs*, p. 333.

[66]*Ibid.*, p. 335.

CHAPTER TEN

[1]Visser't Hooft, *Memoirs*, p. 334f.

[2]Secretariat for Promoting Christian Unity, *Directory for the Application of the Decisions of the Second Ecumenical Council of the Vatican Concerning Ecumenical Matters: Part 1*, United States Catholic Conference, tr. U.S.C.C., Washington,

D.C., 1967. (Hereafter cited as SPCU, *Ecumenical Directory: Part 1*).

[3] SPCU, *Ecumenical Directory: Part 1*, p. 13.

[4] *Ibid.*, p. 1f.

[5] *Ibid.*, p. 2.

[6] *Ibid.*, p. 2.

[7] SPCU, *Ecumenical Directory: Part 1*, p. 2.

[8] *Ibid.*, p. 6. The *Directory* quotes *Lumen Gentium*, Art. 15, here.

[9] SPCU, *Ecumenical Directory: Part 1*, p. 6f.

[10] *Ibid.*, p. 6f. The use of the expressions such as "matter and form" (p. 7) and "*res sacramenti*" (p. 9) remind the researcher that elements of Aquinas' *Summa Theologiae* continue in post-conciliar theology.

[11] *Ibid.*, p. 11.

[12] SPCU, *Ecumenical Directory: Part 1*, p. 18.

[13] *Ibid.*, p. 20.

[14] *Ibid.*, p. 20.

[15] *Ibid.*, p. 21.

[16] SPCU, *Notes On The Application of the Ecumenical Directory* (United States Catholic Conference, 1968), p. 2.

[17] *Ibid.*, p. 2.

[18] SPCU, *Ecumenical Directory: Part II* (Washington, D.C., National Conference of Catholic Bishops, 1970), p. 1.

[19] SPCU, *Ecumenical Directory: Part II*, p. 7.

[20] *Ibid.*, p. 8.

[21] *Ibid.*, p. 8.

[22] Thomas Stransky, "Commentary," *The Decree on Ecumenism*, p. 39.

[23]SPCU, "Declaration on the Position of the Catholic
Church on the Celebration of the Eucharist in Common by
Christians of Different Confessions," *Vatican Council II:
The Conciliar and Post Conciliar Documents*, ed. A. Flannery
(Minnesota: The Liturgical Press, 1975), p. 502.   (Hereafter
cited as *Declaration on Shared Eucharist*).

[24]*Ibid.*

[25]SPCU, *Declaration on Shared Eucharist*, p. 503.

[26]*Ibid.*, p. 505.

[27]*Ibid.*, p. 504.   (emphasis added).

[28]SPCU, *Declaration on Shared Eucharist*, p. 505.

[29]*Ibid.*, p. 506.

[30]*Ibid.*

[31]SPCU, *Reflections and Suggestions Concerning Ecumenical
Dialogue* (USCC, Washington, D.C.:   National Council of
Catholic Bishops, 1970), p. 1.   (Hereafter referred to as
Dialogue Guide).

[32]SPCU, *Dialogue Guide*, p. 7.

[33]*Ibid.*, p. 10.

[34]SPCU, *Dialogue Guide*, p. 12.

[35]*Ibid.*, p. 12.

[36]SPCU, *Dialogue Guide*, p. 18.

[37]SPCU, "On Admitting Other Christians to Eucharistic
Communion in the Catholic Church," *Vatical Council II: The
Conciliar and Post-Conciliar Documents*, ed. A. Flannery
(Minnesota: The Liturgical Press, 1975), p. 554.   (Hereafter
cited as *Instruction: On Admitting to Communion*).

[38]Yves Congar, "Do the New Problems of our Secular World
make Ecumenism Irrelevant?" *Post-Ecumenical Christianity*, ed.
H. Kung (New York: Herder and Herder, 1970), p. 20.   Congar
sees the Eucharist as an act of the Church, not merely as an
act of a person.

[39]SPCU, *op.cit.*, pp. 554, 555, 556, 557, 558,
respectively.

[40] SPCU, *Instruction: On Admitting to Communion*, p. 554f. (emphasis added).

[41] *Ibid.*, p. 555.

[42] SPCU, *Instruction: On Admitting to Communion*, p. 555.

[43] SPCU, Note Interpreting the "Instruction on Admitting Other Christians to Eucharistic Communion in the Catholic Church under Certain Circumstances," *Vatican Council II: The Conciliar and Post Conciliar Documents*, ed. A. Flannery (Minnesota: The Liturgical Press, 1975), p. 560. (Hereafter cited as the *1973 Note on the Instruction About Intercommunion*).

[44] SPCU, *1973 Note on Admitting to Communion*, p. 560.

[45] SPCU, *1973 Note on Admitting to Communion*, p. 558.

[46] SPCU, *1973 Note on Instruction About Intercommunion*, p. 560.

[47] SPCU, *1973 Note on Instruction About Intercommunion*, p. 563.

[48] Pope Paul VI, "An Ecumenical Meeting between the Churches of Rome and Constantinople," *The Teachings of Pope Paul VI: 1975* (citta Del Vaticano: Libreria Editrice Vaticana, 1976), p. 446.

[49] Pope Paul VI, *The Teachings of Pope Paul VI: 1975*, p. 447.

[50] *Ibid.*, p. 446.

[51] Pope Paul VI, "For the Unity of All Christians," *The Teachings of Pope Paul VI*, Washington, D.C. (Libreria Editrice Vaticana, 1975), p. 200.

[52] Pope Paul VI, "For the Unity of All Christians," *The Teachings of Pope Paul VI*, p. 200.

[53] *Ibid.*, p. 201.

[54] *Ibid.*, p. 201f.

[55] Pope Paul VI, "For the Unity of All Christians," *The Teachings of Pope Paul VI*, p. 203.

[56] *Ibid.*, p. 204.

[57] Pope Paul VI, "Who Belongs to the Church?" *The Pope*

Speaks, tr. A. Vaughn (Indiana: Our Sunday Visitor Press, 1966), p. 372.

[58] *Ibid.*, p. 372.

[59] *Ibid.*, p. 373.

[60] Pope Paul VI, *The Pope Speaks*, p. 373.

[61] *Ibid.*, p. 373.

[62] I Corinthians 12: 20f.

[63] Pope Paul VI, "Church's Contribution to Development of the Ecumenical Movement," *The Teachings of Pope Paul VI* (Washington, D.C.:   Libreria Editrice Vaticana/USCC, 1975), pp. 11-14.

[64] Pope Paul VI, "Church's Contribution to Development of the Ecumenical Movement," *The Teachings of Pope Paul VI*, p. 15.

[65] SPCU, *Ecumenical Collaboration at the Regional, National and Local Levels* (Washington, D.C.:   National Conference of Catholic Bishops, 1975).   (Hereafter referred to as *Ecumenical Collaboration*).

[66] SPCU, *Ecumenical Collaboration*, p. 2.

[67] *Ibid.*, passim.

[68] SPCU, *Ecumenical Collaboration*, p. 5.

[69] *Ibid.*, p. 6.

[70] Vatican II, "Constitution on the Church," *Vatican Council II*, ed. A. Flannery, p. 376.

[71] SPCU, *Ecumenical Collaboration*, p. 7.

[72] SPCU, *Ecumenical Collaboration*, p. 7.

[73] *Ibid.*, p. 8.

[74] *Ibid.*

[75] SPCU, *Ecumenical Collaboration*, p. 9.

[76] *Ibid.*, p. 9.

[77] *Ibid.*, pp. 8-11.   (emphasis added).

[78]SPCU, *Ecumenical Collaboration*, p. 13. (emphasis added).

[79]*Ibid.*, p. 18.

[80]*Ibid.*

[81]SPCU, *Ecumenical Collaboration*, p. 18.

[82]*Ibid.*, p. 19. In German, Vatican II is *Konzil*, the World Council is *Rat*. In French Vatican II is *Concile*, the World Council is *Counseil*.

[83]*Ibid.*, p. 19. (This expression of Roman presidency comes from Ignatius of Antioch, who was martyred about 110 AD).

[84]SPCU, *Ecumenical Collaboration*, p. 19.

[85]SPCU, *Ecumenical Collaboration*, p. 20.

[86]This question confronts the World Council, probably because its appearance seems more ecclesial than its constitution. The Toronto Statement addresses this question. WCC, *Toronto Statement*, New York, 1950.

[87]SPCU, *Ecumenical Collaboration*, p. 20.

[88]*Ibid.*, pp. 20-21.

[89]SPCU, *Ecumenical Collaboration*, p. 22; the countries are Denmark, Sweden, the Netherlands, Swaziland, Belize (British Honduras), Samoa, Fiji, New Hebrides, Solomon Islands, Papua-New Guinea, Tonga, West Germany, Botswana, St. Vincent (British Antilles), Sudan, Uganda, Finland, Guyana, Trinidad and Tobago.

[90]*Ibid.*, p. 15.

[91]SPCU, *Ecumenical Collaboration*, p. 22.

[92]*Ibid.*, p. 22f.

[93]*Ibid.*, p. 25, quoting the *Dogmatic Constitution on the Church*, Article 8.

[94]Marcel Lefebvre, "French Prelate Celebrates Latin Mass in Texas," *New York Times*, July 11, 1977, p. 14.

[95]Kenneth Baker, "Editorial," *Homiletic and Pastoral Review*, LXXVI, 11, 1976, p. 96.

[96]James Hitchcock, *The Decline and Fall of Radical Catholicism* (New York: Doubleday, 1972), passim.

[97]Kenneth Briggs, "Some Scholars Believe Vatican III a Necessity, *New York Times*, June 5, 1977, Week in Review, p. 18.

[98]George Kelly, *Who Should Run the Catholic Church?* (Indiana: Our Sunday Visitor, 1975), passim.

[99]SPCU, *Ecumenical Collaboration*, p. 23.

[100]*Ibid.*, p. 21.

[101]SPCU, *Ecumenical Collaboration*, p. 24.

[102]SPCU, *Ecumenical Collaboration*, p. 25.

[103]*Ibid.*, p. 26.

[104]*Ibid.*, p. 27.

[105]*Ibid.*, p. 28.

[106]SPCU, *Ecumenical Collaboration*, p. 28.

[107]*Ibid.*, p. 27.

[108]*Ibid.*, p. 28.

CHAPTER ELEVEN

[1]World Council of Churches, *The First Assembly of the World Council of Churches*, ed. W. Visser't Hooft (New York: Harper and Brothers, 1949), p. 28f.   (emphasis in text). Hereafter cited as *Amsterdam 1948*.

[2]WCC, *Amsterdam 1948*, pp. 195-201.

[3]WCC, *Amsterdam 1948*, p. 197.

[4]*Ibid.*, p. 197.

[5]*Ibid.*, p. 197f.

[6]Bernard Leeming, *The Churches and the Church* (Maryland: Newman Press, 1960), p. 10.

[7] WCC, *Amsterdam 1948*, p. 127.

[8] Central Committee (WCC), *The Church, The Churches and The World Council of Churches*, WCC, New York, 1950. Hereafter cited as the *Toronto Statement*.

[9] *Ibid.*, p. 3, quoting *Amsterdam 1948*, p. 127.

[10] Central Committee (WCC), *Toronto Statement*, p. 5.

[11] *Ibid.*, p. 5.

[12] *Ibid.*, p. 5.

[13] *Ibid.*, p. 6.

[14] Central Committee (WCC), *Toronto Statement*, p. 7. A distinguished professor of ecumenism who worked at World Council headquarters in Geneva affirmed in unpublished lectures that Anglican-structured ecclesiology (episcopal continuity) dominated the Council until Amsterdam, after which free-church ecclesiology (the gathering is the church) prevailed.

[15] Central Committee (WCC), *Toronto Statement*, p. 7.

[16] *Ibid.*, p. 8.

[17] *Ibid.*, p. 8.

[18] *Ibid.*, p. 8.

[19] Central Committee (WCC), *Toronto Statement*, p. 8.

[20] *Ibid.*, p. 8.

[21] *Ibid.*, p. 9.

[22] Central Committee (WCC), *Toronto Statement*, p. 10.

[23] WCC, *Amsterdam 1948*, p. 197.

[24] Central Committee (WCC), *Toronto Statement*, p. 10f.

[25] Central Committee (WCC), *Toronto Statement*, p. 11f. *Extra muros* means 'outside the walls,' *aliquo modo* means 'in some way,' and *ecclesia extra ecclesiam* means a church outside the Church.

[26] Vatican II, "Dogmatic Constitution on the Church, *Vatican Council II*, ed. A. Flannery (Minnesota: Liturgical

Press, 1975), Art. 8, p. 357.

[27] SPCU, *Ecumenical Collaboration*, p. 17.

[28] Pope Paul VI, "Who Belongs to the Church?" *The Pope Speaks*, tr. A. Vaughn, 1966, p. 372.

[29] Roman Catholic Church, "Rite of Reception of Baptized Christians into Full Communion with the Catholic Church," *The Roman Ritual*, U.S. Catholic Conference, tr. International Commission on English in the Liturgy, Washington, D.C., 1976.

[30] *Ibid.*, p. 1.

[31] Roman Catholic Church, "Rite of Reception...Catholic Church," *Roman Ritual*, p. 1.

[32] Central Committee (WCC), *Toronto Statement*, p. 12.

[33] Central Committee (WCC), *Toronto Statement*, p. 13. (emphasis added).

[34] Central Committee (WCC), *Toronto Statement*, p. 13.

[35] *Ibid.*, p. 13.

[36] *Ibid.*, p. 14.

[37] *Ibid.*, p. 15.

[38] *Ibid.*, p. 14.

[39] Central Committee, (WCC), *Toronto Statement*, p. 13.

[40] *Ibid.*, p. 14.

[41] Central Committee, (WCC), *Toronto Statement*, p. 14.

[42] *Ibid.*, p. 16.

[43] *Ibid.*, p. 16.

[44] *Ibid.*, p. 7 and passim.

[45] Central Committee, (WCC), *Toronto Statement*, p. 7.

[46] W. Visser't Hooft, *Memoirs* (Philadelphia: Westminster Press, 1973), p. 217.

[47] *Ibid.*, p. 218.

[48] Central Committee, (WCC), *Toronto Statement*, p. 8.

[49] *Ibid.*, p. 12.

[50] Visser't Hooft, *Memoirs*, p. 255.

[51] WCC, *The Third World Conference on Faith and Order*, ed. O.S. Tomkins (London: SCM Press Ltd., 1953), p. 357 and passim. Hereafter cited as *Lund*.

[52] WCC, *Lund*, p. 348.

[53] O.S. Tomkins, "Implications of the Ecumenical Movement," *Lund*, p. 163.

[54] *Ibid.*, p. 164.

[55] *Ibid.*, p. 166f.

[56] Tomkins, "Implications of the Ecumenical Movement," *Lund*, p. 167.

[57] *Ibid.*, p. 167.

[58] Tomkins, "Implications of the Ecumenical Movement," *Lund*, p. 168. Tomkins was quoting or paraphrasing the Archbishop of Canterbury.

[59] *Ibid.*, p. 169.

[60] *Ibid.*, p. 170f.

[61] Tomkins, "Implications of the Ecumenical Movement," *Lund*, p. 172.

[62] *Ibid.*, p. 173.

[63] Visser't Hooft, "Faith and Order and the Second Assembly of the World Council of Churches," *Lund*, p. 134.

[64] *Ibid.*, p. 135.

[65] *Ibid.*, p. 133.

[66] Visser't Hooft, "Faith and Order and the Second Assembly of World Council of Churches," *Lund*, p. 134.

[67] *Ibid.*, p. 134.

[68] *Ibid.*, p. 135.

[69]*Ibid.*, p. 137.

[70]Faith and Order Conference, Plenary Session, *Lund*, p. 305.

[71]WCC, "The Constitution of the Faith and Order Commission," *Lund*, pp. 359-365.

[72]*Ibid.*, p. 55. (emphasis added).

[73]WCC, *Lund*, pp. 11, 64.

[74]*Ibid.*, p. 297.

[75]The international ecumenical journal *Lumen Vitae* uses this staccato, propositional paraphrasing as a way of covering extensive material quickly.

[76]WCC, *Lund*, p. 11; a later passage characterizes the nature of the Christ/Church/Holy Spirit relationship as primary and decisive for Christian unity, p. 22.

[77]*Ibid.*, p. 15.

[78]*Ibid.*, p. 15.

[79]*Ibid.*, p. 15.

[80]*Ibid.*, p. 15.

[81]*Ibid.*, p. 18.

[82]*Ibid.*, p. 21.

[83]WCC, *Lund*, p. 24.

[84]*Ibid.*, p. 25.

[85]*Ibid.*, p. 25f.

[86]*Ibid.*, p. 26.

[87]*Ibid.*, p. 26.

[88]WCC, *Lund*, p. 33f. Calvin's two churches: *one,* of the predestined righteous alone, known only to God, and *the other,* the visible Church composed of both the elect and the damned, was objected to by Bellarmine who maintained 'there is only one church, not two.' J. Hamer, *The Church is a Communion,* tr. R. Matthews (New York: Sheed and Ward, 1964), p. 83.

[89]*Ibid.*, p. 37.

[90]*Ibid.*, p. 38.

[91]*Ibid.*, p. 39.

[92]*Ibid.*, pp. 39-43.

[93]WCC, *Lund*, p. 49. (In the assembly discussion, Anglicans and Lutherans also strongly opposed intercommunion as reducing profound theological differences to insignificance; it was not a way forward, pp. 281-285).

[94]*Ibid.*, p. 49.

[95]*Ibid.*, p. 54.

[96]*Ibid.*, p. 58.

[97]*Ibid.*, p. 57.

[98]*Ibid.*, p. 58.

[99]WCC, *Lund*, p. 60.

[100]*Ibid.*, p. 60.

[101]*Ibid.*, p. 60.

[102]*Ibid.*, p. 61.

[103]*Ibid.*, p. 64.

[104]*Ibid.*, p. 64f.

[105]*Ibid.*, pp. 33, 37, 54.

[106]WCC, *Lund*, p. 60.

[107]Meredith B. Handspicker, "Faith and Order," *A History of the Ecumenical Movement*, II, ed. H.E. Fey (Philadelphia: Westminster Press, 1970), p. 147f. (Hereafter cited as *H.E.M., II*).

[108]WCC, *Lund*, p. 23.

[109]Ibid., p. 17.

[110]WCC, *Lund*, p. 18.

[111]*Ibid.*, p. 57.

[112] J.C. Hoekendijk, *The Church Inside Out* (Philadelphia: Westminster Press, 1966), pp. 39-43.

[113] W.A. Visser't Hooft, "The Super-Church and the Ecumenical Movement," Reprint from *Ecumenical Review* (Vol. X, No. 4, July, 1958).

CHAPTER TWELVE

[1] H. Kreuger, "The Life and Activities of the World Council of Churches," *H.E.M.*, II, ed. H. Fey (Philadelphia: Westminster Press, 1970), p. 39.

[2] WCC, *Evanston Speaks: Reports of the Second Assembly of the World Council of Churches.* Switzerland, 1955, p. 8. (Hereafter cited as *Evanston Speaks*). (emphasis added).

[3] *Ibid.*, passim.

[4] H. Kreuger, "The Life and Activities of the World Council of Churches," *H.E.M.*, II, p. 40.

[5] WCC, *Evanston Speaks*, p. 16.

[6] *Ibid.*, p. 17.

[7] P. Abrecht, "The Development of Ecumenical Social Thought and Action," *H.E.M.*, II, p. 244.

[8] M. Boegner, *The Long Road to Unity*, tr. R. Hague, (London: Collins, 1970), p. 234.

[9] WCC, *Evanston Speaks*, p. 13.

[10] *Ibid.*, p. 10.

[11] WCC, *Evanston Speaks*, p. 10.

[12] *Ibid.*, p. 11.

[13] *Ibid.*, p. 12.

[14] *Ibid.*, p. 10.

[15] *Ibid.*, p. 11.

[16] *Ibid.*, p. 11.

[17] WCC, *Evanston Speaks*, p. 17.

[18]WCC, *New Directions in Faith and Order*, ed. Lukas Vischer (Geneva: WCC, 1968), p. 164.

[19]WCC, *Evanston Speaks*, pp. 15-17.

[20]*Ibid.*, p. 14.

[21]*Ibid.*, p. 13.

[22]Marc Boegner, *The Long Road to Unity*, tr. R. Hague (London: Collins, 1970), p. 233.

[23]W.A. Visser't Hooft, "The General Ecumenical Development Since 1948," *H.E.M.*, II, Ed. H.E. Fey, p. 34.

[24]WCC, *Lund*, p. 106.

[25]*Ibid.*, p. 75f.

[26]Leonard Hodgson, "The Task of the Third World Conference on Faith and Order," *Lund*, p. 112.

[27]*Ibid.*, p. 119.

[28]W.A. Visser't Hooft, "The Super-Church and the Ecumenical Movement," *The Ecumenical Review*, X: 4, July 1958. The article will be cited as "Superchurch?", *E.R.*, reprint and page.

[29]*Ibid.*, p. 12.

[30]*Ibid.*, p. 13.

[31]Visser't Hooft, "Superchurch?", *E.R.* reprint, p. 3.

[32]*Ibid.*, pp. 7-10.

[33]*Ibid.*, p. 4.

[34]*Ibid.*, p. 9.

[35]Visser't Hooft, "Superchurch?", *E.R.* reprint, pp. 13-17.

[36]*Ibid.*, p. 14.

[37]Visser't Hooft, "Superchurch?", *E.R.* reprint, p. 14.

[38]Visser't Hooft, "Superchurch?", *E.R.* reprint, p. 23.

[39]*Ibid.*, p. 21.

[40]*Ibid.*, p. 22.

[41]Central Committee, *Evanston to New Delhi*, ed. Visser't
Hooft (Geneva: World Council of Churches, 1961).   (Hereafter
cited as CC, *Evanston to N.D.* and page number).

[42]Franklin C. Fry, "Forward," *Evanston to N.D.*, p. 4.

[43]*Ibid.*, p. 5.

[44]Visser't Hooft, "Epilogue," *Evanston to N.D.*, p. 189.

[45]*Ibid.*, p. 190.   (emphasis added).

[46]Visser't Hooft, "Epilogue," *Evanston to N.D.*, p. 190.

[47]*Ibid.*, p. 190.

[48]*Ibid.*, p. 190f.

[49]Visser't Hooft, "Epilogue," *Evanston to N.D.*, p. 191.

[50]Visser't Hooft, "Epilogue," *Evanston to N.D.*, p. 191.

[51]*Ibid.*, p. 191.

[52]Visser't Hooft, "Epilogue," *Evanston to N.D.*, p. 192.

[53]CC, *Evanston to New Delhi*, p. 193ff.

[54]CC, *Evanston to New Delhi*, p. 19 and the prepared
consultations referred to.

[55]*Ibid.*, p. 214ff.

[56]CC, *Evanston to N.D.*, p. 37.

[57]*Ibid.*, p. 42.

[58]*Ibid.*, p. 42.

[59]CC, *Evanston to N.D.*, p. 43.

[60]Visser't Hooft, "The Ground of Our Unity," *The Nature
of the Unity We Seek*, ed. P. Minear (St. Louis: The Bethany
Press, 1957), p. 123.

[61]CC, *Evanston to N.D.*, p. 43.

[62]*Ibid.*, p. 43.

[63]*Ibid.*, p. 43.

                          CHAPTER THIRTEEN

[1]WCC, *The New Delhi Report*, ed. W.A. Visser't Hooft (New York: Association Press, 1962), p. 116.

[2]Faith and Order, "Christian Unity as Viewed by the Eastern Orthodox Church," *The Nature of the Unity We Seek*, ed. P. Minear (St. Louis: Bethany Press, 1958), pp. 158-163. This 'F&O Conference' Official Report contains a succinct, representative statement of the Eastern Orthodox position with reference to the modern ecumenical movement. "F&O' at Oberlin published the Orthodox position more fully than either Evanston or New Delhi. Briefly the Orthodox Church is the Una Sancta (p. 160); others must return to her (p. 161); unity and church are impossible without visible apostolic succession (p. 162); "communion presupposes unity. Therefore, the term inter-communion seems to us an epitome of that conception which we are compelled to reject" (p. 163).

[3]WCC, *The New Delhi Report*, p. 333.

[4]WCC, *The New Delhi Report*, p. 333.

[5]*Ibid.*, p. 135.

[6]*Ibid.*, pp. 116-135.

[7]*Ibid.*, p. 117.

[8]*Ibid.*, p. 117.

[9]WCC, *The New Delhi Report*, p. 117.

[10]*Ibid.*, p. 117.

[11]*Ibid.*

[12]R.P. Barnes, "Introduction," *New Delhi Speaks*, ed. W. Visser't Hooft (New York: Association Press, 1962), p. 9.

[13]WCC, *The New Delhi Report*, p. 124.

[14]*Ibid.*, p. 124f.

[15]WCC, *The New Delhi Report*, p. 125.

[16]*Ibid.*, p. 131.

[17]*Ibid.*, p. 125.

[18]WCC Commission on Faith and Order, *The Old and the New in the Church*, ed. K. Bridston (Minneapolis: Augsburg Publishing House, 1961), p. 90.

[19]WCC, *The New Delhi Report*, p. 125f.

[20]*Ibid.*, p. 126.

[21]WCC, *The New Delhi Report*, p. 126.

[22]*Ibid.*, p. 126f.

[23]*Ibid.*, p. 126.

[24]*Ibid.*, p. 127. The document has "*community* preceding *teaching*" until it mentions scripture with a primacy over all; thus, does teaching precede community?

[25]WCC, *The New Delhi Report*, p. 127.

[26]*Ibid.*, p. 127, passim.

[27]*Ibid.*, p. 127.

[28]WCC, *The New Delhi Report*, p. 129.

[29]*Ibid.*, p. 129.

[30]*Ibid.*, p. 130.

[31]*Ibid.*, p. 130f.

[32]WCC, *The New Delhi Report*, p. 131.

[33]*Ibid.*, p. 132.

[34]*Ibid.*, p. 132.

[35]*The Classic Greek Dictionary* (New York: Follett Publishing Company, 1958).

[36]WCC, *The New Delhi Report*, p. 132.

[37]*Ibid.*

[38]The proposition declares that the WCC does God's Will for the whole Church; this presumably included non-member churches, such as some Orthodox churches and the Roman Catholic Church.

[39]WCC, *The New Delhi Report*, p. 132.

[40]*Ibid.*, p. 133. The pertinent paragraphs imply the 'part/ whole' relationships to the denomination and the 'Una Sancta' toward which its departing member is going.

[41]*Ibid.*, p. 133.

[42]WCC, *The New Delhi Report*, p. 133.

[43]Visser't Hooft, *Memoirs*, pp. 309-318.

[44]*Ibid.*, p. 310.

[45]Visser't Hooft, *Memoirs*, p. 310.

[46]WCC, *The New Delhi Report*, p. 4.

[47]*Ibid.*, p. 7.

[48]Visser't Hooft, *Memoirs*, p. 311.

[49]WCC, *The New Delhi Report*, pp. 152-159, passim.

[50]*Ibid.*, p. 159.

[51]WCC, "The Constitution of the World Council of Churches," *The New Delhi Report*, p. 197.

[52]WCC, *The New Delhi Report*, p. 157.

[53]*Ibid.*, p. 147.

[54]WCC, *The New Delhi Report*, p. 393.

[55]Visser't Hooft, *Memoirs*, p. 392.

[56]WCC, "The Calling of the World Council of Churches," *The New Delhi Report*, p. 6.

[57]Visser't Hooft, *Memoirs*, p. 309.

[58]WCC, *The New Delhi Report*, p. 173.

[59]Visser't Hooft, *Memoirs*, p. 318.

CHAPTER FOURTEEN

[1]John XXIII, "Announcement of Ecumenical Council," *The

Encyclicals and Other Messages of John XXIII, ed. by the staff
of the Pope Speaks (TPS) Magazine (Washington, D.C.:   TPS
Press, 1964), p. 23.   Hereafter cited as the *Teaching of John
XXIII*.

[2] John XXIII, *Teaching of John XXIII*, p. 454.   This volume
contains no index reference to the very young WCC in the
writings or messages of Pope John.

[3] WCC "Report of the Central Committee," *Uppsala 68*, ed.
N. Goodall (Geneva: WCC, 1968), p. 279f.

[4] WCC, "Report of the Central Committee," *Uppsala 68*, p.
283f.

[5] *Ibid.*, p. 458.

[6] E.C. Blake, "Report of the General Secretary," *Uppsala
68*.

[7] *Ibid.*, p. 385.

[8] E.C. Blake, "Report of the General Secretary," *Uppsala
68*, p. 286.

[9] *Ibid.*, pp. 385-393.

[10] *Ibid.*, pp. 286-293, passim.

[11] Blake, "Uppsala and Afterwards," *H.E.M.*, II, p. 413.

[12] Blake, "Uppsala and Afterwards," *H.E.M.*, II, p. 417.

[13] *Ibid.*, p. 445.

[14] *Ibid.*, p. 417.

[15] WCC, "Report of Policy Reference Committee II,"
Uppsala 68, p. 190, emphasis added.

[16] WCC, *Uppsala 68*, p. V.   The parentheses indicate the
origin and character of the sections.

[17] WCC, *Toronto Statement*, p. 11.

[18] D.L. Edwards, "Personal Comment on the Work of the
Section on Worship," *Uppsala 68*, p. 83.

[19] D.L. Edwards, "Personal Comment on the Work of the
Section on Worship," *Uppsala 68*, p. 85.

[20]WCC, "Section I," *Uppsala 68*, p. 7.

[21]WCC, "Section I," *Uppsala 68*, p. 7f.

[22]*Ibid.*, pp. 12f.

[23]WCC, "Section I," *Uppsala 68*, pp. 15f.

[24]*Ibid.*, p. 16.

[25]*Ibid.*, p. 17. (emphasis added).

[26]WCC, "Section I," *Uppsala 68*, p. 17. (emphasis added).

[27]*Ibid.*, p. 17f.

[28]*Ibid.*, pp. 19f.

[29]John Weller, "Personal Comment on the Work of Section I," *Uppsala 68*, p. 19. (Weller, associated with the British Council of Churches and Bible Societies, is an English Congregationalist clergyman.)

[30]WCC, "Section I," *Uppsala 68*, pp. 15-17.

[31]WCC, "Section I," *Uppsala 68*, pp. 15-17.

[32]*Ibid.*, pp. 18f.

[33]*Ibid.*, p. 18.

[34]*Ibid.*, p. 13.

[35]WCC, "Section I," *Uppsala 68*, p. 17. (emphasis added).

[36]Visser't Hooft, *Has the Ecumenical Movement a Future?* (Atlanta: John Knox Press, 1974), p. 47.

[37]WCC, "Section I," *Uppsala 68*, p. 17.

[38]WCC, *Uppsala 68*, p. 17.

[39]WCC, "Report of the Assembly Committee on Faith and Order," *Uppsala 68*, p. 225.

[40]E.C. Blake, "Uppsala and Afterwards," *H.E.M.*, II, p. 423.

[41]Blake, *H.E.M.* II, p. 423. Blake seems to forget that his familial predecessors were Catholics for the eleven ecumenical councils (between 870 and 1545) which he so easily

discards.

[42]W. Visser't Hooft, "The Mandate of the Ecumenical
Movement," *Uppsala 68*, p. 321.

[43]*Ibid.*, p. 316f.

[44]Visser't Hooft, "The Mandate of the Ecumenical Movement," *Uppsala 68*, p. 319.

[45]*Ibid.*, p. 321.

[46]*Ibid.*, p. 322.

[47]Visser't Hooft, "The Mandate of the Ecumenical Movement," *Uppsala 68*, p. 321.

[48]*Ibid.*, p. 321.

[49]WCC, "Report of the Assembly Committee on Faith and
Order," *Uppsala 68*, p. 223.

[50]*Ibid.*, p. 223f.

[51]SPCU, "Uppsala 1968," *Information Service*, No. 6, Rome,
Jan. 1969, pp. 7, 84.

[52]WCC, "Commission on Faith and Order," *Uppsala 68*, pp.
137, 147, 461ff.

[53]WCC, "Statement Concerning Relations with the Roman
Catholic Church," *Uppsala 68*, pp. 177-180.

[54]*Ibid.*, pp. 177f. (emphasis added).

[55]WCC, "Statement Concerning Relations with the Roman
Catholic Church," *Uppsala 68*, p. 178f. The work 'communion'
translates the Greek Koinonia, better than the word, fellowship. (emphasis added).

[56]E.C. Blake, "Uppsala and Afterwards," *H.E.M.*, II, p.
442.

[57]Lukas Vischer, "The Ecumenical Movement and the Roman
Catholic Church," *H.E.M.*, II, p. 338.

[58]E.C. Blake, "Uppsala and Afterwards," *H.E.M.*, II, p.
432. (emphasis added).

[59]Roberto Tucci, "The Ecumenical Movement, the World
Council of Churches and the Roman Catholic Church," *Uppsala 68*,

pp. 323-333.

[60]*Ibid.*, p. 323.

[61]*Ibid.*, p. 329.

[62]*Ibid.*, p. 329.

[63]R. Tucci, *op.cit.*, p. 329. Norman Goodall, *Ecumenical Progress: 1961-1971* perceives pros and cons of RCC Membership similar to those expressed by Tucci, p. 130.

[64]Marc Boegner, *The Long Road to Unity* (London: Collins, 1970), p. 378.

[65]*Ibid.*, p. 378. Visser't Hooft felt that 'working groups,' not membership, was the first approach. *Memoirs*, p. 332.

[66]Tucci, "The Ecumenical Movement, The World Council of Churches and the Roman Catholic Church," *Uppsala 68*, p. 324.

[67]*Ibid.*, p. 325.

[68]*Ibid.*, p. 328.

[69]*Ibid.*, p. 329.

[70]*Ibid.*, p. 325.

[71]Tucci, "The Ecumenical Movement, The World Council of Churches and the Roman Catholic Church," *Uppsala 68*, pp. 325-327, passim.

[72]Norman Goodall, "Editorial," *Uppsala 68*, p. xvi.

[73]*Ibid.*, p. xvii.

[74]Visser't Hooft, *Memoirs*, p. 356.

[75]Visser't Hooft, *Memoirs*, p. 354.

[76]*Ibid.*, p. 366.

[77]Visser't Hooft, *Memoirs*, p. 367.

[78]WCC, *Breaking Barriers: Nairobi 1975*, ed. David Paton (London: SPCK, 1975), passim. (This source will be cited hereafter as *Nairobi 75*).

[79]James B. Simpson and Edward M. Storey, *The Long Shadows*

of Lambeth X (New York: McGraw-Hill, 1969), p. 208. (emphasis added).

[80] WCC, *Central Committee, Twenty-Third Meeting - Canterbury*, ed. E.C. Blake (Geneva: WCC, 1969), p. 184 and footnote. (Hereafter cited as *CC/Canterbury*).

[81] *Ibid.*, p. 40f.

[82] Lukas Vischer, "A Genuinely Universal Council...?" *CC/Canterbury*, p. 183.

[83] Tucci, "The Ecumenical Movement, The World Council of Churches and the Roman Catholic Church," *Uppsala 68*, p. 329.

[84] Vischer, "A Genuinely Universal Council...?", *CC/Canterbury*, p. 182.

[85] Vischer, "A Genuinely Universal Council...?", *CC/Canterbury*, p. 182f. (emphasis added).

[86] *Ibid.*, p. 184.

[87] *Ibid.*, pp. 184-186.

[88] Vischer, "A Genuinely Universal Council...?", *CC/Canterbury*, p. 183.

[89] WCC, *CC/Canterbury*, p. 40f.

[90] *Ibid.*, p. 41.

[91] Lukas Vischer, "The Church - One People in Many Places," *What Unity Implies* (six essays after Uppsala), ed. R. Groscurth (Geneva: WCC, 1969), p. 72.

[92] *Ibid.*, p. 100.

[93] *Ibid.*, p. 100.

[94] Vischer, "The Church - One People in Many Places," *What Unity Implies*, p. 92.

[95] *Ibid.*, p. 83.

[96] *Ibid.*, p. 99.

[97] *Ibid.*, p. 95.

[98] Vischer, "The Church - One People in Many Places," *What Unity Implies*, pp. 77f, 98f, and passim.

[99] *Ibid.*, p. 95. (emphasis added). *Lumen Gentium*, Ch. 3, Art. 23, sustains Vischer's 'Peter, Roman Pontiff, primacy, jurisdiction' point.

[100] *Ibid.*, p. 98.

[101] Vischer, "The Church - One People in Many Places," *What Unity Implies*, p. 98f.

[102] Norman Goodall, *Ecumenical Progress (1961-71)* (London: Oxford University Press, 1972), p. 130f.

[103] *Ibid.*, p. 130.

[104] Goodall, *Ecumenical Progress*, p. 77f.

[105] *Ibid.*, p. 78.

[106] Goodall, *Ecumenical Progress*, p. 78.

[107] *Ibid.*, pp. 72ff.

[108] *Ibid.*, p. 46.

[109] *Ibid.*, p. 50.

[110] Goodall, *Ecumenical Progress*, p. 50.

[111] *Ibid.*, p. 9.

[112] Paul VI, "To World Council of Churches," *Pope Paul VI in Geneva* (Washington, D.C.: U.S. Catholic Conference, 1969), pp. 22f.

[113] Paul VI, "To World Council of Churches," *Pope Paul VI in Geneva*, p. 21.

[114] *Ibid.*, p. 20.

[115] *Ibid.*, p. 21. (emphasis added).

[116] Paul VI, "To World Council of Churches," *Pope Paul VI in Geneva*, p. 21.

[117] Visser't Hooft, *Memoirs*, p. 338f.

[118] Commission on Faith and Order, "Conciliarity and the Future of the Ecumenical Movement," *The Ecumenical Review*, Vol. XXIV No. 1, Jan. 1972, pp. 88f.

[119] Willem A. Visser't Hooft, *Has the Ecumenical Movement*

a *Future?* (Atlanta: John Knox Press, 1974), pp. 76-97, passim.

[120]*Ibid.*, pp. 25-28.

[121]Visser't Hooft, *Has the Ecumenical Movement a Future?* p. 46.

[122]*Ibid.*, pp. 45f.

[123]Oliver Bristol, "Foreword," *Has the Ecumenical Movement a Future?* p. 8.

[124]Visser't Hooft, *Memoirs*, p. 363.

[125]Visser't Hooft, *Has the Ecumenical Movement a Future?* p. 96.

[126]*Ibid.*, p. 96f.   [127]*Ibid.*, p. 96f.

CHAPTER FIFTEEN

[1]WCC, *Breaking Barriers: Nairobi 1975*, ed. David Paton (London: SPCK, 1976), p. v. Hereafter referred to as *Nairobi 75* in parallel with *Uppsala 68*.

[2]WCC, "What Unity Requires," *Nairobi 75*, pp. 59-61.

[3]WCC, "What Unity Requires," *Nairobi 75*, pp. 59, 61, 64.

[4]*Ibid.*, p. 59f.

[5]WCC, "What Unity Requires," *Nairobi 75*, p. 60. (emphasis added).

[6]WCC, "What Unity Requires," *Nairobi 75*, p. 60.

[7]SPCU, *Ecumenical Collaboration* (Washington, D.C.: National Conference of Catholic Bishops, 1975), p. 20.

[8]WCC, "What Unity Requires," *Nairobi 75*, p. 60. (emphasis added).

[9]WCC, "What Unity Requires," *Nairobi 75*, p. 60.

[10]Demetrios Constantelos, *The Greek Orthodox Church* (New York: Seabury Press, 1967), pp. 85, 108, 110.

[11]WCC, "What Unity Requires," *Nairobi 75*, p. 60.

[12] WCC, "What Unity Requires," *Nairobi 75*, p. 60f.

[13] Nils Ehrenstrom, "Survey of Orthodox-Protestant Dialogues Today," *The Orthodox Church and the Churches of the Reformation*, ed. Lukas Vischer (Geneva: WCC, 1975), p. 32.

[14] WCC, "What Unity Requires," *Nairobi 75*, p. 61. (emphasis added).

[15] Cyrille Argenti, "Unite Des Chretiens," *What Unity Requires* (F&O Paper No. 77), (Geneva: WCC, 1976), p. 56f.

[16] WCC, "What Unity Requires," *Nairobi 75*, p. 61.

[17] Philip Potter, "The Report of the General Secretary," *Nairobi 75*, p. 258. (emphasis added).

[18] *Ibid.*, p. 258.

[19] Philip Potter, "Editorial," *The Ecumenical Review,* XXXVIII, No. 1, Jan. 1976, p. 4.

[20] WCC, *Nairobi 75*, p. 297.

[21] WCC, "The Constitution of the World Council of Churches," *Nairobi 75*, p. 317f. (The term 'purposes' was added to the word 'functions' which had headed this section of the Constitution since 1948).

[22] Philip Potter, "Ecumenical Diary," *The Ecumenical Review*, XXVIII, No. 4, Oct. 1976, p. 469.

[23] David Paton, "A Personal Account," *Nairobi 75*, p. 35.

[24] *Ibid.*, p. 18f.

[25] Paton, "A Personal Account," *Nairobi 75*, p. 30.

[26] *Ibid.*, p. 4.

[27] *Ibid.*, p. 24.

[28] Paton, "A Personal Account," *Nairobi 75*, p. 25.

[29] *Ibid.*, p. 30.

[30] *Ibid.*, p. 26.

[31] *Ibid.*, p. 28.

[32] Paton, "A Personal Account," *Nairobi 75*, p. 28.

[33] WCC, "Appendix 8" (Report of Financial Committee).
Nairobi 75, pp. 287ff, 28f.

[34] Paton, *op.cit.*, p. 29.

[35] Philip Potter, "Ecumenical Diary," *The Ecumenical
Review*, XXIX, No. 1, Jan. 1977, p. 85.

[36] *Ibid.*, p. 85.

[37] Potter, "One Obedience to the Whole Gospel," *The
Ecumenical Review*, XXIX, No. 4, Oct. 1977, p. 357.

[38] Potter, "One Obedience to the Whole Gospel," *The
Ecumenical Review*, XXIX, No. 4, Oct. 1977, p. 358.

[39] *Ibid.*, p. 359.

[40] *Ibid.*, p. 359.

[41] *Ibid.*, p. 361.

[42] Yves Congar, "Fifty Years in Quest of Unity,"
Lausanne 77 (Geneva: WCC, 1977), p. 29.

[43] Joseph Ratzinger, "The Future of Ecumenism," *Theology
Digest*, XXV, No. 3, Fall 1977, p. 205.

[44] WCC, "Policy Reference Committee II," *Nairobi 75*,
pp. 199f.

[45] WCC, "Policy Reference Committee II," *Nairobi 75*,
p. 199f. (emphasis added).

[46] WCC, "Policy Reference Committee II," *Nairobi 75*,
p. 201.

[47] JWG, "The Fourth Official Report...," *Nairobi*, p. 275.

[48] JWG, "The Fourth Official Report...," *Nairobi*, p. 275.

[49] WCC, "Constitution," *Nairobi 75*, p. 317.

[50] O.S. Tomkins, "Implications of the Ecumenical Movement,"
Third World Conference of Faith and Order (Lund), ed. O.S.
Tomkins (London: SCM Press, 1952), p. 167ff.

[51] SPCU, *Information Service*, No. 30, 1976, pp. 23ff.

[52] *Ibid.*, p. 24. (emphasis added).

[53]SPCU, *Information Service*, No. 30, 1976, p. 24. (emphasis added).

[54]SPCU, *Ibid.*, p. 24.

[55]SPCU, *Ibid.*, p. 25.

[56]Willem A. Visser't Hooft, "The 1927 Lausanne Conference in Retrospect," *Lausanne 77* (Geneva: WCC, 1977), p. 19.

[57]Visser't Hooft, "The 1927 Lausanne Conference in Retrospect," *Lausanne 77* (Geneva: WCC, 1977), p. 19.

[58]*Ibid.*, p. 19.

CHAPTER SIXTEEN

[1]World Council of Churches, *Breaking Barriers*, (official report of the Fifth Assembly at Nairobi), ed. D. Paton, (Grand Rapids, W.B. Eerdmans, 1975), p. 317f.

[2]*Breaking Barriers*, p. 402.

[3]*Ibid.*, p. 190.

[4]*Ibid.*

[5]*Ibid.*

[6]World Council of Churches, *Nairobi To Vancouver*, (Report of the Central Committee [1975-1983] to the Sixth Assembly of the WCC), (WCC Publications, Geneva, 1983), pp. 71-115.

[7]*Ibid.*, pp. 116-178.

[8]*Ibid.*, pp. 179-213.

[9]These sub-units have been numbered by the writer to help in identifying and distinguishing them for himself and his readers.

[10]*Nairobi to Vancouver,* pp. 116-178.

[11]*Ibid.*, pp. 179-213.

[12]*Ibid.*, p. 179.

[13]*Ibid.*, p. 73f.

[14]*Ibid.*, p. 75.

[15]*Ibid.*

[16]*Nairobi To Vancouver*, "Introduction", xviii; further
on xxiii, the Assembly, which is preeminently THE World
Council, is conceptually distinguished from the Countil which
is other than the Assembly.

[17]Ephesians 3:20, (New American Bible).

[18]*Nairobi to Vancouver*, "Introduction", passim.

[19]*Ibid.*, xvi, xix, xxii.

[20]Code of Canon Law, (Codex Iuris Canonici, Latin/English
edition) tr. under the auspices of the Canon Law Society of
America, (Washington, D.C., 1983), can. 1952, p. 629,
(hereafter CCL).

[21]*Nairobi to Vancouver*, "Introduction", xix.

[22]Philip Potter, "The Churches and the World Council
After Thirty Years, "*The Ecumenical Review*" (April 1979):135,
(dates and emphasis added).

[23]*Nairobi To Vancouver*, "Introduction", xvii.

[24]*Ibid.*, xxiii.

[25]*Ibid.*, p. 139.

[26]*Ibid.*, p. 140.

[27]W. A. Visser't Hooft, "Karl Barth and the Ecumenical
Movement", *The Ecumenical Review*, 32, (Geneva, April 1980),
133.

[28]"Forward", *Nairobi To Vancouver*, p. vi.

[29]The term "convergence" suggests political accomodation,
in which each party yields points to come together; for
Christian believers, the test of final union is the *transmitted
apostolic truth*, even if one party to the dialogue already had
it and could in no way negotiate or 'converge' from it toward
the partner.

[30]*Nairobi To Vancouver*, p. 72.

[31]Faith and Order Commission of the World Council of
Churches, *Baptism, Eucharist and Ministry*, (F&O paper no. 111,
Geneva, 1982), p. x, (emphasis added) (hereafter referred to
as *BEM*).

[32]*BEM*, "Preface" (by W. Lazareth, Director of the Secretariat on Faith and Order, and Nikos Nissiotis, Moderator of the Commission on Faith and Order), x.

[33]Rev. Dr. Wainwright is Professor of Systematic Theology at the Divinity School of Duke University, Durham, NC.

[34]Geoffrey Wainwright, *The Ecumenical Moment*, (William B. Eerdmans Publ. Co., 1983), p. 5. "In January 1982, at Lima in Peru, I was privileged to preside over the establishment of the final text of Baptism, Eucharist, and Ministry, unanimously judged by the plenary Faith and Order Commission to be ripe for transmission to the Churches which had called for it."

[35]*BEM*, p. 2.

[36]*BEM*, "Preface", ix.

[37]*Ibid.*, vii.

[38]L'Osservatore Romano, 13 Sept. 1983, p. 2.

[39]*BEM*, p. 2. (emphasis added).

[40]*Ibid.*, p. 4.

[41]*Ibid.*, pp. 2-7, passim.

[42]J. Jorgenson, "Reflections on the Lima Statement," *St. Vladimir's Theological Quarterly* 24 (Tuchahoe, NY, 1983), 241, (hereafter *SVTQ*).

[43]*BEM*, p. 5.

[44]*Ibid.*, p. 6.

[45]*Ibid.*, p. 10, passim.

[46]*Ibid.*, p. 11, (emphasis added).

[47]*Ibid.*, p. 11.

[48]George Bebis, "The Lima Statement on the Eucharist," *SVTQ*, 1983, p. 268.

[49]*BEM*, p. 12, (emphasis added).

[50]*Ibid.*, p. 12.

[51]*Ibid.*, p. 15.

[52]Christology is commonly qualified as "high" if it
explicitly or implicitly affirms Christ's divinity, pre-
existence, or unique unity with the Father.

[53]Robert Bertram, "Chicago Theologians on BEM", *Journal
of Ecumenical Studies*, 21, (Winter 1984), p. 65.

[54]*BEM*, p. 17.

[55]*Ibid.*, p. 12.

[56]*BEM*, p. 20.

[57]*Ibid.*

[58]*Ibid.*, p. 21, (emphasis added).

[59]*Ibid.*, p. 25.

[60]*Ibid.*, p. 21, (emphasis added).

[61]"The Church", *Vatican Council II*, ed. A Flannery,
(Liturgical Press, Collegeville, 1975), pp. 361, 372
respectively.

[62]*BEM*, p. 30.

[63]Consultation on Church Union, *In Quest Of A Church Of
Christ Uniting*, (Princeton, N.J., 1980), p. 41f, (hereafter
COCU).

[64]*CCL*, Canon 775, p. 285.

[65]Raymond Brown, *Priest and Bishop*, (Paulist Press, N.Y.,
1970), p. 42f.

[66]William A. Jurgens, *The Faith of the Early Fathers*,
(Liturgical Press, Minnesota, 1970), pp. 17-26.

[67]*Ibid.*, p. 21.

[68]*Ibid.*, p. 25.

[69]R. Brown, and J. Meier, *Antioch & Rome*, (Paulist Press,
New York, 1983), p. 211f.

[70]Robert Stephanopoulos, "The Lima Statement on Ministry"
SVTQ, 1983, p. 278.

[71]Martin Hengel, *Acts and the History of Earliest Christiantiy*, tr. by John Bowden, (Fortress Press, Philadelphia, 1980), p. 25.

[72]*Ibid.*, p. 26.

[73]*Peter in the New Testament*, ed. by R. Brown, K. Donfried, J. Reumann, (Augsburg Publishing House, Minneapolis, 1973), pp. 158-166.

[74]*Ibid.*, p. 162.

[75]Raymond Brown, *The Churches The Apostles Left Behind*, (Paulist Press, N.Y., 1984), p. 97.

[76]Wainwright, *The Ecumenical Moment*, p. 5f.

[77]Max Thurian, "The Eucharistic Liturgy of Lima", *Ecumenical Perspectives on Baptism, Eucharist and Ministry*, (World Council of Churches, Geneva, 1983), pp. 225-246, (hereafter cited as *Perspectives*).

[78]*Perspectives*, pp. 225-246., passim.

[79]*Ibid.*, p. 225.

[80]*Ibid.*, p. 226.

CHAPTER SEVENTEEN

[1]*Gathered For Life*, Official Report, VI Assembly, World Council of Churches, ed. by David Gill, (WCC, Geneva, 1983), passim, (hereafter cited as *Gathered*). (In the "preface" General Secretary Potter "heartily commended" editor Gill's report of the VI Assembly.

[2]*Gathered*, p. 43.

[3]David Gill, "Story of the Assembly", *Gathered*, p. 8.

[4]*Ibid.*, p. 17.

[5]*Ibid.*, p. 5.

[6]"Assembly Programme", *Gathered*, p. 171ff.

[7]"Messages", *Gathered*, p. 210.

[8]Pierre Duprey, "Fr. Duprey's address to the Assembly,"
July 25, 1983, *Information Service* 53/4 (Secretariat For
Promoting Christian Unity, Vatican, 1983), p. 103 (hereafter
SPCU, *IS*).

[9]"Table of Contents", *Gathered*.

[10]Gill, "Story of the Assembly" (hereafter "Story")
Gathered, p. 14.

[11]"Taking Steps Toward Unity" (hereafter "Steps")
Gathered, p. 44.

[12]*Ibid*., pp. 45-50.

[13]*Ibid*., p. 49.

[14]*Ibid*., p. 51.

[15]*Ibid*., pp. 51-52.

[16]*Ibid*., p. 52.

[17]Gill, "Story", *Gathered*, p. 9.

[18]*Ibid*., pp. 9 and 12, respectively.

[19]*Ibid*., p. 10.

[20]*Ibid*., p. 11.

[21]Thomas P. Rausch, "An Ecumenical Eucharist For A World
Assembly", *America*, Jan. 21, 1984, p. 28 (hereafter *Ecumenical
Eucharist*).

[22]SPCU, "Impressions On The Sixth Assembly Of The World
Council Of Churches" (hereafter "Impressions") *Information
Service* 53 (Vatican City, 1983), p. 126.

[23]Rev. Robert G. Stephanopoulos, *Guidelines for Orthodox
Christians in Ecumenical Relations*, (publ. by the Standing
Conference of Canonical Orthodox Bishops in America, NY, 1973)
p. 52f. (hereafter *Orthodox Guidelines*) (emphasis added).

[24]*Orthodox Guidelines*, p. 15.

[25]Gill, "Story", *Gathered*, p. 11.

[26]Code of Canon Law (Latin/English edition), translation
approved by NCCB, (Canon Law Society of America, Washington,
DC, 1983), Can. 837, p. 317 (hereafter *CCL*, Canon number).

[27]*CCL*, Can. 838, p. 317.

[28]*CCL*, Can. 908, p. 341.

[29]Pope John Paul II, "Address to the Secretariat for Promoting Christian Unity" *Doing the Truth in Charity*, ed. by T. Stransky and J. Sheerin (Paulist Press, NY, 1982), p. 303.

[30]Rausch, "Ecumenical Eucharist", *America*, p. 28.

[31]"Decree on Ecumenism", *Vatican Council II*, ed. by A. Flannery (Liturgical Press, Collegeville, 1975), art. 23, p. 469.

[32]Rausch, "Ecumenical Eucharist, *"America"*, p. 28.

[33]Gill, "Story", *Gathered*, p. 18.

[34]Philip Potter, "Report of the General Secretary" (hereafter "Report"), *Gathered*, pp. 193-209.

[35]"Biblical References", *Gathered*, p. 355.

[36]Potter, "Report", *Gathered*, p. 199.

[37]*Ibid.*, p. 206.

[38]Potter, "Report", *Gathered*, p. 206f.

[39]"Report of the Assembly Programme Guidelines Committee", *Gathered*, p. 249 (hereafter "PGC").

[40]"Constitution", *Gathered*, p. 324.

[41]"Reviewing The Past; Charting The Future", *Gathered*, p. 127 (hereafter "PRC I"), (emphasis added).

[42]"Steps", *Gathered*, p. 48f.

[43]"PRC I", *Gathered*, p. 113.

[44]*Ibid.*, pp. 112-128.

[45]"PRC I", *Gathered*, p. 118 (emphasis added).

[46]*Ibid.*, p. 118 (emphasis added).

[47]*Ibid.*, p. 119.

[48]Idem.

[49]"Fifth Report of the Joint Working Group Between the Roman Catholic Church and the World Council of Churches", *Information Service*, 53/IV (Secretariat For Pormoting Christian Unity, Vatican, 1983), p. 105 (hereafter JWG "Fifth Report" *IS*).

[50]JWG, "Fifth Report", *IS*, p. 107.

[51]*Ibid*.

[52]"Letter of Cardinal Willebrands" (7/4/83), *IS*, 53/4 (SPCU, Vatican, 1983), pp. 119-121.

[53]*Ibid*., p. 120 (emphasis added).

[54]*Ibid*.

[55]*Ibid*., p. 121.

[56]*Ibid*.

[57]"PRC I", *Gathered*, p. 118.

[58]SPCU, "Impressions", *IS*, p. 12.

[59]*Gathered*, p. 259.

[60]Policy Reference Committee II (hereafter PRC II), "World Affairs in Ecumenical Perspective", *Gathered*, p. 129.

[61]"PRC II", *Gathered*, p. 139.

[62]"Pastoral Constitution on the Church", article 51, *Vatican Council II*, p. 954.

[63]"PRC II", *Gathered*, pp. 129-167, passim.

[64]*Ecumenical Press Service* (hereafter *EPS*), 51/21 (WCC, Geneva, June, 1984), p. 111.

[65]*EPS*, pp. 114-115, (emphasis added).

[66]John Paul II, "Ecumenism and the Role of the Bishop of Rome", *Origins* 14/7 (NC Documentary Service, Washington, DC, June 28, 1984 (cf. Appendix I).

[67]John Paul II, *Origins*, p. 99 (emphasis added).

[68]*Ibid*., p. 101.

[69]*EPS*, 84.06, p. 111.

[70]Pope John Paul II, "A perspective on Communion", *Origins* 14/7, p. 102.

[71]*Ibid.*

[72]Anastasia Toufexis (reported by R. Kroon/Geneva), "A Bridge Builder Takes Charge", *Time,* 7/23/82, p. 101.

[73]*Ibid.*

[74]*Ibid.*

[75]Instruction on the Historicity of the Gospels, Congregation for the Faith, Rome, April 21, 1964.

[76]Many scholars estimate that Matthew included the Risen Christ's teaching in the historical Caesarea-Philippi account (Matt. 16); if this be so, it strengthens the "iure divino" character of the special status promised to Peter.

CHAPTER EIGHTEEN

[1]James O'Connor, *The Father's Son* (St. Paul Editions, Boston, 1984), p. 162.

[2]"Lumen Gentium", *Vatican Council II*, a.18, p. 370.

[3]*The New York Times,* Aug. 21, 1980, p. 1; *Long Island Newsday,* Aug. 22, 1980, p. 67; *New York Catholic News,* April 9, 1981, p. 6. A group of nearly a thousand Episcopalians (about 63 were clergy) recently left their church (because of its ordaining an active homosexual woman) and did "return" or "were reconciled" to the Catholic Church. The clergy, even though married, were later ordained as Catholic priests. One who has written about the change, keyed his decision to wanting the truth.

[4]John Jay Hughes, "I Deeply Love My New Spiritual Home", *Long Island Catholic,* Aug. 22, 1980, p. 67.

[5]Geoffrey Wainwright, *The Ecumenical Moment,* William B. Eerdmans Publ. Co., 1983, p. 5f.

[6]"Decree on Ecumenism", *Vatican Council II,* ed. Flannery, p. 460.

[7]Yves Congar, "Trials and promises of ecumenism", Voices of Unity, Geneva, 1981, p. 22.

[8]*Ibid.,* p. 28.

[9]*Ibid.*, p. 28.

[10]As always with serious inquiry, new questions arise
along with the answers to the questions which started the in-
vestigation:

1) Given the elements of religious conviction expressed
by both the RCC and the WCC, what *model of future relationship*
appears coherent with the data? Only communities of Christians
join, not agencies with churches. What does this say about the
long-range value of such agencies as advocates of, or facilita-
tors of, ecclesial unity?

2) How can each recently formed world *denominational*
Christian bodies (LWF, WARC, etc.) avoid *collision* with the
WCC? If a Lutheran Church leaves the Lutheran World Federation (LWF) where does it go? To the Catholic Church as a
diocese? To the WCC, How? Where?

3) Is the WCC down-playing of the denominational differences
driving reformation Christians toward a free-floating non-denominational Protestantism? Some describe themselves as *non-
denominational Christians*! What is that? Christianity is essentially a koinonia!

4) Did the integration of Faith and Order with the World
Council (dominated by the unavoidable L&W socially-oriented,
and thus dominant, influence) frustrate or advance Charles
Brent's hopes for church unity?

BIBLIOGRAPHY

Abbott, Walter M., ed. *The Documents of Vatican II*. New
    York: Guild Press, 1966.

Adams, Michael, ed. *Vatican II on Ecumenism*. Dublin:
    Scepter Books, 1966.

Adolfs, Robert. *The Church is Different*. New York: Harper
    and Row, 1964.

Ahearn, Barnabas M. *New Horizons*. Indiana: Fides Press,
    1963.

Amann, Abbe. *The Church of the Early Centuries*. Translated
    by E. Raybould. London: Sands and Co., 1930.

Anderson, Floyd, ed. *Council Daybook*. Washington, D.C.:
    National Catholic Welfare Conference, 1965.

Andrews, James F., ed. *Barth*. St. Louis, Missouri: B.
    Herder, 1969.

Anglican/Roman Catholic Commission (USA). *Documents on
    Anglican/Roman Catholic Relations*. Also identified as
    A/RC DOC 1. Washington, D.C.: U.S. Catholic Conference,
    1972.

_____. *Documents on Anglican/Roman Catholic Relations* II.
    Also identified as *A/RC DOC* II. Washington, D.C.: U.S.
    Catholic Conference, 1973.

_____. *Documents on Anglican/Roman Catholic Relations* III.
    Also identified as *A/RC DOC* III. Washington, D.C.: U.S.
    Catholic Conference, 1974.

Aubert, Roger. "Stages of Catholic Ecumenism from Leo XIII to
    Vatican II." *Renewal of Religious Structures*. New York:
    Herder and Herder, 1968.

"The Augsburg Confession," *The Book of Concord*. Translated
    and edited by T. Tappert. Philadelphia: Fortress Press,
    1959.

Bainton, Roland H. *The Age of the Reformation*. New York:
    Van Nostrand Co., 1956.

Baker, Kenneth. "Editorial." *Homiletic and Pastoral Review*
     LXXVI, (1976); p. 96.

Barry, Colman J. *Readings in Church History*, Vol. 1. West-
     minster, Maryland: Newman Press, 1960.

Barth, Karl. *Church Dogmatics: A Selection.* Edited by H.
     Gollwitzer, translated by G. Bromiley. New York: Harper
     Torch Books, 1961.

_____. *Church Dogmatics: A Selection.* New York: Harper
     and Row, 1962.

_____. *Ad Limina Apostolorum.* Richmond, Virginia: John
     Knox Press, 1968.

Baum, Gregory. *The Catholic Quest for Christian Unity.* Glen
     Rock, New Jersey: Paulist Press, 1965.

_____. ed. *Ecumenical Theology Today.* Glen Rock, New
     Jersey: Deus Books, 1964.

_____. ed. *Ecumenical Theology* No. 2. New York: Paulist
     Press, 1967.

Bea, Augustin. *The Unity of Christians.* New York: Herder
     and Herder Co., 1963.

Bebis, George. "The Lima Statement on the Eucharist," *St.
     Vladimir's Theological Quarterly*, 24. New York: SVTQ,
     1983.

Bellarmine. *Catholic Dictionary of Theology.* London: T.
     Nelson & Sons Ltd., 1962.

Bellarmini, Roberti, Cardinalis. *Solida Christianae Fidei.*
     Demonstratio, Antverpii, 1611.

Benedictines of Solesmes. *The Church: Papal Teachings.*
     Translated by E. O'Gorman. Boston: St. Paul Editions,
     1962.

Benz, Ernst. *The Eastern Orthodox Church.* New York:
     Doubleday, 1957.

Berry, George R., ed. *The Classic Greek Dictionary.* New York:
     Follett Publishing Company, 1958.

Bertram, Robert. "Chicago Theologians on BEM," *Journal of
     Ecumenical Studies*, 21. Philadelphia: Temple University,
     Winter 1984.

Bettenson, Henry, ed. *Documents of the Christian Church* 2nd ed. New York: Oxford University Press, 1970.

Bishops' Commission for Ecumenical Affairs. *Recommendations for Diocesan Commissions for Ecumenical Affairs.* Washington, D.C.: National Catholic Welfare Conference, 1966.

_____. *Interim Guidelines for Prayer in Common and Communicatio in Sacris.* Washington, D.C.: National Catholic Welfare Conference, c.1967.

Blake, Eugene Carson. "Address to Pope Paul VI" (on the occasion of his visit to the headquarters of the World Council of Churches on June 10, 1969). *The Ecumenical Review*, XXI (July 1969), 265-266.

_____. *The Church in the Next Decade.* London: Collier-Macmillian, Ltd., 1972.

Bliss, Kathleen. *The Future of Religion.* England: Hazell, Watson and Viney Ltd., 1972.

Boegner, Marc. *The Long Road to Unity.* Translated by R. Hague. London: Collins, 1970.

Bouyer, Louis C. *The Decomposition of Catholicism.* Translated by C. Quinn. Chicago: Franciscan Herald Press, 1969.

Bridston, Keith R. and Wagoner, Walter D., editors. *Unity in Mid-Career.* New York: Macmillan, 1963.

Briggs, Kenneth. "Some Scholars Believe Vatican III a Necessity." *New York Times*, 5 June 1977, p. 18.

Brinton, Crane. *The Shaping of Modern Thought.* New Jersey: Prentice Hall, 1965.

Brown, Raymond E. *Priest and Bishop.* New York: Paulist Press, 1970.

_____. *Crises Facing the Church.* New York: Paulist Press, 1975.

_____. *The Churches The Apostles Left Behind.* N.Y.: Paulist Press, 1984.

Brown, R., Donfried, K., et al. editors. *Peter in the New Testament.* Minneapolis: Augsburg Publishing House, 1973.

Brown, R., and Meier, J. *Antioch to Rome*. New York: Paulist
    Press, 1983.

Brown, Robert McAfee. *The Ecumenical Revolution*. Revised
    edition. New York: Doubleday, 1969.

Brown, R. McAfee and Weigel, Gustave. *An American Dialogue*.
    New York: Doubleday, 1960.

Burns, J. Edgar. "The Roman Primacy in Recent Study." *The
    Ecumenist*, VII (July-August, 1969), 65-67.

Calian, Carnegie S. *Icon and Pulpit*. Philadelphia:
    Westminster Press, 1968.

Calvin, John. *A Compend of the Institutes of the Christian
    Religion*. Edited by T. Kerr, Philadelphia: The
    Westminster Press, 1964.

Calvert, Samuel McCrea. *The American Churches in the
    Ecumenical Movement 1900-1968*. New York: Association
    Press, 1968.

_____. *Church Cooperation and Unity in America*. New York:
    Association Press, 1970.

Central Committee of the World Council of Churches. cf. under
    World Council of Churches.

Classic Greek Dictionary. New York: Follett Publishing Co.,
    1958.

Clarkson, J.F., et. al. translators and editors. *The Church
    Teaches*. Kansas: B. Herder, 1955

Claudia, Sister M. ed. *Dictionary of Papal Pronouncements*.
    New York: P.J. Kenedy and Sons, 1958.

Commission on Faith and Order (World Council of Churches),
    listed under World Council of Churches.

Congar, Yves M.J. "Progress of Ecumenical Dialogue."
    Theology Digest, XI (Summer, 1963), 67-71.

_____. *The Mystery of the Church*. 2nd revised edition.
    Baltimore: Helicon Press, 1965.

_____. *Ecumenism and the Future of the Church*. Translated
    by J.C. Guinness. Chicago: Priory Press, 1967.

_____. *A History of Theology*. New York: Doubleday, 1968.

_____. *This Church That I Love*. Translated by L. Delafuente. New Jersey: Dimension Books, 1969.

Congregatio S. Officii. "Monitum." *Acta Apostolicae Sedis*, 15 Junii 1948, p. 257.

_____. "Instructio: DeMontione Oecumenica." *The Jurist*. Jan. 1950, pp. 201-213.

Constantelos, Demetrios. *The Greek Orthodox Church*. New York: The Seabury Press, 1967.

Consultation on Church Union. *In Quest of A Church Uniting*. New Jersey: COCU, 1980.

Crow, Paul A. *The Ecumenical Movement in Bibliographical Outline*. New York: National Council of the Churches of Christ in the U.S.A., 1965.

_____. *The Ecumenical Movement in Bibliographical Outline: Supplement*. New York: N.C.C., 1969.

Cullmann, Oscar. *Peter: Disciple, Apostle, Martyr*. London: SCM Press Ltd., 1962.

Daniel-Rops, Henri. *The Second Vatican Council*. Translated by A. Guinan. New York: Hawthorn Books Inc., 1962.

Dawson, Christopher. *The Dividing of Christendom*. New York: Doubleday Co., 1967.

De Lubac, Henri. *The Church: Paradox and Mystery*. Translated by J.R. Dunne. New York: Alba House, 1969.

Denzinger, Henry. *The Sources of Catholic Dogma*, 30th edition. Translated by R.J. Deferrari. London: B. Herder Book Co., 1953.

_____. *Enchiridion Symbolorum*. 30th edition. Translated by Roy J. Deferrari. London: B. Herder Book Co., 1954.

Deretz, A. and Nocent A., editors. *Dictionary of the Council*. Washington, D.C.: Corpus Books, 1968.

Dewey, John. *A Common Faith*. New Haven: Yale University Press, 1934.

Dirkswager, Edward J. *Readings in The Theology of the Church*. New Jersey: Prentice-Hall, 1970.

Dodd, C.H. *The Apostolic Preaching and Its Developments*. New York: Harper and Row, 1964.

_____. *The Founder of Christianity*. London: Collier-
Macmillan Ltd., 1970.

Dolan, John P. *Catholicism*. Woodbury, New York: Barron's
Educational Series, 1968.

Duggan, G.H. *Hans Kung and Re-Union*. Cork: Mercier Press,
1964.

Duggan, W.J. "A Comparative Study of Catholic Ecumenism and
Protestant Ecumenism Reflected in the Oberlin Conference."
Unpublished S.T.D. Dissertation, Catholic University of
America, Washington, D.C., 1962.

Dulles, Avery. *A Testimonial to Grace*. New York: Sheed and
Ward, 1946.

_____. *Apologetics and the Biblical Christ*. Maryland:
Woodstock Papers (No. 6) Newman Press, 1966.

Dulles, Avery. *The Dimension of the Church*. Westminster,
Maryland: Newman Press, 1967.

_____. *Revelation and the Quest for Unity*. Washington,
D.C.: Corpus Books, 1968.

_____. *Survival of Dogma*. New York: Doubleday, 1971.

_____. *Models of the Church*. New York: Doubleday, 1974.

Duprey, Pierre. "Address to the [Vancouver] Assembly"
Information Service. Vatican: SPCU (53/4), 1983.

Eagan, Joseph. "Ordained Ministry in BEM" *Ecumenical Review,*
36. Geneva: WCC, July 1984.

Ehrenstrom, Nils. *Confessions in Dialogue* 3rd edition.
Geneva: World Council of Churches, 1975.

Empie, Paul C. and Baum, William W., editors. *The Status of
the Nicene Creed as Dogma of the Church*. Vol. 1.
Baltimore: jointly published by the U.S.A. National
Committee of the Lutheran World Federation and the
Bishops' Commission for Ecumenical Affairs, 1965.

_____. *Lutherans and Catholics in Dialogue*. Vol. II.
Washington, D.C.:   National Catholic Welfare Conference,
1966 (One Baptism).

Empie, Paul C. and Murphy, Austin T., editors. *Lutherans and Catholics in Dialogue*. Vol. III. New York: U.S.A. National Committee for Lutheran World Federation, 1968 (Eucharist as Sacrifice).

_____. *Lutherans and Catholics in Dialogue*. Vol. IV. New York: U.S.A. National Committee for Lutheran World Federation, 1970 (Eucharist and Ministry).

Encyclopedia Americana, 1968 XXII, "Protestantism" by Hugh T. Kerr.

Faith and Order. cf. under World Council of Churches.

Fesquet, Henri. *The Drama of Vatican II*. Translated by B. Murchland. New York: Random House, 1967.

Fey, H. Ed. *A History of the Ecumenical Movement, 1948-1968*. Vol. II. Philadelphia: Westminster Press, 1970.

Finn, Edward. *Brothers: East and West*. Collegeville, Minnesota: Liturgical Press, 1975.

Ford, John T. "Protestant Mergers and Catholic Ecumenism." *The American Ecclesiastical Review*, CLXI, (November, 1969), 359ff.

Forell, George W. *The Augsburg Confession: A Contemporary Commentary*. Minneapolis: Augsburg Publishing House, 1968.

Fry, John R. *The Trivialization of the United Presbyterian Church*. New York: Harper and Row, 1975.

Fullam, Raymond, B. *Exploring Vatican II*. New York: Alba House, 1970.

Gaines, David P. *The World Council of Churches*. New Hampshire: Noone House, 1966.

Gill, David. "Story of the Assembly," *Gathered For Life*. Geneva: WCC, 1983.

Goodall, Norman. *The Ecumenical Movement*. London: Oxford University Press, 1961.

_____. *Ecumenical Progress (1961-1971)*. London: Oxford University Press, 1972.

Grant, Frederick C. *Rome and Reunion*. New York: Oxford University Press, 1965.

Gratsch, Edward J. *Where Peter Is* (Survey of Ecclesiology).
    New York: Alba House, 1975.

_____. *The Credentials of Catholicism*. Washington, D.C.:
    University Press of America, 1976.

Greeley, Andrew M. *The New Agenda*. Garden City, New York:
    Doubleday, 1973.

Hales, E.E.Y. *The Catholic Church in the Modern World*. New
    York: Doubleday, 1960.

Halverson, M. and Cohen, A. *A Handbook of Christian Theology*.
    New York: New American Library, 1974.

Hamer, Jerome. *The Church Is A Communion*. Translated by R.
    Matthews. New York: Sheed and Ward, 1964.

Hardon, John A. *Religions of the World* (2 vols.). New York:
    Doubleday, 1968.

Harvey, Van A. *A Handbook of Theological Terms*. New York:
    The Macmillan Company, 1968.

Hebblethwaite, Peter. *Theology of the Church*. Notre Dame
    South Bend, Indiana: Fides Publishers, 1969.

_____. *The Runaway Church*. New York: Seabury Press,
    1975.

Henderson, Ian. *Power Without Glory*. Richmond, Virginia:
    John Knox Press, 1969.

Hertling, L. and Kirschbaum, E. *The Roman Catacombs and their
    Martyrs*. Translated by M. Costellow. Milwaukee: Bruce
    Publishing Co., 1956.

Hitchcock, James. *The Decline and Fall of Radical Catholicism*.
    New York: Doubleday, 1972.

Hengel, Martin. *Acts and the History of Earliest Christianity*.
    Philadelphia: Fortress Press, 1980.

Hoekendijk, J.C. *The Church Inside Out*. Translated by I.C.
    Rottenberg. Philadelphia: Westminster Press, 1966.

Horton, Douglas. *Vatican Diary*. Philadelphia: United Church
    Press, 1966.

_____. *Toward an Undivided Church*. New York: Association
    Press, 1967.

Hritz, P.J.   "A Phenomenological study of the Ecumenical
    Movement Among Protestant Christians in America Designed
    for Catholics" Unpublished Ph.D. dissertation, Catholic
    University, Washington, D.C., 1962.

Hughes, Philip. *A Popular History of the Catholic Church*.
    New York: Macmillan Co., 1957.

_____. *The Church in Crisis*. New York: Hanover House,
    1960.

Hurley, Michael. *Theology of Ecumenism*. Notre Dame: Fides
    Publishers, 1969.

Jaquet, C.H., ed. *Yearbook of American Churches 1970*. New
    York: Council Press, 1970.

John XXIII, Pope. *Teaching of John XXIII*. Washington, D.C.:
    TPS Press, 1964.

John Paul II, Pope. "Address to the Secretariat for Promoting
    Christian Unity," Doing the Truth in Charity. NY:
    Paulist Press, 1982.

_____. "Ecumenism and the Role of the Bishop of Rome,"
    Origins, 14/7. Washington, D.C.:   NC Documentary
    Service, June 28, 1984.

_____. "A Perspective on Communion," *Origins*, 14/7.
    Washington, D.C.:   NC Documentary Service, June 28, 1984.

Johannes, F.V., ed. *Rethinking the Church*. Translated by E.
    Burke, Dublin: Gill and Macmillan Ltd., 1970.

Johnson, Robert C. "Who is Heinrich Ott?" In *New Theology
    No. I*, edited by M. Marty and D. Peerman. New York:
    Macmillan Co., 1964.

Jones, Alexander, General Editor. *The Jerusalem Bible*. New
    York: Doubleday and Company, 1966.

Jordan, Placid. *The Divine Dimension*. Dublin: Gill and
    Macmillan Ltd., 1970.

Jorgenson, J. "Reflections on the Lima Statement,"
    St. Vladimir's Theological Quarterly, 24. N.Y.: SVTQ,
    1983.

Jurgens, William A. *The Faith of the Early Fathers*.
    Minnesota: The Liturgical Press, 1970.

Joint Working Group (JWG). "Fifth Report of the JWG between
    the Roman Catholic Church and the World Council of
    Churches," *Information Service*, 53/IV. Vatican: SPCU,
    1983.

Kaufman, Gordon D. "On the Meaning of God: Transcendence
    Without Mythology." *In New Theology No. 4.* Edited by
    M. Marty and D. Peerman. New York: Macmillan Co., 1967.

Kee, Howard Clark. "The Gospel According to Matthew." *The
    Interpreter's One-Volume Commentary on the Bible.*
    Nashville: Abingdon Press, 1971.

Kellenberg, Walter P. *Interim Directives for Ecumenical
    Activities in the Diocese of Rockville Centre.* Rockville
    Centre, New York: Diocensan Commission for Ecumenism,
    1966.

Kelly, George A. The Uncertain Future of the American
    Church. A reprint from *Thought.* New York: Fordham
    University, 1972.

_____. *Who Should Run the Catholic Church?* Indiana:
    Sunday Visitor, 1975.

_____. editor. *Reflections on Contemporary Catholic
    Problems.* New York: St. John's University, 1971.

Kerr, Hugh T. editor. *A Compend of the Institutes of the
    Christian Religion.* Philadelphia: Westminster Press,
    1939.

Kloppenburg, Bonaventure. *Ecclesiology of Vatican II.*
    Translated by M. O'Connell. Chicago: Franciscan
    Herald Press, 1974.

Kung, Hans. *That the World May Believe.* Translated by
    Cecily Hastings. New York: Sheed and Ward, 1963.

_____. *The Church.* New York: Sheed and Ward, 1967.

_____. et al. *Council Speeches of Vatican II.* Glen
    Rock, New Jersey: Paulist Press, 1964.

_____. ed. *Post-Ecumenical Christianity.* New York:
    Herder and Herder, 1970.

Lambert, Bernard. *Ecumenism.* Translated by L.C. Sheppard.
    West Germany: Herder and Herder, 1967.

Latourette, Kenneth Scott. *Toward a World Christian Fellowship*. New York: Association Press, 1938.

Lee, Bernard. *The Becoming of the Church*. New York: Paulist Press, 1974.

Leeming, Bernard. *The Churches and the Church*. Maryland: Newman Press, 1961.

_____. *The Vatican Council and Christian Unity*. New York: Harper and Row, 1966.

Lefebvre, Marcel. "French Prelates Celebrate Latin Mass in Texas," *New York Times*, July 11, 1977, p. 14.

Leo XIII, Pope. "Praeclare Gratulationis." *The American Catholic Quarterly Review*. October 1894, p. 779.

_____. "Satis Cognitum." *The Irish Ecclesiastical Record*. Vol. XVII, Dublin, 1896, p. 748.

_____. Divinum Illud. *Translated by J. Bluett*. New York: The America Press, 1897.

Leo XIII, Pope. "Annum Ingressi." *The Great Encyclical Letters of Pope Leo XIII*. Edited by J. Wynne. New York: Benziger Bros., 1903.

Leon-Dufour, Xavier, ed. *Dictionary of Biblical Theology*. Translated by P. Joseph Cahill. New York: Desclee Company, 1967.

_____. *The Gospels and the Jesus of History*. Edited and translated by J. McHugh. New York: Desclee Company, 1968.

Lescrauwaet, J. *The Bible on Christian Unity*. Translated by N.D. Smith. Wisconsin: St. Norbert Abbey Press, 1965.

Lewis, Charleton T. and Short, Charles. *A Latin Dictionary*. Oxford: Clarendon Press, 1879, impression of 1962.

Lortz, Joseph. *How the Reformation Came*. New York: Herder and Herder, 1964.

McBrien, Richard P. *Do We Need the Church?* New York: Harper and Row, 1969.

_____. *Church: The Continuing Quest*. New York: Newman Press, 1970.

_____. *Who is a Catholic?* Denville, New Jersey:
    Dimension Books Inc., 1971.

McCabe, Herbert. *The People of God.* New York: Sheed and
    Ward, 1964.

McClellan, Joseph C.   "Frankfort Profile (Report of the 19th
    General Council, World Alliance of Reformed Churches)."
    The Ecumenist, III (November-December, 1964), 12-14.

McCord, Peter, editor. *A Pope For All Christians?* New York:
    Paulist Press, 1976.

McDonagh, Edna. *Roman Catholics and Unity.* London: A.R.
    Mowbray & Co. Limited, 1962.

McDonnell, John.   "Catholic Action, Its Nature and Beginnings
    on the College Level." Unpublished Dissertation, Niagara
    University, New York, 1951.

McGurn, Barrett. *A Reporter Looks at American Catholicism.*
    New York: Hawthorn Books, 1967.

McKenzie, John L. *Dictionary of the Bible.* Milwaukee:
    Bruce, 1965.

_____. *The Roman Catholic Church.* New York: Doubleday,
    1971.

McNeill, John T. and Nichols, J. *Ecumenical Testimony.*
    Philadelphia: The Westminster Press, 1974.

Macquarrie, John. *Principles of Christian Theology.* New
    York: Charles Scribner's Sons, 1966.

_____. *New Directions in Theology Today.* Vol. III.
    Philadelphia: Westminster Press, 1967.

_____. *Christian Unity and Christian Diversity.*
    Philadelphia: The Westminster Press, 1975.

_____. editor. *Contemporary Religious Thinkers.* New
    York: Farrar, Straus and Giroux, 1972.

Martin, Malachi. *Three Popes and the Cardinal.* New York:
    Farrar, Straus and Giroux, 1972.

Marty, Martin E. *Righteous Empire.* New York: The Dial
    Press, 1970.

_____. *Protestantism.* New York: Doubleday Co., 1974.

Miller, S. and Wright, G. editors. *Ecumenical Dialogue at Harvard*. Cambridge, Massachusetts: Belknap Press, 1964.

Minear, Paul S. *Images of the Church in the New Testament*. Philadelphia: Westminster Press, 1960.

Minear, P. editor. *The Nature of the Unity We Seek*. St. Louis: The Bethany Press, 1957.

Mudge, Lewis S. *One Church Catholic and Reformed*. Philadelphia: Westminster Press, 1963.

Mueller, David L. *Karl Barth*. Waco, Taxas: Word Books, 1972.

Mugavero, Francis J. *Practice of Ecumenism: Revised Interim Directives, 1968 - Diocese of Brooklyn*. Mimeographed copies. Brooklyn, N.Y.: Diocesan Commission for Ecumenism, 1968.

Murphy, William B. et. al. *God and His Creation*. Dubuque: The Priory Press, 1958.

National Conference of Catholic Bishops. *The Program of Priestly Formation*. Washington, D.C.: N.C.C.B., 1971.

National Council of Churches & Christ in the U.S.A.: National Study Commission. *The Ecclesiological Significance of Councils of Churches*. New York: N.C.C.C., 1963.

Neill, Stephen C. *Brothers of the Faith*. Nashville: Abingdon Press, 1960.

Neuner, J. and Roos, H. *The Teaching of the Catholic Church as Contained in Her Documents*. Edited by Karl Rahner. New York: Alba House, 1967.

New Testament of the New American Bible. New York: Catholic Book Publishing Co., 1970.

New York Times, 10 June 1972, article by G. Dugan (religious ads page).

Olin, John C. Editor. *Luther, Erasmus and the Reformation*. New York: Fordham University Press, 1969.

O'Neill, Colman. *Meeting Christ in the Sacraments*. New York: Alba House, 1964.

Ott, Ludwig. *Fundamentals of Catholic Dogma*. Translated by James Bastible. St. Louis: B. Herder, 1958.

Paul VI, Pope. *Ecclesiam Suam*. Translated by N.C.W.C.
     Boston, Massachusetts: St. Paul Editions, 1964.

_____. *Opening Address: Third Session of Vatican II*.
     Translated by N.C.W.S. Service. Washington, D.C.:
     National Catholic Welfare Conference, 1964.

_____. "Discourse of Pope Paul VI to the Observers at the
     Third Session of the Second Vatican Council." *The
     Ecumenist*, III (November-December, 1964), 15-16.

_____. *The Pope Speaks*. Translated by A. Vaughn.
     Indiana: Our Sunday Visitor Press, 1960.

_____. *Seven Addresses on the Church*. Translated by
     U.S.C.C. News Service. Washington, D.C.: United States
     Catholic Conference, 1967.

_____. "The Essence of Ecumenism." *The American
     Ecclesiastical Review*, CLIX (July, 1968), 57ff.

_____. "Allocution of His Holiness Pope Paul VI" (in
     response to the Welcoming address of Dr. Eugene Carson
     Blake on June 10, 1969). *The Ecumenical Review*, XXI
     (July, 1969), 266-268.

_____. *Pope Paul VI in Geneva*. Washington, D.C.: U.S.
     Catholic Conference, 1969.

_____. *The Teachings of Pope Paul VI: 1975*. Citta del
     Vaticano: Libreria Editrice Vaticana, 1976.

Paul VI, Pope and Archbishop Michael Ramsey of Canterbury.
     Joint Statement on Christian Unity. Washington, D.C.:
     N.C.W.C., 1966.

Piper, Otto A. *Protestantism in an Ecumenical Age*.
     Philadelphia: Fortress Press, 1964.

Pius XI, Pope. "Allocutio: Jan. 11, 1927," *Irenikon*, III,
     (1927), p. 20.

_____. *Mortalium Animos*. Translated by R.A. McGowan.
     Washington, D.C.: National Catholic Welfare Conference,
     1928.

Pius XI, Pope. *The Unity of Human Society*. New York:
     American Press, 1939.

_____. *Mystici Corporis*. Vatican Translation. Washington,
     D.C.: National Catholic Welfare Conference, 1943.

_____. *Humani Generis*. Translated by J.C. Fenton. Washington, D.C.: N.C.W.C., 1950.

Potter, Philip. "Editorial." *The Ecumenical Review*, XXVII (Jan. 1975), p. 4.

_____. "Ecumenical Diary" *The Ecumenical Review*, XXVIII (Oct. 1975), p. 469.

_____. "One Obedience to the Whole Gospel." *The Ecumenical Review*, XXIX, (Oct. 1977), p. 357.

Potter, Philip. "Report of the General Secretary," *Gathered For Life*. Geneva: WCC, 1983.

_____. "The Churches and the World Council After Thirty Years." *The Ecumenical Review*, XXXI, (April 1979), p. 135.

Powell, John. *The Mystery of the Church*. Milwaukee: Bruce Publishing Co., 1967.

Pratt, T.B. "A comparative study of the Protestant-Catholic interpretation of the Ecumenical Movement 1943-1963." Unpublished D.S.S. dissertation, Syracuse University, New York, 1965.

Rahner, Karl. *On The Theology of Death*. 2nd edition. New York: Herder and Herder, 1965.

_____. *The Church After the Council*. New York: Herder and Herder, 1966.

_____. *The Church and the Sacraments*. New York: Herder and Herder, 1968.

_____. "Schism in the Catholic Church." *Theology Digest*, XVIII (Spring, 1970), 4-8.

_____. *Theological Investigations*. Vol. 9. New York: Herder and Herder, 1972.

_____. *Theological Investigations*. Vol. 10. New York: Herder and Herder, 1973.

Rahner, Karl. *The Shape of the Church to Come*. Translated by E. Quinn. New York: Seabury Press, 1974.

Rahner, Karl and Ratzinger, Joseph. *The Episcopate and the Primacy*. New York: Herder and Herder, 1963.

Rahner, Karl and Vorgrimler, Herbert. *Theological Dictionary*.
     Edited by Cornelius Ernest, translated by R. Strachan.
     New York: Herder and Herder, 1968.

Ramsey, Paul. *Who Speaks for the Church?* New York:
     Abingdon Press, 1967.

Ratzinger, Joseph. *The Open Circle: The Meaning of
     Christian Brotherhood*. Translated by W.A. Glen-Doeple.
     New York: Sheed and Ward, 1966.

_____. *Theological Highlights of Vatican II*. New York:
     Paulist Press, 1966.

_____. "The Future of Ecumenism." *Theology Digest*, XXV,
     (Fall 1977), 200-205.

Rausch, Thomas. "An Ecumenical Eucharist For A World Assembly,
     America. N.Y.: America Press, Jan 28, 1984.

Robinson, James M. and Koester, Helmut. *Trajectories
     Through Early Christianity*. Philadelphia: Fortress
     Press, 1971.

Rodger, Patrick C. editor. *Ecumenical Dialogue in Europe*.
     Richmond, Virginia: John Knox Press, 1966.

Roman Catholic Church. *Instruction on the Historicity of the
     Gospels*. Vatican: Congregation For the Faith, 1963.

Roman Catholic Church. *The Roman Ritual*. Washington, D.C.:
     International Commission on English in the Liturgy, 1976.

_____. *Code of Canon Law*. Washington, D.C.: Canon Law
     Society of America, 1983.

Rosten, Leo. editor. *Religions in America*. New York: Simon
     and Schuster, 1963.

Rouse, R. and Neill, S.C., eds. *A History of the Ecumenical
     Movement, 1517-1948*. Philadelphia: The Westminster
     Press, 1968.

Rousseau, Richard W. "Is Ecumenism Dead?" *The American
     Ecclesiastical Review*, CLXII (June, 1970) 383-391.

Ryan, H. and Wright, J.R., eds. *Episcopalians and Roman
     Catholics: Can they ever get together?* Denville, New
     Jersey: Dimension Books, 1972.

Rynne, Xavier. *Letters from Vatican City*. New York: Farrar,
    Strauss & Co., 1963.

Sartory, Thomas A. *The Ecumenical Movement and the Unity of
    the Church*. Translated by H.C. Graef. Westminster,
    Maryland: Newman Press, 1963.

Schillebeeckx, Edward. *A Survey of Catholic Theology 1800-
    1970*. Edited by T.M. Schoof. New York: Paulist-Newman
    Press, 1970.

Schlink, Edmund. *After the Council*. Translated by H. Bouman.
    Philadelphia: Fortress Press, 1968.

_____. *The Coming Christ and the Coming Church*.
    Philadelphia: Fortress Press, 1968.

_____. "The Holy Spirit and the Catholicity of the
    Church." *The Ecumenical Review*, XXI (April, 1969),
    98-115.

Schmaus, Michael. *The Church* (Vol. 4). Translated by Mary
    Ledderer. New York: Sheed and Ward, 1972.

Schmidt, William J. "The Morphology of Ecumenism." *New York
    Theological Seminary Bulletin* (1969); 9f.

_____. "The Reformed Stance." *Review of Books and
    Religion*. (Vol. 4, No. 4); p. 12.

Schnackenburg, Rudolf. *The Church in the New Testament*.
    Translated by W.J. O'Hara. New York: Herder and Herder,
    1977.

Schoof, T.M. *A Survey of Catholic Theology 1800-1970*.
    Translated by N.D. Smith. New York: Paulist-Newman
    Press, 1970.

Schroeder, H.J. *Disciplinary Decrees of the General Councils*.
    London: B. Herder, 1937.

Scott, William, ed. *Sources of Protestant Theology*. New York:
    Bruce Publishing Company, 1971.

Secretariat For Promoting Christian Unity. *Directory for the
    Application of the Decisions of the Second Ecumenical
    Council of the Vatican concerning Ecumenical Matters:
    Part I*. Translated by U.S.C.C. Washington, D.C.: United
    States Catholic Conference, 1967.

_____. *Notes on the Application of the Ecumenical
     Directory.* Washington, D.C.:   United States Catholic
     Conference, 1968.

_____. "Uppsala 1968" *Information Service,* January 1969,
     p. 84.

_____. *Ecumenical Directory for the Application of the
     Decisions of the Second Vatican Council concerning
     Ecumenical Matters: Part II.* Washington, D.C.:
     Natinal Conference of Catholic Bishops, 1970.

_____. *Reflections and Suggestions Concerning Ecumenical
     Dialogue.* USCC Washington, D.C.:   National Council of
     Bishops, 1970.

_____. *Ecumenical Collaboration at the Regional,
     National and Local Levels.* Washington, D.C.:
     National Conference of Catholic Bishops, 1975.

_____. "Impressions On The Sixth Assembly Of The World
     Council Of Churches," *Information Service,* 53. Vatican
     City: SPCU, 1983.

Semmelroth, Otto. *The Church and Christian Belief.*
     Translated by T.R. Milligan. New Jersey: Deus Books,
     1966.

Sheerin, John B. *A Practical Guide to Ecumenism.* New York:
     Paulist Press, 1967.

Shehan, Lawrence. "The Priest in the New Testament." *Homiletic
     and Pastoral Review.* November 1975.

Sherwood, Polycarp, ed. *The Unity of the Churches of God.*
     Dublin: Helicon, 1962.

Simpson, James & Storey, Edward. *The Long Shadows of
     Lambeth X. New York: McGraw-Hill, 1967.*

Skoglund, J. and Nelson, J. Fifty Years of Faith and Order.
     New York: Faith and Order Commission, WCC, 1963.

Skydsgaard, K.E. *One In Christ.* Philadelphia: Muhlenberg
     Press, 1957.

Stark, Rodney and Glock, Charles. *American Piety: The Nature
     of Religious Commitment.* Berkeley: University of
     California Press, 1970.

Stephanopoulos, Robert. "The Lima Statement on Ministry,"
    St. Vladimir's Theological Quarterly, 24. N.Y.: SVTQ,
    1983.

_____. *Guidelines For Orthodox Christians in Ecumenical
    Relations*. N.Y.: SCOB 1973.

Stransky, Thomas. *The Decree on Ecumenism With a Commentary*.
    The Decree translated by J. Long and T. Stransky. New
    York: Paulist Press, 1965.

Stransky, T. and Sheerin, J. eds. *Doing The Truth in Charity*.
    N.Y.: Paulist Press, 1982.

Stravinskas, Peter & McBain, R. *The Church After the Council*.
    New York: Alba House, 1975.

Suenens, Leon-Joseph. *The Church in Dialogue*. Notre Dame:
    Fides, 1965.

Swidler, Leonard J. *The Ecumenical Vanguard*. Pittsburgh:
    Duquesne University Press, 1964.

Swidler, Leonard J., ed. *Scripture and Ecumenism*. Pittsburgh:
    Duquesne University Press, 1965.

Swidler, Leonard J., ed. *The Eucharist in Ecumenical Dialogue*.
    New York: Paulist Press, 1976.

Tanquerey. A. *Synopsis Theologiae Dogmaticae Fundamentalis*,
    24th ed. Edited by J. Bord. Paris: Desclee at Socii,
    1937.

Tappert, Theodore G. Trans. and ed. *The Book of Concord*.
    Philadelphia: Fortress Press, 1959.

Tavard, George H. *Two Centuries of Ecumenism*. Translated
    by R.W. Hughes. Mentor Omega Book New York: The New
    American Library, 1962.

_____. *Understanding Protestantism*. Translated by R.
    Attwater. Glen Rock, New Jersey: Paulist Press, 1964.

Thurian, Max. "The Eucharistic Liturgy of Lima," *Ecumenical
    Perspectives on Baptism, Eucharist and Ministry*. Geneva,
    WCC, 1983.

Tomkins, O.S. ed. *Third World Conference of Faith and Order
    (Lund)*. London: SCM Press, 1952.

Torbet, Robert G. *Ecumenism...Free Church Dilemma.* Valley
    Forge, Pa.: The Judson Press, 1968.

Toufexis, Anestasia. "A Bridge Builder Takes Charge," *Time,*
    7/23/82.

Urresti, Jimenez. *Structures of the Church.* New York:
    Herder and Herder, 1970.

Vatican Council I. *Documents of Vatican I.* Selected and
    translated by J.F. Broderick. Collegeville, Minnesota:
    Liturgical Press, 1971.

Vatican Council II. *The Documents of Vatican II.* Edited by
    Walter Abbott and translated by Joseph Gallagher. New
    York: Guild Press, 1966.

_____. *Vatican Council II: The Conciliar and Post
    Conciliar Documents.* A. Flannery ed. Collegeville,
    Minnesota: The Liturgical Press, 1975.

Vatican. *L'Osservatore Romano.* Vatican Polyglot Press,
    Sept. 13, 1983.

Vischer, Lukas. "Some Considerations Regarding the Joint
    Working Group Between the Roman Catholic Church and the
    World Council of Churches." *The Ecumenical Review, XXI*
    (October, 1969), 354-359.

_____. *A Documentary History of the Faith and Order
    Movement.* St. Louis: Bethany Press, 1963.

_____. ed. *The Orthodox Church and the Churches of the
    Reformation.* Geneva: WCC, 1975.

Visser't Hooft, Willem. *The Ten Formative Years 1938-1948.*
    Geneva: WCC, 1949.

_____. "The Super Church and the Ecumenical Movement."
    Reprint from *Ecumenical Review,* July 1958.

_____. "Dynamic Factors in the Ecumenical Situation."
    The Ecumenical Review, XXI (October, 1969), 320-331.

_____. *Memoirs.* Philadelphia: Westminster Press, 1973.

_____. *Has the Ecumenical Movement a Future?* Atlanta:
    John Knox Press, 1974.

_____. "Karl Barth and The Ecumenical Movement." The
    Ecumenical Review XXXII (Geneva, April 1980), p. 133.

Vorgrimler, Herbert ed. *Dogmatic vs Biblical Theology*.
Baltimore: Helicon Press, 1964.

_____. ed. *Commentary on the Documents of Vatican II*.
New York: Herder and Herder, 1968.

_____. ed. *One, Holy, Catholic, and Apostolic*.
Translated by E. Quinn and A. Woodrow. London: Sheed
and Ward, 1968.

Wainwright, Geoffrey, *The Ecumenical Moment*. Grand Rapids:
W.B. Eerdmans, 1983.

Ware, Timothy. *The Orthodox Church*. Maryland: Penguin
Books, 1972.

Witte, J.L. (S.J.) "A Talk With a Giant - Karl Barth."
America, September 25, 1948, p. 568.

Weigel, Gustave. *A Catholic Primer on the Ecumenical
Movement*. Westminster, Maryland: The Newman Press,
1957.

_____. *Catholic Theology in Dialogue*. New York: Harper
and Row, 1965.

Wolf, D.J. & Schall, J., eds. *Current Trends in Theology*.
Garden City, New York: Doubleday, 1966.

World Council of Churches

A. Assemblies

_____. Provisional Committee Report. *The Ten Formative
Years 1938 to 1948*. Edited by W.A. Visser't Hooft,
general secretary. Geneva: WCC, 1948.

_____. *The First Assembly of the World Council of Churches*.
Edited by W.A. Visser't Hooft. New York: Harper and
Brothers, 1949.

_____. *Evanston Speaks: Reports of the Second Assembly
of the World Council of Churches*. Geneva, Switzerland:
WCC, 1955.

_____. *The New Delhi Report*. Edited by W.A. Visser't
Hooft. New York: Association Press, 1962.

_____. *Uppsala 68*. Edited by Norman Goodall. Geneva:
WCC, 1968.

_____. *Breaking Barriers: Nairobi 1975*. Edited by David
Paton. London: SPCK, 1976.

_____. *Gathered For Life* (Vancouver 1983). Ed. by David
Gill. Geneva: WCC, 1983.

B. Central Committee

_____. *The Church, The Churches and the World Council
of Churches*. New York: WCC, 1950. "The Toronto Report."

_____. *Evanston to New Delhi*. Edited by W.A. Visser't
Hooft. Geneva: World Council of Churches, 1961.

_____. *Minutes and Reports of the Eighteenth Meeting of
the Central Committee (Enugu)*. Geneva, Switzerland:
WCC, 1965.

_____. *Minutes and Reports of the Nineteenth Meeting of
the Central Committee (Geneva)*. Geneva, Switzerland:
WCC, 1966.

_____. *Minutes and Reports of the Twentieth Meeting
(Heraklion)*. Geneva, Switzerland: WCC, 1967.

_____. *Minutes and Reports of the Twenty-Second Meeting
of the Central Committee (Uppsala)*. (The minutes of
the twenty-first meeting are added). Geneva,
Switzerland: WCC, 1968.

_____. *The Central Committee, Twenty-Third Meeting -
Canterbury*. Edited by E.C. Blake. Geneva, Switzerland:
WCC, 1968.

_____. *Central Committee of the World Council of Churches
Minutes and Reports of the Twenty-Fourth Meeting*.
Geneva, Switzerland: WCC, 1971.

_____. *Nairobi To Vancouver* (1975-1983). Geneva: WCC,
1983.

C. Faith and Order Commission

_____. *The Third World Conference on Faith and Order*.
Edited by O.S. Tomkins. London: SCM Press Ltd., 1953.

_____. *Baptism, Eucharist and Ministry*, (BEM). Geneva,
F&O paper No. 111, 1982.

_____. *The Nature of the Unity We Seek*. (Oberlin). Edited by Paul S. Minear. St. Louis: Bethany Press, 1957.

_____. *One Lord One Baptism*. Edited by Keith Bridston. Minneapolis: Augsburg Publishing House, 1960.

_____. *The Old and the New in the Church*. Edited by K. Bridston. Minneapolis: Augsburg Publishing House, 1961.

_____. *The Fourth World Conference on Faith and Order* (Montreal). Edited by P.C. Rodger and L. Vischer. New York: Association Press, 1964.

_____. *New Directions in Faith and Order*. Edited by Lukas Vischer. Geneva, Switzerland: WCC, 1968.

_____. *What Unity Implies*. Edited by Reinhard Groscurth. Geneva, Switzerland: WCC, 1969.

_____. *Can Churches Be Compared?* Edited by Steven G. Mackie. Geneva, Switzerland: WCC, 1970.

_____. "Conciliarity and the Future of the Ecumenical Movement." *The Ecumenical Review*, Jan. 1972, pp. 88f.

_____. *Lausanne 77*. Edited by Lukas Vischer. Geneva, Switzerland: WCC, 1977.

_____. "Pope John Paul II Visits The World Council Of Churches," *Ecumenical Press Service*, 51/21. Geneva: WCC, June, 1984.

D.   Studies and Reports

_____. Translation Department. *Ecumenical Glossary*. Geneva, Switzerland: WCC, 1967.

Woywood, Stanislaus. *A Practical Commentary on the Code of Canon Law*. Revised by C. Smith. New York: J.F. Wagner, Inc., 1957.

Wright, John. "Modern Trends in Theological Method." *Current Trends in Theology*. Edited by D. Wolf & J. Schall. New York: Doubleday & Co., 1966.

Young, James ed. *Third Living Room Dialogues*. New Jersey: Paulist Press, 1970.

Zerwick, Max. *Analysis Philologica Novi Testamenti Graeci*. Roma: Scripta Pontificii Instituti Biblici, 1953.

DATE DUE

DE 13 02			